Torn at the Roots

RELIGION AND AMERICAN CULTURE

The Religion and American Culture series explores the interaction between religion and culture throughout American history. Titles examine such issues as how religion functions in particular urban contexts, how it interacts with popular culture, its role in social and political conflicts, and its impact on regional identity. Series editor Randall Balmer is the Ann Whitney Olin Professor of American Religion and chair of the Department of Religion at Barnard College, Columbia University.

Torn at the Roots

THE CRISIS OF JEWISH LIBERALISM IN POSTWAR AMERICA

MICHAEL E. STAUB

COLUMBIA UNIVERSITY PRESS / NEW YORK

Columbia University Press
Publishers Since 1893
New York Chichester, West Sussex

Grateful acknowledgment is made for permission to reprint the illustrations that appear in this book, and full acknowledgments appear with the captions to those illustrations. Every effort has been made to obtain permissions for them. The author and publisher would be interested to hear from anyone not here acknowledged.

Library of Congress Cataloging-in-Publication Data
Staub, Michael E.
Torn at the roots : the crisis of Jewish liberalism in postwar America / Michael E. Staub.
p. cm. — (Religion and American culture)
Includes index.
ISBN 0-231-12374-4 (alk. paper)
1. Jews—United States—Politics and government—20th century. 2. Liberalism—United States. 3. Religion and politics. 4. Social problems. I. Title. II. Religion and American culture (New York)

E184.36.P64 S73 2002
305.892'4073—dc21

2002025687

Columbia University Press books are printed on permanent and durable acid-free paper.

Designed by Lisa Hamm
Printed in the United States of America
c 10 9 8 7 6 5 4 3 2 1

FOR LUCY

Contents

Torn at the Roots

"Making My Jewishness Too Visible": An Introduction

IN MAY 1969 Columbia University's Jewish Advisory Board voted not to renew the contract of A. Bruce Goldman, a Reform rabbi and chaplain to Jewish students. The board, as reason for this dismissal, cited that during the 1968 Columbia strike Rabbi Goldman spoke strongly in favor of student demands and condemned the administration for bringing police onto campus to put it down. In a press interview board chairman Gerard Oestreicher said:

> The university has bent over backwards to allow so many Jewish students to enter. This [Goldman's] behavior is hardly appropriate recognition of the manner in which Columbia welcomed Jewish students. . . . It did not help the Jewish image to have a rabbi calling on students to destroy property. It put us at a disadvantage. If I were a trustee, I would think seriously about keeping the college with a majority of Jewish students from radical backgrounds.

Goldman's support for the strike was the final straw. To be sure, Goldman had antagonized the JAB before. Goldman had, for instance, publicly defended the right of a gentile Barnard co-ed and her Jewish Columbia boyfriend to live together in an off-campus apartment. Having spoken with the young couple, Goldman judged their premarital relationship to be "meaningful," and therefore legitimate, even though it was a technical violation of a Barnard student housing policy (Columbia had no similar student housing code). Goldman offered abortion counseling for Barnard students. He organized demonstrations for Soviet Jewry. Goldman also vehemently opposed the Vietnam War. Goldman was well-known as the "radical rabbi." The phrase was not always used sympathetically.[1]

For some spokespersons in the Jewish community, Goldman was an embarrassment and a liability. Complaints came in that Goldman's views were inappropriate for a rabbi. While Goldman's principled opposition to U.S. foreign policy might have been forgiven, his pronouncements on premarital sex and abortion were taken as entirely improper and out of bounds. The Rabbinical Alliance of America, an organization of Orthodox rabbis, circulated a letter urging the Jewish Advisory Board to "disassociate" itself from Goldman. Furthermore, it requested that Goldman be asked to "desist from such preachments to our college students" because these statements encouraged "promiscuity and free love." Goldman's views were "a direct contravention of the teachings of Judaism," warned the alliance, and consequently "we will feel compelled to urge all Jewish students at Columbia to refuse to visit with Rabbi Goldman."[2] The Jewish Advisory Board's feelings toward Goldman promptly went cold; five members resigned over his remarks about premarital sex, and it was reported that at least one prominent board member (*New York Times* publisher Arthur Ochs Sulzberger) began to explore ways to have Goldman removed.[3]

After Goldman's dismissal, Jewish students responded in outrage. An Ad Hoc Committee for Freedom for University Clergy circulated petitions to students and faculty and protested the rabbi's dismissal by picketing outside the offices of *Newsweek* (in a building owned by realtor Gerard Oestreicher; see figure 1.0). Demonstrations occurred outside the New York Times Building, and a student entered the offices of Oestreicher Realty Corporation to demand a meeting with the board chairman.[4] The newly formed Jewish Committee for Self-Determination also distributed a broadside on campus which made an explicit parallel between black and Jewish identity movements:

> Shalom: . . . the issue is not whether we like or dislike our rabbi. The issue is whether we will determine the matters which will affect us. This issue of control over our own heritage and over our own lives—is as crucial to us as it is to our Black brothers who at campuses all over this country are demanding control.[5]

Goldman became a willing martyr for a new Jewish youth movement that believed the Jewish "establishment" was disinterested in anything but its own prestige and power. An article in the radical Zionist *Jewish Liberation Journal*

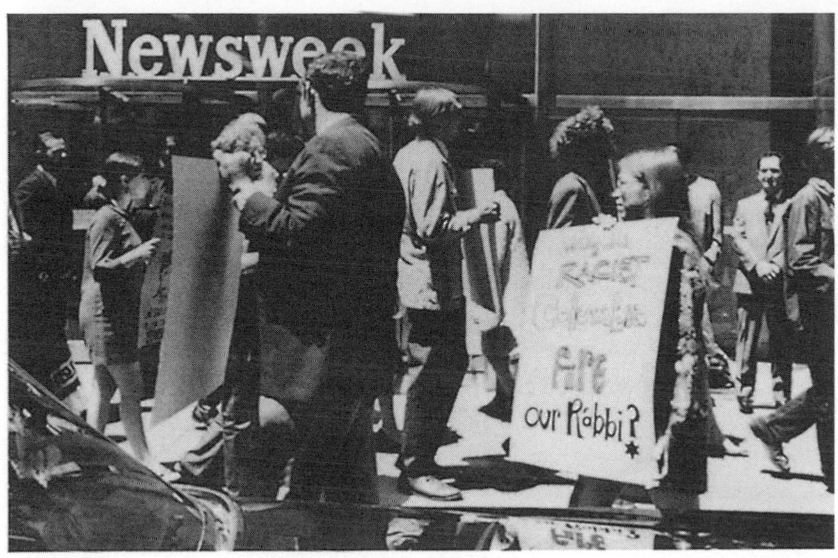

FIGURE 1.0 "Why Did Racist Columbia Fire Our Rabbi?" Students protest the dismissal of Rabbi A. Bruce Goldman by the Jewish Advisory Board of Columbia University. Originally appeared in *Dimensions in American Judaism* 4, no. 2 (Winter 1970). Photograph by Diana Jo Davies.

bluntly put the issues in the hyperbolic language so characteristic of the sixties. According to a Barnard College graduate who called herself Malka Zedek (Hebrew for "queen of the righteous"), "the university's Judenrat, otherwise known as the Jewish Advisory Board (JAB), did some neat dirty work for the administration and trustees: it told Rabbi A. Bruce Goldman, the thirty-three-year-old Jewish chaplain it had hired two years ago, that he better look for another job for the coming academic year." But the ramifications of the incident extended far beyond the Jewish enclave on the Upper West Side of Manhattan: "The Goldman case cannot be considered an isolated and far-out incident involving the paranoia of a bunch of self-hating Jews faithfully ass-licking their WASP masters." To the contrary, Zedek continued, the problem between the JAB and the Jewish students "is unfortunately a microcosm of the American Jewish community as a whole. The self-serving behavior of the JAB, its eagerness to sell out to the WASP power structure, its paranoia, is illustrative of the behavior of the American Jewish establishment and is the epitome of its philosophy and modus operandi."[6] An intracommunal (and intergenerational) battle line had been drawn.

For his part, and possibly to his credit, Rabbi A. Bruce Goldman refused to kowtow. Truth be told, Goldman appeared to revel in the strong reactions his remarks had stirred—perhaps especially from other Jews—and he proceeded to do and say more things he must certainly have known would jettison all possible chance to keep his university position. For instance, Goldman informed the media that the Jewish Advisory Board had "told me to shave off my beard—they said it made me look too Jewish."[7] Goldman said the Jewish Advisory Board was composed of

> white, Anglo-Saxon Jews, people who are only concerned with the image of the Jew in the non-Jewish community. . . . The board felt that I was making my Jewishness too visible, too conspicuous, and that this would raise antisemitic feelings which would jeopardize future admission of Jews to the university.

Goldman said that when he had been hired the JAB had been looking for a "young, forward-looking rabbi," but added, sarcastically, that what that really meant was "the kind [of rabbi] who would lead marches to Mississippi but not to Low Library." Waxing more than a trifle self-important about his new unemployed status, Goldman also observed that

> taking a moral stand is not abandoning my co-religionists. It is affirming Judaism. The prophets, too, were controversial. This is absolute, unadulterated, political reprisal offered as an apology to the Gentiles by a few white Anglo-Saxon Jews whose primary concern is in keeping Jewish students inconspicuous and their rabbi a "court Jew."

As for Oestreicher's comments to the press that Goldman had "overstepped the bounds of a religious man" and had "abandoned his co-religionists," the rabbi responded that the "only abandonment of co-religionists has been done by the Jewish Advisory Board itself."[8] When the Jewish Advisory Board categorically refused to reconsider its decision to dismiss Goldman, Jewish students at Columbia did what they considered to be their ethical obligation: They kept Goldman on by creating their own position for him as their adviser, at personal expense.

THIS IS a book about ideological conflicts between Jews in the post–World War II era.[9] All through the postwar decades, American Jews debated how Jewish identity could and should matter and what political stands Jews should take. Whether the topic under dispute was American anticommunism, activism on behalf of African American civil rights, the purported lessons of the Holocaust for the American context, Israel and Israeli-Palestinian relations, the war in Vietnam, the state of Jewish religious observance, the counterculture, or the women's and gay and lesbian liberation movements, Jews accused each other of being inadequately or improperly Jewish. By providing an intellectual and cultural history of some of the struggles that have most profoundly split the American Jewish community in the three decades after 1945, I hope to provide a better understanding of what American Jewish identity once meant to those who spoke most prominently and passionately in its name. I also hope to clarify how and in what ways the possible meanings for American Jewish identity have changed—and changed dramatically—in the generation after World War II. The ways in which the terms of debate over American Jewishness shifted and reconfigured over the course of the 1940s through the 1970s continues to have significant effects on Jewish communal stances on every pertinent political issue of our day and on innumerable Jews' self-understandings. In particular, the ways in which the 1960s are remembered has a remarkable impact on the boundaries of acceptable intracommunal debate and on present-day assumptions about what constitutes appropriate Jewish identity.

It is routinely noted that, despite their dramatic upward economic mobility in the course of the postwar decades, Jews remained consistently the most politically liberal of white American ethnic groups. Jews, it is said, retained their attachments to liberal values, projects, and policies long past the point when it was no longer to their immediate benefit to do so. The literature on Jewish liberalism is large, and differences between the accounts often hinge on whether they (explicitly or implicitly) see this propensity toward liberalism as a positive or a negative thing. For many it is a source of pride; for others it is a sign that Jews still do not have the good sense unapologetically to defend their own interests. But because the main focus in many studies has been on relationships and/or comparisons between Jews and other groups—rather than on intra-Jewish conflict—the basic story lines and sense of periodization remain the same. Among other things, what gets lost in the standard narrative of Jews' surprisingly tenacious adherence to liberalism is an adequate understanding of how far back into the postwar period the contests over Jewish liberalism—its legitimacy and its content—actually go. Yes, many Jews were, and a considerable number still are, radicals, left-liberals, or more moderate liberals. But without paying attention to intra-Jewish conflict we have no sense of just how embattled these individuals' positions within the community often were, nor of how energetically and creatively antileft and antiliberal arguments were put forward by their critics. For example, Jewish activists who invoked the prophetic tradition of Micah, Amos, and Isaiah to cast Judaism as morally bound to antiracist activism and other social justice issues already came under sharp attack in the mid-1950s. The view that Jewishness and liberalism were at all reconcilable was rejected as early as 1960. And the very meaning of liberalism was subjected to sustained, intricate, and intense debate for the entire duration of the first quarter-century after World War II.

A careful examination of intra-Jewish conflict over liberalism also helps us understand relations between Jews and other groups in more helpful ways. Most accounts of the demise of the black-Jewish alliance, for instance, date the dissolution of that alliance to the growth of black militancy and rising incidence of black antisemitism from the mid-sixties on, rather than to any earlier conflicts between Jews over what Jews' obligations to other groups might be. Along related lines, neglecting intra-Jewish struggles over both Jews' relationships to blacks and Jews' involvement in the New Left obscures from view the early roots of Jewish neoconservatism. Hence we are left with an impoverished understanding of significant developments in the contemporary political scene as well. Meanwhile, and although there is widespread agreement that Jews were disproportionately active in the antiwar and other New Left–affiliated sixties movements, this activity has been described by many commentators as not only a distressing departure from the balanced wisdom of liberalism but also a symptom of self-hatred, masochism vis-à-vis gentiles, and alienation from Jewish tradition. Such a retrospective summary, however, obfuscates what many of the intra-Jewish fights of the late sixties like the battle over Rabbi Goldman at Columbia made clear: that sometimes it was New Left–affiliated student radicals who insisted on making Jewishness more visible, and it was their elders who were resistant to visibility and confrontation with the gentile power elite. The point here is not that the radicals were right and their elders wrong, but that this story—and in the sixties there were many like it—simply cannot be accommodated to our twenty-first-century assumptions and standard retrospective narratives. At the time it was not at all self-evident who was displaying self-hatred and who was properly honoring Jewish tradition. Finally, most accounts make the double argument that while Jews in the 1970s and since have continued to tend more toward liberalism than other whites, the seventies also saw the beginnings of a turn away from and redefinition of liberal priorities among American Jews. While some commentators have expressed sadness or anger at the conservative turn, many others have seen the retreat from older forms of liberalism as a beneficial *re*turning to a concern with Jewish pride and survival. But this aspect of the oft-recounted narrative suppresses once more just how longstanding has been the resistance to liberalism within the American Jewish community; it ignores as well to what extent many of those Jews who were attached to various forms of leftism and liberalism contributed to the sustaining of Jewish pride and survival.

Putting intra-Jewish conflict at the center of our analysis also offers new insights into the history of religion and the relationships between religion and politics in twentieth-century America. Many of the scholarly and popular texts on American Jewry make a point of refuting what they see as a persistent assumption that somehow the Jewish predilection for social justice and liberal causes derives from the Jewish religious heritage. These texts repeatedly emphasize that Jewish activism in progressive causes, far from having religious origins, is better explained by the ways post-Enlightenment Jews identified liberalism, democracy, and a secular state as best meeting Jews' needs. In addition, a number of scholars over the years have argued that Jews' attraction to liberalism in the U.S. can be effectively understood either as the result of an effort to gain respect within the larger gentile culture through a demonstration of their superior adherence to American democratic ideals or as the product of the struggle to reconcile conflicting desires to acculturate and yet maintain some distinctiveness as a social group. Yet, as sensible as the impulse is, the frequent effort to reject connections between Jewish religious tradition and Jewish liberalism has also had the unfortunate effect of causing us to lose sight both of just how important the belief that there *were* such connections was to many Jewish commentators and activists throughout the postwar period *and* of how powerfully the ensuing arguments among Jews over this belief contributed to the formulation of contemporary ideas about American Jewish identity.

Most important, what is missing in most of the studies stressing the need to disassociate Jewish liberalism from Jewish religious heritage is the recognition that, from the mid- to late 1960s on, an increasing number of commentators also from the middle to the right of the ideological spectrum began to invoke aspects of Jewish religious tradition for political ends. Rather than insisting that religion and politics had nothing to do with one another, or that those advancing a notion of prophetic Judaism had falsely politicized religion, a variety of more conservative commentators entered into debate over what the lessons of the religious tradition were. The later 1960s saw a remarkable efflorescence of the phenomena of invoking Torah and Talmud, marshaling theological arguments, and adapting religious rituals to make political statements—by leftists, liberals, conservatives, *and* right-wing militants. These phenomena could themselves be written off as misappropriations of religion for political ends, but that too would be missing the bigger point, for this "religification" of politics coincided with an extraordinary renewal of religious life and communal devotion. Occasionally, writers pointed out that Judaism, in this way unlike Christianity, was not "just" a religion but a whole way of life; others noted that the concept of religion did not exhaust the meanings of Judaism, for (again unlike Christianity) Judaism always had an ethnic or national or sociological dimension as well. But these intermittent objections did not alter the fact that a transformation of the terms of debate was steadily underway, and often the very same writers who raised the objections also found themselves joining everyone else in arguing over *halakhah* (Jewish law), or presenting a story from the Talmud, to lend emphasis to the specific political view they hoped to advance. Just as secularity could be found among Jews of almost all political persuasions, so also, and now increasingly, Jews on the left, right, and middle could be found making claims about what God's expectations for human beings were and/or what it meant to treat Judaism as a sacred inheritance.

One of the most notable aspects of the intracommunal postwar debates is the way that reference to the Nazi genocide of European Jews was made by all sides—and for a great diversity of political purposes. The standard view is that from 1945 until the first half of the 1960s Jews remained reticent to speak about the destruction of six million European Jews.

> During the 1950s, Jewish communities did not sponsor Holocaust commemorations, the Jewish lecture circuit did not feature speeches on the Holocaust, no Holocaust centers existed in the United States, and there was little public discussion among Jews regarding the fate of European Jewry,

wrote American Jewish historian Edward Shapiro in 1992.[10] *Commentary* senior editor Gabriel Schoenfeld, in 1999, wrote that "it is striking to recall that in the first decade and a half after World War II, the destruction of Europe's Jews was a subject shrouded in taboo and seldom discussed in public or print." It was a silence that only "began to dissipate in the 1960's, first with the trial of Adolf Eichmann in Israel in 1961, and then with the six-day war in June 1967."[11] Peter Novick's *The Holocaust in American Life* (1999) has argued for a similar chronology. On the first page of his book, Novick categorically states that the Holocaust was "hardly talked about for the first twenty years or so after World War II."[12] Out of shame or a misguided desire to protect their children, or hesitant to disrupt a fragile sense of hard-won security, postwar Jews steered clear of this most devastating subject. Mournfully, but respectfully, Irving Howe wrote of this immediate postwar generation, "Perhaps they had driven their memories deeper beneath the surface of consciousness than was quite seemly . . . There was nothing to do but remember, and that was best done in silence, alone."[13] Jewish studies scholarship in recent years has begun tentatively to revise the notion that the Holocaust was a taboo or suppressed topic for postwar Jews. For instance, Stuart Svonkin states that Jewish professionals active in the intergroup relations agencies (like the American Jewish Committee, American Jewish Congress, and Anti-Defamation League) "were profoundly influenced by the cataclysmic events of the 1930s and 1940s," and that "the Holocaust, as it eventually came to be known, was arguably the touchstone of their identities as Jews."[14] And in his study of the Holocaust on American television, Jeffrey Shandler notes: "Although generally characterized as a period of American Jewish silence on the Holocaust, the immediate postwar years saw a considerable amount of activity in response to this as-yet-unnamed subject: pioneering historical scholarship, the writing of the first of hundreds of personal and communal memoirs, the establishment of the earliest memorials."[15] Shandler also powerfully documents the presence of the Holocaust on American television even before the 1960s—in newsreels and in fictionalized dramas—and analyzes the complex ways in which the dramas in particular negotiated issues of antisemitic prejudice and Jewish identity. But there were yet other forums in which the murder of European Jewry was continually invoked in U.S. public discussion.

Far from being silent, either out of horror at the magnitude of the Nazi crimes or out of respectful sensitivity toward the trauma of survivors, commentators of all political persuasions made analogies to the mass murder of European Jewry when debating political issues in the U.S. or invoked its purported "lessons" for the American context. Although it may seem incomprehensible in hindsight, now that we are much more attuned to the Holocaust's horrific specificities, and the inappropriateness of facile comparisons, such sensibilities were not operative for much of the postwar period. Almost at once in the years after 1945 the Nazi genocide of European Jews became crucially instrumental to (and instrumentalized in) intra-Jewish communal debates. There was never any agreement on what the lessons for the American context were, but all agreed that there were lessons, and that the Nazi genocide was a logical reference point from which to draw conclusions about the situation in the U.S. as well. The notion that it might be indecent to engage in such invocations and lesson making would not be articulated until the later 1960s. What requires analysis, then, are the immensely complicated processes by which those purported lessons were contested and renegotiated. Already by the first half of the 1960s, for example, assumptions about the lessons of Nazism for U.S. race relations had gone through at least three distinct stages. And it is only against the background of the battle lines drawn in these earlier conflicts over African American civil rights and black-Jewish relations that we can appreciate adequately what was at stake, for instance, in the conflicting ways the Holocaust would subsequently be invoked in arguments over American Jews' appropriate stances on the war in Vietnam or the state of Israel.

Precisely because of the painful paradoxical doubleness of increasing security and prosperity in the U.S. alongside the acute awareness of the potential ferocity and tenacity of antisemitism, postwar American Jews struggled over the issues of assimilation and acculturation with particular anguish and ambivalence. As Jonathan Sarna has observed, the tension between assimilation to American society and the maintenance of Jewish identity is "probably the foremost challenge of American Jewish life," pitting as it does "the desire to become American and to conform to American norms against the fear that Jews by conforming too much will cease to be distinctive and soon disappear."[16] As many thoughtful writers have testified, Jews coming of age in the 1950s and 1960s were subjected to profoundly mixed messages about how to behave and who to be. Fitting in among gentiles was important, but so too was loyalty to the Jewish family and community. But how should one demonstrate loyalty? What did Jewishness and Judaism stand for? Should Jews identify with that other manifestly oppressed American minority, blacks? Or should they either aspire to and/or take the responsibility for being whites? What did they owe themselves and each other? How did, or should (some though not all) Jews' increasing economic and geographic mobility—out of the working and lower middle classes and into the middle and upper middle classes, out of the cities and into the suburbs—affect Jews' sense of commitment to social justice issues? Did rising comfort mean they had more to give or more to lose? Both the young and their elders reconciled these conflicts in extraordinarily diverse ways—always, however, struggling to persuade each other with moral arguments. And hanging heavy over all the conflicts was the uncertainty as to whether antisemitism really was in permanent decline.

Many older Jews were marked by memories of violence and discrimination. As the journalist Charles E. Silberman would recall: "When I was growing up in New York in the 1930s, for example, brown-shirted members of the German-American Bund used to sell their virulently anti-Semitic newspaper just a few blocks from where I now live; the synagogue my family attended was frequently defaced with swastikas and crosses; an elementary school classmate who ventured onto alien turf had a swastika cut into his hand with a penknife." As Silberman also added: "No wonder the operative principle on which my generation of American Jews was raised was 'Shah!' [be quiet] and that our Jewishness was a source of anxiety and discomfort."[17] How could a talented and ambitious young Jewish man make it in America? For Norman Podhoretz, who matriculated at Columbia University in 1946, the path to American Jewish success was proposed to him with bitter clarity: "Become a facsimile WASP!"[18] Behaving Jewish, looking Jewish, and being Jewish were not credible or reasonable options. Making it in America still meant fading in. Even with the defeat of fascism, the founding of the state of Israel, and the decline of antisemitism and overt forms of discrimination in the U.S., Jews continued to feel their doubleness as both insiders and outsiders to American society. Jewishness remained for many a fact it would be unwise to make too visible. "We don't want a Jewish president," anthropologist and American Studies scholar Riv-Ellen Prell recalls her father saying to her as a child in the 1950s. " 'Why?' I asked in astonishment. Because, he explained, 'If things go wrong then the Jews are blamed.' "[19]

While the challenges posed by conflicting desires for assimilation and distinctiveness in a climate that has been by turns hostile and welcoming are regularly alluded to in both scholarly and popular accounts of American Jewish history, the many fierce battles of the postwar decades over wherein exactly Jewish distinctiveness lay have gone underdiscussed or, in many cases, unmentioned. Jews are routinely enjoined to be concerned about Jewish survival, but there is much less debate than there once was about what that survival should mean. In 1960, in an address to the B'nai B'rith Hillel Foundation, Rabbi Abraham Joshua Heschel of the Jewish Theological Seminary (Conservative) in New York opened with the perspective that the "central problem of our time is *emptiness of the heart*," adding that it was deeply discouraging that American Jews seemed increasingly anaesthetized to the hurt and suffering of the world. Jews, Heschel argued, were becoming a people who "do not know how to cry, how to pray, or how to resist the deceptions of the hidden persuaders." Given such indifference, the future of Jewish youth was cause for particular worry. As Heschel put it, no good would come from "the *high standard of living* the young people enjoy," if their elders did not "demand in return a *high standard of doing*, a *high standard of thinking*."[20] In 1963 historian Arthur Hertzberg, like Heschel a Conservative rabbi, also found "emptiness" as he assessed the prospects for American Jewry. In a tone of bleak foreboding, Hertzberg argued that in view of "the emptiness of contemporary Jewish religion," he was left finally only to "pray that God has not taken us on this long journey through the centuries [so] that Judaism might die in these United States in a 100 years or so." In response to the question "Will the Jews continue to exist in America?" Hertzberg suggested that "any estimate of the situation based on an unillusioned look at the American Jewish past and at contemporary sociological evidence must answer flatly—No." Hertzberg's negative assessment was primarily based on what he saw as the main values prevailing among Jewish youth, whose flight from faith to atheism, preoccupation with "enjoyment of their parents' money," tendencies toward intermarriages and low birth rates, and "thinness of Jewish knowledge and emotion . . . bodes ill for the quality of the Jewish life in the next couple of generations." But in contrast to Heschel's central concern with indifference to the sufferings of others, Hertzberg worried in passing about the opposite: the "drift of the Jewish young away from Jewish activity into liberal politics."[21] The tensions *and* conjunctions between the views represented by Heschel and Hertzberg and the complex question of whether social justice activism and serious attachment to Jewish identity were profoundly at odds with one another or mutually reinforcing, are among the themes pursued in this book.

Just as significant, however, is the way in which the terms of debate over these questions were transformed in the late 1960s, not least by that supposedly so self-involved generation of young people that had worried both men. By the time sociologist Seymour Martin Lipset confirmed in 1969 that "the available data indicate that the student left in the United States is disproportionately Jewish," it was more than likely a fact most Jewish parents of college-age children had gleaned for themselves.[22] Numerous observers in the late 1960s noted that it was no great surprise that Jewish youth raised with superficial knowledge of their own heritage and now largely living in secular college and university settings should prove so susceptible to the lures of "beatnik" rebellion, countercultural experimentation, and radical politics. Bemoaning a lost generation of Jewish youth became a frequent refrain, and parents fretted endlessly over "interdating," premarital sex, widespread drug use, and involvement in revolutionary activism. But this is far from the full story. While Jewish members of the New Left were typically seen as both secular and highly assimilated, there were notable exceptions. The late 1960s and early 1970s witnessed the emergence of numerous youth groups that maintained *both* a commitment to New Left activism and cross-racial causes *and* fostered strong Jewish religious and ethnic identification.

New Jewish spiritual communities called *havurot* emerged within, not against, the counterculture. The same years, moreover, saw the growth of a radical Zionist movement on college campuses across the nation as well. Radical Zionists organized scores of campus organizations and published dozens of student newspapers, working consistently to engender Jewish pride and greater identification with Jews in Israel and the Soviet Union. While Jewish community spokespeople continued to pronounce on young people's inadequate devotion to Jewishness and Judaism, the young often turned their anger on their elders. Radical Zionist Jonathan Braun, for example, writing in 1970, did not necessarily disagree about the dangers of the New Left, but he thought parents had only themselves to blame. Braun assailed the previous generation for having "allowed their ghetto-like fears to render themselves impotent" and having "replaced the Sabbath meal with the TV dinner, the chalah with the package of cheese doodles, the synagogue with the bowling alley."[23] What Jewishness and Judaism should stand for became contested by an ever broader array of commentators, many of them speaking for what they saw as theretofore neglected constituencies. As the Orthodox rabbi Yaakov Jacobs poignantly summarized the trends of the time in 1968: "Jews are today locked in civil war; we contend with each other as to who is more authentically Jewish."[24]

Furthermore, it was not just diverse constituencies of young people who were entering the fray. Also within the older generation, self-defined liberals and their (often ex-liberal and soon to be labeled neoconservative) opponents could no longer determine the boundaries of debate. Suddenly, or so it seemed, Jewish establishment leaders could expect challenges from multiple directions. The year 1968, for example, did not just mark the heyday of the international New Left student rebellions. It was also the birth year of Meir Kahane's right-wing extremist Jewish Defense League. While it remained relatively small in formal membership, and was publicly condemned by virtually every major Jewish establishment organization, the JDL nonetheless became tremendously influential, garnering financial and popular support from diverse political and religious quarters. Reform and Conservative rabbis also now found their historic ability to speak on behalf of an inchoate entity known as the "Jewish community" vigorously disputed not just from the left but also the right. In the triple contexts of the Vietnam War, the rise of Black Power, and the growing impact of the sexual revolution, increasing numbers of Orthodox leaders and organizations shed their prior reluctance to opine publicly on contemporary political issues. Some Orthodox leaders, like Rabbi Irving Greenberg and Rabbi Henry Siegman, were strongly involved in the antiwar movement, but the majority announced themselves as far more politically conservative. Many Orthodox leaders in fact vocally endorsed U.S. military policies in Vietnam. In one especially influential 1968 essay, Rabbi Bernard Weinberger, president of the Rabbinical Alliance of America (Orthodox), called into sharp question the Jewish loyalties of liberal and left-wing Jews who opposed the Vietnam War or marched for black civil rights. Presenting his views as dissenting from conventional wisdom, Weinberger offered the "perhaps shocking countercharge that those Jews who *are* thus involved in the social clashes of the day may well threaten the survival of the Jewish community in America."[25] The sexual revolution, and the supposedly immoral practices that accompanied it, were also a source of particular worry for many Orthodox spokespeople. Here too, as in the civil rights and antiwar movements, Jews named other Jews as a major problem. One commentator, for example, decried the "deterioration of a Torah-less Jewish society that has already produced the Jewish hippie and the Jewish theologian who preaches the New Morality of sexual promiscuity."[26] Taking a more overtly spiritual tack, Orthodox Rabbi Jacobs, in his 1968 essay entitled "To Picket . . . Or to Pray?" argued that "the crisis which lies at the root of all the social, economic, and political problems of modern man is his alienation from G-d. The enemy is not discrimination or war; the enemy is the tidal wave of secularism." In Jacobs' view the sixties cry for "relevance" was a pathetic attempt by Reform Jews to copy "social-gospel" trends in Protestantism. The truth was that activism on behalf of racial desegregation in housing or against the Vietnam War was contrary to the "divine teachings of Torah." Only "through the practice of chesed and tsedakah on the individual and communal level" could the worldly and otherworldly be made one. Torah, Jacobs argued, "offers no corporate solutions to the problems that plague the world; it does offer a divine program of mitzvah-action which creates the climate in which man and society can overcome human greed and lust."[27]

Those committed to a view that Judaism was commensurate with radical New Left politics could not have disagreed more, either on where the main problems lay in the American Jewish community or on the teachings of Torah. Michael Tabor, for example, leader of the antiracist organization Jews for Urban Justice (JUJ), founded in Washington, D.C. in 1967, saw his group as "engaged in a struggle of *Jewish* survival against the acceptance by Jewish establishment leadership and their following of the worst principles of the Pharaohs—racism, their domination, cutthroat competition, exploitation—as their own."[28] While Jacobs argued that a search for "relevance" weakened Judaism, JUJ saw the whole matter from the opposite perspective:

> We feel the unique responsibility not only to articulate the moral imperatives of Judaism but the compelling need to translate these words into actions which will stimulate change in our community. . . . Our purpose is to breathe new life and meaning into such words as *mitzvah* (moral imperative), *tzedek* (justice) and *hesed* (loving-kindness).[29]

Importantly, as this statement suggests, JUJ was moved by the very same terms from Jewish tradition that had animated Jacobs' account as well.

As the intra-Jewish civil war heated up in the late 1960s and early 1970s, not only religious lessons but new Holocaust lessons proliferated. Many American Jews had interpreted the Six-Day War in 1967 between Israel and the Arab nations as constituting a second potential Holocaust, and some had even viewed Israel's victory as a divinely ordained, at least partial redemption of the murder of the six million. Quite a few (one in four according to a poll taken at the time) also articulated support for the Jewish Defense League. Many agreed that the JDL slogan "Never Again!" meant never again would Jews be on the receiving end of violent attack rather than responding in kind—also in the streets of America's cities. Surprisingly, numerous commentators also resuscitated the popular theory—which had been strongly promoted by the widely read studies of Bruno Bettelheim, *The Informed Heart* (1960), and Hannah Arendt, *Eichmann in Jerusalem* (1963)—that Jews had been too passive under Nazism.[30] Rather than dissent from or refute Bettelheim and Arendt's highly problematic views—although numbers of Jewish thinkers had already and brilliantly done exactly that in the course of the 1960s—leading antiliberal Jewish spokespersons now chose to reinforce the "passive Jew" myth, specifically to lend weight to their efforts to advance Jewish power in their present, both in Israel and the U.S.

However, other commentators sought to revive older liberal interpretations of the lessons of Nazism for the American context. These writers were often concerned about Jews' withdrawal from antiracist activism. For instance, in a 1969 book on black-Jewish relations the left-leaning journalist Nat Hentoff summarized what he still saw as the pertinent riddle: "We are, all of us who are white, the *goyim* in America. The further question is: Which among us are the Germans?"[31] Along related lines, Bill Novak, editor of the Jewish countercultural journal *Response*, in 1971 put his concerns about meaningful Jewish survival in a post-Holocaust light as well:

> Several years ago, during the civil rights movement, there were those who said disdainfully, "nobody helped us" and "let them pull themselves up by their bootstraps like we did." These reckless comparisons are being repeated now in new forms, as if we must give the world tit for tat, as if there were no special obligations, no sense of destiny, or of mission, that Jews have always possessed. And as long as we are here, it is our duty to make life in America better for all people; and this needn't be at the expense of ourselves. For we must assert it loudly: Mere existence, for Jews, *even in the wake of Hitler*, is simply not enough.[32]

Yet in the 1970s issues of mere existence did often take center stage. Jewish leaders repeatedly cited the need for Jewish families to have four children (or more) or risk allowing Hitler a posthumous victory. Indeed, a Reform rabbi in 1971 said exactly this: "Each Jewish family should have at least four children," at least until the year 2000, at which point "we can reevaluate our situation." If this did not occur, and Jewish families had only two children, it "would mean fixing our numbers at the level established by Adolf Hitler."[33]

If subtlety had ever been an element in these disputes, it was sorely lacking by this time. In the rush of new Holocaust analogies the charge of complicity with evil was now linked with ever more themes, among them Vietnam and Israel. In 1970, when the Radical Jewish Union of Columbia University interrupted religious services at Temple Emanu-El (Reform) to demand that the synagogue publicly declare its opposition to the Vietnam War, it said the temple should go on record "identifying Israel's struggle for survival and self-determination as synonymous with that of the Vietnamese people."[34] When the temple's rabbi saw to it that the protesters were arrested, the students furiously labeled the action as being like those taken by the *Judenrat* in a Nazi-controlled ghetto. Meanwhile, Harvard sociologist Nathan Glazer, one of the foremost authorities on ethnicity in America, repeatedly liked to suggest that Jewish radicals had something in common with Nazi perpetrators. In 1969 Glazer had said that although "I do not want to deprive blacks of all the credit for the mood of violence that hangs over the country," much of the blame should be squarely placed where it belonged—with "Jewish intellectuals," who "rationalized violence" and whose diatribes against the middle class meant that "the Jews, the most middle-class of all, are going to be placed at the head of the column marked for liquidation."[35] In 1971 Glazer asserted pithily that "the New Left likes final victories and final solutions."[36]

Contradictory invocations of the Holocaust now fairly saturated intra-Jewish dissent; references to it became the lingua franca of intracommunal contest. In 1972 the director of the Hillel-Jewish Service Center at Kent State University wrote to the *Cleveland Jewish News* about his ethical opposition to the Vietnam War. He compared American Jewish silence on atrocities in Vietnam to German complicity under Nazism, juxtaposing the disregard German Christian church leaders had shown toward tortured and murdered Jews with remarks on American Jews' inevitable entanglement in the Vietnam War's brutalities through their cooperation with the draft and with war taxation. "No one is an innocent bystander," he wrote. In the wake of the outrage and controversy that followed—which included charges that he was a "silly, emotional, unrealistic young man with deranged ideals" who "should be removed from his position immediately"—the director resigned his Hillel post.[37] On the other hand, when Breira, an American Jewish center-left coalition group comprised of rabbis and Jewish intellectuals and writers, counseled in the mid-seventies that American Jews should work toward a peaceful solution of the Middle East crisis and urged that Israel help establish a sovereign Palestinian state, the countercharges from right-wing American Zionists did not hesitate to bring in the Holocaust, either. The rabbis affiliated with Breira should be fired, Yaakov Riz of the Jewish Identity Center in Philadelphia wrote in 1974, because they were "acting as the 'Yudenrat' in the Nazi concentration camps where my family perished."[38]

Identifying where exactly the differences lay between left-wing and right-wing Jewish activist perspectives was not always so simple, not least because an ardent concern for Judaism sometimes led both sides to articulate similar concerns. Sounding remarkably like the most earnest Jewish New Leftists, for example, Jewish Defense League leader Meir Kahane wrote in 1968: "Swaddled in mutation mink and choked with pearls the woman of the nouveau riche sit in artificial gaiety and frantic insecurity. Driven by greed and status seeking they and their husbands claw frantically for houses above their means for neighborhoods that they cannot afford to have and yet cannot afford not to have." This, Kahane concluded, "is modern man. This is the enlightenment. This is the world of non-Torah."[39]

THIS, THEN, is a book about politics, religion, and racial and ethnic relations in the U.S., but it is also a book about the remarkable intricacy and complexity of meaning-making processes. It is not possible to understand how American Jewish political commitments splintered, shifted, and intensified without attending closely to the manner in which people made their arguments. The postwar history of American Jews' running conflicts with each other is a deeply emotional one, and only by taking emotions seriously can we make sense of it. This also means retraining our ears to hear fully what exactly was being said and reentering the imaginative universe of past decades. It means becoming attuned to rhetorical strategies as well as overt claims, noting the unexpected echoes and overlaps between conflicting positions and letting go of our contemporary presumptions about what many key concepts—among them faith, loyalty, and survival, assimilation and adherence to tradition, self-hatred and self-affirmation—were once thought to mean. Reconstructing the complex texture of intra-Jewish debates over painful and divisive issues also reveals just how intimately interwoven seemingly disparate controversies were in their time and how important it is to read these debates with and against each other. Only then does the full significance of these debates become clear.

Finally, this is a book about the importance of ideology and the necessity of taking into account splits within ethnic communities rather than assuming that there is any self-evident link between someone's ethnic position and their political views. In this way, although the book concerns Jewish politics, it also raises questions relevant to scholars of ethnicity, religion, multiculturalism, and American political life more generally. Too often relations *between* ethnic groups are seen as the sole locus for the making of ethnic identities. This approach not only takes for granted that which needs to be explained but also elides the way it was precisely *the interplay between* left, liberal, conservative, and right-wing elements *within* ethnic communities that provided a key site for the production of post-1960s "identity politics." For the formation of what now count as ethnic identities, in short, and thus the shape of important aspects of the contemporary political landscape, intraethnic conflicts have been as important as interethnic ones.

1 "The Racists of America Fly Blindly at Both of Us": Atrocity Analogies and Anticommunism

The word "atrocity" is acquiring new connotations.
—Marie Syrkin, 1945

THE RACISTS OF AMERICA FLY BLINDLY AT BOTH OF US

In May 1958 the American Jewish Congress invited Dr. Martin Luther King Jr., a minister from Montgomery, Alabama and the leader of a local bus boycott, to Miami Beach to address its national biennial convention (figure 1.1). In several important respects this was a memorable event. For one thing, it was the first time the American Jewish Congress, one of the foremost American Jewish defense organizations, held its national convention in the South. What is more, it was the first time Dr. King had been invited to speak before an audience of both African Americans and whites at an integrated Miami Beach function. Those in attendance at the AJCongress convention no doubt fully recognized the powerful emotional and historic significance of Dr. King's presence on the podium.

Additionally, and no less significantly, the opportunity in 1958 to celebrate Dr. King in Miami Beach had particular meaning for Miami's Jewish community. The occasion helped Miami Jews close an uncomfortable and ambivalent chapter in their own political history. As Deborah Dash Moore has amply documented, the Jewish community in Miami had not acted quite as honorably in defense of African American civil rights as it might have liked to remember. Locally, Jews were not at the forefront of desegregation efforts during the 1950s. By and large, they had not challenged segregation openly. Indeed, as recently as 1956 the largely Jewish Miami Beach Hotel

Owners Association had worked to cancel an African Methodist Episcopal Church convention because of a fear that so many black clientele in Miami Beach might have negative consequences on their mortgage loans. In 1957 and 1958, during a period when more than forty African American homes and institutions were bombed, the Miami Jewish community maintained a cautious public silence on the crimes of southern white supremacists. Wishing to sidestep conflict, Miami Jews often chose, whenever possible, to avoid country clubs and hotels likely to refuse them as well.

Only the relatively small Jewish left-wing organizations spoke out vocally against segregation during these years—and suffered withering and persistent harassment and prosecution from anticommunist witch-hunts as a result. When these pro-integration Jewish radicals beseeched the general Jewish populace to rise to their defense in the name of civil liberties, their pleas often fell on deaf ears. Few in the Jewish community were willing to risk a communist taint during the cold war fifties, and most chose rather to keep a careful distance from any close identification with desegregation efforts. Only in March 1958, after an enormous dynamite blast struck a prominent Miami synagogue, did some Miami Jews conclude that they could no longer avoid a more activist stance (even while an official for the Anti-Defamation League maintained that the synagogue bombing did not constitute an "emergency"). Still, as the cause of civil rights took hold nationwide in the later fifties, Miami Jews managed to assert themselves rather more, although even then they advanced the cause of religious freedom rather than racial equality.[1]

Martin Luther King Jr. did not address the history of local Jewish ambivalence toward African American civil rights activism, although he did angrily chastise the spread of what he called "a quasi-liberalism" which has "developed a high blood pressure of words and an anemia of deeds." Instead, King approached the sensitive subject of Jewish support for black civil rights through an analogy he surely knew would strike a deep chord with an AJ-Congress audience. Drawing a lesson for domestic race relations from the genocidal policies of the Third Reich, Dr. King said:

> One of history's most despicable tyrants, Adolph Hitler, sought to redefine morality as a good exclusively for the Aryan race. He bathed mankind in oceans of blood, murdering millions of Jews, old and young, and even the unborn. Negroes saw that such hideous racism, though not immediately applied to them, could sooner or later encompass them, and they supported the struggle to achieve his defeat.

FIGURE 1.1 Speakers at the American Jewish Congress national biennial convention, held in Miami Beach from May 14–18, 1958. *From left to right:* Nahum Goldmann, Israel Goldstein, Joachim Prinz, Thelma Richman, Walter Reuther, Justine Wise Polier, Martin Luther King Jr. Reprinted with permission from *Congress Weekly* 25, no. 11. Copyright © 1958 American Jewish Congress.

King then moved from the past to more recent events—and back again. He continued:

> Every Negro leader is keenly aware, from direct and personal experience, that the segregationists and racists make no fine distinctions between the Negro and the Jew. . . . Some have bombed the homes and churches of Negroes; and in recent acts of inhuman barbarity, some have bombed your synagogues—indeed right here in Florida. As the Nazis murdered Catholic Poles and Jews, Protestant Norwegians and Jews, the racists of America fly blindly at both of us caring not at all which of us falls.[2]

With this analogy King hoped most powerfully to encapsulate for a predominantly Jewish audience the potential *and* actual evil consequences of white racism. No one could claim safety from the tactics of white supremacy until all were safe. Yet, along the way, King also made reference to another history—a prouder history—of an African American commitment during the Second

World War to the "Double V," that is, the intertwined aims of many black Americans to see a victory both over fascism overseas and racism at home. Black Americans had ably fought against Nazism and in so doing had risked their lives to put a stop to Hitler's final solution. Now it was only just that Jews fight alongside African Americans in the unfinished struggle for integration and racial equality in the U.S.

King's line of argument and his invocation of lessons from the experience of Nazism for the situation of blacks in the U.S. had historic roots in the popular African American press dating back a quarter-century. Moreover, the notion that Nazism was a relevant reference point for making sense of U.S. racial realities was articulated in the immediate postwar years in both left-wing and liberal Jewish venues. But under the impact of the rise of anticommunism, the kinds of analogies that seemed acceptable in the first postwar years were abandoned in favor of comparisons between Nazism and Soviet Communism.

As Stuart Svonkin has shown in his careful and comprehensive study of postwar American Jewish defense and intergroup relations organizations, the rise of a liberal anticommunist consensus had a deleterious impact on the Jewish left.[3] The consolidation of public American Jewishness with liberalism was accompanied by the expulsion of suspected communists from all major Jewish organizations. It was in justifying this process that analogies to Nazism were reworked and Stalinism replaced white American racism as the scourge most comparable to Nazism. Not insignificantly, moreover, the liberal anticommunist consolidation had a crippling impact on grassroots leftist Jewish anti-racist activism. The anticommunist consolidation also brought with it a crucial reformulation of the available terms of debate about ethnic and racial identities. As leftists were increasingly demonized, their ability to speak for, or even consider themselves as belonging to, the Jewish and black communities was called into sharp question. All of these reconfigurations were to have lasting consequences.

JIM CROW FOR JEWS NOW

Since the early 1930s influential black commentators had expressed moral outrage and anguish at *both* German fascism and American racism and often drew direct parallels between the two forms of oppression. Indeed, already in the early thirties this analogizing between Jewish and black suffering achieved the status of rhetorical common sense for many African Americans. For instance, a 1933 editorial in the *Afro-American*, "Jim Crow for Jews

Now," compared the segregation of Jews in Nazi Germany to discrimination policies against American blacks, while an African American newspaper in Washington, D.C. said Hitler was nothing more than the "master Ku Kluxer of Germany."[4] Meanwhile, a notable black intellectual concluded an extended comparison between black and Jewish oppressions in 1936 with these words: "In America the Negro is often lynched and burned at [the] stake, not so much for his crime, but on account of his color. The German people have not yet reached such depths of depravity nor reverted to such primitive barbarism."[5] Comparisons and analogies like these continued to appear in many prominent African American periodicals throughout the war years. Many black leaders argued that African Americans had a special responsibility to combat German fascism because it was an especially virulent white racism; they also believed it to be little more than setting a double standard for white Americans to pretend that American white racism and German fascism were not two sides of a coin, and they pointed to especially noxious examples of racism and antisemitism in the U.S. government.

Most outrageous was Senator Theodore G. Bilbo of Mississippi, with his colleagues Representatives John E. Rankin and James O. Eastland, also Mississippians, tagging close behind in their shameless bigotry. Bilbo, for instance, noting that some "of the best friends I have in the world are of the Jewish faith," repeatedly made reference to "kikes" and "niggers" in his speeches; the *Crisis* merely reprinted the Congressional Record, letting Bilbo's racism speak for itself.[6] The public statements in particular of congressmen like Bilbo and Rankin were disturbing reminders that "negrophobia" and "judeophobia" lingered powerfully into the later 1940s. Rankin considered *Jew* and *communist* interchangeable words and thought "long-nosed reprobates" were orchestrating the civil rights struggle. Rankin also denounced black men as "vicious" fiends eager to rape white women. Into the immediate postwar period, efforts to implement antidiscrimination legislation, notably a move to establish a peacetime United States Fair Employment Practices Committee (FEPC), foundered against the hostility of Bilbo and Rankin. Rankin decried the FEPC as "the most dangerous and brazen attempt to fasten upon the white people of America the worst system of control by alien or minority racial groups that has been known since the Crucifixion."[7] And the FEPC failed to secure appropriate funding partly as a result of the strenuous and openly bigoted campaign against it.

For many in the African American community Bilbo and Rankin were proof positive that Nazism's specter flourished even in the hallowed halls of Congress. And in the immediate postwar years the *Crisis* continued to draw heavily upon the Nazi genocide of European Jewry as *the* analogy for racist conditions faced by American blacks. For instance, against congressmen like Bilbo and Rankin, "who unashamedly proclaimed their hatred of Negroes and Jews" as a way to block FEPC funding, an August 1945 editorial in the *Crisis* raged back:

> This is not representative government. This is not democratic government. The will of the people on an issue was not permitted to be asserted. This was fascism operating behind a facade of parliamentary skulduggery, parading boldly under a panoply of racial and religious screamings reminiscent of Hitler and Goebbels.[8]

In the months that followed the *Crisis* hammered often and hard with precisely this sort of Nazi-laden imagery at segregation policies and white racism. After a brutal incident in Columbia, Tennessee of antiblack mob violence marked by police passivity, the *Crisis* angrily responded that if "Negroes may not depend upon any authority, local, state, or federal, for equal protection under the law, then we will have terror, riots, bloodshed, and death—and Storm Trooper Fascism in the flesh."[9] After prison guards shot and killed eight black convicts at a prison camp in Georgia, an editorial in the *Crisis* sarcastically concluded: "And America gagged at Nazi concentration camp cruelties!"[10] When an African American veteran of World War II was attacked (and blinded) by a South Carolina police chief, the *Crisis* titled its commentary on the assault, "Southern Schrecklichkeit [Southern Horrors]."[11] And in introducing an article on Ku Klux Klan activities, the *Crisis* noted bluntly how the "notorious Nazi Nuremberg racial decrees aimed at the Jews were patterned on Dixie's 'techniques of racial oppression.' "[12] Even an event as relatively minor—though certainly deplorable—as a black woman finding herself the victim of job discrimination became sufficient justification for the *Crisis* to invoke memories of the war against German Nazism. It rhetorically asked, "Did we win the war, or did Hitler? If we won, was our victory to free only the peoples across the world, or did that victory include, also, 13,000,000 loyal American Negro citizens?"[13]

There are at least two things especially striking about the *Crisis* and its frequent use of German fascism as the most ready analogy for white racism in the U.S. First, as the influential periodical of the National Association for the Advancement of Colored People (NAACP), the *Crisis* had a unique historic relationship with American Jewry because of the prominent role Jews had played (and continued to play) in the political evolution of the NAACP since its formation in 1909. Put simply, the NAACP was the heart of an institutional coalition between African Americans and Jews. As Hasia Diner has shown in detail, the day-to-day operation, funding, and policy making of the NAACP all reflected a cross-racial partnership that managed to stay viable for almost half a century.[14] Many leading American Jewish spokespersons (e.g., Louis Brandeis, Felix Frankfurter, Jack Greenberg, Louis Marshall, Henry Moskowitz, Julius Rosenwald, Jacob Schiff, Lillian Wald, Rabbi Stephen Wise) participated actively in NAACP projects over the years. Additionally, in its early years the NAACP had seen two Jews (Arthur Spingarn and Joel Spingarn) serve as president, and Jews made up nearly half of the organization's legal committee through the 1930s.[15] While American Jewish historians have debated what motivated Jewish NAACP involvement, there is no dispute over the remarkable extent of this support.[16] Thus, and while the NAACP remained an organization with a definable focus on African American politics, the analogizing between American racial problems and German fascism—which found its fullest expression within the pages of the *Crisis*—was being formulated with Jewish participation and awareness.

Second, it is noteworthy that some of the leading Jewish periodicals in the immediate postwar era also adopted the analogy between German fascism and American racism long championed by the *Crisis* and other voices for the black community. For instance, after race riots "directed against the presence of Negro students in racially mixed schools" broke out in several Northern cities in late 1945, the Labor Zionist publication *Jewish Frontier* observed how those "who are familiar with the rise of Nazism" would immediately recognize that "most of the white troublemakers" were "boys with bad scholarship and attendance marks, the perfect Hitler material."[17] Jewish commentators did not hesitate to draw direct lessons from "a Nazi extermination program" in order "to explain a southern lynching," as Leo Pfeffer, a lawyer on the staff of the American Jewish Congress's Commission on Law and Social Action, wrote in 1946. Just "as Hitler well knew," a lie "will be believed, no matter how big it is, if only it is repeated often enough," the "continued repetition of the fairy tale that Negro blood is different from and inferior to Caucasian has caused millions of uneducated or partially educated poor whites to consider Negroes an intermediate species between simian and human." This dynamic also explained ordinary German citizens who

> participated or acquiesced in mass murder of Jews because for years they had been exposed to the lie that the Jews were their enemy and that all would be well when Jewish blood would flow. Race libels do not usually

> have immediate recognizable results, but their cumulative effect when compared with defamation of individuals is as atomic fission to the explosion of a fire-cracker.[18]

Along similar lines, the widely respected new journal *Commentary*, sponsored by the American Jewish Committee, used a version of the Nazism analogy on several occasions to dramatize disapproval with racial discrimination, especially in housing and employment practices. Arguing that a tradition of libertarianism in the U.S. did not give property owners a legal right to refuse to sell their homes to "non-Caucasians" (which would also include Jews), a 1947 essay in *Commentary* entitled "Homes for Aryans Only" put a distinctly Americanized spin on the possible lessons of Nazism for the contemporary scene: "Eighty years after Gettysburg, and two years after Hitler, the proposition that all men are created equal is again being whittled down, and in the area perhaps most crucial for a future democratic America—the area of our neighborhood life."[19] Likewise, a 1948 essay in *Commentary* bearing the ominous title "Alaska's Nuremberg Laws" attacked that state's recent legislation (directed at Indians) legalizing the seizure of the "possessions of Americans solely because they belong to a minority race."[20] Indeed, and even while it also began to suggest the cold war liberal attitudes soon to blossom within its pages, *Commentary* still in 1948 could stress the "painful theme" of an American "double standard" when it came to race relations after the victory over fascism.

> In the aftermath of World War II it became apparent that segregated war memorials and prewar Jim Crow patterns would not be submissively accepted as the fruits of democratic victory. These resentments have deepened. In a worldwide war against Nazism the survival of racism in America undercut our propaganda and caricatured our liberations. The anomaly is no less devastating in an era of new political conflict between democratic and totalitarian symbols—especially since the contemporary commissars officially reject the racism the brownshirts proclaimed.[21]

WAKE UP, AMERICA! PEEKSKILL DID!

Yet there was one additional noteworthy element to the frequent use both in Jewish and African American journals of German fascism as the most available analogy for white American racism: the analogy was pointedly abandoned by the *Crisis* in the late 1940s. While it is more difficult to document why a position may have been dropped than it is to analyze its usage, there are a number of clues—all of which point directly to the NAACP's avid endorsement of a cold war liberal anticommunism. Indeed, this move toward (what Arthur Schlesinger in 1949 approvingly named) the "vital center" found elaborate expression in the periodical's redirected editorial tone.[22] In an early 1949 editorial, for instance, the *Crisis* now attacked American communists as "only incidentally" interested in the "support of Negro rights." The communist movement was engaged in a "campaign of infiltration, disruption, and destruction of other organizations such as the NAACP." And the NAACP membership, the editorial warned, needed to be "on guard against this campaign."[23]

Also in 1949, the pro-communist political activism of the African American singer and performer Paul Robeson inadvertently provided the *Crisis* with a first real test of its new cold war liberalism. In April of that year Robeson spoke in Paris at the World Peace Conference, which was attended by two thousand delegates from fifty countries. In a widely reprinted Associated Press dispatch of his speech, Robeson reportedly said:

> We denounce the policy of the United States government, which is similar to that of Hitler and Goebbels . . . It is unthinkable that American Negroes would go to war on behalf of those who have oppressed us for generations against a country [the Soviet Union] which in one generation has raised our people to the full dignity of mankind.[24]

Public outcry against Robeson's remarks—and most especially his suggestion that black Americans refuse to fight a war against the Soviet Union if called upon to do so—was swift and decisive. The House Un-American Activities Committee determined that it was high time to collect testimony from important black leaders in order to investigate possible unpatriotic or seditious sentiments within the African American community.

At the same time, the *Crisis* added personal insult to these official injuries. It suggested that Robeson's earnest altruism or heartfelt political conviction was just another fraudulent role play from the gifted performer. It went on to itemize the jet-set lifestyle that attested to Robeson's fakery:

> He made great phonograph records, gained fame and fortune on the legitimate stage and in the movies. He lived in England, traveled and sang abroad, put his son in a fashionable school in Switzerland. He was a lion at social affairs, moving in very select British and Continental society. He went to Rus-

> sia. . . . So Mr. Robeson has none except sentimental roots among American Negroes. He is of them, but not with them.

The singer might be black, the *Crisis* scathingly concluded, but skin color was likely the only thing he shared with the "everyday life of colored people." Robeson possessed "tremendous talents" and "great personal charm," the editorial said, but he used those qualities to establish an exclusive world where an "expensive country place in Connecticut, unlisted telephone numbers, and the sifting of all correspondence by a mid-town Manhattan lawyer all kept 'the people' at a safe distance." Such details *proved* Robeson was a con artist; two decades later, in his satiric attack on American upper-class left-wing affection for black militants, New Journalist Tom Wolfe would call this phenomenon "radical chic." Wolfe mobilized class resentments in his mockery of Black Panthers and their white (and often Jewish) supporters; here the *Crisis* anticipated those antileft jabs with similar techniques in its denunciation of Robeson.[25]

By the end of the summer of 1949 two bloody riots in quick succession widened a new ideological chasm between anticommunist liberals and procommunist activists, and revealed these groups' starkly divergent responses both to white U.S. racism and antisemitism. And this new cold war chasm would have unquestionable consequences specifically on the professional *Jewish* response to racial and ethnic hatreds. Once again the leftist singer Paul Robeson became the center of controversy. On August 27, 1949, the singer was scheduled to perform the fourth in a series of popular annual concerts held on picnic grounds near Peekskill, New York. Typically the concerts were attended primarily by Jewish leftists and communist sympathizers who vacationed in the region during the summer months and among other things appreciated the black singer's performance of popular Yiddish folk songs. African Americans also attended and, in the past, the interracial concerts had been free of incident. However, in 1949 year-round residents—most of whom were white blue-collar workers—advertised their intentions to prevent what they dubbed an "un-American" event. War veterans—including members of the Jewish War Veterans group—as well as local members of the Veterans of Foreign Wars (VFW) and the American Legion planned to protest the concert with a parade.[26]

The results were disastrous. As concertgoers congregated on the picnic grounds, they were met by angry hecklers yelling "dirty commie" and "dirty kike" as well as "God bless Hitler and fuck you nigger bastards and Jew bastards!" They were pelted with bricks and rocks. Local police stood by, some smiling, and did nothing. A melee ensued; the concert stage was smashed, more than a dozen concertgoers ended up in the hospital, and a cross was burned on a nearby hill. No one was arrested.[27]

Refusing to be intimidated, Robeson and his supporters vowed to return to Peekskill on September 4 to see the concert performed. The rescheduled concert found an audience of twenty thousand met by a protest parade of eight thousand. Anticommunist protesters hung banners everywhere: "Wake Up, America! Peekskill Did!" Robeson sang this day; the troubles began only afterward. On their way home concertgoers were dragged from their cars and cries of "Go back to Jew town" were heard. State police participated in the assault on the volunteer guards who attempted to protect concertgoers from the violence. Twenty-five volunteer guards were arrested. The following day, during a press conference, Robeson said the state policemen had acted no better than "Fascist storm troopers who will knock down and club anyone who disagrees with them." In the weeks that followed, however, New York governor Thomas Dewey blamed the Peekskill riot on the concertgoers, whom he labeled "followers of Red totalitarianism." When a grand jury ended an investigation into these events the next month, it also concluded that Robeson's pro-communist statements had provoked the riots. Efforts by Robeson and his supporters to wage a lawsuit either for personal injuries or property damages sustained in the riots were subsequently dismissed by a judge on the New York Supreme Court.[28]

Jewish Life, a leading pro-communist Jewish periodical, shared Robeson's furious reaction to the riots. And a lengthy *Jewish Life* editorial based on an eye-witness account began by drawing explicitly upon the nightmares of an extremely recent past:

> It was the summer of 1937. The train from Paris to Zurich had halted on the outskirts of the Swiss town of Basel, at the border line of France, Switzerland and Germany. All of us left the train to walk over the border to the customs house on the Swiss side. From the German town nearby we could hear the beat of marching feet and the strains of singing. Soon a group of *Hitler-jugend* [Hitler Youth] drove into sight and came to a halt a few hundred yards from us. Their arms raised in the Hitler salute, they concluded their song with the cry *Deutschland, erwache*!—"Germany, awake!" Then they spotted a bearded Jew in our midst. They rushed forward to the border posts, venom and hate exuding from their faces, shouting obscenities, spitting in our direction and filling the air with their cries of *Verfluechte Jude* [Damned Jew].

That scene came back to me on Sunday, September 4, 1949, in Peekskill, U.S.A., on my way to the Robeson concert.[29]

In the months that followed, *Jewish Life* published several equally outraged reactions to the Peekskill riots and their aftermath. A significant contribution came from novelist and antifascist activist Howard Fast, who had witnessed both Peekskill riots. Fast was especially outspoken in his condemnation of the press coverage, much of which argued that Robeson and his supporters had brought the mob violence on themselves. In response to a particularly blunt expression of this position (which had appeared in a western Massachusetts newspaper), Fast angrily wrote:

> I can only think of the exhibition of soap that appeared in New York City last year—little cakes of green soap, good for hard water and soft water, but made out of Jewish flesh, a simple nazi byproduct of 6,000,000 Jews who went to the gas chambers. Would this miserable newspaper of Pittsfield, Massachusetts, charge that the Jews had sought this?[30]

Or as Fast recalled the night of the first riot in his expanded book-length account, *Peekskill: USA*, he had watched as anti-Robeson forces set fire to the chairs and concert stage: "Then they discovered our table of books and pamphlets, and then it was, that to crown our evening, there was re-enacted the monstrous performance of the Nuremberg book burning which had become a world symbol of fascism."[31]

The antiracist pro-communist trajectory of *Jewish Life* through the late forties is not incidental here. Established in late 1946 by the Morning Freiheit Association, *Jewish Life* announced its immodest intention to

> dedicate itself to strengthening the ties of the Jewish people with labor, the Negro people and all other oppressed groups, for a common struggle against anti-Semitism, discrimination, lynching and jimcrow; for a common struggle against fascism and war, against labor-baiting and the persecution of minorities, political and national.[32]

Already in its inaugural issue *Jewish Life* analogized between a resurgence in U.S. white racism and the rise of German Nazism. It noted how the "recent activity of the Klan is reminiscent of the SS terrorism before 1933," and added, "Like the SS, the Klan specializes in beatings, terrifying torch parades, burnings and lynchings."[33] In the months that followed, and much like the *Crisis* in

1946–47, *Jewish Life* continued to draw upon the analogy of German fascism with American antisemitism and white racism. For instance, *Jewish Life* condemned key members of the Republican party for their "Bilboism" and for "spreading Hitler's poison."[34] It questioned whether the discriminatory "quota system" in higher education was not just the "embryo of the maniacal 'solution' to the Jewish problem which Hitler put into effect."[35] Again in a style that closely echoed the *Crisis*, a 1947 *Jewish Life* editorial quoted several racist, antisemitic, and anticommunist statements only to add sardonically that they "are not a translation from the German" but had been "spoken by John Rankin, an alleged Congressman from Mississippi." The editorial then asked rhetorically, "Is it necessary for Jews to prepare more millions of corpses from among their own depleted ranks before they grasp fully what Rankin went out of his way to prove: that anti-communism and anti-Semitism are inseparable?"[36]

Thus, references specifically to the genocide of European Jewry formed a significant and recurring trope in the early *Jewish Life*. A long editorial in early 1947 saw "symptoms of the alarming situation" that "led to the rise of Hitlerism in Germany" disturbingly present in the U.S. as well. The editorial expressed the deep hope it

> is not necessary to pay once again with six million Jews and with countless millions of other people to learn this lesson once more—that anti-communism and anti-Semitism lead only to the disaster of all people. Jews must not only not indulge in Red-baiting, which can only inevitably lead to anti-Semitism. They must positively reject anti-communism. They must fight sharply against it wherever attempts are made to inject it. They must precisely offset the efforts of reactionary Jews who by peddling anti-communism seek to win "safe passage" by playing fascism's game.[37]

Throughout the remainder of the forties, *Jewish Life* continued to document a direct analogical link between racism and antisemitism in America and German fascism. At all points it made abundantly clear that attempts to suppress or deny the civil liberties of American communists were really one crucial early signal that domestic capitalist forces (many of whom, *Jewish Life* claimed, had profited from their investments in German companies successful during the Third Reich) intended to follow through on a plan to institute an American-style fascist state.

In the process of putting forth such explicit pro-communist text, initial discussions in *Jewish Life* of white racism against African Americans sometimes functioned awkwardly. Incidents of white racism against blacks immediately translated into one more opportunity to argue in support of communism. By mid-1947, however, *Jewish Life* worked to modify its stilted (and self-serving) analysis of white racism, adopting a conclusion long held by the African American press—that the analogies of American racism to German fascism meant *all* Americans—white *and* black—had a moral responsibility to combat white supremacy if they cared about the fate of U.S. democracy. For *Jewish Life* this meant it still put the Ku Klux Klan and Hitler into an analogical relationship, but it now did more to detail what it saw as a crucial lesson of Nazism, particularly for the American Jewish community:

> Skillfully promoted anti-Semitism in nazi-Germany helped to *brutalize* certain elements among the German people and to create the conditions under which the annihilation of Jews and the bestial destruction of millions of members of other nations was made possible. In the same way American lynch-breeding jimcrowism leads to the brutalization of significant sections of the American masses and may create the necessary conditions and sentiments for a new Hitlerite destruction of the Jews in America. In the interests of the security of Jewish life, of the future of the Jews in America, we must fight with all our strength *all* forms of race prejudice and discrimination against the Negro people, as American citizens, as neighbors, as workers, as fellow-members of unions.[38]

From 1948 onward, as media reports also in the Jewish press began to amass a mountain of evidence that the USSR was fostering a campaign of vicious antisemitism, *Jewish Life* fiercely defended the Soviet Union against these charges. A typical *Jewish Life* article from this time chose instead to rhapsodize over how the "Jewish people of the Soviet Union have become an equal among equals in the great fraternal family of peoples of the USSR. . . . In hand with all equal peoples of the USSR, the Jews of the Soviet Union will continue to build with enthusiasm and passionate love the glorious structure of communism for our homeland."[39] These expressions of blind faith would come back to shatter the pro-communist Jewish community in 1956 when official communist (including Jewish communist) sources as well confirmed Stalin's destruction of Jewish institutions and murder of Jewish writers and intellectuals since 1948.[40]

Then Peekskill happened. And, such as it was, and despite whatever deep ideological flaws it certainly had, *Jewish Life* again articulated with passion the necessity for American Jewish antiracist activity in the wake of the Nazi destruction of European Jewry. To put it mildly, however, and despite the overtly racist and antisemitic abuses witnessed by so many at Peekskill, the pro-communist Jewish perspective suddenly found itself more isolated than ever before.

Again an editorial in the *Crisis* took the lead in the condemnation of Robeson, concluding that he and his communist supporters were "the arch-enemies of civil rights." Even more significant, the *Crisis* also took the opportunity to disassociate itself thoroughly from the very same German Nazism/white American racism analogy it had so forcefully—and repeatedly—promoted for much of the previous fifteen years. In the aftermath of Peekskill the *Crisis* now ridiculed the "Communist fabricated hysteria that it was a 'storm trooper mob violence' " that had fueled the anti-Robeson protesters. Such inflamed rhetoric from communists "already shrieking 'fascist violence' and 'would-be lynching' throughout the world" merely "furnished new grist for the Kremlin propaganda mill." It represented, in short, a dramatic and decisive reversal in perspective from the *Crisis* in its newly minted anticommunist liberal campaign.[41]

Many prominent voices in the American Jewish press followed suit in their interpretation of the Peekskill riots and their aftermath. For instance, and importantly, the Labor Zionist *Jewish Frontier*, edited by Hayim Greenberg and with well-known liberal Jewish intellectuals like Ben Halpern and Marie Syrkin also on its masthead, articulated a position that would quickly achieve the status of common sense for many in the professional Jewish community. Communism, the *Jewish Frontier* admitted, certainly had scored some success "among underprivileged racial and religious minorities," but overall it was "extremely unpopular among all sections of the American people—including Jews." Indeed, *Jewish Frontier* went out of its way to stress how truly *Americanized* virtually all Jews had become also in political terms. In this way American Jews had merely followed the example of the "more representative sections of the American people" in their rejection of left-wing values, which a few "immigrants with a Socialist background [had] brought over from Europe." These "immigrants" included among their ranks "some Jews (particularly when the trauma of the Hitler era destroyed faith in the stability and security of the democratic system)," in addition to some "Negroes who could no longer bear to wait patiently for a gradual improvement of their position in the United States." But, for the overwhelming number of Jews, the "last remnants of faith in the superiority of Soviet over so-called 'formal' democracy" had been thoroughly eliminated.[42]

So far as *Jewish Frontier* was concerned, Robeson's decision to give his concert in Peekskill unsurprisingly aggravated local white racists who were under no obligation "to accept lovingly" an influx of pro-communist Jewish outsiders. Indeed, Robeson and his communist "comrades" merely "cast the dynamite stick" into an already tense situation when they insisted on going through with the concert, for it only provided local racists "their opportunity to swing free those fists that are usually under stiff control."[43] In short, *Jewish Frontier* largely concurred with the official inquest that the irresponsible conduct of Robeson himself was primarily responsible for the antisemitic and racist violence that broke out.

But arguably the most striking moment in this *Jewish Frontier* account of the Peekskill riots and their aftermath bore only an incidental connection to either. Instead, it was a report by the author Shlomo Grodzensky on a conversation he'd recently had with an "old friend of mine, a Negro working woman of fine intelligence" who said she felt that "at bottom" Robeson was "not playing fair with the Negro people." At some length Grodzensky then proceeded—though without quotations—to speak with the authority of an authentic black perspective:

> Robeson is world-famous and rich—he can afford to do all sorts of things which would be beyond the means of the average Negro. If Robeson didn't wish his son to be brought up in a country where children with colored skins are discriminated against, he could easily send him to a school in Moscow. If one day Robeson should lose patience entirely with life in America, he can very easily move to some other country which does not suffer from American prejudices. But the general run of Negroes in America cannot afford such luxuries. They must live here, and they have to be careful in choosing their methods for achieving their full civil and human rights. Mr. Robeson's Communism is the personal luxury of a well-meaning, but privileged member of his race. He can allow himself to ignore the consequences of his actions.[44]

Grodzensky's black woman friend—or possibly Grodzensky himself—certainly seemed to have followed the anticommunist twists and turns in the editorial policy of the *Crisis* pretty closely that summer.

The most elaborate, detailed, and (in many respects) influential discussion of the Peekskill riots in the Jewish press, however, appeared the following year in *Commentary*, itself now also cleansed of the very same German fascism/American racism analogy it too had found applicable on occasion in the immediate postwar years. James Rorty and Winifred Raushenbush's "The Lessons of the Peekskill Riots," published in October 1950, subjected to scrutiny the perspective that "what had happened, apparently, was that the pattern of hatred and rioting that had preceded Hitler's capture of power in Germany had been repeated for the first time on American soil—and not in the deep South, but in Peekskill, on the outskirts of the New York metropolitan area." Much like the *Crisis* had done already the previous year, this *Commentary* article exhaustively attempted to repudiate such analysis. In a cool and serious tone, Rorty and Raushenbush stated that while a "muddy brew of anti-Communism, anti-Semitism, and anti-Negroism" had "boiled out of the crowds" after the initially scheduled Robeson concert, and there had been considerable "name-calling," many of the anti-Robeson forces themselves "were dismayed and shocked" when circumstances took a more violent turn. In the aftermath of the first riot, it really was the "wholly hypocritical" and "bellicose tub-thumping" statements of the "Communist-controlled Civil Rights Congress" (which had sponsored the Robeson concert) that stirred up further trouble. Rorty and Raushenbush explained this communist strategy:

> Those familiar with the Communist program have long recognized that it requires the exploitation of the civil rights issue only with the objective of polarizing extremist passions and sowing the seeds of discord—the more violent the better—that will disrupt the democratic process. What the Communists wanted was another propaganda harvest which would be all the greater if a second veterans' demonstration led to another round of violence and another flare-up of racism.

And this was—according to the *Commentary* reporters—more or less exactly what would happen. The "second Robeson 'concert' " (as Rorty and Raushenbush mockingly referred to it) resulted in "a horrifying spectacle of mob violence at its ugliest." In the final analysis, though, and according to Rorty and Raushenbush, the worst atrocities might truly have occurred in the verbal jousting during the days and months long after the physical violence ended. It was then that communists and their supporters repeatedly invoked the fascism analogy in an attempt "to make the Peekskill riots appear as part of the major Negro struggle for emancipation." In truth, the entire communist effort was to create a "new American myth" in which "Negroes, Jews, and Communists are arrayed against the rest of the country." And, the authors cautioned, "as yet the Jewish community seems only vaguely aware of the potential viciousness of the formula."[45]

From here, Rorty and Raushenbush abandoned entirely their play at objectivity to proffer what emerged as their own most daring proposition. Apparently, it was not sufficient merely to argue that the American Civil Liberties Union report on the riots was marked by "naivety" and "a rather cavalier, and partial, handling of facts," as well as describe Communist and left-leaning reports on the incidents as "wholly unreliable" or as confusing matters "in a blaze of outrageous lies." What was required now was nothing less than a revised interpretation of the possible lessons of the past for a new decade in which American Jewish politics would be dominated by cold war liberalism. Turning the ideological tables on the seemingly immovable German Nazism/American racism analogy, Rorty and Raushenbush elaborated a different set of equivalencies.

> That the Communists pose as the chief defenders of Jewish and Negro rights forms only a deceptive distinction between them and the Nazi agents. The slogans of anti-anti-Negroism, despite the sincerity with which individual Communists may still utter them, have simply become their most effective weapons in attacking the American government and people and in weakening this country before the Soviet attack—just as anti-Semitism became the chief weapons of the Nazi propaganda offensive.[46]

What Rorty and Raushenbush argued, then, was not solely that the Communists and their sympathizers provoked the mob violence in Peekskill. The lasting significance of their message was that—although many commentators had believed that antiracism, especially after the Holocaust, was a moral imperative—actually here it was the antiracists themselves who were most comparable to Nazis.[47]

"ANTI-SEMITISM" AND THE ROSENBERG CASE

Commentary did not abandon a public stance against white racism during the cold war, though its coverage generally was both diminished and downplayed. An exception to this rule, however, was "The Time Bomb That Exploded in Cicero," an impassioned report by Charles Abrams on the racist reaction in 1951 from an all-white Illinois town when a black family attempted to desegregate an apartment house in the community: "Flares, bricks, and burning torches were thrown into the house, radiators and walls were ripped out, furniture thrown from the windows, and trees torn up by the roots to be burned as the mob cheered."[48] More typical, though, would be James Rorty's reflections that the "neo-Nazi anti-Semites, the Stone Age fundamentalist exhorters, the ultra-nationalist fanatics, crackpots, and racketeers" had all but been eliminated as "a serious political force" as a result of the Supreme Court desegregation ruling in 1954. "Nothing succeeds like success," Rorty blandly predicted, "and now desegregation can begin to feed on its successes."[49]

The overall strategy *Commentary* adopted toward antiracist activism was to place it into a crucial broader context, one that articulated invigorating confidence in American democratic principles. Segregation and racial discrimination might persist in everyday American life, as *Commentary* editor Elliot Cohen wrote in 1952, but such societal ills hardly told the whole story. In his homage to the American way Cohen glowingly noted how the "citizen of Jefferson's dream . . . who was to be at the same time the eternal rebel and the eternally responsible, who was to tear down and to build up, who was to know no higher good than the satisfaction of his own selfish needs and impulses and at the same time to join with others and to sacrifice all for his brother and the common good" was today "more alive and kicking than ever." When Cohen looked around at cold war America, what he saw was a society in essentially fine working order:

> If the American Christian does not meet the Jew or the Negro in his church or his club, he will meet him in his parent-teacher association or his union local. There are still gaps and evils: there are large areas where, shamefully, racial exclusion and discrimination powerfully operate, but in the interplay of the little communities with the great community, aided and abetted by organized protest, education, legislation, and the needs and general give-and-take of production and commerce, we have a dynamic process at work whose progress forward is steady and accelerating. Most on our conscience is the Negro: but even here we need hardly grovel in guilt before the other nations. Which society that has had the same problem has had greater success in weaving widely different "ethnic" groups into a national community: South Africa, Russia, India herself?[50]

Indeed, pro-Americanism represented a major theme in *Commentary* during the cold war. If "Communism is twentieth-century Americanism" had been U.S. Communist Party leader Earl Browder's Popular Front slogan in the mid-thirties, here *Commentary* seemingly transmogrified the phrase into "Jewishness is twentieth-century Americanism."

The reasons for this had already been implied early in 1948 by Sidney Hook, chairman of the philosophy department at New York University. In effect, Jews made the best and most loyal cold war Americans precisely because they had suffered a holocaust that—above all else—had taught them staunchly to defend U.S. democracy against the excesses of totalitarianism in all its pernicious forms. Simply titled, "Why Democracy Is Better," Hook's essay noted how a "stable pluralistic community" required "religious freedom and toleration" for it to thrive, but "its existence has been threatened all along the line, first by Hitlerism and now by Soviet Communism." Hook elaborated:

> Whoever believed that Nazi expansionism constituted a threat to the survival of democratic institutions must conclude by the same logic and the same type of evidence that Soviet Communism represents today an even greater threat to our survival, because the potential opposition to totalitarianism is now much weaker in consequence of the war, and because the Soviet government commands a fifth column in democratic countries stronger than anything Hitler or Franco ever imagined possible.[51]

Commentary in fact became fairly obsessed with how to dramatize the synergy of Jewish and American values—and the mutual abhorrence of both for communism. As *Jewish Frontier* had also concluded, if the communist was most likely either the immigrant who held unassimilated (and subversive) convictions or a member of an underprivileged minority, then the Jew embodied the most hospitable and modern of ethnics whose traditions would only strengthen the fiber of American democracy. Jews were so adaptable to democracy because only democracies permitted Jews to live freely as Jews. And, as it turned out, woe to those who challenged the neat symmetry of this pro-American scenario. Within a few years, Sidney Hook would argue in the *New York Times Magazine* that college professors who invoked the fifth amendment when called to testify about membership in the Communist Party be dismissed from their jobs. *Commentary* voiced similar opinions.[52]

It would be difficult to overstate the consequences of an increasingly uncompromising and embittered cold war liberalism on this influential Jewish journal in the years that soon followed. One after another, *Commentary* writers applied the lens of a new and terrifying analogy between Soviet communism and Nazi fascism as they sought to dramatize their stark vision of current political realities, both domestic and abroad.[53] In addition, liberals in particular were warned that any sympathies they might still feel for communists or any anxieties they might have about the damage anticommunist policy could do to American civil liberties were both misplaced. Robert Bendiner, for example, an associate editor of the *Nation* and a prominent expert on civil liberties, warned his fellow liberals in the pages of *Commentary* against a "self-defeating tolerance." Bendiner defended proposed legislation designed to root out American communism, even if it compromised constitutional freedoms, since the "fullest measure of liberty will normally be found where there is the greatest degree of social stability." According to Bendiner, it was wrong to conclude that a law denying "the 'rights' claimed by Communists" also diminished civil liberties. On the contrary, acknowledged communists "not only have no 'right' to government jobs but are in fact incongruous in the role of trusted workers for a government they have every desire to undermine and supplant." The careful exercise of curbs on constitutional freedom was good, especially since, as Bendiner wrote, the "obvious truth is that there can be no complete freedom short of anarchy."[54]

More extreme in his conclusions was Irving Kristol, *Commentary*'s managing editor, who made a celebrated conceptual leap forward when in early 1952 he argued that defending the civil liberties of communists was no different from defending the civil liberties of Nazis. Challenging liberals to ask themselves if they would find nothing objectionable in having Nazis able freely to promote their views in the U.S., also within schools and universities, Kristol maintained that removing communists and communist sympathizers from their jobs was entirely appropriate. Especially intent on demolishing any lingering notions that some American communists were motivated by high-minded "generous idealism," Kristol invoked the Holocaust as he worked to convey what he saw as the too often concealed threat of communism to American values:

> Many of us have known Communists, and most of them conveyed no impression of being conspirators. But then, some of us have known Nazis too, and they conveyed no immediate association with gas chambers. It is quite impossible to judge a political movement by the personality of an individual member. Roosevelt certainly didn't see in Stalin any symptoms of blood lust. Hermann Goering in jail struck one as a clever clown. And there are still plenty of people who can't believe that Alger Hiss ever did any such thing.[55]

The most potentially insidious fact about American communists was that they could *seem* so well-intentioned and decent; it was in reality just a latter-day (and updated) version of the ways the *Crisis* had smeared an African American communist like Robeson. Here Kristol gave the smear a distinctly Jewish spin. For the Jewish readership of *Commentary*, imagining the dapper (and gentile) Hiss—a high-ranking State Department official who was convicted of perjury in 1950 and subsequently denounced as a treasonous communist spy—to be a con artist would not have been such a stretch. But circumstances soon dictated that similar suspicions be leveled against Julius and Ethel Rosenberg, New York Jews whose most distinguishing characteristic was their overwhelming ordinariness.

Indicted on charges that they had conspired to commit espionage, Julius and Ethel Rosenberg were left-wing sympathizers who steadfastly denied that they were communist spies or that they had planned to pass classified data about the atomic bomb along to the Soviet Union. As their trial unfolded during the height of the cold war, and while the Jewish community "as a whole distanced itself from the Rosenberg case," primarily as a way to demonstrate by its silence that the Rosenbergs' Jewishness had no bearing on the government's allegations, the couple was convicted and sentenced to death in April 1951.[56] Although an international campaign sought to have the death sentences commuted, President Eisenhower denied a final clemency plea, and Ethel and Julius Rosenberg were executed in the electric chair on the evening of June 19, 1953.

How did the "Jewish issue" figure in the Rosenberg case? After the espionage trial had concluded, but before the death sentences had been carried out, *Commentary* gave the task of analyzing the case in light of Jewish communal concerns to Lucy Dawidowicz, a staff member of the Library of Jewish Information of the American Jewish Committee. Her resulting essay, "'Anti-Semitism' and the Rosenberg Case," emerged as an instructive model of cold war Jewish liberal thought. As far as Dawidowicz was concerned, if Jews responded sympathetically to the Rosenbergs because they were Jews this amounted to an error of near incalculable proportions. Dawidowicz was appalled at all appeals to rabbis and mainstream Jewish communal leaders on the Rosenbergs' behalf. Pointing out that it had taken quite a bit of time for American communists to begin arguing that the convictions were motivated by antisemitism, Dawidowicz argued that this time lag proved the insincerity of the campaign to save the Rosenbergs. Nor did she find the Rosenbergs themselves innocent of this strategy employed in the campaign. Indeed, Dawidowicz saw Ethel Rosenberg as herself taking the lead in an "attack" on "bona fide Jewish leaders" for the supposed treason to the Jewish cause exemplified by their unwillingness to defend the Rosenbergs. In disgust, Dawidowicz quoted Ethel Rosenberg, who reportedly called out when her sentence had been upheld (by a Jewish judge): "This is the way the *Judenrat* performed for the Nazis in the Warsaw Ghetto."[57] But Dawidowicz cautioned that this reference represented nothing more than a strategy of mobilizing the Holocaust in a manner that masked a far uglier reality.

For Julius and Ethel Rosenberg posed the worst kind of threat to the anticommunist movement within the Jewish community precisely *because* they could tug on postwar Jewish liberal sentiments. However, Dawidowicz argued, any Holocaust rhetoric that emerged from the mouth of Ethel Rosenberg (or her communist supporters) was similar to communist rhetoric decrying as an instance of "anti-Semitism" the suspension of Jewish schoolteachers in New York who had "refused to deny Communist party membership": such rhetoric was "intended merely as a trial balloon to test the new technique," and was a calculated means to "pick up sympathy and support from individual Jews who may be suckers for this particular bait."[58] It was paramount to grasp this "Jewish" campaign to save the Rosenbergs for what it actually represented: a stark reminder of communism's cynical talent for heartless exploitation. As cultural critic Andrew Ross has written in his incisive critique of the cold war witch-hunt: "Signs of normality and of social conformity could now be regarded, by alert neighbors and friends, as the most insidious signs of treachery, since, in the Jekyll and Hyde spy syndrome, they are the most telling signs of deception."[59] Thus the ordinary-seeming Rosenbergs, as Dawidowicz sarcastically observed, were really part of a hideous confidence game rigged

> to persuade the world at large that the American government is in the hands of an anti-Semitic conspiracy which is inexorably working up to the extermination of American Jewry, and that the conviction of Ethel and Julius Rosenberg for espionage is a 1952 version of the Reichstag fire, prelude to an American version of Auschwitz.

As Dawidowicz concluded, "It is obvious that the Communists, by such propaganda, aim to enlist Jews in defense of Communists and their interests."[60] This agenda, she argued, was deeply insidious, for it ran the risk of making all Jews appear potentially guilty of communist sympathies.

Even after the Rosenbergs were executed, the journal asked its readers to maintain their resolve against the couple and all they had represented. As *Commentary* associate editor Robert Warshow summarized it, posthumous efforts to "vindicate" the couple as Jewish victims and martyrs were misguided precisely because the Rosenbergs were total frauds: "Since the propaganda built up around the case emphasized the fact that the Rosenbergs were Jewish, they simply adopted the role that was demanded of them." Warshow coolly noted, "If something else had been needed, they could as easily have taken up the pose of Protestantism or Catholicism or Gandhiism."[61] In short, it was the journal's view that the Rosenbergs had deserved neither sympathy nor compassion from American Jews because they had not been *real* Jews, a fact they proved especially when they attempted to pretend that they were persecuted Jews for whom the Holocaust was a relevant touchstone. It was exactly their misapprehension and misapplication of Holocaust meanings and legacies for American politics and postwar American Jewish identities that in the end determined the Rosenbergs be shut off from legitimate access to all Jewish communal support. Their deaths (at least in *Commentary*'s considered judgment) were just.

Reaction from the pro-communist Jewish press to this intense red-baiting was always swift, but remained largely ineffective. After the Peekskill riots, for instance, the *Jewish Fraternalist*, the publication of the pro-communist Jewish People's Fraternal Organization, wrote in early 1950: "The Peekskill fascists and hoodlums claimed it was their 'anti-Communism' that prompted the attacks on the Robeson concert audience, but it was 'kill the Jews and kill the Negroes' that they shouted as they threw rocks and overturned cars."[62] Likewise, also early in 1950, *Jewish Life* retaliated against *Commentary* and its sponsoring organization, the American Jewish Committee, by labeling the AJC "the agency of the big bourgeoisie," and therefore one that could never be counted upon to "become a component of the general people's anti-fascist front."[63] In short, *Jewish Life* came close to saying outright that *Commentary* itself was a front run by Jews for American fascist propaganda.[64] After the "Rosenbergs were killed as an offering to the cold war," *Jewish Life* condemned those responsible as "trying speedily to kill the Bill of Rights, tear the Constitution to shreds and to bring fascism to our country."[65] The Jewish community in cold war America was scarcely prepared to align itself with such dangerous views in the early fifties, and although *Jewish Life* continued with undiluted passion to argue that "the Jewish people of the United States know, with varying degrees of clarity and of will to action, that their own security is essentially connected with the struggle of the Negro people to achieve status as first class citizens," a Jewish audience for such appeals continued to decline.[66] By 1952, when *Jewish Life* eulogized Joseph Stalin for "his leadership in the liberation of peoples, including the Jewish people," its ideological credibility in nearly all sectors of the American Jewish community dipped toward zero.[67]

Perhaps not surprisingly, almost irreversibly tainted in this process was any ability to argue aggressively against racism or domestic antisemitism through using references to the Holocaust. Analogizing between black and Jewish suffering had been at the core of the "Double V" campaign as well as antiracist arguments found also in Jewish periodicals (like *Commentary*) in the immediate postwar era, but an association with communism appeared to hasten its demise as an acceptable liberal rhetorical device. During the height of the cold war, parallels between German fascism and domestic expressions of white racism and antisemitism simply no longer found widespread expression in the Jewish press. This would continue to be true for most of the decade. By 1958, then, when Martin Luther King Jr. reinvoked memories of the Holocaust as a means to underscore the moral rectitude of the black American civil rights struggle at the national convention of the American Jewish Congress, and to encourage Jewish participation in that struggle, he was using an analogy already freighted with a complicated and ambiguous history. With its roots in the African American press of the early 1930s, and a trajectory that spanned the postwar period where it was found abandoned in large part due to cold war realpolitik, then resuscitated by pro-communist Jews, and only later (as we shall see in chapter 2) readopted—in an altered form—by the less fiercely antileftist elements of cold war liberalism, this analogy already reflected the many inner tensions of an often ambivalent postwar American Jewish politics of race.

References to the Holocaust and its purported lessons for the American context became less frequent in the course of the fifties—precisely because of the dynamics and pressures of anticommunism charted here. Yet, by the end of the decade, as King's remarks suggest, and by the beginning of the sixties, as the next chapter will show, invocations of the Holocaust resurfaced with renewed force. When they did they emerged in competing and mutually irreconcilable forms. In order to make sense of how and why this was so, it is necessary to reconstruct other debates where Jewish leaders sought to work through the proper relationship of the Jewish community to the black struggle for equality. But the conflicting assessments of the relevance of the Holocaust to the subject of American Jewish antiracist activism in the early sixties cannot be fully understood without attention to the later 1940s/early 1950s background described here in chapter 1. It is not only crucial to register that a certain kind of Holocaust analogizing, contrary to conventional assumptions, already existed in the U.S. in the 1940s. It is also significant that the origins of this version of the lessons of fascism lay in the black press and the black-Jewish alliance, and especially that the onset of the cold war made this particular formulation of the possible relationship between Holocaust analogizing and black civil rights activism increasingly untenable.

Yet another important outcome of the conflicts in the late forties and early fifties was the intensifying effort to redraw the boundaries of acceptable racial and ethnic identities along ideological lines. In a very specific sense the

Crisis could say things about a prominent African American—just as *Commentary* slurred the Rosenbergs—that no nonblack journal (or, in the instance of the Rosenbergs, non-Jewish journal) could say without being decried as bigoted. The *Crisis* and *Commentary* both advanced a crucial and interrelated thesis—however debatable—about racial and ethnic identity: it was not just something you had and kept forever. It was also something you could squander or lose, allow to wither or trade away. Appropriate ethnic and racial identity was intimately tied to ideology.

It would become increasingly commonplace in the postwar years for spokespersons within a particular ethnic or racial minority to evaluate others within their group as either suitably group-identified and ethnic enough, or inadequately so. With such judgments came the beginnings of a fresh paradigm about the meanings of ethnic and minority identities. Politics, and perhaps especially radical left politics, could compromise minority status. One could indeed become less black or less Jewish if one accepted radicalism. While the terms of conversation would shift many times in the years ahead—and by the later sixties, one could become *more* black, if still *less* Jewish, if one embraced left radicalism—there would remain this odd notion that politics of a certain (though always historically changing) kind and racial or ethnic identities of a certain (though always shifting) kind bore a definite interrelationship.

2 "Liberal Judaism Is a Contradiction in Terms": Antiracist Zionists, Prophetic Jews, and Their Critics

How can we condemn the millions who stood by under Hitler, or honor those few who chose to live by their ideals, when we refuse to make a similar choice now that the dilemma is our own?
—*Rabbi Jacob M. Rothschild, 1958*

AMERICA MUST NOT REMAIN SILENT

On August 28, 1963, at the March on Washington rally held at the Lincoln Memorial, Dr. Joachim Prinz, rabbi of Temple B'nai Abraham in Newark, New Jersey and president of the American Jewish Congress, gave a brief address entitled "The Issue Is Silence." At Prinz's side stood Dr. Martin Luther King Jr., who delivered his "I Have a Dream" speech that same afternoon and had spoken so memorably at an AJCongress convention in Miami Beach five years earlier. (It was also during the 1958 convention that Prinz was elected to the AJCongress presidency.) In August 1963 Prinz now drew directly on an earlier chapter in his own personal history: his service from 1925 to 1937 as rabbi in the Berlin Jewish community. By the mid-thirties, and until his expulsion by the Gestapo, Prinz had been (as one Berlin congregant put it decades later) "something unheard of in Germany of that period—an ardent, devout and militant Zionist" who "resolutely and unflinchingly" spoke out "against the rising tide of National Socialism" even as he "urged the immediate emigration of Jews from Germany to Palestine, unmasked the shallowness of assimilation, and appealed, again and again, for identification of German Jewry with the eternal fountainhead of the Jewish people and with the upbuilding of its ancient homeland."[1] With the authority of this background, on that late summer day in 1963 before a crowd of two hundred thousand, Prinz recalled his experiences as intimate witness to the advance of Nazism and then revitalized an analogizing link between German fascism and American racism that had all but been obliterated during the early fifties by Jewish anticommunist liberals.

Prinz began simply: "I speak to you as an American Jew." Yet, in the speech that followed, Prinz repeatedly used "we" and "our" and so indicated a self-conscious sense that these words might also serve as a voice for *all* American Jews. He said:

> As Americans we share the profound concern of millions of people about the shame and disgrace of inequality and injustice which make a mockery of the great American idea.
>
> As Jews we bring to this great demonstration, in which thousands of us proudly participate, a twofold experience—one of the spirit and one of our history.

Prinz explained that for Jews "neighbor" is "a moral concept" that "means our collective responsibility for the preservation of man's dignity and integrity." Jewish history tells the story of an ancient heritage of oppression that "began with slavery and the yearning for freedom." American Jews felt "not merely sympathy and compassion for the black people of America" but "above all" a sense of "complete identification and solidarity born of our own painful historic experience."[2]

As Prinz elaborated why Jews struggled for U.S. racial justice after Auschwitz, he presented a different sort of pro-civil rights Holocaust reference than the one put forth by the *Crisis* or *Jewish Life* in the 1940s or King in 1958:

> When I was the rabbi of the Jewish community in Berlin under the Hitler regime, I learned many things. The most important thing that I learned under those tragic circumstances was that bigotry and hatred are not the most urgent problem. The most urgent, the most disgraceful, the most shameful and the most tragic problem is silence.
>
> A great people which had created a great civilization had become a nation of silent onlookers. They remained silent in the face of hate, in the face of brutality and in the face of mass murder.
>
> America must not become a nation of onlookers. America must not remain silent. Not merely black America, but all of America. It must speak up and act, from the President down to the humblest of us, and not for the sake of the Negro, not for the sake of the black community but for the sake of the image, the idea and the aspiration of America itself.[3]

In short, what Prinz was formulating here was a kind of Holocaust analogizing that might best be described by the term *bystander anxiety*: the concern that in failing to work on behalf of African Americans, other Americans, including American Jews, might be behaving no better than most non-Jewish Germans had under Nazism.

These were sentiments that had already begun to find expression in rabbinical and other Jewish circles in the previous several years, as the epigraph from Rabbi Rothschild suggests, though with nowhere near the public prominence of Prinz's speech. In 1962, for instance, in an indicative turn of phrase, gentiles who had rescued Jews from the Holocaust were honored as "Freedom Riders."[4] And earlier in 1963 Rabbi Richard Rubenstein reported on a debate that broke out at the convention of the Rabbinical Assembly (Conservative) after a rabbi proposed that an institute be established whose aim was "to document altruistic deeds done by non-Jews to save Jews during the Hitler holocaust." Rubenstein wrote:

> The proposal touched an understandably sore nerve. In the midst of the debate, one rabbi queried why we were concentrating our energies on what had happened twenty years ago. . . . Then, almost as an afterthought, the rabbi asked whether the Rabbinical Assembly was doing the right thing by meeting together rather than adjourning to Birmingham, Alabama, to aid Dr. Martin Luther King and his followers in their struggle for human rights.[5]

Increasingly, then, rabbis who saw social justice concerns as integral to their faith found in the Holocaust a reference point that underscored the moral righteousness of antiracist activism in the present. As a rabbi who attended the March on Washington told a reporter from *Hadassah Magazine*, Prinz's speech closely reflected his own feelings: "Had this march taken place in the 1930s in Germany, there might never have been the mass murder of Jews. The conscience of the Christians in Germany might have been awakened as our consciences are being awakened today."[6] As chapter 3 will demonstrate, these were far from isolated statements. The years 1963–64 would witness the flourishing of this line of argument.

Yet, before those developments of 1963–64 can be fully understood, it is important to grasp also how Prinz's formulation that compared German and American bystanders to brutality was itself the outgrowth of a complicated and elaborate set of historic developments. For one thing, the historic roots of Prinz's speech need to be traced back to an often angry dispute in the American Jewish communal leadership since the mid-fifties over how best to respond to the crisis of southern Jewish communities hit by antisemitic violence. Notable Jewish defense agencies like the American Jewish Committee, for example, had counseled then that active pro-integration Jewish agendas would place southern Jews at greater risk of extremist right-wing attack. Most southern Jews also made this argument and resented northern Jewish liberal intrusions into their local affairs; closely related to this stance was an argument that the significance of Jewish identity lay in the realm of religion, not politics. In this context Prinz's contention that Jews must remain active in southern desegregation efforts clearly reflected a dissenting position. But Prinz's remarks also need to be understood in the context of the American Jewish Congress and its own postwar priorities; since the late forties the organization had specifically identified its American Zionist mission as inseparable from active support for African American civil rights. Additionally, Prinz's words need to be seen in light of the concerted efforts by a few southern activist rabbis on behalf of racial justice. This was a movement that believed the essence of Jewish faith demanded solidarity with pro-integration activities.

The politics of American Zionism underwent dramatic revision in the course of the twentieth century. At the start of the twenty-first century American Zionism is typically portrayed as a movement whose dedication to Israel's survival completely outweighs all other issues. It would be ludicrous to suggest that Zionists support African American civil rights in equal measure to their support for the state of Israel. Yet this sharp and narrow sense of what Zionism stood (and now stands) for is a product of the late 1960s and early 1970s; the Six-Day War in 1967 and the Yom Kippur War in 1973 exerted tremendous pressure on Zionists to recast their priorities. After that time Israel stood alone at the center of Zionist concerns.[7] Before it, during the fifties, as in earlier decades, American Zionism embraced a more fluid and internally diverse range of ideological commitments. At times secular, at other times religious (with strong ties to the Reform but also the Conservative movements), what bonded one American Zionist to another was a Jewish pride; otherwise, it was not unusual to find that the Zionist identification with a Jewish Palestine (and later Israel) came together with an active involvement in domestic social justice issues. In hindsight this may be most striking when it came to the Zionist dedication to antiracist activism. A strong statement of this dedication came in April 1956, when Dr. Israel Goldstein, a Conservative rabbi who had been president of the Zionist Organization of America and was now president of the AJCongress, stressed in no uncertain terms that the "fulfillment of the American dream" and the "fulfillment of the Zionist dream" were each inseparable from the "problem affecting the American Negro." Goldstein went on explicitly to criticize those more "timid members" of the American Jewish community who advised on the issue of antiracist activism that "'this is not a problem for Jews. We have enough of our own headaches. We ought not take upon ourselves the additional burden of fighting for the Negro.'" Goldstein countered,

> We in the American Jewish Congress act against any evil that is practiced on other men with the same conviction and vigor as if we ourselves were the victims. We must defend the rights of the Negro as zealously as we would defend our rights as Jews whenever and wherever these might be threatened. This is a moral issue from which we dare not avert our faces because of reasons of expediency. It is an American problem in the solution of which all Americans should feel that they have a common stake.[8]

Nor were progressive Zionists in the AJCongress alone in their advocacy of racial justice; an overlapping Zionist commitment to civil rights was also clearly evident during this era in the more openly left-wing Hashomer Hatzair youth movement.[9]

A second antiracist activist movement emerged in the 1950s from within the ranks of the Union of American Hebrew Congregations (UAHC), the major synagogue organization for Reform Judaism in the United States. This movement drew directly from the ancient Jewish prophets to argue that Judaism was a religion committed to social justice. Considered a basic tenet of the Reform movement since the nineteenth century, prophetic Judaism gained renewed relevance in the mid-1950s. One defining postwar expression came in February 1955 when Rabbi Maurice N. Eisendrath, president of the UAHC, addressed the organization's biennial assembly in Los Angeles. Eisendrath said that it was incumbent upon all Jewish leaders to "translate our preachment into practice, our dogmas and doctrines into deed, our creed into conduct, our prayers into programs of moral righteousness and social justice, our invoking of God's name—too frequently in vain—into the establishment of His Kingdom on earth."[10] The following year, Rabbi Eisendrath elaborated that there might be "those who today would partition the synagogue, Judaism, religion itself, from life," but that such divisions were wrong. Instead, the "Torah, its teachings, its moral mandates, touched every facet of human living," for Judaism was far more than "rites and rituals, diet and dishes." Eisendrath preached that the very key to Judaism's survival was its ability to serve as "a concrete guide and tangible aid whereby each synagogue and every member thereof might become a true and living Temple of the Lord."[11] Not surprisingly, many Reform rabbis and laypersons committed to prophetic Judaism were at the forefront of the civil rights struggle during the 1950s, several years before a surge of support developed among Jewish students on college campuses in the early sixties. Nor was it unusual to find these same rabbis and laypersons self-identified as American Zionists as well; the ideals of prophetic Judaism and those of American Zionism were not mutually exclusive.

Studies of postwar American Jewish political thought do recognize the American Jewish Congress as primarily a Zionist organization and note also that the AJCongress was the most fervently antiracist of Jewish defense organizations. However, the fact that these dual allegiances were felt at the time to be inseparable is not discussed. To learn that a Zionist agenda was once conceived to be integrally linked to antiracism (or that a disciple of prophetic Judaism might also be Zionist) might well strike the contemporary observer as disjunctive. This is all the more reason to document these forgotten linkages here. In the later fifties American Zionist antiracism and the rabbinical movement for a prophetic Judaism increasingly found common ground, and together they steadily gained supporters especially among young northern Jewish students. Without understanding this crucial context, moreover, it makes little sense to learn that already by 1960 these activist liberal movements experienced the beginnings of a backlash from influential, more moderate liberal Jewish sources. These sources, in particular *Commentary* magazine, played a major role in setting forth anti-activist arguments that decried the misguided and simple-minded idealism of those Jews strongly involved in black civil rights. Furthermore, in this moderate backlash against the righteousness of Jewish civil rights militancy, one more instrumentalization of the Holocaust for the contemporary American politics of race got voiced. This moderate argument suggested that antiracist activist Jews were insensitive to their own histories as Jews, and most especially to the history of Jewish victimization under Nazism. And it was against this moderate backlash, in turn, that the bystander anxiety argument now began finally to find wider expression, as in the speech by Joachim Prinz.

Most standard accounts of postwar American Jewish history, not to mention most studies of Jewish involvement in black civil rights, tend to leave these historical intricacies underacknowledged, or even unmentioned. Uncovering these disputes among Jewish liberals over support for black civil rights, and the accompanying shifting perspectives on the potential import of the Holocaust for the U.S. context, complicates the familiar portrait of

Jewish support for African Americans as pervasive and unproblematic until the advent of Black Power. Attending to these intra-Jewish conflicts shows that the quality of that support was in fact hotly contested: while all Jewish liberals articulated their commitment to black civil rights, many were actually not convinced that antiracist activism was itself a great idea. Focusing on these neglected elements reveals a fuller portrait of the 1950s and early 1960s Jewish community as bitterly at odds with itself over fundamental social justice concerns.

In addition, it remains the case that general studies of Jewish-black historic relations tend to minimize (or denigrate) the significance of prophetic Judaism as well as the central role it played especially for those southern rabbis who actively opposed segregation during the fifties. Detailing the movement's very existence and the ways it formulated Jewish-black relations, however, is essential for making sense of the urgency with which those hostile to prophetic Judaism would subsequently work to redefine the lessons of the Holocaust for American politics. To reexamine the backlash against antiracist Zionism and prophetic Judaism reveals that these critics advanced a multiplicity of argumentative strategies against both. There was no consensus around how to deal with or address the challenges of these more progressive impulses within the Jewish community. Furthermore, it is crucial for a twenty-first century reader to understand that the key counterargument to prophetic Judaism at the time was that Judaism was a religion and nothing more. In the process, then, of making an argument that prophetic Jews had falsely politicized Jewish identity in order to promote liberal activism on behalf of African American civil rights, what it meant to be a liberal Jew itself underwent a slow but fundamental redefinition. Charting all these complex developments—and reconstructing the mounting ideological hostilities among Jews with respect to antiracist activism—becomes essential if we are to grasp how embattled Prinz's position was when he made his March on Washington speech in August 1963.

In short, then, as Prinz addressed the March on Washington demonstration, and asserted the shamefulness of being a bystander to injustice, he was taking a stand in an already divisive contest about Holocaust legacies, their relationship to the African American civil rights struggle, and the meaning of a *proper* American Jewish identity in relation both to Auschwitz and antiracist activism. Prinz's speech in August 1963 represented a culmination and a turning point in a drawn out and often intense debate within the ranks of professional Jewish leadership about whether it was either wise or expedient for American Jews to become widely identified with antisegregation activism. By giving a most public airing to what had previously been a largely internal and private American Jewish quarrel, Prinz was no doubt well aware of what was at stake—and of how fractured the progressive liberal Jewish alliance in support of civil rights had become. For, from 1960 on, and most dramatically by early 1963 when *Commentary* editor Norman Podhoretz brought up Auschwitz in a confessional essay in which he declared his personal dislike of black men, moderate liberal Jews were finding in the Holocaust a most intense reference point from which to suggest how more progressive Jews were not adequately attuned to the tragic memories of the recent past.

This was an odd twist, yet its popular appeal was undeniable, for it allowed Jews who were skeptical of pro-integration activism a morally righteous riposte of their own. Here was a self-defined liberal (and yet simultaneously antiliberal) Jewish perspective on the Holocaust and its lessons for a politics of race that would only gain ground over the course of the decade. When commentators from the 1980s to the present repeat the now conventional view that Holocaust consciousness in the U.S. only flourished in the aftermath of the Six-Day War in 1967, then, they not only erase the presence of various earlier and more progressive ways to interpret the possible lessons of the Holocaust with respect to racial justice. They neglect as well the early antiprogressive versions of the Holocaust's supposed lessons and the specific context of discomfort with civil rights activism within which these versions were first articulated.

WE KNOW THAT RACISM ENDS IN CHARRED BODIES

Immediately after the 1954 *Brown* decision, which had outlawed the "separate but equal" doctrine, and also after the 1955 Supreme Court ruling that desegregation should proceed with "all deliberate speed," there were divisions among national Jewish organizations over what stands and leadership roles Jews in the North and the South should take on racial issues. Some professional spokespersons for national Jewish defense organizations stated how most especially those tiny Jewish communities in the American South could suffer dearly at the hands of white supremacist groups if Jews got lumped with blacks in the struggle for civil rights, while other Jewish leaders—among them members of the American Jewish Congress and rabbis and laypersons committed to prophetic Judaism—argued both that Jews had a moral obligation to risk themselves in defense of blacks and that (if unchecked) racist violence would eventually hit Jews as well.

As American Jewish historian Naomi Cohen has noted, an overwhelming percentage of southern Jewish leaders resented the encroachment of national Jewish defense organizations into their local affairs when it came to race relations. They actively pressured those organizations to adopt a restrained approach toward antisegregation activism and to couple their efforts with "those of many other non-Jewish organizations, so that civil rights would not be interpreted as primarily a Jewish cause."[12] After all, most Jews in the South now led a relatively untroubled existence; the 1915 lynching of Leo Frank in Georgia was mostly a forgotten nightmare. Southern Jews argued that active engagement—or even the *perception* of active engagement—with civil rights in the mid-fifties could undo their separate peace with southern gentiles virtually overnight.[13] Prominent southern Jews who advocated a policy of moderation also often contended that northern liberal Jews who strenuously called for civil rights were hypocrites because "northern schools were segregated too, in fact if not by law," which meant that "northerners could hardly justify their holier-than-thou attitude."[14] " 'Judge not thy neighbor until thou hast stood in his place,' " editorialized a southern Jewish newspaper in 1956 about these northern Jewish liberals.[15] Given also a perpetuation of a cold war mentality that liked to use words like *communist, nigger-lover,* and *kike* interchangeably, many Jewish leaders considered it both foolhardy and self-destructive for Jewish organizations to risk even deeper association with African Americans or their freedom struggles.

When terrorist violence against Jews did occur, many spokespersons in the Jewish community took this as one more confirmation that Jews and their national organizations *must* avoid too close a connection with civil rights activism after the Supreme Court desegregation decision. In just over four years after 1954 there were eighty-three bombings in the South, including seven bombings and attempted bombings of Jewish institutions. Scores of people were killed or injured and millions of dollars of property were destroyed. On one day in March 1958 a synagogue in Miami and the Nashville Jewish Center were bombed. Other seemingly coordinated attacks on southern synagogues also occurred elsewhere during these years. However the single most horrifying moment may have been when fifty sticks of dynamite blew apart the Temple, the oldest synagogue in Atlanta, in the predawn hours of October 12, 1958. Set alongside a brutal pattern of racist assaults against the southern African American community during these same years, this systematic campaign of antisemitic actions represented what Melissa Fay Greene has called the "lunatics' reply to the *Brown* decision."[16] For many

Jewish leaders both inside and outside the American South, there seemed no response the Jewish community could reasonably make against such naked expressions of lawlessness and terror except to retreat sensibly to a cautious posture from which to protect itself as best as it could.

This policy of moderation toward desegregation activism received considerable support from the leadership of important national Jewish agencies, especially the American Jewish Committee and the Anti-Defamation League of B'nai B'rith (ADL). These were the same professional American Jewish groups that previously had lobbied most fiercely for the active cooperation of American Jews with McCarthyism. (For instance, when Congressman Harold H. Velde of the House Committee on Un-American Activities requested in 1953 that representative religious leaders testify on how the "three faiths" were conducting their war against domestic communism, the AJC shared its files on suspected Jewish communists, telling the Velde Committee that "Judaism and communism are utterly incompatible.")[17] These two Jewish defense groups also had followed (what their critics called) a "shah-shah" (or hush-hush) policy when it came to violent antisemitic activities. Better not discuss antisemitism too openly, the hush-hush policy contended, as it might only give antisemites the publicity they desired, and so fuel their dangerous bravado. Now, after 1954, a new "quiet" policy on civil rights activism emerged as an updated variant on the older hush-hush policy. Better to remain silent in public about racial discrimination, the "quiet" strategy advised, so that behind-the-scenes dealings might achieve slow (but less costly) gains.

It is important to note, furthermore, that this diplomatic approach toward a Jewish politics of racial justice located its justification in a particular interpretation of what it meant to be a Jew. As one American Jewish historian wrote in 1961, these same organizations—the AJC and ADL—both represented the most affluent (and politically moderate) bloc within the American Jewish community and both understood Judaism "strictly as a religious grouping" and not "the ethnic and national channels of Jewish expression." To be Jewish meant to be an adherent of the Jewish faith and had little or nothing to do with politics. Not coincidentally, this was the bloc within American Jewry that prided itself most on its "modern and enlightened" American identity—entirely shed of its immigrant traits. These were, in short, the Jews "most integrated into American life."[18] Thus, these professional Jewish agencies (and the thinkers most associated with them) argued against a view of Jewishness associated *necessarily* with either liberalism or social justice concerns. Significantly, moreover, this disengaged political understanding of Jewish identity got promoted more fiercely as the African American civil rights struggle awoke.

Some of the most concerted arguments against a "quiet" Jewish presence in the fight for African American civil rights came from social justice-oriented American Zionist spokespersons like Joachim Prinz and others long associated with the American Jewish Congress. As the sole major Jewish defense organization profoundly dedicated both to social activism and Jewish nationalism, the AJCongress occupied a unique position on the American postwar scene. As Stuart Svonkin has noted, this dual commitment to Zionism *and* progressive politics meant the AJCongress existed in "relative isolation" among Jewish groups; however, this dual allegiance also spoke for a significant minority in the American Jewish community. It was a double allegiance that garnered tremendous support especially from more left-leaning (though also overwhelmingly anticommunist) American Jews who believed that a domestic campaign against racial injustice was integral to an American Zionist faith.[19]

The conceptual connection between struggles *against* American racism and *for* Jewish nationalism dated back already to the immediate postwar period and marked another chapter in the internal history of American Jewish thought about racial justice after Auschwitz that deserves fuller attention. In November 1949, for instance, political commentator Max Lerner made such a connection between an advocacy for Jewish nationalism and against American racism in his address to the AJCongress biennial convention just as the organization moved to expel members who also belonged to pro-communist groups. A well-respected journalist, educator, and intellectual who had, earlier in the decade, considered the Soviet Union a worthy antifascist state, Lerner had by 1949 soured completely on Stalinism. Thus Lerner represented well a cold war mood experienced throughout the Jewish liberal community. Yet he refused to choose between conflicting ways to analogize from Nazism. At one and the same time Lerner took on board the new anticommunist consensus that Stalinism and Nazism were comparable evils and elaborated comparisons between antisemitism in Germany and antiblack racism in the U.S.

For example, Lerner condemned the "totalitarianism of the left" whose aim "to win the world or to win America" would inevitably mean for Jews that "the basic spirit that we have stood for in our history would have to be extinguished." And he intoned dramatically: "There is something about a Jew that hates a storm trooper of any kind; and there is something about a storm trooper that hates a Jew." Most of Lerner's address, however, celebrated the AJCongress for its leadership role both as a champion of Jewish nationalism and a supporter of American social justice. This dual leadership role, Lerner said, was "the only way to fulfill this organic sense of being at once Americans and Jews." As a former pro-Soviet intellectual, Lerner suggested, he had come to recognize this "organic sense" neither easily nor quickly. Rather, Lerner said, before he realized the "relation between myself and Jews elsewhere in the world, six million of my brothers and sisters had to die." Lerner elaborated with stories of his recent trips both to Germany—especially his visit to Dachau—and to Israel. He discussed a recent day in Jerusalem when he witnessed the funeral of Theodor Herzl, the spiritual father of the modern Zionist movement. It was a tremendous spectacle with persons of all races gathered together as a people in this new democratic nation. Only U.S. heritage offered anything analogous:

> As I looked at these people, my mind went back to Walt Whitman who had once seen another group and nation growing like this, and who said, "This is not a nation, this is a nation of nations."
>
> And as I looked at the Jews, I said again, "This is not a nation, it is a nation of nations."

As both an American and as a Jew, some might argue that he "ought to be a split personality," Lerner said, though the actual effect was the opposite. "I feel more normal because of what has happened in Israel, because that has helped to normalize my life."[20]

This was Lerner's message: a pride in Israeli statehood meant American Jews could be "better fighters for democracy" at home, enabling them to stand against those "primitives in America, basically illiterate in the language of the human heart," who "light joyous fires in their hearts when misguided veteran groups in a town like Peekskill go around beating and clubbing people." Even though Lerner was fiercely anticommunist, then, he still identified with the leftist victims of the Peekskill riots. Furthermore, presaging a progressive argument that would only gain wider currency a decade later, Lerner argued how the cause of Jewish nationalism and the struggle for U.S. racial justice were indissoluble after Auschwitz:

> The new pride that I have in being a complete personality makes me, I think, a better fighter in America for democratic causes, because I have come to understand the true inwardness of what anti-democratic movements mean. I now understand that they are not just jokes. They are a grim thing that ends

in the furnaces of Auschwitz and Dachau. We have come to understand what the meaning of racism is. We know that racism ends in death. We know that racism ends in charred bodies.[21]

JUSTICE AND JUDAISM

The other significant strand within American Jewish thought in the mid-fifties arguing that Jews should stand at the forefront of the civil rights struggle was the Reform movement of prophetic Judaism. The core beliefs of prophetic Judaism were elaborated in the landmark book *Justice and Judaism*, which appeared in 1956 and was reprinted four times by 1959. Written by Albert Vorspan and Rabbi Eugene Lipman, directors of the UAHC's Commission on Social Action, *Justice and Judaism* made its point plain and simple: "A synagogue which isolates itself from the fundamental issues of social justice confronting the community and the nation is false to the deepest traditions and values of the Jewish heritage." As evidence, the authors returned to the words of the prophets Isaiah, Amos, and Micah and found there that a "passionate belief and concern for justice for all men is inherent in Judaism." For instance, they quoted approvingly this proclamation of Micah:

He has told thee, O man, what is good;
And what doth the Lord require of thee,
But to do justice and to love mercy
And to walk humbly with thy God. (6:8)

The authors further noted that throughout Jewish history it was to the synagogue the poor would come "to receive, not charity, but *tse'dakah* their righteous due. To the synagogue came the lame and the sick, to be cared for in community hospices. To the synagogue came the sinned-against to cry out against injustice, and to receive justice." In the American fifties, the authors went on to argue, a prophetic Judaism righteously demanded of all Jews that they struggle actively for African American civil rights. Southern Jews had often urged "neutrality," the authors wrote, but the "bombings of Jewish institutions in the South should have shattered the illusion that the Jewish community can be 'neutral' or 'safe' when the fabric of law and order disentangles."[22]

Indeed, with the American South becoming the major site for an embittering disagreement over the appropriate place of Judaism in the struggle for civil rights, it was especially those southern Reform rabbis who were members of the UAHC's Commission on Social Action who took the lead in preaching a Jewish social activism. They alone among southern Jewish leaders articulated prophetic Judaism as *the* reason why racial justice was integral to their Jewish faith. For instance, there was Dr. William Silverman, an activist rabbi in Nashville, Tennessee, who in early 1958 emphasized that a Jewish strategy of silence toward racial integration was immoral. "If we are to be true to our heritage of prophetic Judaism," Rabbi Silverman told his congregation, "then not only we in Nashville, but every congregation must stand and be counted to live by our faith and implement its moral ideals." Silverman explained why so much was at stake in the U.S. struggle for racial justice:

> Much more is involved than an attack upon the Negro. The Negro is the symbol to galvanize the mobilization of the bigots for warfare against all spiritual values. The ultimate objective is to attack the principles and precepts of the Judeo-Christian way of life. There is a time when silence is cowardly. There is a time when our faith must commit us to moral action. Now is such a time.[23]

Likewise, in a withering denunciation of segregation delivered as part of a Yom Kippur service in Alexandria, Virginia, in 1958, Rabbi Emmet Frank said: "When those who are not afraid to speak, even when thousands of citizens who felt secure in the law have been silenced because of fear of reprisals, when those who are not afraid to speak sound like a voice crying in the wilderness—it is our moral obligation as Jews not to desist from being a light unto the nation."[24] And there was Rabbi Charles Mantinband of Hattiesburg, Mississippi, who wrote, also in 1958, how it was "the moral evil of segregation" that obligated Jews "to stand up and be counted."[25] As Melissa Fay Greene has pointed out, it was largely because of the antiracist activism of these few southern rabbis that "the phrase 'prophetic Judaism' entered the modern lexicon of the Reform movement."[26]

Almost immediately, however, efforts were underway to downplay and quell the potential impact of calls for a prophetic interpretation of Judaism. One influential strategy was to stress that religion and politics bore no relationship to one another while nonetheless reporting the self-congratulatory news that American Jews were predominantly liberal and supported a civil rights agenda. Nathan Glazer's *American Judaism* (1957) provided one important articulation of this approach. Glazer's intellectual pedigree more than suggested the leaning of his thought; he had been on the editorial staff at *Commentary* from its first issue in 1945 until 1954, and *American Judaism* not only warmly acknowledged a deep debt to *Commentary* founding editor Elliot Cohen but also subtly advanced an American Jewish Committee perspective on Jewish engagement with African American civil rights activism. On the one hand, Glazer went out of his way to note that American Jews were "almost universally to be found among the defenders of civil liberties and civil rights" and were also "generally against the segregation of Negroes." On the other hand, he emphasized pointedly that it was "hard to see direct links with Jewish tradition in these attitudes." Glazer further held that "it is specious to say" that American Jews expressed religious attitudes through their concern for social justice. The one had nothing to do with the other. "Indeed," Glazer concluded, "it is one of the most remarkable things about American Judaism, as distinct from American Jews, that it is not particularly concerned with social problems." If Jews happened to be liberal, then that liberalism derived from exposure to traditions and values other than religious ones (such as the liberalism and leftism brought from Europe by immigrants). As factually accurate as Glazer's assessments may have been, his assertions nonetheless had ideological implications in the context of his day. Ignoring the prophetic Judaism movement of his own time, for example, Glazer at one point announced he found "surprising" the "failure of a Jewish 'social gospel' movement to develop among Reform Jews."[27] Glazer also neglected to mention the social justice agenda—let alone the existence—of the American Jewish Congress, *the* organization that represented, as one American Jewish historian has written, "the most militantly de-segregationist of national Jewish communal organizations" at the precise historic moment Glazer was preparing *American Judaism*.[28]

In their local contexts advocates of a prophetic Judaism found themselves severely reproached by other southern Jews. As one Alabama rabbi told Jacob Rothschild, the activist rabbi of the Temple in Atlanta, he wouldn't risk "one hair on the head of one of my members for the life of every *shvartzeh* in this state."[29] Or as another southern Jew angrily reprimanded a representative from a progressive national Jewish organization for meddling in local southern affairs: "You people are like Hitler. You're stirring up anti-Semitism down here."[30] Resistance like this was customary, and the few activist rabbis willing to stand up for racial justice found themselves isolated, upbraided, or out of work.

In 1957, for instance, Harry Golden, editor of the *Carolina Israelite* and a widely respected commentator on Jewish life in the South, recounted the case of one Rabbi Seymour Atlas who had served the congregation Agudath Israel of Montgomery, Alabama for almost a decade. The previous year

Rabbi Atlas had joined together with a Roman Catholic priest and an African American, Reverend Ralph Abernathy, for an interfaith Brotherhood Week program. Abernathy had just participated in and been arrested for his participation in a local bus boycott, and a photograph of the three clergymen appeared in *Life* magazine alongside a story about the boycott. Golden outlined the fallout from these events:

> The board of trustees of the synagogue were chagrined at this publicity. They were angry at *Life*, at Rev. Abernathy, at the bus strike; but they were particularly angry at their Rabbi Atlas. They ordered him to demand a "retraction" from *Life*. He was to explain that the Brotherhood Week had been purely coincidental; that it had nothing to do with Negroes, Rev. Abernathy, Supreme Court decisions, or with the Montgomery bus strike. The rabbi of course refused to be a party to any such nonsense; and the trustees were in for yet another shock at the very next Sabbath service during which Rabbi Atlas offered up a prayer for the success of the bus strike against racial segregation.

After continued harassment from the board of trustees—which included the "silent treatment" ("they literally turned their backs as he passed them in the synagogue or on the street") and then a demand that he submit his sermons to the trustees before he could deliver them—Atlas resigned. "The trustees accepted his resignation," Golden wrote, "and voted unanimously that the next rabbi must sign a pledge not to discuss Negroes or the segregation issue 'in any manner, shape or form whatsoever.' "[31] A story like this was clearly designed at least to shame those who had failed to speak out in Atlas's defense as well as anyone else who might have remained silent under similar circumstances.

As the fifties came to an end, prophetic Judaism gained credence within the more progressive elements of the national Jewish community. It was an approach to Jewish identity that preached an intimate interconnection between personal behavior and political action, and it thus represented for many Jews what would become the wellspring for much sixties activism. In other words, it argued that the personal involvement of every single individual in struggles for social justice was a moral obligation—even if whatever difference that involvement made was not immediately evident. It also spoke of sacrifice. At a major conference on religion and race early in 1963, for example, Rabbi Abraham J. Heschel, a professor at the Jewish Theological Seminary, said that the religious commandment to equality "means my being hurt when a Negro is offended." Heschel defined the struggle for civil rights activism as a properly Jewish activity and added, emphatically, "Let there be a grain of prophet in every man!"[32]

In September 1963 the UAHC distributed to its more than 650 congregations "A Call to Racial Justice," which, among other things, recommended for congregational adoption and implementation "practices designed to promote racial justice in the lives of the congregation's individual members."[33] Although its preaching often sounded abstract to its critics, those who promoted prophetic Judaism insisted it was just the opposite. It was a belief system that brought all elements of Judaism together, and it enabled Jews to identify the special relevance of their religion in the modern world. As the director of the Commission on Interfaith Activities for the UAHC, Rabbi Balfour Brickner, observed: "Judaism's involvement in the quest for racial justice is motivated by the twin propellants of faith and experience." American racism was not the "exclusive responsibility of any single group," conceded Brickner, but, nevertheless, "we who every Passover still relive the painful lash of the taskmaster, who still recall the sting of slavery and who will never forget 'that the ghetto was first invented to segregate Jews,' feel quite naturally that we have a special stake in this newest American revolution."[34]

In the midst of these discussions, also from the mid-fifties onward, assertions about the legacies of the Holocaust and the lessons of German fascism for an American context began subtly to be revived. One notable example came from historian Louis Ruchames when he informed an audience during Negro History Week in February 1955 that "we Jews have known within our lives and the lives of our fathers the problems which have confronted the Negro." He elaborated: "And in our own day, the lesson that men have had to relearn in every generation, that the rights of all men are inter-related, that no minority group is safe while others are the victims of persecution, has been seared into our minds and hearts through the burning flesh of six million of our brethren in Europe."[35] The following year, an editorial from *Congress Weekly* bitterly attacked a House of Representatives subcommittee whose public hearings into "reported low standards in the schools" had devolved into a "persistent allegation . . . that Negroes are inferior in innate intelligence." As the editorial immediately noted, "What is so depressing about the tack taken by the subcommittee is that it comes perilously close to reviving exploded Nazi-like race theories."[36] And, also in 1956, and most explicit in its call for a Jewish identification with pro-integration activism, the resolutely left-wing (if by now non-Stalinist) journal *Jewish Life* quoted respected sociologist Arnold Rose, who had earlier noted similarities between the nationalist aims of Marcus Garvey and Theodor Herzl. Speaking at a National Community Relations Advisory Council meeting, Rose went so far as to argue that unless Jewish leaders took a "courageous" stand in the fight against southern segregation "they are playing the same role as the collaborationist Jews played in Europe during the Nazi period."[37]

Especially as terrorist violence in the South grew more intense, articulations of a bystander anxiety argument similar to the one Joachim Prinz would express in August 1963 found increasingly broad expression. Such views appeared, for example, in a 1958 *Congress Weekly* essay addressed to those southern Jews who advocated the "expediency of silence." It made this Holocaust comparison:

> We have all gratefully honored those Christians who, at the very risk of their lives, aided Jews to survive the holocaust of Hitlerism. It would be ironic if after expressing our admiration for those who helped save the Jews we should now condone the rationalization that we ought to do nothing on behalf of the Negro because it may jeopardize Jewish security.[38]

At the same time, however, there was caution in applying these rhetorical analogies to fascism too blithely. Rabbi Prinz himself, for example, observed in the immediate aftermath of the Temple bombing in Atlanta that there could be no direct analogy made between events in Nazi Germany and recent antisemitic violence in the U.S. In a November 1958 address marking the twentieth anniversary of the *Kristallnacht* pogroms when his own synagogue in Berlin had been among fourteen hundred burned and pillaged, Prinz advised listeners to keep in mind the tremendous differences between 1938 Germany and present-day America. "Germany went mad," Prinz said, while here "in America just the reverse is true. From President Eisenhower on down the American people have been shocked at these bombings and expressed outrage and shame at them." Hysteria was inappropriate, he continued, and those who "raise the spectre of a rising anti-Semitism in America" deserved to be "condemned as reckless and irresponsible. They are doing the community a disservice."[39] World events would, however, soon change—seemingly irreversibly—the possible ways to interpret the lessons of the Holocaust for the present.

THE LIBERAL JEW OF TODAY IS IN A DILEMMA

On December 24, 1959, a swastika was painted on a synagogue in Cologne, Germany. Two days later the first similar incident occurred in the

United States; antisemitic vandalism also occurred repeatedly in other German cities, and the pattern then spread to other European countries. For nine weeks after the end of December 1959, swastikas appeared on Jewish synagogues, on Jewish community centers, on sidewalks, automobiles, churches, storefronts, walls of schoolrooms, and college campuses. There were over six hundred incidents altogether.[40]

This was followed in May 1960 by the announcement that Adolf Eichmann, the highest Nazi official in direct contact with Jewish leaders and the man most responsible for the transport of Jews to the death camps, had been arrested in Argentina by the Israeli intelligence and security police. David Ben-Gurion, the Israeli prime minister and leader of Mapai (Labor), announced that Eichmann would stand trial before an Israeli court on charges of genocide. It was this decision to try Eichmann in Jerusalem that provoked much dissent and debate, for it was, as Israeli journalist Tom Segev has observed, a decision motivated by deep political need. Ben-Gurion wished nothing less than to have the Eichmann trial "remind the countries of the world that the Holocaust obligated them to support the only Jewish state on earth." In other words, the Eichmann trial would give Ben-Gurion's Mapai administration the opportunity to demonstrate "its control over the heritage of the Holocaust," control that had long been contested within Israel by political parties on both the right and the left.[41]

Meanwhile, during this same period, progressive American Zionism faced an internal crisis of its own. As Milton Himmelfarb put it rather ruefully in the summer of 1960, the American Jewish Congress might call itself the leading American Zionist organization, but its president was more interested in civil rights activism than Zionism and its membership voiced "strong proud-to-be-a-Jew feelings" even though these "feelings are without content and in fact are more attached to civil-rights rhetoric than to Jewish religion, education, or culture." In truth, he averred, it was "inconclusive" whether the AJCongress was "a Jewish organization with a civil-rights program or a civil-rights organization whose members are Jews," and it appeared quite likely "a split was in the making."[42]

The split occurred later that same year. At the World Zionist Congress in Jerusalem held in December 1960, Prime Minister Ben-Gurion declared that the "Judaism of the Jews of the United States and similar countries is losing all meaning, and only a blind man can fail to see the danger of extinction, which is spreading without being noticed." Ben-Gurion's scorn for Jews in the Diaspora (and especially in the U.S.) was nothing new, but here he raised it to a new level. As Ben-Gurion forcefully put it, "Since the day when the

Jewish State was established and the gates of Israel were flung open to every Jew who wanted to come, every religious Jew has daily violated the precepts of Judaism and the Torah of Israel by remaining in the Diaspora." Indeed, he continued, "Whoever dwells outside the land of Israel is considered to have no God."[43] While nearly all leading American Zionists (including the influential leadership of Hadassah and Labor Zionism) refrained from public criticism of Ben-Gurion, Joachim Prinz promptly wrote, "Zionism is—for all practical purposes—dead." Prinz cut his support for the World Zionist Congress, and concluded that Zionism was a movement "no longer capable of responding to the new needs of a new generation. Attainment and fulfillment are killers of dreams, and this, not to belabor the point, is precisely what has happened to the Zionist movement."[44] Prinz recommitted the resources of the American Jewish Congress to African American civil rights activism. Only Prinz's small American Zionist allies on the left in Hashomer Hatzair shared these priorities, for they too rejected Ben-Gurion's negation of Diaspora Zionism. As the Hashomer Hatzair newspaper, *Israel Horizons*, editorialized earlier in 1960 during Ben-Gurion's U.S. visit, the prime minister wanted only "two things in the American Jewish community: Its money, and its youth."[45] Not incidentally, this internal debate over the proper priorities of American Zionism coincided with a more broad-based move to call into question certain strategies of young antiracist liberals.

For instance, already in the spring of 1960, as northern Jewish students took a more prominent role in the struggle for African American civil rights, prominent Labor Zionist intellectual and *Jewish Frontier* editor Marie Syrkin questioned the wisdom of some of their actions in print. It would be inaccurate to label Syrkin's position as antiliberal; she made it absolutely clear that the "heroic struggle for civil rights waged by Negro students calls for the maximum of assistance," and she furthermore underscored her unstinting admiration for "our young intellectuals 'engaged' in a cause instead of ostentatiously disengaged." Yet, at the same time, Syrkin's overarching point was to question the move to picket outside Woolworth stores in the North as a protest against the chain's discriminatory practices in the South. Syrkin felt that this tactic "raises serious questions as to its common sense and effectiveness." As a "gesture," Syrkin said, it was "too trivial to produce a change of heart or view." Furthermore, such protests in northern cities could easily have a counterproductive effect. After all, Syrkin asked,

> What is the effect on the average passer-by in the North when he sees bright-faced young students marching with placards in front of a store at whose

> counter a Negro may be seen sitting side by side with white customers. The sympathy of the average citizen in this instance is more likely to be with the store manager "who is doing the right thing"—serving Negroes—than with the marching picketers, who seem to be "making trouble" needlessly.

The "battle of the Negro is too serious and tragic to be utilized as a pedagogic tool," Syrkin critically observed, and if students wanted to make a difference they would do better to engage in "meaningful, as well as risky, protest" like the "sit-down demonstrations at a segregated counter in the South."[46]

Also in 1960, fellow Labor Zionist and *Midstream* editor Shlomo Katz wondered whether civil rights activism wasn't simply faddish because it allowed students to engage in cathartic social guilt-releasing bouts of group therapy. Katz concurred with Syrkin's disparaging assessments of the long-distance liberal activism performed by white Northerners on behalf of racial justice. Katz concluded that such risk-free protests represented merely a "salve for the conscience" of the sort that was becoming the "fashion among liberals and self-proclaimed radicals alike." Katz added sarcastically that it was a lot easier—not to mention, safer—for northern intellectuals to "write brilliant editorials ridiculing the Governor of Arkansas (if only he would read them he would die of shame, but he doesn't read them and isn't even aware of their existence)" than it was to struggle against de facto segregation in their own northern neighborhoods.[47] It took no guts to engage in northern liberal protests or to write moving editorials against segregation, and perhaps that was why such actions—however pointless—were becoming so popular. (And was it simply a coincidence, as Syrkin and Katz no doubt must have known, that Dr. Joachim Prinz had himself marched in a Woolworth's anti-segregation picket line alongside those same "bright-faced young students" in New York?)

Skepticism about the new "fashion" for antiracist protest also appeared in *Commentary* magazine. In June 1960 it published the testimonial of a disillusioned University of Chicago undergraduate who had enthusiastically picketed in front of a local Woolworth's store. "Most of our activity accomplishes little," the student now despondently concluded. "We achieve none of the small victories which might encourage us to believe that we are not wasting our time."[48] While, throughout the fifties, Jewish social activists had been on the offensive with their argument that timidity, or cowardice, prevented the American Jewish community from confronting racial injustice more resolutely, in 1960 a reversed perspective made its appearance. Now some prominent Jewish liberals suggested that idealistic Jewish liberals or Jewish radicals were so invested in appearances they flinched when called upon to challenge liberal pieties no matter how inane they were. And what brand of courage did that take?

After Norman Podhoretz became its editor in February 1960, *Commentary* presented its critique of progressive Jewish liberalism from a number of interrelated angles, even as it also continued to voice general support for integration and civil rights. However, the idea that Podhoretz advanced an anti-left agenda from 1960 onward is hardly the standard view. On the contrary, most typically Podhoretz is assumed at that time to have been a radical with left-wing sympathies. Historians seem mainly to take Podhoretz's own later retrospective rendition at its word; for instance, one historian uncritically cites Podhoretz's "self-identification as a radical," and another observes that when "Podhoretz took over [*Commentary*], he brought the magazine to the left."[49] Yet these conclusions merely disguise concerted attacks already launched by *Commentary* in 1960 and 1961 against a Jewish engagement with racial justice concerns. While most scholars and journalists assume that the so-called backlash among Jews against liberalism began only when blacks were understood to be becoming more militant—i.e., in 1964–65—the evidence from *Commentary*, like that from *Jewish Frontier* and *Midstream*, suggests that—although the views put forward were often mutually inconsistent—a remarkable variety of antiprogressive arguments were already being formulated at the very beginning of the sixties.

For example, and although Lucy Dawidowicz's contribution to *Commentary* in 1960 mainly rehashed what Nathan Glazer had argued in his 1957 book, *American Judaism*, she did cannily update Glazer's analysis for the sixties. Observing that the "modern Jew's concern with social justice does not, I think, derive from the ethical teachings of Judaism," Dawidowicz continued:

> The modern Jew's impulse to help the wronged and the oppressed springs, it seems to me, from the fact that he associates his own security with a democratic, liberal, and secular society. He looks upon a threat (even if not directed specifically against him) to any of these aspects of the society he lives in as an evil to be combatted. To be sure, Jewish advocates of good deeds and social welfare draw upon the teachings of the Torah and the prophets to stimulate Jewish involvement. But chapter and verse merely serve to adorn the will to self-preservation.[50]

If Syrkin and Katz conjectured that Jewish social justice activism in reality lacked the courage of its own abstract convictions, Dawidowicz doubted whether the call to selfless sacrifice embodied by Jewish activism represented true altruism. What better way to challenge self-styled altruists than to accuse them of selfishness? More important, in stressing the *lack* of logical connection between Jewish faith and Jewish activism, Dawidowicz once again implicitly challenged the very core of prophetic Judaism.

Rabbi Emil Fackenheim made an even stronger claim than Dawidowicz, although ultimately with a completely different emphasis. At the age of twenty-two, Fackenheim had been imprisoned in Sachsenhausen concentration camp; he subsequently was ordained as a Reform rabbi in Berlin in 1939 and escaped to Canada the following year. Writing in *Commentary* in 1960, Fackenheim condemned prophetic Judaism outright for its insistent pleas for social justice. Such an interpretation of Judaism was false and, Fackenheim predicted, would collapse under its own internal inconsistencies. "The liberal Jew of today is in a dilemma," Fackenheim wrote, because the liberal Jew will have to confront the "possibility that he might in the end have to choose between his Judaism and his liberalism; that, as critics on both right and left have charged all along, liberal Judaism is a contradiction in terms." The teachings of Jewish liberalism, moreover, Fackenheim contended, produced "broad-minded, pluralistic, and tolerant" young Jewish people unable to articulate the traditional values of Judaism even if their lives depended on it.[51]

In a sense Fackenheim meant this last point quite literally. Progressive Jewish youth, in his view, neither seemed to know or even care what the German Nazis had done to the Jews. He illustrated this dramatic conclusion with the disturbing story of a recent experience teaching a confirmation class in a liberal synagogue.

> I would cite extreme and repellent examples of conflicting belief. "What about cannibalism? What about Nazism? Wouldn't you say that at least these are absolutely wrong and false beliefs?" On this some of the students would surrender. But others were prepared to regard even Nazism with relativistic "impartiality." "*We* may think we are right and they are wrong. But *they* think the exact opposite. So who is to make an impartial decision?"

Young Jews were now so "liberal" they hesitated to condemn fascism! If teachers of Judaism and Jewish leaders allowed such appalling perspectives to go unchallenged in the name of "tolerance" or "liberal humanism," Fackenheim warned, then Judaism itself might soon cease to exist in any meaningful sense. Preaching Judaism as merely "a way of life" that should advocate social justice was "highly problematic" because this "progressive" view of Judaism damaged Jewish faith with its "relativism." What would come next? Fackenheim made his dire predictions: "Passover would become just another 'festival of freedom,' the Sabbath just another 'socially progressive institution,' and Yom Kippur—heaven only knows what; and what is specifically Jewish about these festivals would reduce itself to 'folklore,' 'customs,' 'ceremonies.' "[52]

Again along a different line, though with related effect, *Commentary* also ridiculed Harry Golden, the longtime champion of southern Jewish antiracist activism. Theodore Solotaroff, an associate editor, dismissed Golden's prose because it dished out to "bland, homey Americans" a folksy blend of "affable flatulence" designed to "soothe anxieties, provide a confident if vague sense of direction, and preside over the evasion of issues." Golden's writing was not simply bad because it represented Americans' more general tendency toward "soft, sloppy, equivocal thinking" or was itself "so soft that any heavy commitment is unable to stand upon it for more than a paragraph." Solotaroff finished his damning appraisal of Golden's writing by comparing it to Republican party rhetoric in the fifties:

> For all the supposed vitality and alertness in Golden's writing, there is a softness in his prose and his thought, a steady veering away from complexity and controversy to the safe banality or the nice sentiment, and a power of accommodation that eventually occupies both sides of the question, which give his books much of the eery feeling of an Eisenhower press conference or a Nixon speech.[53]

Meanwhile, Milton Himmelfarb, whose regular *Commentary* column on American Jewish communal affairs began in 1960, arguably went one step further when he maintained that Jewish liberals lacked a healthful self-respect. In August 1960 he pondered how liberal Jewish lawyers for the American Civil Liberties Union could defend the constitutional rights of George Lincoln Rockwell, commander of the American Nazi party: "One thing puzzles me: what moral or professional obligation led *Jewish* lawyers to volunteer?" Himmelfarb suggested that this "liberal" impulse was a potential threat to American Jewish communal survival.

> It will not happen here, almost certainly; but the possibility of its happening is increased if the only impulse a Rockwell arouses in us is to defend his dubious rights and help him emulate Hitler and Goebbels.

For myself I am disturbed by the unreal, detached—or hostile?—stance of so many Jewish liberals in the Eichmann and especially the Rockwell matters. Is it a simple failure of the imagination that is responsible? Is it repression, or distortion, or diversion of affect? Probably something more complex and obscure; and troubling.[54]

What was emerging, then, in the analysis of Himmelfarb (as in that of Fackenheim) was an antiprogressive liberal strategy that raised its eyebrows at extreme examples, but then cast them as symptomatic or typical cases. In the process progressive liberalism looked ridiculous—or worse. From this perspective, Fackenheim could conclude that all Jewish progressive liberals were wishy-washy when it came to German fascism, while Himmelfarb could argue that those same Jews were so anxious to protect Rockwell's First Amendment rights they forgot their own heritage.

This strategy, which generalized that an extreme example was representative and thus suggested that all progressive Jews spoke with the same voice and marched to the same drummer, also found its way into the opinions of Norman Podhoretz himself. He too incisively linked his own skepticism of progressive liberalism to the survival of the Jewish people after Auschwitz. In spring 1960, and with a brilliant gift for passionate argument, Podhoretz introduced an excerpt from the memoirs of journalist Arthur Settel, the lead piece in that issue of *Commentary*. In 1951 Settel had witnessed the hanging of Oswald Pohl and other leading Nazis, and Podhoretz took the occasion to defend the idea of capital punishment in these cases. The executions might have been made easier if Pohl and the other men "would have walked to the gallows with their crimes etched on their faces and their bodies disfigured into monstrous shapes, so that they could be robbed of the power to exert a claim on our sympathies." But instead these men "looked and acted like men, ordinary run-of-the-mill men." Podhoretz detailed the atrocities each executed man had committed, and then wrote:

My own view is that to a Jew the possibility that anything short of death should be meted out to these men ought to be no less (and perhaps no more) outrageous than the spectacle of the hangings themselves. I believe that any Jew who so far permits himself to forget what the Nazis were and did as to condemn the executions altogether is committing a kind of violence against his own humanity that may be more deeply barbaric than the events described by Mr. Settel—barbaric in the way that the young father in Philadelphia was last year when he publicly trotted out all the clichés of liberal en-

> lightenment to plead for "understanding" of the boy who had assaulted and murdered his four-year-old daughter the day before. The Nazis dehumanized themselves in carrying out their mass slaughters; and any Jew who indulges the inclination to forgive and forget is countering that dehumanization with a species of his own—a species not at all comparable in kind or degree or quality, but one that can be called dehumanization nevertheless.[55]

If the American Jewish Congress since the late forties said antisemitism and white racism were the principal dangers to Jewish security, and the American Jewish Committee in the early fifties named communism as the central threat, then Podhoretz at the start of the sixties looked to the psychopathological demons within. Auschwitz had left scars on every Jew, but they were seldom if ever visible to the naked eye. As dramatized by the nightmarish allegorical tale of the "liberal" father who asked that his daughter's murderer receive "understanding," Podhoretz believed that each Jew was in a pitched internal struggle to reclaim emotional well-being after the Holocaust, whether that individual knew it or not. Indeed, a lack (or denial) of consciousness that there even existed a struggle was arguably the surest sign that there was. Jews after Auschwitz had to grasp that the genocidal campaign the Nazis waged against them was not over. The genocide had merely moved to a more ambiguous place, one that involved the health and emotional security of each Jew's own mind.

FEAR TURNED TO HATRED

Podhoretz's fascination with the psychology of the liberal Jewish mind was not short-lived, as evidenced by his remarkable and memorable essay, "My Negro Problem—And Ours," which appeared in February 1963. This essay foreshadowed many of the arguments that would become so prevalent in the second half of the sixties. Podhoretz believed liberals were internally divided. Alluding to the phenomenon of white flight from the inner cities, for example, Podhoretz summarized what he saw as the disconnect between liberal creeds and liberal deeds. "Thus everywhere we look today in the North," Podhoretz wrote, "we find the curious phenomenon of white middle-class liberals with no previous personal experience of Negroes—people to whom Negroes have always been faceless in virtue rather than faceless in vice—discovering that their abstract commitment to the cause of Negro rights will not stand the test of a direct confrontation." Podhoretz also described liberals suddenly "judiciously considering whether the

Negroes (for their own good, of course) are not perhaps pushing too hard; we find them clucking their tongues over Negro militancy; we find them speculating on the question of whether there might not, after all, be something in the theory that the races are biologically different." Such ruthless observations flaunted liberal convention, but they represented only a starting point. What made this essay so controversial and breathtaking had far more to do with its reflections on contemporary American Jewish identity. To achieve the effect he sought, Podhoretz used a framing device: the essay began and concluded with a case study of an emotionally inhibited Jewish boy in Brooklyn terrified he might be a "sissy" ("that most dreadful epithet of an American boyhood").[56] Yet he lived a life dominated by a desire to please his mother and his teachers, indicating the boy was becoming that which he most feared. Furthermore, when resentment at his successes led black boys in his class to beat him up, the little Jewish boy remained too scared to squeal on them. He could not let go of these humiliations, and so could not overcome his discomfort with black men. This case study was derived from Podhoretz's own childhood memories. Then came the middle section of the essay, representative samples of which are quoted above. There was not one mention of Jewishness. Only at the end did Podhoretz return to the framing story.

Grown to manhood, and now an accomplished intellectual, Podhoretz confessed that he still carried inside himself the trauma of his childhood humiliations, but he was now also a good liberal with a well-developed superego that dictated he articulate a need for racial justice. Podhoretz wished above all somehow to reconcile these educated convictions with his own repressed past. Yet he had been so often a scapegoat for black boys eager to find someone to blame for their own deficiencies and mistakes; he confessed he still had "twisted feelings about Negroes." Podhoretz remained annoyed at white liberals who, in his view, "romanticize Negroes and pander to them" or who "permit Negroes to blackmail them into adopting a double standard of moral judgment, and who lend themselves . . . to cunning and contemptuous exploitation by Negroes they employ or try to befriend." In the end, and peculiarly, Podhoretz invoked Auschwitz as a means for grasping how possibly the racial crisis in the United States should be overcome:

> Did the Jews have to survive so that six million innocent people should one day be burned in the ovens at Auschwitz? It is a terrible question and no one, not God himself, could ever answer it to my satisfaction. And when I think about the Negroes in America and about the image of integration as a state in

> which the Negroes would take their rightful place as another of the protected minorities in a pluralistic society, I wonder whether they really believe in their hearts that such a state can actually be attained, and if so *why* they should wish to survive as a distinct group. I think I know why the Jews once wished to survive (though I am less certain as to why we still do): they not only believed that God had given them no choice, but they were tied to a memory of past glory and a dream of imminent redemption. What does the American Negro have that might correspond to this? His past is a stigma, his color is a stigma, and his vision of the future is the hope of erasing the stigma by making color irrelevant, by making it disappear as a fact of consciousness.

From here Podhoretz concluded—however idiosyncratically—that only complete miscegenation could result (eventually) in a world where the races would "*in fact* disappear."[57]

As a means of inoculating himself against charges that he was mocking or ridiculing the earnest efforts of liberal antiracist activism, Podhoretz dramatized (or fantasized—one could never be entirely sure) the pathos of his own youth. If nothing else, little Norman had been a *nebbish*; bullied and cursed, forced to wear scratchy clothes and eat spinach soup, Norman was the quintessential Jewish momma's boy. He was not likeable, nor was he intended to be. Podhoretz's alter ego was so persuasive—and credible—precisely because the author rendered himself in such an unappealing, even infuriating, light. Furthermore, since it had everything to do with having his manhood stunted in adolescence both by the subtle horrors of a matriarchal Jewish home and the violent clashes with dark-skinned boys on the street, Norman's grown-up rants against African American men openly invited a pop Freudian analysis. This represented nothing new to *Commentary* readers. After all, one of Podhoretz's first acts as editor had been to publish three lengthy excerpts from Paul Goodman's *Growing Up Absurd*, which (as one psychologist critiqued it) was "a long, anguished, soul-rending cry of pain for the crucified adolescent."[58] With the added touch of negrophobia, almost the same could be said about Podhoretz's study.

After all, here was the sort of "honest" reportage that would soon sweep the sixties as self-exposure—or self-involvement, depending on your perspective—became a benchmark for the New Journalism. Most obviously, it was titillating and voyeuristic. Less well-understood was that it was also almost always a *political* project; in this case, "My Negro Problem—and Ours" sought to denigrate liberal Jewish antiracist activism while it also shamelessly—via its shamefulness—presented sentiments just one shade shy of white racism. Yet Podhoretz was just being true to his identity; it was a moment in history when the shedding of inhibitions (at least in print) seemed itself cause for celebration. With daring bravado, what this particular case study of uninhibited self-expression camouflaged—however thinly—was blunt antileft and antiblack ideology. The dozens of rapturous letters to the editor *Commentary* published in the months afterward, many specifically applauding Podhoretz's courage and honesty, suggest how powerfully his essay had touched a sensitive nerve.[59]

Certainly, however, not all responded with glowing praise. Perhaps the most impassioned and detailed counterattack on Podhoretz, aiming to undercut his essay's potential impact on an already splintered liberal Jewish civil rights alliance, appeared almost immediately in *Congress Bi-Weekly*. Entitled "Fear Turned to Hatred," it was written by Judge Justine Wise Polier, chairman of the executive committee of the American Jewish Congress (and daughter of founding president Rabbi Stephen S. Wise) and Shad Polier, a vice president of the AJCongress and chairman of its Commission on Law and Social Action.

While Podhoretz had mocked those masochistic whites "who romanticize Negroes and pander to them," the Poliers identified *Podhoretz*'s version of Jewishness as lacking in appropriate self-respect. They found Podhoretz's confession to be not only "woefully insensitive" to the larger context of black lives but also "suffused with self-pity" and "infantile self-appreciation." The Poliers also cuttingly declared: "One cannot but wonder whether the doubt later expressed by Podhoretz concerning the value of Jewish survival does not stem from a preference, conscious or unconscious, to be part of the powerful white *goyim* who could oppress, rather than to be part of any minority which might suffer oppression."[60] Was it Podhoretz, the Poliers implied, who might really be ashamed he was a Jew?

The Poliers also reiterated the need for Jewish solidarity with black civil rights struggles and declared themselves particularly aghast at Podhoretz's invocation of "the ovens of Auschwitz" for the purpose of criticizing black efforts to survive as a group. With these remarks on Auschwitz, the Poliers said,

> the writer reveals his own moral bankruptcy. Conformity achieved through the bulldozing of all differences and the surrender of individual and group contributions to human development is apparently not too high a price—in Podhoretz's value scale—to pay for individual physical comfort and survival. . . .

> The concept of loving oneself not in the terms of narcissism but in terms of self-respect and the ideal of loving one's neighbor and the stranger, the great themes of Judaeo-Christian ethics, are to be cast aside.

Seeing in Podhoretz's writing an "admission of self-contempt," the Poliers accused him as well of the "rejection of the Jewish and American ideal." And they concluded that it was precisely the "great heritage" of Jews' commitment to the ideal of "human brotherhood" that had "made the survival of the Jewish people meaningful to Jews as men, and to those lands in which the Jews have lived."[61]

The tensions between the visions of Podhoretz and the Poliers would grow even more acute in the years that followed, when the very meaning of Jewish liberalism would become the subject of overt and extended controversy. Chapters 3 and 4 will take the story to 1967 when the Six-Day War shocked many Jewish liberals into a deepened appreciation of Israel's vulnerability and when many of these liberals would begin more forcefully to name their Jewish identities as the reason they could no longer support African American civil rights. But as this chapter has shown, the shift toward a redefinition of Jewish liberalism was already well underway in 1960–61; the consequences of that shift for Jewish involvement in black civil rights would only intensify in the years ahead. Chapter 3 will chart debates in the course of 1963 and 1964 over school and neighborhood integration, conflicts about the proper role of Jewish communal service organizations, and the growing hostility of moderate Jewish liberals both to black militancy and to the persistence of radical Jewish support for it. In all these disputes comparisons between American racial politics and the Holocaust now got tossed back and forth with regularity. Meanwhile, during the same period, many Jewish observers also began to highlight the purported social pathologies of the black community. These black pathology statements spanned ideological perspective; they could be served up to defend the need for integration or they could be cited as evidence that, if integration were to be implemented, black deficiencies would disrupt Jewish communities and undermine the development of Jews' supposed special skills and talents. The Holocaust was never too far from these debates about pathology either. Progressive Jewish commentators dramatically compared the black ghetto to Dachau or elaborated comparisons between concentration camp internees and descendants of slavery; conservative observers more routinely (and for the first time) explicitly linked black antisemitism, and even black militancy in general, to German fascism. Already by the midpoint of the sixties, there was virtually no consensus on how to respond to the revolution in black America—even as all sides drew on increasingly hyperbolic Holocaust references to make their points. What has come to be seen as the turning point of 1967 in American Jewish history—and in many respects it *was* a turning point—also marked a boiling over of circumstances that had been in the making already for several years.

3 "Artificial Altruism Sows Only Seeds of Error and Chaos": Desegregation and Jewish Survival

The American Jew who wants to go to Little Rock cannot simply hop on a bus and go there, not even on a Freedom Riders bus. His road to Little Rock is a long one and leads by way of Warsaw and Auschwitz. It is a long and a roundabout road, but it is the only one that will get him there—if he is to come there bringing true gifts of sympathy and help and understanding, and not merely in search of a bit of heroic self-glorification.
—Shlomo Katz, 1962

CHANGING LESSONS

The first half of the 1960s was a time of tremendous uncertainty, ambivalence, and internal divisiveness for American Jewish liberalism. The divisiveness was especially evident in communal debates over the appropriateness of Jewish support for civil rights activism. On the one hand, and as Jews during this period often noted, young Jews predominated among white Americans willing to fight alongside African Americans in Freedom Summer and voter registration drives in the South. Northern rabbis also began increasingly to take a public stand in their synagogues and in the streets against de facto segregation in their communities. On the other hand, there was increasing evidence that Jewish communities were surprisingly resistant to the accelerated pace of the civil rights movement because of an uneasy perception that "Jewish" schools and neighborhoods were among the first to be targeted for desegregation. Furthermore, there was a growing sense that blacks were not "worthy" of the gains they demanded because they sought to have handed to them advantages that Jews had worked incredibly hard to achieve. There was also the perception—unevenly applied and hotly contested—that blacks were antisemites who took out their resentments and frustrations most especially on the Jew whom they saw only as a different shade of white person. Nor was it clear to many Jews at the grassroots why rabbis preached that Judaism required Jews to support civil rights activism. And more and more rabbis soon began to heed the cautious tones of their congregations. Increasingly, an antiliberal perspective began to find articulation among the rabbinate; some rabbis now sought to define Judaism as antithetical with American liberalism precisely because they saw liberalism as a doctrine whose "enlightened" views on humanity undermined or opposed entirely the particularities of Jewish identity. Indeed, Jewish difference could not survive in a pure liberal democracy because it demanded the erasure of all group difference, or so the argument went, and the complete integration of all peoples.

During these years the Holocaust and its lessons were often cited in the pronouncements made by Jewish commentators in discussions of Jewish civil rights activism and liberal politics. Yet, to be sure, there was little consensus: the Holocaust continued to be named (as Joachim Prinz argued at the March on Washington in 1963) as a sharp reminder that Jews could not remain bystanders in the struggle for racial equality in America. But increasingly the Holocaust also functioned in other—often mutually irreconcilable—ways as well. One set of debates revolved around the meaning of Jewish manhood. Would Jews be only passive subjects in a struggle for freedom and perpetuate the myth that they were afraid to resist injustice—as some insisted they had been under Nazism? Or would Jews only fight on behalf of others, and refuse to stand up as men in the struggle to preserve Jewish heritage and tradition? Were blacks really the Jews of American society as they got beaten by southern segregationists who behaved just like German fascists? Or were blacks themselves like Nazi hooligans as they pillaged Jewish stores and attacked Jewish merchants in their irrational and militant rage against U.S. society? Did American Judaism need to adjust in a post-Holocaust era to the demands and pressures of social injustice or risk losing and alienating its young people who increasingly saw Jewishness as irrelevant to the social conflicts of the day? Or did Judaism need to defend itself through a conscious process of "self-ghettoization" in a democratic pluralistic society whose ideals urged a leveling of all difference between various subgroups? These were just some of the opposing viewpoints advanced during the first half of the sixties.

In seeking to understand these developments it would be a mistake to underestimate the impact made by Jewish intellectuals and leaders who placed Jewish survival at the center of their analysis. By 1966 the argument that Jews would find themselves wiped out soon enough if they did not attend more conscientiously to the demands of communal survival was gaining in prestige and populist influence. It was a perspective with long-lasting consequences. For one thing, this position slowly but consistently aimed to sever the meaning and legacy of American Zionism from its often quite liberal or left-leaning origins. Zionism had unquestionably been a movement encompassing a range of ideological tendencies; a survivalist perspective sought to link Zionism solidly and solely to an antiliberal agenda. This perspective also hoped to cast American Jewish identity in a manner that stood necessarily opposed to a prophetic tradition exemplified by the more politically progressive elements within Reform Judaism. Significantly, this perspective often accomplished its goal by paying special attention to the "race revolution," as its spokespersons questioned the financial resources and institutional commitments Jewish organizations and individuals provided to this revolution. In other words, this position set the demands of the black civil rights movement in opposition to the needs of Jewish survival, and it interpreted (or reinterpreted, depending on one's political point of view) Zionism and American Jewishness as obligated *above all* to defend Jewish values it perceived as threatened to the point of extinction.

Certainly not all Jewish leaders accepted this particularist version of American Zionism, and prophetic Judaism with its social justice agenda, as well as a left-leaning Zionism, which the American Jewish Congress (above all) continued to articulate, resisted these inroads against their liberal views. In addition, an increasing number of commentators tried to put into words the notion that the essence of being a Jew was being an outsider, that Jews could take pleasure and pride in their outsider status, and that to abandon one's liberal or radical edge and become "like everyone else" amounted to assimilation. Sometimes this argument was put forward in theological terms, as a new way of making the case that Jewish religious tradition demanded social justice activism. However, the argument was voiced most strongly by secular Jews who saw in outsider status some more indefinable but nonetheless powerful sociocultural quality of Jewish ethnicity.

Yet, over the course of these several years during the mid-sixties, especially as the civil rights movement was understood to be demanding that northern neighborhoods integrate, and even more as demands on school desegregation moved ahead, Jewish agency spokespeople and religious leaders who wished to further a liberal agenda now found that their constituencies and congregations were no longer open to a language of social justice. Liberalism was now cast as a threat, not the solution, and Jews wished above all to hold onto societal gains they felt were still fragile. A popular resentment against the preaching of liberal causes gained a strong foothold, as the perceived abstraction of civil rights became a reality. Still, as this chapter seeks to illustrate, this represents far from the whole story.

Chapter 3 examines these critical years of flux and contest over the meaning and direction of Jewish support for civil rights and liberal programs and policies. It starts from the premise that Jewish leaders across the political spectrum wished to advance what they believed were positive American Jewish values, but it also shows that there was no accord whatsoever about what those values should be and that Jews were internally quite divided and conflicted about what was the right or just or ethical thing to do. The chapter focuses on three central debates that galvanized Jewish intellectuals and leaders during these years: how to respond to a trend in the Jewish community toward greater conservatism, what to do about a widespread sense that American Jewish youth were increasingly alienated from Judaism and their Jewish identity, and how to address the embittered conflict over school desegregation and its possible consequences for Jewish children. At all points the chapter focuses on *how* Jewish leaders and intellectuals said what they believed as a means of casting light most especially on the *assumptions* behind their ideas and political perspectives. The aim is to explicate the shifting terrain on which those assumptions were being made. Jewish leaders were competing for authority in a landscape where there was no sense which perspective would gain dominance; as a consequence, perhaps, there was no consensus about argumentation even within points of view that tended to agree about conclusions and goals. Conflicting arguments got deployed for similar goals; similar sounding arguments were put forward toward divergent ends. This was, in other words, a period of trial and error, of rapidly changing ideological tensions, and of internal crisis and competition over the future meaning of American Jewish political values and identity.

PROBING THE PREJUDICES OF AMERICAN JEWS

By the early 1960s commentary in Jewish venues would begin repeatedly to register that there existed a mounting "Jewish backlash" against liberal social programs and policies. Most often these discussions focused on a decline specifically among Jews in support for African American civil rights. One notable example of this commentary was a 1964 essay by Manheim S. Shapiro, director of Jewish Communal Affairs for the American Jewish Committee. Shapiro's essay reviewed a 1962 survey of Jewish racial prejudices in an unnamed city. The survey's findings were sobering. On the one hand, while it found Jews voiced support for civil rights in theory, it also uncovered far more qualified responses when Jews were asked about "the prospect of direct personal contact between themselves and Negroes." Specifically, the survey found that four in five interviewed said Jewish organizations should work for desegregation in the schools. Yet it also found that "52% of our entire sample said they would object to having Negroes move into their neighborhood." These results were reported to be typical; similar surveys of other Jewish communities revealed even higher percentages of Jewish respondents opposed to racial integration. To dramatize these results, Shapiro told the story of a Jewish Community Center director in an unnamed city. The JCC director had announced publicly that "while the Center was intended to serve Jewish purposes, its only requirement for membership was that applicants be of good character." After his remarks were widely—and correctly—interpreted among the Jewish membership "as meaning that Negroes of good character could also become members," the director saw one hundred Jewish families resign or drop their memberships—even though not one black actually did apply for JCC membership.[1]

Other observers reported comparable stories of a Jewish reaction against liberal programs and desegregation policies. In one widely discussed 1963 essay, titled "The White Liberal's Retreat," Murray Friedman, an intergroup relations official for the American Jewish Committee, confirmed that there existed a "growing estrangement" from civil rights among northern Jewish liberals who "worried about Negroes' moving into their neighborhoods, which are often the first to be broken in the Negro advance."[2] Also in 1963, Albert Vorspan, director of the Commission on Social Action of Reform Judaism and a longtime civil rights activist, stated with open dismay that while American Jews "continue to speak and to vote as liberals," they were now "about like everybody else when it comes to concrete behavior on racial matters." Vorspan condemned as dangerously misguided the assumption "that our smug suburbs *will* ride out the tornado of racial change whipping through the world." And in searing language he asked:

> Is it quixotic to expect American Jews to be different from everyone else, to rise above the level of a sick American culture and to stand for racial justice as the Quakers do for world peace? Perhaps it is. But if that is the case, we should be more honest with ourselves. We should stop talking about the mission to Israel. We should stop boasting to the rafters that our forebears gave the world the concept of the unity of mankind as the children of One God. We should stop preaching sermons at each other and at America. We should cleanse our prayer books of those words like justice and brotherhood which our mindless repetitions have long since robbed of all meaning. And we should stop pretending to be Jews.[3]

In the fall of 1964, the *New York Times* reported that almost half of Jewish New Yorkers interviewed felt the civil rights movement should "slow down."[4] That December Richard C. Hertz, rabbi of Temple Beth El in Detroit, echoed Joachim Prinz's sentiments at the March on Washington the previous year. According to Hertz, Jewish nonactivity on behalf of civil rights was especially shameful in light of the Holocaust: "Jews and others must speak up and act, otherwise be as guilty as the non-Nazis in Germany were who looked the other way when Jews were persecuted."[5] And in January 1965, in a B'nai B'rth publication, *National Jewish Monthly*, Henry Cohen, rabbi of Philadelphia's Beth David Reform Congregation, wrote: "For a Jew to use Jewish experience to justify the withholding of basic human rights from the Negro—this not only makes a mockery of Judaism but also reveals a dreadful misunderstanding of our history." Cohen was "particularly disturbed by the Jewish version of the white backlash: 'We Jews may have been poor, but our children were not delinquents. We earned our rights! We worked hard, studied hard, and deserved our freedom! Let the Negro stop demanding and start earning his rights!' " Like Rabbi Hertz, Cohen argued that the Holocaust cast a huge shadow over these intra-Jewish civil rights debates because it meant Jews shared with blacks a history of oppression: "Must we be reminded of the death toll in the suffocating box cars bound for Auschwitz or of the tearing of children away from their mothers' arms?"[6] Or as A. James Rudin, assistant rabbi of Congregation B'nai Jehudah in Kansas City, Missouri, preached in his Yom Kippur sermon in 1965: "How ironic to see Jews often blocking the Negroes' way," given that "our children under the Hitler regime in Germany went to segregated schools, until there were no more schools for them to attend—until there were only shower rooms and crematoria available to them."[7]

Yet there were strong reactions against these calls for sustained Jewish civil rights activism. One letter to the editor of *National Jewish Monthly* in response to Henry Cohen, for instance, argued that the rabbi's essay represented "an insult to our Jewish people," while another letter writer said she was most appalled by Cohen's invocation of the Holocaust in defense of civil rights; she saw quite opposite lessons from the memories of Nazism: "Does the rabbi see no similarity between the picketing of Jewish stores in Hitler days, and the Negro racists in New York who picket Jewish storekeepers with signs proclaiming the stores should belong to Negroes?"[8] And the April 1965 issue of *National Jewish Monthly* published an essay by Robert Gordis, the influential and widely respected Conservative rabbi of Temple Beth El in Rockaway Park, New York, and professor of Bible at the

Jewish Theological Seminary, which presented what could also be seen as his response to Cohen's liberal challenge. Gordis sidestepped entirely the possibility of a Jewish conservative backlash. Instead he underscored how "American Jews have, by and large, demonstrated their genuine commitment to this epic struggle," and emphasized (with italics) that now the "*Negro leadership has a moral obligation to do far more effective work in combating anti-Semitism within the Negro community than has been evident thus far.*"[9]

These reactions against the truisms of liberalism all indicate a conservative shift among Jews already during the first half of the 1960s. Nor would the existence of this shift merely vanish from memory in later years. In 1968 Richard G. Hirsch, a rabbi and director of the Union of American Hebrew Congregations Religious Action Center in Washington, D.C., recalled the "battle" that had "raged within the Reform movement for two years" over whether the UAHC should establish a Religious Action Center dedicated to social activism. In the end the center had been overwhelmingly endorsed. Yet for Hirsch what was memorable in retrospect were the "typical statements" made by those who had bitterly opposed the center's establishment: " 'When I joined a congregation, I did it for religious reasons.' 'I join a political party or a citizen's group if I want to express my views on politics.' 'The task of religious leadership is to speak *to* the members, and not *for* the members.' " These sentiments were, or so it seemed to Hirsch, clear portents of a trend toward an increased Jewish conservatism. The UAHC debate over the center had taken place from 1959 to 1961.[10]

Thus observers agreed (or illustrated by their example) that there was already in the several years leading up to 1965 a conservative trend among American Jews and a movement away from liberal support for desegregation policies and civil rights activism. Yet they did *not* agree on what precisely were the causes of this trend. Even more significant, perhaps, and as the range of opinions already cited suggest, neither could observers agree on whether this new Jewish conservatism signaled a shift to be mourned or welcomed.

CONSERVATIVE TRENDS IN AMERICAN JEWISH LIFE

In the fall of 1963 an early and highly suggestive conversation on the new Jewish conservatism took place in the New York editorial offices of *Judaism*, a publication of the American Jewish Congress. The board of editors had invited Melvin M. Tumin, a professor of sociology and anthropology at Princeton University and an authority on attitudes toward desegregation, to offer his analysis of political trends in contemporary American Jewish life. Tumin informed the *Judaism* editorial board of what they no doubt already suspected from reports and stories circulating among Jewish leaders: as a community American Jews were increasingly becoming "conservative, security-seeking, status-minded, and apolitical." Jews were, in Tumin's view, adopting values that would assure "a smooth fitting in of Jews into American life at its middle-class worst—and on precisely the same terms as the Presbyterians, Baptists, and all others." Tumin identified at least two intra-Jewish—and paradoxical—tendencies that contributed to this (in his view) most unfortunate trend. On the one hand, Tumin observed how those Jews who argued for "increased self-ghettoization" as the way to ensure Jewish survival did so with "demands that Jews make on each other to 'return to the fold' and bear witness by joining in Jewish communal activities, most particularly the center and the synagogue." Such demands for increased religious observance assumed a "morally dubious notion that one's neighbors will respect one more if one is religious" and they negated the authenticity of the secular Jewish identity. In Tumin's opinion, these demands sought to turn the Jew into "an all-rightnik in the American host community" whose politics mirrored the "100-percent community-cum-church posture of the non-Jewish American." On the other hand, Tumin argued that unaffiliated Jews who said Judaism was "irrelevant" to their social and political lives were engaging in "a form of ostrich-like make-believe 'I don't exist' " attitude; this perspective denied that Judaism should "stand for something, and something vital and alive on the American scene." In short, Tumin reiterated scornfully, these two (otherwise) opposing elements within Jewish life *both* put forth positions whose "net impact so far" has been to see the American Jew spout opinions "exactly as much all right as other status-quo-minded, status-anxious, politically conservative, eye-on-the-main-chance, non-Jewish Americans."[11]

The third alternative for Jewish identity was what Tumin clearly favored. It involved "those other Jews"—"relatively small in number by comparison, who either remain totally outside" the centers of American institutional power, "or have come in only half way," and who were able to offer a "morally radical position on the political spectrum." Such "outsider" Jews avoided all "institutional loyalties" that represented "the obvious antipathies" of the "forces which make social and cultural change possible." What "outsider" Jews confronted, however, was the "most vitriolic scorn" from the far more numerous "insider" Jews who defended the status quo, and who had elected themselves the "full-fledged—so they think—institutionalized and bureaucratized defenders of the official faith." Given the high stakes of intra-Jewish tensions over the appropriate meaning and direction of Jewish identities, Tumin voiced pessimism for what was becoming of American Jews in the early 1960s:

> The American Jewish community seems to be living on the rapidly shrinking psychic income from the capital investment of Jews of the last two thousand years—or the last thirty years. What can it mean, in all honesty, for the average Jew in America to claim he comes from a heritage and tradition of social justice, of respect for knowledge and learning, of concern for culture? He appears today to care for these things no more than anyone else around him.[12]

In the discussion that followed, several editorial board members expressed some sympathy for Tumin's analysis. Maurice Friedman, a professor of philosophy at Sarah Lawrence College and a self-characterized "unreconstructed liberal," observed how he had been "much gratified" when he saw Jewish students and rabbis who "have not been afraid to stick their necks out and to do things" for the civil rights movement. Yet Friedman also conceded that he thought it remained an open question whether "a Jewish commitment can and should lead in the direction of a Jewish radicalism or at least a Jewish social witness." Steven S. Schwarzschild, a Reform rabbi and the editor of *Judaism*, more clearly echoed Tumin's formulation when he said: "The Jew, it would seem to me, is required by definition to be the outsider." A radical Jewish intellectual, Schwarzschild questioned why Tumin tended to lump liberal and radical action together: "When in the freedom movement we call for radicalism, we mean precisely the revolt against the mealy-mouthed liberalism that has prevailed, I suppose, ever since the early 1930's." Or, as Leo Pfeffer, now director of the American Jewish Congress Commission on Law and Social Action, put it:

> I believe that ultimately there is no justification for Jewish survival unless there is that separateness, that outsidedness, that being the goad of the universal conscience. I don't think, realistically, that theology itself will long be adequate to maintain Jewish survival. To justify his survival as Jew the Jew should be the radical, the malcontent, the one who sparks revolutions. That, for better or for worse, is his mission in society.

And meanwhile, Henry Schwarzschild, publications director of the Anti-Defamation League (and Steven's brother), also defended Jewish radicalism, linking radicalism to Jewish theology. Decisively distancing himself from "Marxian utopianism," Schwarzschild nonetheless forcefully called for a "radicalism not as obedience to ideology but as obedience to God."[13]

These progressive assessments of Jewish identity also prompted sharp critique, however. At least two *Judaism* board members dissented wholly from the assumption that American Jews bore a decisive connection either to liberalism or to radical activism—or that they should. And in some respects, it could be argued that these dissenting perspectives represented the clearest indicators of what was yet to come. First, Marshall Sklare, director of the Division of Scientific Research of the American Jewish Committee, attacked Tumin for neglecting to note how tragic the alliance between Jews and the left had historically been. Furthermore, Tumin himself was simply a biased malcontent: According to Sklare, Tumin "is unsympathetic to all institutions within whose confines a distinctive Jewish vocation could be nurtured" because he was "an intellectual whose convictions were forged on the anvil of American radical politics." It was not surprising, Sklare scornfully said, that Tumin, "from his secular-radical vantage-point," would reject Jewish separatism since "Jewish radicalism has always called for a cessation of all parochialisms, among them Jewish parochialism"; nor could it be counted a surprise that Tumin saw "present-day Jews as inauthentic: inauthentic because he believes they support the status quo, inauthentic because he believes they are becoming the insider's insider." However, Sklare contended, "Prof. Tumin's view of the Jew as being chosen for Marxian witness" and "his homage to Jewish secular radicalism" were deeply problematic, most especially since "such radicalism contained many cruel and terrifying aspects to which he did not allude."[14]

But the most damaging challenge to Tumin's ideas about Jewish identity and liberalism may have come from Michael Wyschogrod, assistant professor of philosophy at the City College of New York. Wyschogrod did not take issue with Tumin's thesis that there had been a conservative shift among American Jews; instead Wyschogrod—like Sklare—considered Tumin's reactions to this shift both naive and misguided:

> I can understand that it dismays him but that it surprises him I cannot. What is more natural than the process he describes? College students are sometimes radical. But when they grow up, have a family and a job, they begin to develop a stake in the system, they come to have something to conserve and consequently they become a bit more conservative. . . . The process Prof. Tumin describes is a most natural one that ought not to occasion surprise.

Wyschogrod did not stop there. Stating again that "the process we are discussing is a perfectly natural one," and that "the society which has most personified radicalism in this century has turned out to be a monstrous tyranny that is in the process of committing cultural genocide against the Jewish people," Wyschogrod challenged Tumin's "lament" at the recent "Jewish swing to the right." Wyschogrod asked: "Is loyalty to any institution, per institution, all that abominable? Aren't there good institutions worthy of loyalty and preservation? Must we always oppose, criticize, find fault just as a matter of principle? Isn't there something adolescent and immature about rebellion for the sake of rebellion?" Furthermore, Tumin appeared not to understand his Judaism terribly well. Wyschogrod concluded:

> Judaism has never been radical in the economic or political sense of that word. It has been a religion of law against anarchy, of reverence for the past and love for its traditions and heritage. It has always had a very realistic appraisal of what lurks in man and the necessity for social and political bounds within which responsible freedom is exercised. We need only to bring to mind the Talmudic dictum that every day men should bless God for the government because without it they would devour each other alive. That is a rather conservative statement entirely irreconcilable with any sort of anarchist utopianism. It is the radicalism of the last century that has been the aberration in Jewish history.[15]

THE CHALLENGE OF JEWISH YOUTH

Given such sharp political divisions within even the more self-styled liberal wing of the American Jewish leadership (which is precisely what the American Jewish Congress had long represented), not to mention the Jewish rank and file, young Jewish activists often quickly found that a commitment to radicalism could be a barrier between themselves and other (nonactivist) Jews. At times such barriers left the activist with odd feelings of familial or communal estrangement. A striking expression of this alienating experience appeared in 1965 in *Conservative Judaism*. Paul Lauter, a former director of Peace Studies for the American Friends Service Committee and a college professor of English, reflected on his family's indifference to his civil rights activities. Lauter wrote that although his family "has a Bulletin which reports the activities of family members to all the others," no one in the family "thought it of sufficient importance or interest to report on my work in Mississippi last summer or to write of my jailing in Montgomery. Somehow,"

Lauter added rather ruefully, "all of that fell too far outside the periphery of their normal existence for them to see it as relevant, or of general family interest." Then in satiric stream of consciousness, Lauter imagined what a member of his own family might have been thinking as Paul returned home from Freedom Summer:

> Maybe you can't really trust a lawbreaker who gets arrested (who in the family ever did that? or who works for a *goyish* organization and thinks *goyish* thoughts). It would be hard to talk to him. At any rate, he would probably make you feel uncomfortable over what you said about Negroes (What does *he* know? They don't work for *him*!), or because you don't want to sign things (What does *he* remember? All of those Jews who had trouble because they signed too much thirty years ago . . .) or because a war in Vietnam doesn't seem to be troublesome (Does he mean we shouldn't have fought Hitler or Nasser? What kind of Jew is that?).[16]

Another young Jew who linked his Jewish identity to radical politics and a commitment to civil rights activism was Paul Cowan. For Cowan (as he remembered it subsequently in the early 1980s), his participation in the civil rights struggle against segregation had grown out of what he learned from his mother's "secular messianism: a deep commitment to the belief that we had a lifelong debt to the six million dead." According to Cowan, it was specifically this sense of debt that led directly to his involvement in voter registration drives during Freedom Summer.[17] In July 1965, Cowan, a graduate of Harvard University and already a civil rights worker for three years, was an invited panelist at a conference in Israel sponsored by the American Jewish Congress on the theme of "The Challenge of Jewish Youth: Israel and America, 1965." Cowan quickly found the terms of debate did not especially invite perspectives like his own on Jewish radical political activities; much of the conversation turned on the desirability of American aliyah. Beginning his presentation with the statement that "there are many different sorts of Jews," Cowan defied those who pressed for American aliyah, making clear "that a commitment to the civil rights movement is a greater moral duty than coming to Israel merely because one is a Jew." Cowan said that it was through political protest and social activism that he expressed his Jewishness: "*That* is my own way of resisting assimilation." Cowan was asked to define those Jewish values: "How does civil rights activity, even if prompted by some sort of Jewish impetus, contribute to Jewish continuity?" He responded:

> I don't have an answer, but, then, I don't agree with the question, either. For myself, I just cannot believe that to be a good Jew means to act only in a certain way. I don't think that every Jew who puts on a prayer shawl is a good Jew, nor do I think every Jew who works in the civil rights movement is a good Jew. What is important is that a man take some part of his tradition which is agreeable to him, and work within that part creatively and honestly.[18]

In the course of the conference's three-day discussion, held first in Tel Aviv and then also at Kibbutz Givat Brenner, Cowan's views on American Jewish identity and its connection to civil rights activism provoked harsh criticism from the other American participants and audience members. Yet these dissents did not necessarily agree with one another. For David Berger, a rabbinical student at Yeshiva University, the key issue was religious observance; Berger said that there was "no question that the essential aspect of Jewishness, historically, has been the religious aspect." Therefore, Berger acknowledged, on the one hand, that "as for the Jewish civil rights worker in Mississippi, there is no doubt that the person working to attain an ethical goal is fulfilling a very vital aspect of Judaism." But the point, so far as Berger was concerned, was that there is "one thing that is missing here, and that is the motivation for the action. It is difficult to apply the term Jewish to the particular action if its motivation is not consciously Jewish." A second American panelist, Jane Satlow Gerber, was even more dismissive, noting "that the burning issue for the Jews in America is to find some kind of relevance within their tradition. This is a more imminent problem," Gerber argued, "than that of a few thousands of Jews in the civil rights movement." And one U.S. audience member was still more critical: "The activities of civil rights, and all the other American responsibilities have nothing to do with Judaism; and I don't think you have the right to be so idealistic as to say: 'I am a Jew, and the Jews, because of their Jewish background, because of their idealism, have been committed to these movements.' " Nor were the Israeli participants receptive by and large to Cowan's point of view; as Benjamin Kedar, a history student at Hebrew University, succinctly put it: "I cannot take seriously the claim that the civil rights movement is a true outlet for Jewish activity."[19]

TO BIRMINGHAM, AND BACK

Yet it was not only secular-minded young Jewish radicals like Lauter or Cowan who worked in the civil rights movement. When rabbis joined the civil rights struggle, their statements often reflected how their social activism flowed directly from deep convictions about their moral role as spiritual leaders in the Jewish community. One early and profoundly influential example of this expression took place on Tuesday, May 7, 1963, at the Annual Convention of the Rabbinical Assembly (Conservative). It began when Harold M. Schulweis, rabbi of Temple Beth Abraham in Oakland, California, made the proposal to establish an institute that would document altruistic deeds done by non-Jews to save Jews during the Holocaust. Later that same day it was suggested that the convention not focus solely on the past but also apply the lessons of the past to present-day events in Alabama. As a rabbi attending the convention later remembered: "That very day, the front page of the newspapers showed police dogs let loose on peacefully demonstrating men and women in the South. Reports of the brutal use of high-pressure fire hoses and electric cattle-prods against praying school children aroused the conscience of millions."[20]

In the debate over how to respond to the events in Alabama, Rabbi Moshe Cahana from Houston made clear to the assembly—with reference to the Schulweis proposal—that it had to do something about Alabama if it genuinely took to heart the memories of the Holocaust: "This morning we condemned the non-Jewish people who were silent when our brothers in Germany were chased by dogs. We will also be condemned for doing nothing."[21] In the end the assembly passed the Birmingham Resolution, which called for volunteers to travel to Birmingham as a delegation. The resolution read: "Resolved, that The Rabbinical Assembly, in convention assembled, enthusiastically endorse the action of members of The Rabbinical Assembly who in its name volunteer to go to Birmingham to speak and act on behalf of human rights and dignity."[22] Nineteen rabbis volunteered, leaving for Birmingham immediately and arriving in the predawn hours the following morning.

Jack Bloom, rabbi of Congregation Beth El in Fairfield, Connecticut, discussed his decision to join the Birmingham delegation at a Conference on the Moral Implications of the Rabbinate in fall 1963. "I had no history of standing up for Negro rights," Bloom confessed. "I don't like to stick my neck out." But he added: "At the convention, when the critical situation in Birmingham was being discussed, I finally felt that I should put up or shut up." Bloom described how he had come from "a northern, 'lily-white,' Jewish middle class home," the sort of place where he'd only known blacks as maids and servants. "The verbal commitment of the environment demanded racial equality," Bloom said, "but on the hidden agenda the Negro remained a *schvartzer*." Before Birmingham, Bloom had privately questioned the demands of the civil rights struggle:

> The Negro was equal, of course, but . . . Is he ready for equality? And what about the high crime rate? Will the value of my property go down if a Negro moves in? Would you want your daughter to marry a Negro? I shared the image and stereotypes of the Negro common to the liberal white community. I did not experience the Negro as a living brother. At best, he was an abstraction.[23]

In another testimonial on his experiences as a member of the rabbinical delegation to Birmingham, Andre Ungar, rabbi of Temple Emanuel in Westwood, New Jersey, wrote that he was saddened to find the Birmingham Jewish community standing "squarely on the side of reaction, of what, in that great confrontation, is the side of wrong against right." Ungar then described the difficult encounter between the visiting rabbis and Birmingham's Jewish leaders:

> We caught ourselves in the role of self-righteous little angels on the one hand, and posturing as pompous *shtadlanim* on the other. But all along, unspoken but unmistakably felt, there was, on their side, an accusation. "Boychiks, we know you are right, but still, how could you do this to us, your brothers?" and on our part, an exalted silence, "Jews, dear scared little Yidden, how can you side with racism, with Hitler's heritage; and yet, and yet, you are our brothers, and we love you, we love you, forgive us, please."[24]

Despite his self-critical qualms, Ungar concluded his account fully confident that what he and the rabbinical delegation had done by traveling to Alabama was not merely justified but necessary: "In contributing to the moral solution of Birmingham, or its future equivalent, a handful of human beings may indeed leave their worthy mark. Who is more called upon than Jews, God's chosen, and among them rabbis, the chosen people's chosen ones, to fulfill that holy task?"[25]

In the years that followed, however, it would probably be the statements by Richard L. Rubenstein, chaplain to Jewish students at the University of Pittsburgh, that would be cited most frequently. In his Birmingham account Rubenstein acknowledged that his motivations for joining the delegation had been "mixed" and came in part from his selfish urge as a writer to "get a good story." Yet—and with veiled reference to Hannah Arendt's much reviled articles on the Eichmann trial for the *New Yorker*—Rubenstein quickly added: "There were other, better, reasons for going to Birmingham. I've been a little sick and tired of the recent refrain that 'Jews were passively compliant in their own downfall under Hitler,' which some of our slickest magazines have been feeding us. I wanted to be an actor in events rather than a spectator or commentator."[26]

Once in Alabama, however, such high-minded intellectual poses fell away as Rubenstein found himself feeling genuine shock and revulsion at the stark parallels between what he saw before him in the contemporary American South and what had occurred a generation earlier to Jews in Nazi Germany. "This was fascism in everything but name," Rubenstein wrote. And he provided this incisive analysis of southern white manhood:

> The men from nowhere, the radicals outside society, had triumphed for the moment over the forces of compromise and social order in Birmingham, as they had in Hitler's Germany and elsewhere in Europe. As I walked through the streets, I saw hundreds of arch-segregationist Alabama Highway Police who had been sent by Gov. Wallace "to maintain law and order." They were tense, violent, and frightened men. Their presence was provocative. They were really in Birmingham to create violence rather than to suppress it. . . . These men were largely "rednecks," lower middle class petty officials with little but the sense of whiteness to give them a feeling of identity. They were pathologically dependent upon the myth of Negro inferiority for their own human dignity. Were that lost, they would face the most awesome of all psychological problems—the problem of self-confrontation. They were prepared to assault and to murder rather than give up the Negro as the standard whereby they could be assured of their own worth.[27]

When they returned to their communities, many members of the rabbinical delegation were met by their congregations with "a veritable hero's welcome."[28] The overwhelming public response was also to praise and congratulate the Birmingham delegation for its courage and moral guidance. For some like Connecticut Rabbi Bloom, what was most gratifying about his return home was a single seemingly minor encounter. Bloom described it:

> One of my congregants is a contractor who employs day labor. He is a devoted, hard-working congregant who in four years has missed one Friday evening service. He has heard me speak about a multitude of topics, including Little Rock, Arkansas and Jackson, Mississippi. About a week after I came back from Birmingham and had spoken about the trip in the synagogue, he came to me and said, "You know, Rabbi, this is kind of hard to admit. . . . This week, as a result of what you did, I employed some Negroes

on the job, and you know something, for the first time in my life I didn't see them as monkeys."[29]

However, at least one member of the Birmingham delegation experienced far less enlightened reactions once back home. He got obscene phone calls and hate mail and found his congregation vehemently opposed to his participation in the civil rights struggle. "Jewish circles treated him as an outcast," Andre Ungar reported. "They looked past him, avoided him, and when they spoke to him, it was from a distance and with a meticulous blindness to the Birmingham trip as if it were a shameful lapse from morality."[30] It was, as it turned out, only an early sign of what would soon become a factious intra-Jewish debacle.

JEWISH LIBERALS, ALAS!

In early 1964 Harold Schulweis, the rabbi whose proposal on Holocaust resistance among non-Jewish Germans at the 1963 Rabbinical Assembly had resulted indirectly in the Birmingham Resolution, published a scathing indictment of Jewish liberalism entitled "Jewish Liberals, Alas!" Schulweis disparaged "the flagrant inconsistency" of Jewish liberals who were "normally articulate impassioned defenders of Mexican braceros, Buddhist priests and atheists, Negroes and liberation movements, [yet] turn morosely silent on Jewish issues." It was, Schulweis made clear, Judaism itself that was being betrayed by the Jew who set the needs of others above the needs of his own community. Of the "universalistic Jewish liberal who reacts to Jewish issues with a conscious neutrality or negativity," Schulweis concluded: "It is no surprise to those of us nurtured in the realistic tradition of Judaism to find that artificial altruism sows only seeds of error and chaos."[31]

Only a few months earlier, Richard Rubenstein had made the point that he volunteered to go to Birmingham because he wished to counter a perception of the post-Holocaust Jew as enfeebled and passive. Schulweis turned that analysis on its head, utilizing the memory of Nazism to insult the self-respect of Jewish liberals who were willing only to stand up for others but never for themselves or their own people. Indignantly, Schulweis wondered whether it might be a fear of antisemitism in the wake of Auschwitz that had led to the present-day popularity of "dichotomized Jewish liberals." With sarcastic sympathy for their difficult plight, Schulweis wrote: "The fear of some Jewish liberals is real and understandable. It is less than three decades after Auschwitz and the smoke of the past clings to us all. That memory has made some Jews stronger, more determined than ever to resist Jewish destruction; others have been made weaker, more bent on escape from Jewish identity."[32]

Other critiques of the idea that Jewishness and liberal activism might have something in common soon followed. One especially powerful argument came from Conservative rabbi Arthur Hertzberg of Temple Emanu-El in Englewood, New Jersey, author of *The Zionist Ideal.* In 1964 Hertzberg publicized his challenge to American Jewish liberalism, a challenge that depicted the ideals of U.S. democracy as a corrosive force for Jewish survival. This was an important new theme among Jewish intellectuals, and it marked a strong departure from the *Commentary*-style position that Jewishness and American democracy were especially compatible.

Hertzberg believed (in a manner that closely echoed Melvin Tumin's position, though in support of an opposing conclusion) that the politics of Jews in the U.S. "are indeed becoming just like everybody else's, which means that there has been a perceptible lessening of any specific passion about other Jews." As far as Hertzberg was concerned, American Jews needed to wake up fast to their American dilemma. In the pages of the Labor Zionist *Jewish Frontier,* Hertzberg argued that

> the next generation is settling down in America, to behave like a university trained segment of the big city bourgeoisie, indeed to be a major component of it. What shocks the Jewish Establishment in this image is the fear that it must see itself, on this evidence, not as a solution to the question of Jewish life in a democracy, but as a way station on a slow, seemingly inevitable road to evaporation.[33]

At a one-day symposium on February 5, 1964, in New York City, Hertzberg brought his message to more than three hundred Jewish communal workers from the New York metropolitan area. Organized by the National Conference of Jewish Communal Service, the symposium's timely theme was reflected in its title: "Changing Race Relations: Impact and Implications for Jewish Agencies." The conference organized a series of workshops on a range of Jewish communal services such as Jewish community centers, Jewish schools, and Jewish casework agencies. The symposium focused its attention on three questions as it sought to examine "the 'reciprocal influences' of Jewish communal services and the Race Revolution":

1. How can and should Jewish agencies participate in the race revolution?
2. How can and should Jewish agencies help their members or clients to deal with their attitudes and behavior toward Negroes?
3. How will this affect the agencies' primary Jewish purposes and services?[34]

The major address at the symposium was given by Hertzberg. He opened by stating that it required "no great moral courage to assert, and even to mean, that every American who lays claim to personal decency must be involved in the struggle for the equality of the Negro." Hertzberg also said that civil rights was an issue which "would seem to be very simple," certainly also for an organized Jewish community that saw "the mandate of this generation" as placing it "in the forefront in the solution of the problem." But Hertzberg emphasized that while such moral absolutism had "many virtues," it really represented only "a partial truth." The appropriate role of the Jewish community toward black civil rights activism was *not* a simple matter, Hertzberg contended, and although one hazarded being labeled "a white 'Uncle Tom' " if one was "anything less than vocally doctrinaire" in support of the black freedom struggle, nonetheless, "this danger must be risked." This risk was necessary, Hertzberg argued, because the American Jewish community found itself at a dangerous crossroads, and it was the relationship of Jews to blacks that "goes down to the very root of the meaning of Jewish identity, both personal and communal."[35]

From this dramatic opening, Hertzberg proceeded to map the difficulties inherent in unfettered Jewish communal support for black activism. First, putting Jews into a "popular front" intergroup alliance united against prejudice and bigotry defined Jewish identity in solely negative terms, for it represented a defensive position that meant "a lessening of one's own dignity, that is inevitably involved when a minority pleads with a majority not to hate it." Second, a "non-sectarian" communal approach toward bigotry allowed American Jews to skirt deeper *internal* communal concerns; this activism on behalf of others had a most unfortunate result as it became only "a way of attempting to fill the void left by the evaporation of positive Jewish content within Jewry."[36]

It was true, Hertzberg continued, that "some flavor of their own ancient tradition" motivated American Jews' engagement in social activism and philanthropy, and a social mission was undeniably "a useful and honorable thing, for it involves the Jewish community in making an important contribution to the wider democratic society." But problems arose almost immediately whenever Jews revealed even a hint of "Jewish particularism," because this was perceived as "both immoral and anti-democratic," especially if it meant "a locking of the door to some degree to non-Jews, and even perhaps to their misery." But here history—like the French Revolution—proved instructive, Hertzberg said, for history showed that there were indeed moments when "democracy itself can become a form of totalitarianism," especially when it demanded the "leveling" or "considerable refashioning of identities." Noting that "we are now at the nub of the issue," Hertzberg then asked, "Is the primary purpose of the Jewish community to help itself disappear, or is it to help itself survive? What is the meaning of that survival?"[37]

Hertzberg said that Jews had to be willing to acknowledge that there existed "a crucial difference between the Jewish and the Negro communities." In formulations about black-Jewish cultural distinctions that oddly echoed those Podhoretz had put forward in 1963, and despite the considerable and striking other differences in the two men's positions, Hertzberg elaborated that Jews had a distinctive cultural heritage many wished to preserve. Not so the American black, however:

> There is some, and perhaps even a growing, amount of feeling in Negro circles that there is a positive and distinctive Negro culture, and that it is a necessary function of the Negro community to foster it. This is as yet not the dominant view. The total stance of the Negro community is in the other direction, towards the assertion that the Negro has no culture other than the general American one, and that whatever pertains specifically to him as a Negro will and should disappear in some future generation which will be color-blind.

This, according to Hertzberg, meant that when liberal Jews fought on behalf of black civil rights, they fought also on behalf of their own "further entry into the white majority," and thus these activities inexorably hastened the dissolution of the Jewish community's particular traditions.[38]

As far as Hertzberg was concerned, Jews must maintain "the apartness of the Jewish community." For one thing, without "apartness," "Jewish learning" would be lost, and certainly the "transmission of that learning is important." For another, given the pull of American public schooling toward "the larger American society," Jewish communal agencies found themselves obligated to provide young Jews "with a specifically Jewish counterpull." In sum, "some amount of conscious self-ghettoization" was essential for American Jews if they were to resist the "high-road to assimilation." In stark contrast, then, to liberals like Justine Wise Polier and Shad Polier or radicals like

Melvin Tumin, who saw antiliberalism among Jews as a sign of problematic assimilationism, Hertzberg advanced the opposite contention. Hertzberg further argued that Jewish communal associations "should not permit a cycle of evaporation" and should not "become neighborhood centers or camps, financed by Jews for everyone." To allow this to happen would mean that Jewish organizations would, in effect, be "engaged in committing their own institutional suicide." However, Hertzberg concluded, shifting from alarmism to confidence, this dire outcome was unlikely; instead he predicted (more hopefully, in his view) that "the day of the Jewish-financed organization representing the Jewish community in the civil rights field, despite all the seeming verve of the moment, is soon to come to an end."[39]

Hertzberg's insistence that the Jewish liberal advocacy for civil rights posed dangers for Jewish group survival quickly became part of a more general wave. Extremely important support—albeit, and significantly, from a non-Zionist position—came from Nathan Glazer who, in the course of 1964, argued that black demands for equality and integration, if met, would destroy Jews' ability to maintain the integrity of their own communities.[40] Always denying that Jews had anything resembling the hateful feelings toward blacks that he claimed blacks had toward Jews, Glazer insisted that exclusionary behavior by Jews was not racist, but merely an unproblematic "part of the standard Jewish ethnocentrism," or just reflective of good business sense. Jews, in his view, had advanced in American society according to "the principle of measurable individual merit," while "it is clear that one cannot say the same" about blacks.[41] Glazer repeatedly echoed stereotypes about both blacks *and* Jews, linking blacks with violent tendencies and poor scholastic skills and Jews with financial aptitude and superior intelligence. Thus, as Glazer concluded, "Jews find their interests and those of formally less liberal neighbors becoming similar: they both have an interest in maintaining an area restricted to their own kind; an interest in managing the friendship and educational experiences of their children; an interest in passing on advantages in money and skills to them."[42]

At the 1964 Annual Meeting of the National Conference of Jewish Communal Service held in Los Angeles in early June, Glazer made a presentation that outlined concerns that—there can be little doubt—had a lasting impact on the terms of the debate over Jewish communal service. Like Hertzberg, Glazer began ominously, stating that Jews in America have "lived in some comfort for the past ten or fifteen years," but that this security "has now been fatally challenged by the Negro revolution." Having advanced into the more affluent and acculturated suburbs, Jews—like all other groups—had also managed to maintain "a distinctive social life." But this delicate balance between acculturation and distinctive group identity was now under siege because "the Negro, focused exclusively on the absolute barriers that were once raised against him, sees nothing, absolutely nothing, in the Negro group that requires defense—that requires separate institutions, group loyalty, residential concentration, or a ban on intermarriage." With such attitudes so prevalent within the black community, Glazer added, the rules by which every other group had advanced would now have to be rewritten:

> It is my feeling that with the Negro revolution there has been a radical change in this pattern of group advancement within an accepted structure of group distinctiveness. It is my feeling that Negro demands now involve the end of the American community as we have known it. . . . If one looks at these demands for equality . . . one must come up with the conclusion—the sub-community has no right to exist. It either protects privilege, or creates inequality. This is certainly the force of present day Negro demands—and this is why I say they present quite a new challenge to the Jewish community, or to any sub-community.

And it was this "new challenge," Glazer said, that "certainly helps explain the discomfort of Jews over many present-day Negro demands." The problem, however, would not find "simple solutions," though one had first to acknowledge how unfortunate for Jewish cultural survival—and ultimately threatening—black demands really were. Glazer concluded:

> Let me sum up by saying that the Negro now demands entry into a world, a society, that doesn't exist, except in ideology. This is the world in which there is an American community and in which heritage, ethnicity, religion, race, are only incidental and accidental personal characteristics. There may be reasons for this world to come into existence. Among them is that it is necessary in order to provide full equality for the Negroes. But if we do move in this direction it will be very hard to maintain any justification for Jewish exclusiveness and particularity in America.[43]

YOU CAN DROP OFF THE WORD JEWISH

Hertzberg and Glazer's lines of argument did not go uncontested. After Hertzberg's paper, for example, Albert D. Chernin, director of community consultation for the National Community Relations Advisory Council (NCRAC), worried aloud whether Hertzberg's position (which he summarized as "Retreat from the civil rights struggle; otherwise, jeopardize the future of Jewish survival!"), might, in turn, "be seized upon by some as justification for turning aside from the problem searing American society." While Chernin noted (like Hertzberg) how "a Jewish ethos" might possibly "be evaporated into an amorphous universal cloud that ultimately will disappear," Chernin strongly opposed Hertzberg's sectarian program for Jewish survival in America: "The particularism of Jews cannot be separated from its universal function without destroying both. They are mutually dependent; obverse sides of the same coin. Compartmentalizing the individual into the universal man and the particularistic Jew would both destroy universal commitment and convert the prophetic role of Judaism into tribalism."[44]

At the 1965 Annual Meeting of the National Conference of Jewish Communal Service held in Philadelphia in late May and early June, there were further challenges to Hertzberg and Glazer. Arnold Aronson, director of program planning for NCRAC in New York, observed that much of this intra-Jewish discussion about the proper role of Jewish organizations seemed propelled by an "increasing nostalgia for a return to tradition or at least for some emotional identification with a group that embodies the continuance of a tradition." Challenging perspectives that called for more "sectarianism," Aronson wondered whether "more intensive or more inclusive Jewish education will necessarily lead to wider or deeper Jewish identification," an assumption for which "there is no empirical evidence." Rather, Aronson concluded, if Jewish organizations wished to draw "the unidentified, the alienated and the indifferent" back into the Jewish community, that meant "establishing the relevance of religion to the realities of contemporary life." Aronson concluded:

> There is something almost paradoxical about this. For the prophetic tradition and the historic experience of the Jewish people are laden with relevance to Selma and Montgomery, to the war upon poverty, to the issues of religious freedom and church-state separation, to the work of the Peace Corps, to the struggle for world peace. Somehow, we have failed to implant that relevance in the minds and hearts of Jewish youth—perhaps because we have been too much immersed in the elucidation of that relevance and not enough in active involvement by our community and our communal services in the struggles of our time.[45]

However, no one presented more forceful opposition to the sectarian arguments for Jewish survival than Albert Vorspan, who continued throughout this period to mobilize the most passionate arguments in defense of vigorous Jewish social activism.[46] At the 1965 annual meeting, and presaging Jewish New Left critiques by several years, Vorspan spoke harshly of how Jews, "carrying their synagogues on their backs into the homogenized white suburbs of our nation," have become "intoxicated with words—resolutions, sermons, dialogues, conferences—but the Racial Revolution has already bypassed this stage and has taken to the streets and to other forms of direct action." From their "segregated flesh-pots," Vorspan said, "we hear, increasingly, the weary refrain from Jews: why can't they (Negroes) pull themselves up by their bootstraps the way we did," along with expression of "a thankfulness complex . . . Why don't they thank us?" It was a sorry state of affairs, Vorspan added: "Jewish complacency in suburbia is matched only by Jewish accommodation to affluence and the challenge of golf, stocks, and trips abroad." And matters were only made worse by the "lapse into hysteria when integration plans seem to threaten the academic standards of their children's schools," as well as the way a "generalized anxiety seeps through the Jewish consciousness, distorting and confusing reality" any time there is an incident "of Negro evil-doing, especially anti-Jewish activities."[47]

On the other hand, Hertzberg and Glazer also won approval. Already at the spring 1964 annual meeting, Charles Miller, director of community planning for the Federation of Jewish Agencies of Greater Philadelphia, noted that with respect to "the integration struggle," Jewish communal organizations were "like a government without a clear foreign policy," quite unlike the "Negro social revolution [which] is active and well led." In other words, Miller said, sectarianism among black Americans was routinely validated because it permitted blacks to organize and unify in their quest for equality, and because to object "would be to object to a basic minority right in a pluralistic democracy." The same rules simply did not apply to Jews, who held themselves to a different standard. "We still have to reach the point where we can accept our sectarianism as valid in a pluralistic democracy," Miller concluded in regret.[48] Morris Grumer, executive director of Jewish Vocational Service in Los Angeles, agreed. Grumer said that the Jewish community should "establish safeguards to insure that in making a contribution toward the Negro community we are not watering down our service to the Jewish community, and that we are not acting in a manner which begins to destroy our identity as part of the Jewish community."[49]

Other speakers strove to find middle ground in what was emerging as a mounting internal dispute on the implications of black civil rights demands on the Jewish community. They succeeded perhaps only in sounding ambivalent. At the New York City regional meeting of the National Conference of Jewish Communal Service held in New York at the end of March 1965, Manheim Shapiro indicated that the sort of "dichotomy" offered by Rabbi Hertzberg the year before was "an over-simplification and an over-polarization." Judaism in America needed to respond to current social problems like black civil rights, Shapiro maintained. Yet, he added, "we must still confront the dilemma of whether our agencies may not indeed be undertaking a process leading to the dissolution of the Jewish group."[50] Similarly, at the 1965 annual meeting, Ben Halpern, associate professor of history at Brandeis University, saw "a certain futility to this inner Jewish debate" over the "proper limits of sectarian activities in America" because it only offered Jewish communal workers paradoxical nonchoices. To follow the lead of "our left wing sectarians (or non-sectarians?)" and "provide non-self-serving, altruistic services on a non-sectarian basis" were "signs of growing confidence in the security of the Jewish position in America"—though this was, "of course, an illusion." To follow the advice of the "ultra-right sectarians," who thought "the only real Jews, or at any rate, the only good Jews, are believing and practicing observers of Judaism," meant that Jews should "model themselves increasingly on the American Catholic church" and that they were merely in "imitation of more secure Christian sects." Halpern concluded, "Jews have got to make a deliberate effort to overcome the present centrifugal tendencies in our communal life. We have got to come closer, to talk to each other and listen to each other, to get into one another's skin."[51]

Such conciliatory gestures were not always shared by other participants. At the 1965 meeting, Eli Ginzberg, professor of economics at Columbia University, told this anecdote:

> I have written several books about the Negroes and I am closely connected with several of their major organizations. However, nothing shocked me more than when a few years ago, the American Jewish Congress called up and asked me if I would go to Boston to talk. I said, "Yes, but what's the occasion? What do you want me to talk about?" They said they wanted me to talk on the Negro. I refused. I said, "I'll talk on the Negro if the NAACP asks me or the National Urban League. Why should I talk on the Negro under the auspices of the American Jewish Congress?"

Ginzberg was in complete agreement with proposals that Jews needed above all to fight for their own survival as a group. "As an individual," Ginzberg added, "I feel compelled to contribute money and effort to help the Negro."

But this was utterly different from the most important role of Jewish organizations: "Jewish organizations must be first, foremost and always concerned with the deepening, furthering, and survival of specific Jewish values, or they have no raison d'être. Otherwise you can drop off the word Jewish."[52]

CAN MINORITIES OPPOSE "DE FACTO" SEGREGATION?

In late 1963 the New York City Board of Education announced its intentions to "pair" two elementary schools five city blocks (or a quarter-mile) apart in Queens, New York in an effort to reduce "racial imbalance." Modeled after a similar school desegregation effort implemented in Princeton, New Jersey already in the mid-fifties (which came to be called the "Princeton Plan"), this desegregation proposal was a first for public schools in New York. At the time of the proposal, the school in Jackson Heights was nearly ninety percent white, while the other school in neighboring Corona was approximately one hundred percent minority (mainly black, but also Puerto Rican). Initially suggested by parents in Jackson Heights, the desegregation proposal was scheduled to take effect in the school year 1964–65. But already in the fall of 1963, after this suggestion, but *before* any official commitment to the plan had been made, a neighborhood controversy raged among families whose children attended the largely white school. As a result of this neighborhood controversy, and quite possibly because the white school was also predominantly Jewish, the American Jewish Congress sponsored a study by Kurt Lang and Gladys Engel Lang, two sociologists who had formerly lived in Jackson Heights, to investigate more fully "the social base on which much of the northern resistance to school desegregation proposals rest." In the fall of 1963, with AJCongress financial assistance, the Langs conducted "systematic participant observation" research into "early resistance to the plan" among the families who lived near the white school in the pairing. They began to circulate their findings in professional sociological circles in 1964, and the findings were first published in 1965.[53]

Although this was a local neighborhood conflict, the Langs emphasized that it had far broader social implications in part because the Queens plan proved "one of the first testing grounds" for school desegregation in the North, and also because several more prominent figures "on both sides of the local controversy quickly rose to citywide leadership in the struggle as it spread throughout the City of New York." In addition, they observed several factors that made this neighborhood controversy distinctive but no less significant as a result. For instance, the physical proximity of the two schools meant virtually no children would face busing. Also, the proposed plan included "provisions for upgrading the educational facilities in *both* schools." The proposed school pairing would result in a dramatic drop in class size (which was often more than three dozen students in the white school) to an average of twenty-seven students. Finally, the Langs noted class differences between Jackson Heights and Corona as "no 'Gold Coast and the Slum' situation," for "the discrepancies" between the adjacent communities "are not as great as some might believe."[54]

The Langs found that better educated Jewish respondents were more likely to favor the desegregation plan. Supporters of the plan demonstrated "greater sensitivity to the *quality* of education their children were receiving," the Langs observed, and the supporters stressed "values" learned in school over "grade achievement."[55] This appeared to contradict conventional wisdom about how communities respond to school desegregation, the Langs concluded, since neighborhood anxiety about *declining* educational standards was usually cited as a key reason a community might *oppose* school desegregation.

Yet only 28 percent of the Jackson Heights Jews the Langs polled in the fall of 1963 favored the desegregation plan—compared with 33 percent of the far smaller number of Catholics in the neighborhood. And concern about educational standards *was* cited by the opponents, although their reasoning struck the Langs as possibly not reflective of the whole story:

> Despite their many public protestations that the plan was being rejected solely because it was educationally unsound, opposition seems to have been based on, or at least related to, underlying attitudes concerning contact with outgroups. . . . The inference to be drawn is that the opposition by Jews represents a form of ethnocentrism, directed not solely against Negroes but reflecting, in part, a pro-ghetto outlook. The Jewish ingroupishness is dramatically expressed by the woman who phoned the local city councilman, after he had publicly endorsed the pairing, to scold him: "How could you, Mr. Councilman, do this to us, a nice Jewish boy like you?"

Jewish respondents who opposed the plan "stressed the fact that they (and others) had worked hard to get here; it was a good neighborhood and they wanted nothing to spoil it." These Jewish opponents also " 'belong to or regularly attended' a synagogue" more often than did Jewish supporters of the plan. While supporters were less observant Jews, they nonetheless more routinely "considered themselves members of a minority group." Their research led the Langs to suggest a need to rethink the truisms about a Jewish liberal "backlash" against black civil rights:

> The image of the white liberal—Jewish or not—torn between liberal "instincts" and an overriding concern for the educational welfare of his own child, who ultimately comes to oppose the drive toward school desegregation when the issue becomes salient, simply does not fit this situation. The "backlash," for the most part, does not represent a selfish resolution of a moral dilemma. The more "liberal," the more sensitive to the ingredients that enter into a good educational milieu, the more likely was the respondent to favor this particular [desegregation] proposal.[56]

A more personal though no less analytical response to the Jackson Heights controversy was offered by Myron Fenster, Conservative rabbi of the Jewish Center of Jackson Heights, who documented with clear dismay his neighborhood's resistance to the school desegregation plan. Writing in *Midstream* in early 1964, Fenster described his first encounter with neighborhood resistance at a public meeting held in Jackson Heights the previous September:

> Shouting became the order, as speakers were repeatedly interrupted, especially if they indicated approval of the integration plan. One parent vehemently suggested that he would fight to the end to see to it that his child would not be bussed into Harlem—though nobody suggested bussing children to Harlem. I began to look around, concern now coupled to curiosity, to see who these people were. Some of them looked faintly familiar, others I knew well. There was my neighbor, whose son played with mine, and she was apparently rooting with the opponents. There was a girl who sang in our Synagogue choir, also among the opponents. . . . They summoned all the rhetoric of democratic individualism to prove that it was right to send their children to the nearest school. All denied feeling any prejudice against Negroes. Finally, one young man stood up: "I happen to be a Jew and so I know something about prejudice. I think we should go out of our way to help the Negroes instead of fighting them." But a few moments later, another speaker countered, "If the Negroes want to get ahead why don't they work hard the way we Jews did? Where I went to school there were only Jews and we did all right. Nobody gave us anything. Why can't they get ahead the same way?"[57]

"Princeton Plan in the Garbage Can" chanted Jackson Heights protesters outside the Board of Education that fall. As a response, Rabbi Fenster chose to devote his sermon on Kol Nidre to the themes of intergroup tension and atonement to the black community for past injustices. In the weeks that followed, Fenster received hate mail, some of it unsigned, urging his resignation. "Would the Negroes help us if we needed their help? Where were the Negroes during the Hitler regime?" asked one anonymous letter writer. Another challenged that Fenster's view "was not the opinion of the Jewish Community of Jackson Heights," its author speculating that there was "no doubt in my mind that you were influenced by a few Communist members of your congregation." Having touched this raw nerve of intra-Jewish hostility around race relations raised disturbing questions for Fenster about the correct role of a rabbi when his community did not accept his stance as reflecting popular opinion. Rabbi Fenster concluded rather mournfully that his position as a leader in the Jewish community was hardly made any easier when "many of the people in my congregation still think of the Negroes as *schvartze*—especially among the older generation."[58]

In the course of 1964 several prominent Jewish intellectuals rejected a liberal Jewish analysis of school desegregation plans. In the March 1964 issue of *Atlantic Monthly*, for instance, Oscar Handlin, professor of history at Harvard University, and author of *The Uprooted* (for which he won the Pulitzer Prize in 1952), among other works, asked rhetorically, "Is Integration the Answer?" According to Handlin, integration was admirable in theory but untenable and potentially undemocratic in practice. Handlin observed simply that segregation in northern cities—quite unlike in the South—was not the result of "overt prejudice" since it was "not imposed by ordinances or by organized community pressures; it is de facto, the result of separate residential districts and the product of a cycle in which lack of skill condemns the Negro to inferior jobs, low income, poor ghetto housing, and slum schools." The demands for "positive integration" or "de facto integration" may appear desirable, Handlin continued, but there was no denying that it amounted to "favoritism" or "preferential treatment" in "the nature of reparations to compensate in part for the injustices of the past." Yet Handlin added that the "hidden costs of such remedies are high." Desegregation confronted ethnic groups with a legitimate problem, Handlin wrote:

> "Positive integration" sacrifices important communal values embedded in the neighborhood and in the ethnic institutions within which Americans have in the past organized their urban life. It threatens to reduce the individid-

ual to an integer to be shuffled about by authority without reference to his own preferences or to the ties of family and other social groupings.

Typical northern suburban parents opposed desegregation plans in their children's schools because they grasped its consequences on educational standards, Handlin explained. This set up a terrible conflict: "In practice, the demands for de facto desegregation threatens the education of their own children, who would be compelled by schemes for racial balance to share classrooms with boys and girls from the slums."[59]

Then, in the spring of 1964, Abraham G. Duker, an editor of *Jewish Social Studies* and a professor of history at Yeshiva University, spoke at a conference on Negro-Jewish Relations at the headquarters of the Union of American Hebrew Congregations in New York City. Although Duker did not address the school desegregation plans in New York directly, his remarks could well be understood as at least partially relevant to that context. Duker's speech was a remarkable and prescient presentation. He both sought to revise what it meant to have proper Holocaust consciousness and denigrated Jewish involvement in civil rights activism. Acknowledging the motivations of those he was about to criticize, Duker stated that one of the key "causes of this intensive interest in the Negro struggle on the part of so many Jews . . . stems from the Jewish tradition of social justice (usually called 'prophetic' tradition)." Moreover, he noted, "the impact of the nazi holocaust that has cost the lives of six million Jews has heightened the sensitivity of Jews to inequality and minority positions." However, he insisted, it was necessary also to take into account the consequences of such interest, for "in many cases Jewish communal involvement in integration" has come "at the cost of neglecting . . . Jewish survival." Suggesting further that blacks were turning on Jews because of their own "disappointments with the pace of integration," Duker continued that "Jewish survival" was at risk if Jews did not recognize that black "demands on Jews are sometimes veiled with threats" and "are remindful of prolegomena to quotas, robberies, confiscations and pogroms." He averred: "Demands for 'Negroization' of Harlem stores are viewed by some Jews as too similar to 'Aryanization' propaganda in Germany." Furthermore, Duker warned that "genocidal Negro extremists have been given respectability and recognition" and reminded his listeners, "That is what happened to antisemites in Germany, and the world is still paying for it." Duker was no less harsh on Jews who advocated the rights of blacks (describing them as having a "masochistic approach to their own people") and, through an extended chain of associations, brought together Holocaust imagery with Jewish involvement in civil rights:

> The gas chambers and crematoria have proved at least to one generation the bankruptcy of assimilation in Europe. Nevertheless, the pressures of acculturation, Jewish deculturation and thereby de-Judaization have been increasing, with hedonism and deracination as their most visible hallmarks. Departure from the community through intermarriage and indifference follows. . . . In the United States escapism from Jewishness has also found expression in the integrationist movement. I know of cases of escapist identification of Jews with the integration struggle to the extent of extreme *jüdischer Selbsthass* and active antisemitism.[60]

Yet it was most probably editor Marie Syrkin's essay in the September 1964 issue of the New York-based *Jewish Frontier*, the major voice of a traditionally left-leaning Labor Zionist movement in America, that would arouse the greatest reaction from liberal Jews. In the essay, "Can Minorities Oppose 'De Facto' Segregation?" Syrkin suggested several reasons why a civil rights push for desegregation "is not only self-depreciating but deflects energy from more meaningful demands." Syrkin, an associate professor of English at Brandeis University and a widely respected intellectual commentator on modern-day Jewish concerns, saw her essay's appearance coincide with the start of a new school year—and the first month of the Queens desegregation plan—which necessarily magnified its immediate impact. While not naming the local controversy, Syrkin instead cited, abstractly, "the case of elementary schools" as linked to "the idea of the neighborhood school," a concept "deeply embedded in American educational practice." No doubt Syrkin wished her contribution to have broader social and cultural relevance, and she made explicit and striking references to her post-Holocaust Jewish identity and how it directly influenced her thoughts on desegregation:

> Any point of view which runs counter in any significant respect to the current Negro civil rights program is bound to be suspect. For this reason I preface my comments with the statement that I am impelled to write not as a white liberal, though I believe the label fits, but as a member of a minority which knows more about systematic discrimination and violent persecution than any group in history. In the immediate as well as historic experience of Jews, a ghetto is not a metaphor; it is a concrete entity with walls, stormtroopers and no exit save the gas chamber. And wherever Jews have lived varying

> gradations of bias and social exclusion have been their daily diet. I offer these credentials to indicate Jewish expertise in what it means to be a suffering minority. However brilliant his individual success, Auschwitz is in the consciousness of the modern Jew, reinforcing historic memories of catastrophe.

With her ethnic "expertise" established, Syrkin warned that black activists should not pursue strategies likely to result in the "resentment of groups formerly in agreement with Negro goals." Careful at every step not to advocate or prescribe civil rights policy, Syrkin instead noted she wished only to document actual events and quite real obstacles facing the ongoing struggle for racial equality. Yet her analogies and examples nonetheless revealed a wholly negative view of school and neighborhood integration efforts. Demanding full and total integration, Syrkin indicated, amounted to a societal "*reductio ad absurdum.*" The situation was comparable, according to Syrkin, to riding public transportation and "discover[ing] that most of my fellow passengers on some bus routes or subway trains happened to be Jews. Would I then be justified in protesting *de facto* segregation on my bus?" It was also comparable to the hypothetical—and equally ridiculous—demand that she "be expected to travel to Harlem in the interests of integrated dining."[61]

But there was another, no less important side to this debate. For, like Duker, Syrkin introduced the theme of self-hate. If we have learned anything about the minority experience from the history of the Jewish people, Syrkin stated, it is "how it [a minority] survives," and survival could—and should—mean a *desirable* degree of voluntary communal separateness. "Self-respecting" Jews knew this. After all, as she wrote, "only self-hating Jews" ever viewed de facto segregation of the Jewish community "as oppressive" and, "except for avowed assimilationists, Jews have never made complete integration a goal." As Syrkin pointedly asked, "A minority may justly oppose the quality of housing, schooling or job opportunities available to it, but with what grace can it object to a preponderance of its own people?"[62]

Finally, school integration had already proven itself a failure. Syrkin observed that "an unhappy result has been achieved" in "some communities which have adopted schemes for the transfer of students for better integration." When schools become integrated, teachers can hardly be expected "to abandon academic standards," and the transferred black children just "found themselves in the majority in 'slow' classes." The fuss over desegregation only had "a very undesirable outcome" since black kids just got segregated all over again through tracking (this time, *within* an "integrated" school), which proved the genuine inefficacy of such "mechanical solutions."[63]

That November, *Jewish Frontier* published overwhelmingly negative reactions to Syrkin's essay from several prominent Jewish intellectuals and community leaders. Yet what is remarkable is how—even in their opposition to de facto segregation and to Syrkin's support for it—the respondents relied primarily upon the *differences* they saw evident between Jewish and black culture and history and the conclusions they drew from these differences. Syrkin's remark that "Jewish expertise in what it means to be a suffering minority" informed her analysis of black life in America brought her repeated criticism. In effect, her critics noted, Syrkin wished to suggest that Jews and blacks had experienced comparable histories, an assumption that allowed her to conclude blacks—like Jews—required a degree of separateness in order to survive as a minority group. Her critics, in their arguments in *support* of desegregation, noted that Syrkin's assumption about the commonalities of Jews and blacks was nonsense. It was because the black experience was completely *unlike* Jewish history that blacks deserved and required integration. Leon Jick, for example, a rabbi in Mount Vernon, New York, said just this: that the "experience of the Negro in America is not like that of the [Jew]" was a fact reflected in how, for instance, "the appetite for achievement which America nourished in Jews, it destroyed in Negroes." Daniel Mann, executive director of the Labor Zionist Organization of America, concluded that the "elimination of *de facto* segregation is a legitimate, albeit long-range, goal" precisely because the American black "does not have a validly unique history, religion, or culture to make him proud though rejected."[64]

Richard Rubenstein voiced similar sentiments in his response to Syrkin. Certainly Rubenstein still went on line in favor of greater equality for blacks and expressly worried that Syrkin's essay might offer justification to others for "their own indifference or hostility to the problem of equality of educational opportunity." But Rubenstein also here began to formulate concerns that foreshadowed his formal renunciation of Jewish civil rights activism several years later. Amplifying the notions of black-Jewish cultural difference advanced by Podhoretz, Hertzberg, and Mann, Rubenstein too suggested that "Negro identity has as its goal its own ultimate dissolution." This goal had never been shared by Jews, who had always possessed "the ability to maintain themselves as a distinct entity." Indeed, in Rubenstein's view, blacks belonged to a community

> formed through captivity, violence and degradation. It is a community too uprooted from its non-verbal [*sic*] African past to be able to create an identity through a return to an historic heritage. American Negro social order has

> been largely matriarchal and matriarchates are usually anhistorical. Spiritually, the American Negro has no place to go but into the American middle-class, but there is no way in which he can realistically find himself there.

Blacks, in short, "cannot learn from Jewish experience because their own has not been comparable."[65]

Yet it was probably the most detailed response, written by Ben Halpern, that best articulated (without reconciling) the tangled ambivalence of a "liberal" Jewish stance toward civil rights activism:

> If you ask a Negro how far he would like to see integration go, you will most likely hear the indignant retort that he doesn't want to marry your daughter, and doesn't want the Negroes to be white men. Negroes, like Jews who resentfully tell you they are proud to be Jews, can also fiercely defend their identity. But has anyone ever seen Negro leaders who fearfully contemplate the assimilation of their people? This fear, on the other hand, is very real among the Jews; and Jewish "survivalism" is a live and important theme in all our thinking. To oppose *de facto* segregation is, in the eyes of a Jewish survivalist, to support compulsory assimilation. This is easy to understand. But cannot Jewish leaders have enough empathy with the Negro situation to understand if this reaction is not shared by the Negro leadership?[66]

This *Jewish Frontier* discussion included only two respondents who argued that it was *similarities* in the historic conditions of Jews and blacks that demanded integrationist policies. First, Philip Bernstein, a rabbi in Rochester, New York, reminded Syrkin of their own shared past in postwar Germany and indicated an alternative Holocaust lesson for Jewish-black relations:

> In 1947 as Adviser on Jewish affairs to the United States military commanders in Europe, I invited Marie Syrkin to Germany to record the story of the Jewish displaced persons. She will recall that although ultimately they were their own emancipators, extraordinary efforts were required to normalize and to redeem the lives of these Jews precisely because of what they had been through. The analogy to the Negro situation is quite clear.

It was only Balfour Brickner, director of the Commission on Interfaith Activities of the Union of American Hebrew Congregations, however, who avoided entirely the idea that black culture was pathological and criticized the wrongheadedness of Syrkin's underlying assumptions:

> Negroes are not in "slow learners" groups because they are innately intellectually inferior; they are there because they have not had a chance to develop their intelligences at the same rate as their white peers. . . . Inconveniences in travel and the loss of the "neighborhood school" are small prices to pay when measured against the goal of an equal, educated and culturally more mature America.[67]

Brickner's position was the minority one not just in *Jewish Frontier*. In January 1965 *Commentary* columnist Milton Himmelfarb offered his views on the desegregation matter as well, strikingly beginning by declaring that Melvin Tumin's ideas about the growing conservatism of the Jewish community were "all false." Yet Himmelfarb nonetheless went on to attack the liberal Jewish stand on school desegregation, arguing (not unlike Handlin and Syrkin) that any Jewish parent opposed to elementary school desegregation only articulated "educational self-interest" and could hardly be blamed for doing so. After all, when there were black kids in a class it really *did* lower educational standards—which meant bright Jewish kids suffered. With sentiments almost indistinguishable from Handlin's, Himmelfarb concluded "that as things stand now, there is in fact and in principle a tension, or outright conflict, between the requirements of justice for the Negroes and the requirements of first-rate education."[68]

"The Princeton Plan as a solution to New York City's problems of racial imbalance is through," wrote Myron Fenster in June 1965.[69] A group calling itself Parents and Taxpayers (PAT) orchestrated a "crusade" against school desegregation in Jackson Heights and, in October 1964, brought their children back to the "neighborhood" Jackson Heights school. Met by dozens of police, sixty-five PAT members, including several mothers with babies in their arms, were arrested. These protests persisted, Fenster noted, even though many parents, including some initially opposed to the plan, now agreed their children were receiving a better education because of it. Regardless, however, by the summer of 1965, and principally due to a Jewish community's resistance, the Board of Education retreated almost completely from an initial intention to pair forty city schools on the Princeton desegregation model.[70] The "Princeton Plan is dead," Fenster wrote, adding with a hint of foreboding: "The question is, will its ghost come back to haunt us?"[71]

Yet it is not at all clear that Fenster's anxieties about the future were especially warranted. As American Jews retreated from an activism on behalf of social justice, they did so oftentimes with self-justifying rhetoric that made their retreat appear not only appropriate but ethical in its own right. As the next chapter demonstrates, by 1965 the terms of debate had shifted so thoroughly that from then on political progressives and advocates of prophetic Judaism were decidedly on the defensive.

Disappointments and setbacks had a painful and divisive effect on activists in the civil rights movement as well. Already in 1964 and 1965, but most publicly during the summer of 1966, splits within the Student Nonviolent Coordinating Committee (SNCC) over the goals and tactics of the civil rights movement led to the emergence of a demand for Black Power. In part because of the sense that the federal government's support for a voting rights act had been half-hearted, in part because of a widespread grassroots perception that Martin Luther King Jr. had taken credit for SNCC's laborious toil in the field, and in part because of a view that white liberals hoped to control the movement's growing desire for self-determination, Black Power advocates like Stokely Carmichael tapped frustrated sentiments when they said they were no longer willing to play by rules established without their cooperation or consent. For many white observers, including many Jews, the rise of this new black militancy signaled an end to an interracial civil rights coalition and led slowly (and then more swiftly) to renunciations of its confrontational and radical style.

And yet, however paradoxically, for most observers 1965 was also the zenith of interreligious cooperation and interracial solidarity in the movement for African American civil rights. Jewish leaders and leading Jewish organizations remained highly visible in their advocacy of a civil rights agenda. Most memorably, in March of that year the American Jewish Congress, the American Jewish Committee, the Anti-Defamation League, and the National Community Relations Advisory Council all sent large delegations to the mass march from Selma to Montgomery, Alabama, organized by SNCC and led by Martin Luther King Jr. Alongside Dr. King at the head of the march was Rabbi Abraham J. Heschel of the Jewish Theological Seminary. In addition, an Orthodox presence at the march was so significant that some black participants also wore yarmulkes, calling them "freedom caps." Among the numerous rabbis who joined the final march into Montgomery were Maurice Davis, Maurice Eisendrath, Everett Gendler, Richard Hirsch, Wolfe Kelman, S. Gershon Levi, Eugene Lipman, and Seymour Siegel. Publicly, at least, and so far as most Americans could tell, the Jewish-black alliance for civil rights remained very much alive.

4 "Protect and Keep": Vietnam, Israel, and the Politics of Theology

I get worried when the Jewish position is a popular position.
—Albert Vorspan, 1966

WHY SHOULD WE SURVIVE AS JEWS?

At the end of 1965 a sociological inquiry into Jewish attitudes toward black civil rights argued that there existed no newly minted Jewish "backlash" against integration. But the reasons sociologist B. Z. Sobel and historian May L. Sobel gave for this conclusion were unexpected. Citing both substantial anecdotal and quantifiable evidence, the Sobels said that American Jews were quite similar to other whites when it came both to racial prejudices and social commitments. The perception that Jews were more liberal than other whites, the Sobels contended, rested largely on the activism of Jewish agency professionals; the American Jewish community as a whole, however, exhibited a "general lethargy and/or rejection of such activist involvement." In many respects refining the analysis about conservative trends in the Jewish community proposed two years earlier by Melvin Tumin, the Sobels wrote that "we are, at this juncture, convinced that the large majority of the Jewish community does not feel a communality of purpose with the Negroes; that if Jews desire civil-rights legislation—and by and large they do—they do not support integration." Most striking, the Sobels continued, a widespread Jewish disaffection with civil rights was *not* a recent phenomenon due to black antisemitism or black militancy. On the contrary, the Sobels argued that most American Jews had "never favored integration; and that what we are hearing is *not* really *a change* in attitude, but is the old attitude being voiced vigorously for the first time in reaction to a new problem."

In other words, there cannot be a "backlash" if support never existed in the first place. Thus, the Sobels found that the so-called contemporary Jewish backlash against civil rights should more accurately be understood "not as a retrenchment of civil-rights support, but rather as a new expression of old integrationist opposition."[1]

The Sobels's recommendations for action were unambiguous. They believed the Jewish community needed strong leadership; it needed to be instructed that its anti-integration values were not ethical, and diminished Judaism. Not to challenge Jewish resistance to integration, no matter how widespread it might be, raised serious questions precisely about the prospects for Jewish survival. This was true, in their view—and here their position differed forcefully from that of conservative survivalists—because for Jews, "a mission to live the Torah, to speak to the world of the one true God" involved an obligation "to bear the message of prophetic justice and social melioration." In the contemporary American moment, this largely meant to struggle for racial justice. For the Sobels said that Jews needed to respond *as Jews* to social injustice as a way also to counter the pressures of acculturation and assimilation. "If the faith is lost, the ritual dead, authority absent, what is there to lay hold of loyalties?" they asked. For if Jews now "react as 'whites' in their reaction to Negroes, fearing and castigating the strangers in the gates," this meant that they had abdicated a crucial piece of their Jewishness and their Judaism. And it was now up to the rabbinical and organizational leadership to stand up to the community and instruct it on the un-Jewishly error of its ways—even if this entailed running afoul of its popular demands. The Sobels concluded:

> There appears to be no way out: community leaders must act as a goad and a rod to prod and push the Jewish community into action. The historic Jewish response has always been: *na'aseh v'nishma* (*Exodus* 24:1)—we will do and then understand. This was the traditional answer to those with doubts, and it must be the present answer, too.[2]

Yet such a pro-activist perspective on the responsibilities of the rabbinate and the Jewish organizational leadership in the struggle for civil rights was almost immediately rejected by a broad range of Jewish spokespersons, communal leaders, and cultural commentators. Indeed, far from wanting to push the Jewish rank and file into a more activist position, many commentators now argued that those Jews who did remain active in civil rights work were not only utterly misguided but actually posed a threat to the well-being of their coreligionists. The debate increasingly no longer centered on the financial priorities of official Jewish organizations. Instead the focus of conflict involved those Jews—many (though not all) affiliated with the New Left, many of them young, a few of them older—who engaged directly in antiracist activism and other forms of social protest.

For example, and in this sense like the Sobels, Rabbi Arthur Hertzberg too demanded, in a widely circulated and much debated essay published in early 1966, that the American Jewish leadership take more forceful action and be more directive with its constituency. Hertzberg, like the Sobels, believed that the question facing Jews in its "starkest form" amounted to the question "Why be a Jew at all?"[3] But the path he proposed was diametrically opposite to the one urged by the Sobels. There *was* a serious threat to faith among American Jews, Hertzberg concluded, and a need especially for strong rabbinical leadership. But rabbinical activism for black civil rights was a symptom of a problem confronting Judaism in America—not its salvation.

It was true, Hertzberg noted, that the American rabbinate had traditionally been dedicated to social justice, on behalf of both Jews and other underprivileged groups. But circumstances in America were different from other nations. In the United States Jews had actually achieved what they had only wished for elsewhere, namely, their equality. With this personal battle "now over," the American rabbinate addressed its ethical concerns "to other communities, especially to the Jews of Israel and to the Negroes in America." Yet in both instances, and for different reasons, they found the going pretty rough. In the case of Israel it was hard for an American rabbi to pay more than lip service to the cause because "Zionism becomes a threat" to "the rabbi of today [who] is expected to symbolize the new Jewish role as part of a new American 'we' "; he risked the label of "subversive" if he actually followed through on his convictions and preached aliyah to his congregation (or abandoned his comfortable existence and made aliyah himself). In the case of black civil rights the typical rabbi was here hampered both by his own ambivalence and by "the ambivalence about the Negro that abounds among the laity." Yet the solution to such grassroots resistance was *not* stepped-up activism—nor should it be—because the civil rights cause did not advance the Jewish cause, argued Hertzberg. Instead what it accomplished was greater social contact between Jews and Christians, and what this brought about was increased intermarriage—not to mention more *interracial* intermarriage. (And Hertzberg opined, almost sarcastically, that the synagogue "has certainly not yet arrived at the point of welcoming the phenomenon.")[4]

Thus Hertzberg arrived at the heart of the matter. Rabbis not only had to heed the warnings of their congregations when they dragged their heels in the struggle for civil rights. Rabbis had an obligation to listen to and learn from that resistance. Although he did not name names, Hertzberg's argumentation was an affront to the social activism of prophetic Judaism, especially as interpreted by the Reform leadership of the Union of American Hebrew Congregations and many in the American Jewish Congress. Hertzberg put it this way: he understood how many activist rabbis "are convinced that it is their moral duty to help the Negro advance," but these rabbis also had to see how social activism only eroded *further* the already "constantly diminishing" role of the rabbi as a "leader of the Jews in a hostile world." What the activist rabbi did was nothing less than depreciate Judaism itself. Hertzberg explained:

> The rabbis even know that their presence in the Civil Rights movement is making them encounter many Jews, especially of the younger generation, who are entirely committed to this struggle. What makes the rabbis uneasy, and what, therefore, makes it impossible for them to find their fulfillment in civil rights, is the feeling that they are not thereby bringing peripheral Jews back to any of the parochial Jewish concerns. On the contrary, a rabbinic effort to identify contemporary Judaism primarily with the struggle for justice may well serve to confirm a notion that few rabbis could possibly want to strengthen: that all that is "in-group" within Jewry is irrelevant and dead.

Indeed, when "young Jews they never see in synagogue" found activist rabbis "on the picket lines carrying the banners against segregation," these sidewalk encounters did not inspire Jewish secularists to find their way back to the Judaism of their childhoods, Hertzberg argued. Instead, these encounters between alienated Jew and liberal rabbi merely reinforced sentiments among disaffected Jews that might best be summarized in the oft-repeated question: "Why should we survive as Jews?"[5]

Other commentators soon put their critique of the persistence of Jewish involvement in black civil rights causes in ever more florid terms. In a special December 1966 *Midstream* symposium on "Negro-Jewish Relations in America," for example, a number of contributors voiced explicit hostility and ridicule toward Jewish antiracist activists, while elaborating highly condescending notions about blacks. In her contribution, for instance, Lucy Dawidowicz not only analogized black militancy with Nazism (at one point remarking that it was "hard to distinguish Black Power from Black Shirts") but also reminded readers of the way young Russian radicals in the nineteenth century had whipped up the antisemitism of the serfs in the hopes of winning the rural masses for the longed for revolution. Thinking about black-Jewish relations in the 1960s, in her opinion, was "like watching an old Russian movie about the 1870's." Dawidowicz thought the antisemitism of the peasants then had a lot in common with modern-day black antisemitism: "Like the Russian serfs in many respects, these poor Negro masses share with them also a primitive religiosity embedded in superstition and a distrust of urban mercantile society and of a money economy." Meanwhile, in her opinion, Jews who denied that blacks were truly antisemitic were "Jewish cheek-turners" and "chronically (or is it acutely?) embarrassed about being Jewish." Furthermore, she suggested, the Jewish "boys and girls in Students for a Democratic Society, Northern Student Movement, white friends of SNCC [Southern Nonviolent Coordinating Committee] and CORE [Congress of Racial Equality]" were all "alienated" from their own heritage, "spitting in the wells from which they drank." Dawidowicz even surmised that "today's radical Jewish youth may be providing their non-Jewish (Negro) comrades with the ideological rationalizations and psychological justifications for anti-Semitism."[6]

In the same *Midstream* symposium the widely respected literary critic Leslie Fiedler treated Jewish radicals as simply pathetic, while being quite direct about his disrespect for black intellect. Fiedler mocked the young Jews who "tried to assimilate to a world which mythologically rejects them by linking arms with Negroes in protests and demonstrations." He indicated that "though young Jews have an affinity not only for protests but for folksongs, jazz and marijuana," they have "trouble making it across the legendary line—remain always in danger of being told that they cannot *really* commit themselves to the Movement, cannot *really* make authentic jazz, cannot *really* sing the blues." Referring to the notorious antisemitic remarks of a CORE leader—"Hitler made a mistake when he didn't kill enough of you"—Fiedler amplified his notion that black antisemitism might be a sort of "culture-climbing," a "belated and misguided" effort to "emulate WASP style," just as WASPs were, in his view, abandoning anti-Jewish racism. Fiedler managed to put down blacks more generally as well. The world into which young radical Jews sought entry, Fiedler opined, was profoundly different from the Jewish world. Fiedler expounded on the contrasts he saw between blacks and Jews: "It is no secret, surely, that in America the Jewish community has largely committed itself to a life of logos, a cultivation of the ego and the whole Gutenberg bit . . . while the Negro community in large part continues to live (even to make its living) in the world of sub-literacy, unrationalized impulse, and free fantasy."[7]

Fiedler's essay also contained an extended critique of "anti-liberal Bolshevik 'Humanism,' " identifying any Jew's attachment to Marxism as a sign that he was "politically obtuse" and "recusant," unconcerned with "the fate of his own people." Fiedler appropriated a leftist argument as his own, asking rhetorically whether it might not be that " 'liberalism' " was in fact "only a camouflage for a special sort of privilege." But embedded in his enlargement of this argument was, once again, a derogation of black ability. Commenting on how "dismayed" many Jews had been to find blacks turning against "the whole body of 'Jewish Liberalism,' " Fiedler elaborated that the pain had to do with more than having one's personal assistance rejected:

> Worse, much worse, is the fact that the Negroes, whatever their avowed credo, challenge by their very existence a basic article of the Liberal Faith: equality of opportunity will not grant very many of them, brutalized by long brainwashing and bred by a kind of unnatural selection, a decent life or the possibility of prosperity. What they demand, not so much by what they say as by how they are, how they test, how they perform, is *special privilege* rather than equality if they are to make it at all in the very world in which the Jews have so preeminently flourished.[8]

As the quite different arguments put forward by Hertzberg, Dawidowicz, and Fiedler in 1966 suggest, references to Jews' involvements in black civil rights were starting to get intertwined with discussion of other kinds of social and political issues, from attitudes toward Israel to attitudes toward Marxism. Although blackness and black rights, and Jews' relationships to both, would continue to function as rhetorical reference points, these would not long remain the main foci of intra-Jewish ideological conflict. Comments about race relations would continue to surface in the midst of other discussions, but the main emphases of these discussions began to lie elsewhere: on Vietnam, on Israel, on questions of post-Holocaust theology, and on a more general need for Jewish power and for particularist—even biologistic—interpretations of Jewish survival. These were the sites in and around which answers to Hertzberg's question, "Why should we survive as Jews?" were now primarily elaborated.

From 1965 on, as U.S. military involvement in Vietnam escalated, Jewish leaders took ever more vocal stands for and against the war. Meanwhile, the perception that Israel's security was increasingly threatened had a number of American Jewish commentators linking Israel's survival with a U.S. victory in Southeast Asia. The events surrounding the Six-Day War in June of 1967, and especially the Israeli victory in that war, changed the quality of discussion about Jewish survival in the U.S. yet again, irrevocably reconfiguring the terms of debate about Jewish identity and appropriate Holocaust consciousness. At the same time, beginning already before the Six-Day War but growing in intensity in its wake, specifically theological arguments about the lessons of the Holocaust were pursued ever more fervently and forcefully. Theology, indeed, became interwoven with politics still more explicitly, as commentators across the ideological spectrum invoked religious tradition to buttress their opposing stances. Although in 1965 the tradition of prophetic Judaism had remained a reference point not only for antiracist activists but also for opponents of the Vietnam War, this particular religious movement had fewer and fewer defenders in subsequent years. More and more articulately, leading Jewish intellectuals found ways to express the paramount *moral* importance of pursuing Jewish self-interest and worked to make those who called for altruism or self-sacrifice look not just ridiculous, and not even only obnoxiously self-righteous, but also genuinely dangerous. Leftism and liberalism were both presented as being inherently at odds with Judaism and Jewishness. The nonactivism of much of the Jewish laity was not a cause for alarm, but rather taken as a sign of that laity's good common sense. A new language of "realism" emerged, which treated idealism and a sense of social responsibility toward members of other groups as either wrong-headed or reprehensible—or both. Rather than arguing that Judaism and politics had nothing to do with one another, as previous incarnations of antileftists and antiliberals had, numerous Jewish leaders and intellectuals now began explicitly to draw conservative—even right-wing—political lessons from religious sources. Throughout the second half of the 1960s, as this chapter and those following will show, Jewish involvement in left-wing and liberal activism persisted. But the tide had begun to turn. Over and over again, socially engaged left-wing and liberal activists found both their Judaism and their Jewishness being cast into doubt.

JUDAISM AND WORLD PEACE

In late 1965 and early 1966 social activist Jewish leaders began to say publicly how deeply dismayed they were by the evasive response of the American Jewish community to the urgent issue of the Vietnam War. In his December 1965 keynote address to the National Conference for Progressive Israel, Avraham Schenker, founder and national chairman of Americans for Progressive Israel–Hashomer Hatzair, argued that it was "sad that people are so ostrich-like and refuse to see the world as it is," and sadder still that so many of the uncommitted were American Jews. According to Schenker, Jews had an ethical and historic call to social action. "What does a Zionist organization have to do with the war in Viet Nam?" Schenker asked. The answer resided in history. Since "we are a people which was decimated in a holocaust, because we are a people which suffered more proportionately as few other people have suffered in history," Jews "have an obligation never again to remain silent, never again to take anything for granted." Jews had to defend the rights of Soviet Jews *and* support the establishment of a Palestinian state; they also had to march with the antiwar movement. American Jews "have an obligation, along with all others who seek peace, to express ourselves frankly and firmly for the withdrawal of troops from Viet Nam and for allowing the Vietnamese people their right to fashion their own destiny," Schenker argued.[9]

Likewise, in March 1966, an outspoken Reform rabbi on Chicago's North Shore, Arnold Jacob Wolf, wrote in the column he contributed to his temple's weekly bulletin that he "found the unwillingness to discuss the issues" surrounding the war "by far the most depressing and pervasive fact" facing him as a rabbi. (When congregants remonstrated that it was not the place of Jews to discuss controversial political matters, Wolf responded, "This objection is straight out of the ghetto.")[10] And also in 1966, Albert Vorspan objected that "*as a Jewish community* we have largely been tepid and silent on the great issues of war and peace." This ethical inertia represented a clear sign that American Jews had chosen status quo values over the imperatives of Judaism. "We are so *in* that we are losing that special angle of vision which comes from being *out*, from being alienated, from being *part of* but *apart from* the general society, subjecting it to judgment and to criticism," Vorspan lamented.[11] Like Justine Wise Polier and Shad Polier in their critique of Norman Podhoretz in 1963, like Melvin Tumin in his 1964 assessment of political trends within American Jewry, or like the young Paul Cowan explaining his civil rights activism in 1965, Vorspan too saw affirmations of status quo values as unfortunate signs of craven assimilationism.

At the same time, and even while the Jewish community at large may have been chastised by some for its hesitancy, several Jewish rabbinical and communal organizations were indeed moving decisively to voice their opposition to the war in Vietnam. Already in June 1965 the Central Conference of American Rabbis, representing nine hundred Reform rabbis in the U.S. and Canada, passed a resolution calling for a cease-fire and a negotiated settlement. By the fall, after reports that Reform rabbis were being intimidated by congregational boards not to speak in public against the war, CCAR president, Rabbi Jacob J. Weinstein, himself a Zionist, reiterated his organization's stance, stating that "we commend our colleagues for holding fast to the integrity and freedom of the pulpit and for trying to make relevant in our day the vision of the prophets in the coming of a time when nations would convert the arsenal of war into instruments of healing and prosperity and seek the resolution of conflict at the conference table."[12] At its biennial assembly, held in November 1965, the UAHC also adopted a resolution calling for a cease-fire in Vietnam. In January 1966 the Governing Council of the American Jewish Congress issued its policy statement calling for an immediate cease-fire. It began: "The dream of the Hebrew prophets was of eternal peace, of a world in which men would turn swords into plowshares, and nations would not learn war any more."[13] Later that month, and arguably most influential of all, came a policy statement on Vietnam from the Synagogue Council of America, the coordinating agency for the Conservative, Orthodox, and Reform rabbinic and congregational organizations, representing three million Jews. Signed by the presidents of the CCAR, the UAHC, the Rabbinical Assembly (Conservative), the United Synagogue of America (Conservative), and the Union of Orthodox Jewish Congregations of America, the statement called for the withdrawal of American troops from Vietnam and urged that all sides convene a peace conference.[14]

In February 1966 the Synagogue Council of America held a one-day conference on "Judaism and World Peace," and heard speeches against the war from several prominent rabbis, including Irving Greenberg (Orthodox), Seymour Siegel (Conservative), and Balfour Brickner (Reform). Brickner, director of Interfaith Activities of the UAHC, directly criticized President Lyndon B. Johnson as a leader who "has no clear mandate to engage in, much less to escalate, *an undeclared* war in Vietnam, particularly when such an involvement is based on assumptions which are at best subject to question and at worst immoral."[15] And Brickner declared that only when the "voice of organized religion" showed a willingness "to shape American thinking on social issues" would the peace movement succeed in ending the war.[16]

In his memorable speech from the conference, Arthur J. Lelyveld, Reform rabbi of Fairmount Temple in Cleveland, laid out most clearly how his faith instructed his antiwar activism. Lelyveld noted that "we certainly cannot determine our position by pointing to what the Bible or Rabbinic literature says," but he added that "study of the entire corpus of our tradition should enable us to distinguish between that which is normative in it and that which is atypical." Lelyveld continued:

> Life may be taken only to preserve life or to protect that human dignity which the Divine Presence in life makes supremely precious. Anything else is *chamas*—cruel violence. Modern mass warfare is in the category of *chamas* because it inevitably depreciates life. . . . When we read the history of our involvement in Vietnam the word that comes to mind is *yosher*—the folk-insistence on equity or simple fairness. When we read what is happening to the peasants of South Vietnam, however, we confront that depreciation of life which in the light of our conviction as to its supreme value is intolerable. In the Talmud, the principle of respect for human beings (*k'vod ha'b'riyot*) outweighs every negative command of the Torah.

Lelyveld concluded with a call for the U.S. to "desist" in Vietnam, and he quoted Isaiah: " 'Cease to do evil. Learn to do good.' We must cease to do evil before we can learn to do good."[17]

Thus it was most usually an interpretation of the tradition of prophetic Judaism that reinforced the antiwar pronouncements of American Jewish leaders. As Albert Vorspan argued, "It was our prophets who gave the world the vision of universal peace," and in contemporary American political life this meant Jews needed to stand in opposition to the corporations and think tanks that masterminded military operations in Southeast Asia. "We do not need a Jewish desk of the Rand Corporation," Vorspan said, referring to the leading research organization for the U.S. military. He added: "No, America and the world need Jews, who are really Jews, to keep man human, to remind us again that man is a precious thing, that there is only one family of man, that the spilling of blood is something more serious than cracking a nut, that he who saves a life saves a world, and that man has a higher destiny than that revealed in the cesspool of Vietnam."[18]

For some, such forthrightness expressed sentiments too long suppressed within the Jewish community. "As a Jewish college student who has long been troubled by the relative silence of the Jewish community on the Vietnam issue, I was proud to read Mr. Vorspan's article," wrote Ellen Bernstein. "It is high time the Jewish community came out from behind middle class respectability."[19] Yet praise for this antiwar analysis of Judaism was far from universal, and many came to see it less as an expression of moral truth and more like a very bad error in judgment.

Initially, it appeared as if established Jewish intellectuals were less apt to oppose an antiwar reading of Judaism per se than they were to pursue the neutral conclusion that Judaism in itself offered no definitive political analysis. Trude Weiss-Rosmarin editorialized in the *Jewish Spectator* (while actually praising those rabbis who "have the courage to proclaim that God's will is peace"), "American Jews are in the mainstream of the Jewish and the American traditions by following the dictates of conscientious judgment in taking a stand on our Government's Vietnam policy—in either supporting it or opposing it."[20] Michael Wyschogrod, philosophy professor at City College in New York, wrote in his open letter to Arthur Lelyveld: "If your conclusion is—though you are not really clear on this point—that normative Judaism stands for pacifism and the rest is atypical, you are simply not right. Judaism abhors war but it also considers it necessary to wage war against evil when there is no other way to contain it. I find nothing inconsistent in this attitude."[21] The title for a lead editorial in the Labor Zionist *Jewish Frontier* late in 1966 reinforced a similar point: "No 'Jewish' Position on Vietnam."[22] Thus there was care not to endorse a war effort on behalf of Judaism so much as to divorce Judaism from some sort of automatic antiwar stance; still, in effect, and as would become only more apparent in a short time, this "neutral" reading of Judaism amounted effectively to a rejection of the prophetic Judaism articulated by the leadership especially of many within Reform Judaism.

From a rejection of prophetic Judaism as a false interpretation of the central core of Judaism's teachings, some Jewish intellectuals moved to a position that Jews really ought to affirm U.S. military policy in Southeast Asia—*as Jews*. It was not a question of what the Hebrew prophets may or may not have said. By late 1966 a burgeoning pro-war Jewish position argued that to support the war was to place oneself squarely in the American *and* Jewish traditions; on the other hand, those Jewish leaders with antiwar sentiments were out of touch with both. It was a vocal and combative Jewish populism that began to find expression within the Jewish community, and it stated time and again that it truly represented the rank and file of the American Jewish community. As one letter to the editor in reaction to Vorspan's essay put it, Jews were not interested in pleas for pacifism, adding "that the 'organized' Jewish community (whatever that may be) is not about to fall into line with [the UAHC] and propose that we hand over millions of Vietnamese to the enemy." This writer concluded: "Jews value freedom too highly for that." Along the same lines, another critical letter said the Vietcong were just like the Nazis. And American Jews had now to challenge *all* totalitarian regimes: "Had we defended against Hitler early—millions of lives would have been saved."[23] But more damaging to the antiwar cause among progressive Jewish leaders than a letter or two was the dissenting maneuver at the "Judaism and World Peace" conference from the Rabbinical Alliance of America (Orthodox). In its independent policy statement these Orthodox rabbis said they had "deepest confidence" in the Johnson administration's military decisions, and observed that the peace activism of Jewish leaders "did not represent majority opinion of the Jewish community."[24] Indeed, here was one matter on which Jewish doves like Wolf, Vorspan, and Schenker could agree with Jewish hawks: there was a distinct impression all around that the Jewish community was not committing itself overly much to the peace movement—and apparently had no real plans to do so.

In September 1966 American Jews received a distressing shock from the White House after President Lyndon Johnson met with pro-war members of the Jewish War Veterans. President Johnson told the JWV members that he was frustrated by Jewish opposition to his administration's policies in Vietnam. According to a *New York Times* account, the president "knew Jews to be highly moral and compassionate, among the best-informed on foreign affairs, deeply concerned about Communist rule in other nations and eager for the United States to support other small countries, such as Israel."[25] Then the shock happened; the president reportedly asked how American Jews could expect the United States to continue its unqualified commitment to Israel if they were unwilling to back U.S. war efforts in Southeast Asia. While the administration later declared that the president had not made these remarks or that his remarks had been misinterpreted in the press (the denials were themselves contradictory), it remained unclear what the president had meant to say. In any event, the confusion over the incident provoked both anxiety and anger from many Jewish communal leaders.[26]

In the wake of this controversy—and in ambiguous slant to it—soon afterward, in November 1966, two thousand delegates at the Union of Orthodox Jewish Congregations of America (UOJCA) biennial convention voted to endorse the American war effort in Southeast Asia. It is difficult to imagine that the presidential linkage between the security of Vietnam and the security of Israel was not firmly in these rabbis' minds. As the president of the UOJCA explained, "The spread of Communism, we have found to our sorrow, has usually been accompanied by the suppression of Jewish religious and cultural life."[27] But if the link between Israel and Vietnam was only alluded to in the official position of the major Orthodox organization in the U.S., it was soon made overt in the organization's first significant essay on the subject.

THE JEWISH INTEREST IN VIETNAM

In its winter 1966 issue, *Tradition*, a journal sponsored by the UOJCA, published as its lead article, "The Jewish Interest in Vietnam," written by

Michael Wyschogrod, a member of *Tradition*'s editorial board. Put mildly, the essay revised substantially the author's previous position from the spring of 1966 when, although he had clearly criticized Arthur Lelyveld, he had also said among other things that: "As Jews, we cannot be hawks."[28] Now Wyschogrod argued that American Jews should above all recognize that there were both moral and religious imperatives at stake for them in Vietnam—and that Jews *must* back the U.S. military effort in Southeast Asia.

As its framing device, and amidst a rambling philosophical meditation on the appropriateness of smoking a pipe in the classroom, Wyschogrod's essay mockingly summarized the "unwritten premise" of the "liberal Jewish intellectual": "Our cause is justice, not self-interest." For the philosophy professor Wyschogrod, this was pretzel logic:

> So the Jewish seeker for justice comes to shy away from causes in which the search for justice might conceivably be tainted with individual or group self-interest. He concentrates on the defense of the rights of groups to which he does not belong. His cause is then pure, whether it be the civil rights movement or the struggle for peace. The Jewish community laments the fact that the loyalty of much of its youth is drawn into those causes which are not specifically Jewish, though at the same time it cannot fail to be proud of the proclivity of Jews for the cause of justice.

It was a "fallacy" for Jews to oppose the Vietnam War, Wyschogrod continued. And he was characteristically blunt in his assessment of the Jewish peace movement. Antiwar gestures were "an act of moral dereliction on the part of American Jews" and "symptomatic of a malaise in American Jewish life which, if not checked, can seriously threaten Jewish existence."[29] From here Wyschogrod went on to explain in some detail what any of this really had to do with Judaism.

Wyschogrod said there were essentially three reasons that American Jews had to support the American military in Vietnam. First, and like one of the letter writers who denounced Vorspan, there was the legacy of Nazism to consider. Wyschogrod reminded readers especially of Soviet totalitarianism and its ongoing threat to extinguish the religious life of its Jewish population: "In a generation that witnessed the physical extermination of six million Jews, such a danger of cultural extermination, while of a different order from the physical extermination of Nazi totalitarianism, is a potential catastrophe that is naturally of the gravest concern to Jews." The ideological bridge from Moscow to Hanoi was clear, Wyschogrod argued, especially "in view of the deep Soviet involvement in the Vietnamese war and the inevitable prestige that would accrue to the Soviet Union in case of a Vietcong victory." Thus, it was "not at all unreasonable to assume that should Communism score a series of major successes in the Far East, the stability of Europe and even the United States would very likely be affected and to this extent Jewish existence would be placed in jeopardy."[30]

Yet it was the direction of Wyschogrod's argument from this point that charted new—though no less emotionally charged—territory. Citing as his second reason that "Israel is an Asian country," Wyschogrod maintained that "Asian events will therefore not leave Israel unaffected." There were unavoidable parallels between the political realities of Vietnam and Israel:

> In both cases the theme of national liberation is heard: the Arab infiltrators, often of Palestinian origin, who spread death and destruction in Israeli villages, like to think of themselves as liberating their country just as the Vietcong see themselves liberating their country from the American invaders and their local supporters. In both cases the sympathy of the world Communist movement is on one side, while the Western world by and large supports the other.

If the American military decided to quit Vietnam, Wyschogrod argued, it would boost the Palestinian cause, "cast a deep shadow" over "the credibility of American commitments," and mean that "no small nation surrounded by hostile neighbors such as Israel can put any trust in American guarantees."[31]

Finally, and not least of all, Wyschogrod cited theological justifications for an American military victory in Vietnam. Given that Jewish self-interests would be served by a defeat of communism in Southeast Asia, and given that justice would also be served by this defeat, Wyschogrod turned to the Talmud to corroborate his political views. The Talmud told a story of two travelers in the desert who only had enough water to save one life. Wyschogrod elaborated:

> Must they share the water and both perish or may one of them drink it and live, though the other perish? The Talmud's answer is simple and straightforward: if the water is jointly owned, neither party may appropriate more than his proper share because to do so would constitute robbery which, in this particular case, would result in the death of the companion. But if the water is owned by one, it is not incumbent upon him to give part of it away if, by so doing, his death will result. If the water is his, he has the right to prefer his interest over that of the other because the alternative is either sharing it, which

> will result in the death of both, or bestowing the water as a gift on the other. But this is not required because no man need prefer the life of another over his own if he can save his life without stealing from the other. In this case, the interest of the self takes precedence.[32]

American Jews were like the man with water in the desert, Wyschogrod argued, and according to Talmudic law were obligated never to sacrifice themselves to save another. In contemporary terms this meant that Jewish self-interest had to be defended when it came to the war in Vietnam—and *this* meant supporting the U.S. military operation. There was no other option, even though *in reality* American Jews appeared only too willing to sacrifice their lives for others. As Wyschogrod saw it, "large segments of the American Jewish community lack the almost instinctual reflexes that come into play when vital interests of a group are threatened" because they "no longer identify as Jews on this visceral level." Yet, as an Orthodox Jew, Wyschogrod concluded, he could never give his life or sacrifice the lives of his people, for "to the believing Jew the Jewish people's will to live is intimately connected with God's will in history and His use of this people, in its biological identity, as the instrument of His plan," and "to the believing Jew this gives to the defense of Jewish existence a special, theological significance." Given that a North Vietnamese victory would be "catastrophic to Jewish interests," Wyschogrod saw the political lessons of his faith as utterly clear.[33] American Jews had to defend and support the war effort in Vietnam to defend both Israel and Judaism; there was no other acceptable course of action.

The events of the Six-Day War in mid-1967 hardened divisions between Jewish hawks and doves. In his dissenting response to Wyschogrod, Charles S. Liebman, professor of political science at Yeshiva University and another *Tradition* editorial board member, noted that his comments had been drafted before the Six-Day War, but added that the "current crisis in Israel" only strengthened his argument on behalf of the peace movement. Although he did not elaborate, Liebman said it was "particularly deplorable that when Orthodox groups finally have taken a stand, it has been on the wrong side." In effect, according to Liebman, Wyschogrod had argued that Orthodox rabbis should "wrap themselves in the American flag and wallow in self-righteousness, and this precisely at a time when a sense of genuine moral revulsion has gripped the most sensitive personalities throughout the world in protest against American intervention in Vietnam." It was unconscionable for the Orthodox community to identify with the war effort.

> We are accused of being concerned only with the letter of the law and not its spirit, with ignoring moral issues of a universal nature, and of being entirely self-serving. Doesn't Wyschogrod's article in *Tradition* give substance to these charges? Bad enough that the first article which *Tradition* publishes on Vietnam is a defense of American policy, but even worse, this defense is based on the narrowest grounds of group self-interest rather than on any moral, halakhic, or philosophical position. There would be far less objection to such a piece appearing in *Congress Bi-Weekly*. The American Jewish Congress people could use a touch of Jewish leavening in the self-righteous moral eclairs they are always baking. But in *Tradition*?[34]

But Wyschogrod expressed only disgust for Liebman's concerns for the public image of Orthodox Judaism. "I do not for a moment accept the view that Orthodox thought should be inhibited by misinformed or malevolent stereotypes concerning the nature of Orthodoxy," Wyschogrod wrote. Nor did the Six-Day War attenuate the moral rightness of Wyschogrod's hawkish views. On the contrary, given that the same New Left "peace-at-any-price movement" now backed "the 'progressive' forces in the Arab world represented by Nasser and his cohorts in their murderous assault on Israel," the need for Jews to accept military solutions had only grown more apparent. Wyschogrod concluded: "Anyone who has gone through the past months without learning who our friends are and who our deadly enemies, will never learn that difference."[35]

In the months and years ahead it became standard practice for Jewish commentators who defended the American military effort in Vietnam to tie the prospect of a North Vietnamese triumph in Southeast Asia to escalating threats on Israeli survival. The most persistent proponent of this position may have been Meir Kahane, the right-wing Zionist rabbi who would later co-found the militant Jewish Defense League. Over and over again, Kahane pounded home the intimate link between Vietnam and Israel in his regular column for the Brooklyn-based Orthodox weekly newspaper, the *Jewish Press*. For instance, Kahane wrote in mid-1967:

> United States forces are today fighting in Vietnam to check Communist aggression. All Americans have a stake in this grim war but Jews have a very special interest in the successful outcome of this struggle. For, wherever the Communist machine achieves power, not only are political, social and economic rights swept away, but spiritual persecution is inevitable and mercilessly practiced. Because of this, it is vital that the Jew realizes the danger to his very sur-

> vival as a free human being should Communism ever achieve victory. . . . The principle of great power intervention on behalf of the small state is one that all men of justice must fight for—IN ISRAEL AND IN VIETNAM.[36]

Other Jewish observers essentially concurred with this analysis. Using far more measured and careful tones, for instance, historian Walter Laqueur nonetheless floated the prospect (in *Foreign Affairs*) early in 1969 that "American setbacks in Vietnam have strengthened Maoist-Castroist tendencies" in Arab countries, and that in view of the unpredictability of the Soviets—for whom the "Israeli victory of 1967 was an enormous aggravation"—Arab leaders were "under renewed pressure to act against their better judgement."[37] More blunt was a Jewish commentator in 1970 who raised the image popularized by pro-war factions: "If we abandon Vietnam and the Asian dominos begin to fall—as they will—America will have set a precedent for gradual abandonment of all our commitments. If there is a subsequent confrontation in the Middle East it will be termed only 'another Vietnam' and all the pretexts of the Vietnam 'doves' will be trotted out against supporting Israel . . . The Leftist cry of 'No more Vietnams' means no more Israel."[38] This domino theory, as it was called, made U.S. military involvement in Southeast Asia inseparable from an unstable situation in the Middle East. Although it remained hotly debated within the Jewish community, the substance of a pro-war American Jewish analysis was put firmly into place; Jews had an ethical obligation to stand up for the administration's military strategy. From this ideological vantage point, or so it was contended, to pursue an antiwar position meant to oppose Jewish self-interest and to place at heightened risk the always fragile security of the state of Israel.

THE SIX-DAY WAR

On May 16, 1967, Cairo Radio announced: "The existence of Israel has continued too long. We welcome the Israeli aggression, we welcome the battle that we have long awaited. The great hour has come. The battle has come in which we shall destroy Israel." In the two weeks that followed, Egypt demanded that the United Nations remove its troops from the Sinai Peninsula and from the Strait of Tiran, which permitted access to Israel's Red Sea port of Eilat. When the U.N. evacuated its forces, Egypt mobilized its infantry and air force, and Egyptian president Nasser declared a blockade of all Israeli ships through the Strait of Tiran. Nasser further stated that Egypt should be prepared for "total war on Israel," and Jordan joined Syria in a defense agreement that tied their armies to the Egyptian command.[39] Other Arab nations also committed soldiers to the Egyptian cause against Israel.

On the morning of June 5 fighting began between Arab and Israeli forces. Under the leadership of General Moshe Dayan, newly appointed minister of defense, Israeli troops captured the Gaza Strip and the West Bank and reopened the Strait of Tiran within three days. On June 8 Israel took the Sinai, and Egypt surrendered. On June 10 Syria agreed to a cease-fire but continued shelling until Israel took the whole of the Golan Heights. On the evening of June 10, the war officially ended.

In the immediate aftermath of the Six-Day War, left-wing Jewish commentator I. F. Stone observed that "Israel's swift and brilliant military victory only makes its reconciliation with the Arabs more urgent." Stone called upon the world Jewish community, which had undertaken a "huge financial effort to aid Israel" in a time of war, now to use those funds for "a constructive and human cause." This meant, Stone wrote, "to find new homes for the Arab refugees, some within Israel, some outside it, all with compensation for their lost lands and properties." Stone added:

> It was a moral tragedy—to which no Jew worthy of our best Prophetic tradition could be insensitive—that a kindred people was made homeless in the task of finding new homes for the remnants of the Hitler holocaust. Now is the time to right that wrong, to show magnanimity in victory, and to lay the foundations of a new order in the Middle East in which Israeli and Arab can live in peace. . . . The first step toward reconciliation is to recognize that Arab bitterness has real and deep roots. The refugees lost their farms, their villages, their offices, their cities and their country. It is human to prefer not to look at the truth, but only in facing the problem in all its three dimensional frightful reality is there any hope of solving it without new tragedy.[40]

Yet Stone's interpretation of the Six-Day War—especially his reading of the Holocaust and its lessons—was not to be heeded by the vast majority of American Jews. In her thorough essay on U.S. public response to the war, Lucy Dawidowicz summarized the dominant mood among American Jews in the wake of the war as "a new kind of pride in being Jewish, in the aura that radiated from General Moshe Dayan, his ruggedness, vigor, determination. Many Jews took pride in the changed image of the Jew, no longer seen as victim or the historic typification of a persecuted people."[41] Dawidowicz cited extensive anecdotal evidence that indicated how many young Jews, whose strongest political identifications had been with the antiwar and civil rights movements, now "discovered the importance of being Jewish" in the wake of war in the Middle East. Suggestive of this intense heartfelt Jewish pride—and the ways it was linked to the Holocaust—Dawidowicz quoted at length a letter from a young Jewish woman to the *Village Voice*:

> I think it must have been this way for many of my generation, that the Israeli-Arab collision was a moment of truth. For the first time in my grown-up life, I really understood what an enemy was. For the first time, I knew what it was to be us against the killers.
>
> Us. Two weeks ago, Israel was they; now Israel is we. I will not intellectualize it. . . . I will never kid myself that we are only the things we choose to be. Roots count.
>
> And I will never again claim to be a pacifist; I will never again say that if I had been an adult during World War II I might have been for non-intervention, or, if a man, been a conscientious objector. I have lost the purity of the un-tested, and when someday my children are very pure with me about how there is no reason for us not to buy a Porsche, I will argue with them the way my parents have had to argue with me: impurely, from the heart.[42]

Likewise, *Commentary* editor Norman Podhoretz observed that the tremendous catharsis experienced by most American Jews after the Six-Day War "was to reinforce a thousandfold a new determination we had already tasted as a saving sweetener to the bitter sensation of isolation and vulnerability." So far as the Holocaust was concerned, Podhoretz added that the emotional American Jewish response to Israel's military victory "can, I believe, be understood to have represented the recovery, after a long and uncertain convalescence, of the Jewish remnant from the grievous and nearly fatal psychic and spiritual wounds it suffered at the hands of the Nazis."[43]

Even those Jews who openly questioned whether the Six-Day War should lead them to reconsider the primacy of their left-wing allegiances recognized nonetheless that this was precisely the effect the war and its aftermath were having on many New Left Jews. Noting in late 1967 how Jewish radicals "are being forced out of the movement" by "the orthodox notion of Israel as 'imperialist' or as a neo-imperialist instrument," a disillusioned Martin Peretz wrote:

> It is precisely because so many of the Left rank-and-file feel both existential and rational ties to the people of Israel, while the radical ideologues at the top are in almost complete sympathy with the politics of Israel's enemies, that

> there have developed within every part of the peace and rights constituency fissures shattering the fragile unities cemented by the war in Vietnam.[44]

It was becoming apparent that these fissures were widening, and that antiwar activists had carefully to articulate opposition to the Vietnam War in a context that also negotiated the consequences of that position for Middle East realities. Indicative of these pressures, for instance, was a statement from Balfour Brickner in 1970 expressing his anger at the ways many American Jews were being manipulated into muting their opposition to U.S. military policy in Vietnam for fear that their antiwar stance could be used as an excuse to lessen U.S. government support for Israel. Brickner said: "The Vietnam war must not be used as a club with which to beat into silence those in the American Jewish community" who both criticized U.S. military policy in Southeast Asia and were pro-Israel.[45] In this way, and however indirectly, Brickner was acknowledging how profoundly intertwined both issues had become and how critically they were influencing the acceptable ways American Jewish political identities could be and were being expressed.

Often the assumption has been that the Six-Day War in June 1967 changed dramatically how American Jews understood their relationship to the wider (hostile) world, recalled Jews to the urgent need above all to defend themselves, contributed mightily to their inward turn away from social justice activism on behalf of blacks and other dispossessed groups, and brought the fact and memory of the Holocaust (and the concomitant imperatives of Jewish survival) into sharp relief. Yet the effects of the war were rather different than the now conventional narratives might suggest. For one thing, the assumption that Holocaust consciousness came into full flowering only in the context of the war—and the assumption that the central meaning of that consciousness involved Jewish self-defense and identification with Israel's vulnerability and triumph—obscures the existence of the longstanding conflicts among American Jews over what the Holocaust's lessons for them might be (not to mention shields from view the depth and duration of Jewish resistance to black civil rights activism and to Jewish involvement in it). Thus it would be more accurate to say that the Israeli victory over the Arab nations in 1967 tended more to consolidate agendas and arguments whose foundations had already been set before. As the previous chapters have shown, an eloquently articulate and morally impassioned defense of the need for Jewish particularism—and an insistence that Jews who remained involved in pro-black activism were not authentically Jewish—had been put forward with increasing fervor and success already from the earliest 1960s onward. In the wake of the Six-Day War, and Israel's victory, the stakes in these ongoing debates only became more agonized and internally combative, so that by the end of the 1960s it became virtually impossible to resist a mood bordering on the apocalyptic when intra-Jewish discussions turned to the future prospects for Judaism and Jewish survival.

JEWISH VALUES IN THE POST-HOLOCAUST FUTURE

More than two months before the June 1967 war, *Judaism* editor Steven S. Schwarzschild, himself a refugee from Nazism, convened a symposium on the future of Jewish ethics after Auschwitz entitled "Jewish Values in the Post-Holocaust Future." In his introductory remarks Schwarzschild repeated questions that he had posed to Holocaust survivors in Europe already in 1949: "What new knowledge of God has risen out of the chimneys of Auschwitz? . . . By what values shall we try to live that have been seared into our flesh in Bergen-Belsen? What new Jewish actions have been commanded by the loudspeakers in Buchenwald? What new words have been pressed on our lips by the whips and boots of Theresienstadt?" Describing the Holocaust as "the enactment of absolute and historical evil" that could not be compared "quantitatively or qualitatively" with any other experience, Schwarzschild outlined the need of the symposium to address itself to the times ahead: "We *are* asking, and asking in all seriousness: Knowing what we do, having become what we are, seeing the world as it is—by what values are we to act among ourselves and in relationship to the world at large in our future?"[46] There were several speakers that day, including the literary critic George Steiner, the philosopher Richard H. Popkin, and the Holocaust survivor and author Elie Wiesel. But what emerged as most significant from this symposium were the remarks of Emil Fackenheim. For here Fackenheim introduced "the fact that Hitler did win at least one victory—the murder of six million Jews," a fact that now resulted in what "I will boldly term a 614th commandment: *the authentic Jew of today is forbidden to hand Hitler yet another, posthumous victory.*" Fackenheim continued:

> If the 614th commandment is binding upon the authentic Jew, then we are, first, commanded to survive as Jews, lest the Jewish people perish. We are commanded, second, to remember in our very guts and bones the martyrs of the Holocaust, lest their memory perish. We are forbidden, thirdly, to deny or despair of God, however much we may have to contend with Him or with belief in Him, lest Judaism perish. We are forbidden, finally, to despair of the

> world as the place which is to become the kingdom of God, lest we help make it a meaningless place in which God is dead or irrelevant and everything is permitted. To abandon any of these imperatives, in response to Hitler's victory at Auschwitz, would be to hand him yet other, posthumous victories.[47]

Much subsequent debate over the future ethics of Judaism after Auschwitz and the imperatives of Jewish survival would often circle back to Fackenheim's formulations at the *Judaism* symposium. The very phrase that Jews were "forbidden to hand Hitler yet another, posthumous victory" soon became standard usage in conversations about the primary ethical commitments of modern-day Jews. Indeed, Fackenheim's phrasing would soon become shorthand to mean that Jews needed above all to defend and protect themselves and their own interests even if it came at the expense of social obligations to others. Given such assumptions, it is all the more important to clarify that this was not a completely fair summary of Fackenheim's initial meaning.

In the discussion following his remarks, Fackenheim was pressed to specify what he meant by a Jewish imperative to oppose "other, posthumous victories." Its political implication was not taken as self-evident. Steven Schwarzschild, for instance, appeared to suggest how Fackenheim's commandment might be seen in the activism of rabbis who traveled to Alabama to march for black civil rights. It was not, as Shlomo Katz had said a few years earlier, "that the American Jew goes to Selma via Auschwitz." Rather, Schwarzschild argued, "I would hold that the reverse is equally true." He explained: "Selma is not Auschwitz—far from it—but, even a glance or a song or an experience can be the 'ought,' can be the signpost towards Auschwitz. So I would hold that one can also say that the American Jew, or many American Jews at least, can go to Auschwitz via Selma." For his own part, however, Fackenheim stressed that it was the "radical absurdity" of Auschwitz that modern-day Jews had to confront and address. This did not mean that "we are forbidden to compare the suffering of Jewish and non-Jewish children." But it did mean "this kind of consideration doesn't grasp the issue at all." Fackenheim then sought to clarify the implications of his commandment:

> Nothing was further from my mind than to suggest that the Jew should not fight oppression and murder in South Africa, Indonesia, or here at home. What I did and do suggest is that the Jew abuses Alabama and Vietnam if he uses them as an excuse for trying to be the mythical-man-in-general, i.e., as

an excuse for not facing up to the forces which have singled him out as a Jew in this century.[48]

Fackenheim refused to be misread as someone who advocated only particularism, but he also stressed that the habit of analogizing between different kinds of oppression fundamentally lost sight of the enormity and demonic specificity of the Holocaust. In stressing this point about the Holocaust's radical noncomparability, Fackenheim introduced a new and very important version of Holocaust consciousness. While insisting that "I don't want to be pushed into an anti-universalist position," Fackenheim went on to say that there simply could be no comparison between "the unprecedented attempt to wipe methodically, systematically, every single member of a people off the face of the earth" and all the many other evils the world had faced. For when "Eichmann sent the extermination-trains to Auschwitz, though they were urgently needed for military purposes," he had performed "evil for evil's sake, not for the sake of gain or power or lust." Fackenheim concluded, "This is the incredible shock of Auschwitz, and we must face it. And I would say, to face and respond to this fact is the greatest test for the Jew in our time."[49]

What subsequently obscured the inner complexity of the ongoing debate over the future of Jewish values after Auschwitz, however, was how quickly Fackenheim's precise distinctions were forfeited. Fackenheim had made an existential, even ontological claim. And although he himself had drawn specific political and theological lessons from that claim—insisting for example on the imperative of Jewish biological survival, while also demanding that Jews retain their faith in God despite the Holocaust—his point about Auschwitz's "radical absurdity" as an "evil for evil's sake" stood as a crucial warning against facile lesson making from any direction. But this was not the trend of the time. The outpouring of emotion in the aftermath of the Six-Day War linked Holocaust consciousness to Jewish power ever more explicitly. And as this line of thinking evolved, it became increasingly difficult to tell whether a Jewish spokesperson was making a theological or a political contribution—distinctions between the two having lost the importance they were said to have had a few years earlier.

THE RULES OF NAKED POWER

In this regard, the public declarations of Richard Rubenstein took on special significance, for he spoke both as a former activist in the civil rights movement and as a leading theologian of the post-Holocaust condition. Fundamentally at odds with Fackenheim on the question of God—Rubenstein was the leading Jewish figure in the "God Is Dead" movement of the 1960s—Rubenstein was at one with Fackenheim on the radicality of the challenge posed by Auschwitz. At a session organized by the American Jewish Congress in Rehovoth, Israel on July 30, 1968, Rubenstein furthered his bleak critique of liberal Jewish politics in a presentation called the "Imperatives of Survival." It represented a new—and frankly machismo—development in Rubenstein's thinking.

Rubenstein's core argument concerned the utter necessity of embracing Jewish power. His logic for this argument had several threads. First, according to Rubenstein, there existed in the wake of (and despite) the Holocaust a chronic misinterpretation of antisemitism as something belonging to "the category of emotional abnormality." In truth, however, "there may be something altogether predictable and even normal about the antipathy often expressed towards Jews." To place antisemitism on the shelf with abnormality was to minimize the way in which it continued to saturate the contemporary world, something Jews did only at great risk to their continued well-being as a people. Only Zionists, Rubenstein continued, had correctly understood antisemitism, and responded to it by seeking to create a Jewish national homeland. One consequence of Jewish nationhood was that Jews had to learn new skills and deploy new methods to defend their new state.

> In a word, the re-entry of the Jewish community into the realms of nationhood and territory meant a re-entry into the domain of the intelligent use of violence. For two thousand years, the Jewish community had been the passive recipient of aggression. Immense transformations were required in order that the Jewish community attempt to survive in the world of naked power and violence. Secular society's messianic promise had failed. It was succeeded by tribal nationalism to some degree everywhere in the world.

Without power, especially in a world that respected little else, Jews emasculated themselves. The "realities of naked power" were phenomena, Rubenstein noted, that Israelis recognized all too well. Sadly, Jews in the Diaspora, imbued with a self-destructive "Jewish messianic optimism," had come to consider powerlessness itself sort of "a special virtue." But to accept a self-abnegating view toward power "after the gas chambers" was a risk of tremendous proportions. Rubenstein said:

> After the European Holocaust, the entailments of powerlessness should have proven so degrading and frightening that no Jews with a measure of inner dignity would ever want to be placed in that position again. Powerlessness can mean that the lives and the honor of one's women, one's children and one's person are subject to the good graces of others. Faith in the continuous virtue of men, at least in the ways in which they confront Jews, seems hardly justified by recent history. We do not wish to suggest that imminent danger now threatens the American Jewish community. We merely suggest that its inability to comprehend the question of power is rendered problematic by recent Jewish experience.[50]

Embedded in this argument on Jewish power was Rubenstein's elaboration on what he perceived to be the illustrative example of black American militancy. For black militancy exposed the wrongheadedness of continued Jewish faith in liberal politics. "*Blacks have real power*," Rubenstein said, because their "threat of guerilla warfare in America's cities is not empty." Furthermore, black demands for "preferential quotas" would necessarily be at the expense of Jews. These were not demands that Jews should meet. Instead, Jews should recognize what many black leaders were now acknowledging, namely, "the impossibility of integration and of the need to create a distinctive, separate black community with its own power base," which could only be effectively countered from a position of comparable Jewish strength. This, in turn, could only be obtained through a reinvigorated "Jewish self-consciousness" exemplified by "the assertion of explicit national identity on the part of the Israelis." Regrettably, too many American Jews ("lacking real insight into their own identities as Jews") had continued pathetically to cling to an elusive belief in "messianic liberalism" that had left them both "indifferent to the Arab determination to annihilate Israel" and "shocked at the fact that Israel has had to live by the rules of naked power and interest."[51] However, Rubenstein concluded, the lessons of European history revealed quite clearly that only the agency of power could prevent complicity in self-destruction.

THEN I CAN HAVE NO PART IN IT

Rubenstein's remarks elicited sharp criticism from at least one other participant at the American Jewish Congress conference. The next morning, Steven Schwarzschild offered his fierce and searing dissent from Rubenstein's paean to Jewish power and the realpolitik of Jewish identity in a brave new world of tribal nationalisms. First, Schwarzschild said that Rubenstein's summary concerning Jewish passivity under Nazism managed "to rekindle the invidious considerations put before us by Hannah Arendt and others over the past several years." Second, and "contrary to all his fancy and self-assertive words," Rubenstein's accomplishment was to "defame and undermine the very moral substance of the victims of the Holocaust." Schwarzschild said, "That's not security; that's insecurity. That's not self-assertiveness and pride in one's identity; that's pathology." Schwarzschild then offered his own summary of what Rubenstein's historical and theological perspectives truly implied:

> From this basically pathological reaction to Jewish existence, be it in Israel or abroad, Dr. Rubenstein arrives at a dreadful position. I must now, reluctantly, use a term which I would have liked to avoid, a word which sends a chill down my spine as I know it sends a chill down all our spines. But after the kind of language we heard last night, I can no longer forbear putting it on the table. I think that a spade finally has to be called a spade. It seems to me that the kind of outlook on life and on Jewish history and on the Jewish people that Dr. Rubenstein presented to us last night can be called by only one word—and it now finally has to be uttered. The word is "Fascism."[52]

Nor did Schwarzschild end there. He challenged Rubenstein's definition of Zionism, noting that it "has to do not so much with survival as with the opportunity to test and incarnate Jewish values on the soil of Israel." He said that the true meaning of Jewish identity had to be "to prevent us from becoming the natural men of the new Fascism, to keep us the men of spirit that the Jewish people have always been." And he averred that while he was "as committed as anybody on earth can be to the sanctity of every inch of the Holy Land—*aval lo zu haderech*, this is not the way." And finally, Schwarzschild said, if it were the case that Jews chose to follow Rubenstein's imperatives for survival, then

> I also feel constrained to say, as a Jew and as nothing but a Jew: "If that's the way it's going to go, then I can have no part in it." Or, to rephrase it differently, in the words of the maligned Stokely Carmichael: "Hell no, I won't go." If this is the kind of Jewish existence we are offered . . . I know tens of thousands of Jews, here as well as elsewhere, who "won't go." If that is how the conversation is going to be ended, it will be a great pity. It will have been a marvelous adventure that has extended over 4,000 years, and it will all have been in vain.[53]

In his brief response to Schwarzschild, Rubenstein repeated the essence of his argument: "The overwhelming fact is that, as far as Jews are concerned, if they are not capable of saving themselves, they will not be saved." Although Schwarzschild appeared "unconcerned with this problem," Rubenstein added that he did not share Schwarzschild's "sociological position, which allows him the luxury of his unconcern." Rather, Rubenstein said, it was a fact that "in the course of ensuring your own survival, you find you must dominate the lives of others in order to have that survival." There was no alternative, Rubenstein said.

> If you think that the better alternative for the Jewish people in June, 1967 would have been for the Arabs to have overwhelmed Israel, with all that that entails in the way of gas chambers and the rest, then I say, "Have your virtue and be dead with it." I do not think it is all that neurotic to want to survive. What we Jews are finding out for the first time in two thousand years is that he who enters real life and real politics must decide to get dirty hands. I for one will not shrink from those dirty hands; neither will I glorify in them.[54]

ON THE THEOLOGY OF JEWISH SURVIVAL

At the end of the sixties, Jewish spokespersons who had championed a theology of social responsibility faced inexorable pressures to reconsider those values. For one thing, there was inflamed anxiety over black and New Left antisemitism, which cast the perceived exodus away from liberal social causes as a healthful sign of Jewish self-respect. (Although, as the Sobels argued, the retrospective notion that this was an exodus may have been more self-congratulatory than real, given long-standing communal opposition to social action.) Connected intimately to these concerns was a growing self-consciousness about American Jewish identities, in part as a response to black pride and other minority consciousness movements; quite often this self-consciousness translated into a redefined Zionism and heightened sense of connection to the fate of Israel. Here again, a new form of Holocaust consciousness took strong hold. Taken together, and in uneven development one to the other, these factors all contributed to American Jews' strenuous reconsideration of who they believed they were and who they believed they wished to be. In this context, however, it is essential to remember that the answers to the questions about Jewish identities and Jewish survival were never self-evident. Those answers, if it can be said that these questions ever achieved anything resembling resolution, emerged only after the most contentious ideological *and theological* struggles.

In this light, it is crucial to reconstruct the challenges put forward by Emil Fackenheim, most especially after 1967 when he began to elaborate what he saw as the implications of his argument that the Holocaust was a unique event with unprecedented consequences for the future of Judaism and the Jewish people. In a 1968 lecture series Fackenheim presented at New York University, which he published subsequently in the book *God's Presence in History: Jewish Affirmations and Philosophical Reflections* (1970), Fackenheim enumerated in detail why antiwar activists who named the Holocaust as a reason for opposing the war in Vietnam, or student radicals who compared conditions in the United States to those in Hitler's Germany, or black militants who equated the history of slavery to the Nazi genocide, were all engaged in an egregious and wanton disregard of the historical record. Nothing like the Holocaust had ever occurred in Jewish existence, nor had anything like it happened before in the history of humanity. This did not mean that horrible things had not happened to other peoples in the world, or that those things should not be protested or denounced. It meant that the sort of "violent and indiscriminate talk of genocide" one heard so often in those days was reckless, cruel, indecent, and beyond. But just as significant, the uniqueness of the Holocaust entailed a recognition that it was not possible to be a Jew without finding one's Jewishness defined in some essential relation to that past. This was unavoidable, Fackenheim argued, for the religious and secular Jew alike; indeed, Auschwitz "united in kinship" all Jews "with all the victims" and "against all the executioners." All Jews inescapably had to heed "the Voice of Auschwitz" together, and this meant that they were not permitted to complete the horrible task Hitler left uncompleted. Hitler had been victorious even in military defeat, Fackenheim said, echoing closely the formulation he had made already in early 1967, but to close one's ears to the commanding Voice of Auschwitz meant that "Hitler has succeeded in murdering, not only one third of the Jewish people, but the Jewish faith as well." Jews could never strive for humanity again with a blind conviction that progress was inevitable; nor could Jews ever despair of humanity after Auschwitz. It was a contradiction Jews must endure, Fackenheim wrote, but it was also commanded after Auschwitz for Jews *to survive* as Jews. The Jew was forbidden to "sacrifice Jewish existence on the altar of future humanity." This meant that if a Jew found a gun in his hand, and saw an armed adversary before him, he might wish idealistically to heed

> all sorts of advice from his progressive friends, but not that he allow himself to be shot for the good of humanity. Perhaps he has listened for a moment even to this advice, for he hates a gun in his hand. Perhaps he has even wished for a second he could accept it, feeling, like many of his pious ancestors, that it is better to be killed than to kill. Yet he firmly rejects such advice, for he is *commanded* to reject it; rather than be shot, he will shoot first when there is no third alternative. But he will shoot with tears in his eyes.[55]

The further political implications of Fackenheim's theology were not lost on such newly conservative Jewish leaders as Seymour Siegel, a Conservative rabbi and professor of theology at the Jewish Theological Seminary. Although he had been active in the civil rights movement, and had earlier opposed the Vietnam War, Siegel was by 1969 moving away from many of his former commitments.[56] Now Siegel situated his vision of a "post-Auschwitz God" alongside an endorsement of a new "post-liberal Covenant." Above all, Siegel wrote, Jews had to see themselves as capable of adjusting to the practical responsibilities that came with power. "For the past two thousand years, Jews have found it to be their lot to fulfill the Covenant as best they could under conditions of powerlessness," wrote Siegel, but this was no longer true. With the establishment of a Jewish state, Jews could no longer embrace an idea of covenant "conceived outside the terms of concrete reality, including the reality of politics." To accept this idea of covenant only perpetuated a "flawed" image of Jews as "too 'good' to participate in wars and military activities," Siegel concluded, and this in turn only fueled Christian resentments and hostilities when Jews (as in the Six-Day War) demonstrated their superior military strengths.[57]

Nor did Fackenheim himself hesitate to extrapolate political prescriptions from his post-Auschwitz theological argument. On the contrary, Fackenheim found his parable on Jewish power communicated unambiguous lessons for Jewish political life. In the harshest terms, he denounced progressive and New Left Jews. Radical Jews embraced perspectives that undermined the Jewish people, Fackenheim wrote, perspectives that led them to "cheer when the odd black extremist asserts that not enough synagogues have been burnt." Such "craven cowardice" could *never* be an expression of authentic Judaism but rather was a "moral and emotional disease" whose cure could only be found "in our response to the nadir of Jewish existence, the holocaust." After Auschwitz, Fackenheim argued, the Jew "must commit himself to the struggle for survival, freedom and security waged by his own as well as other peoples; for he can be an authentic witness to Harlem and Vietnam only if he is also a witness to Warsaw and Jerusalem." In actuality, however, Jewish existence had far less to do with Harlem or Vietnam and much more to do with Warsaw and Jerusalem. Pointing the way toward his own evolving Zionist militancy, Fackenheim concluded that the Jew had to commit "his whole existence with the most radical Jewish truth of our time—*Am Yisrael Chai*, the People Israel lives."[58]

There were those Jewish intellectuals who were tremendously disturbed by Fackenheim's post-Auschwitz theology and its implications for Jewish political life. Notably, furthermore, these challenges spanned a left-right political divide. On the right wing of Jewish thought, and despite the seeming parallels between Fackenheim's gun parable and his own Talmudic story of water in the desert, Michael Wyschogrod found that Fackenheim's theology trivialized Jewish faith. It was inexcusable to place the Holocaust at the center of Jewish existence, Wyschogrod wrote, and then spin Judaism around it. Jews could not be *commanded* to devote themselves to Judaism because of Auschwitz. Wyschogrod offered this analogy:

> Let us imagine that there arises a wicked tyrant who sets as his goal, for his own depraved and psychotic reasons, the extermination of all stamp collectors in the world. It is clear that it would be the duty of every decent person to do everything in his power to frustrate the scheme of that tyrant. Let us further imagine, however, that before the tyrant is made harmless, he succeeds, in fact, in murdering a large proportion of the world's stamp collectors. Does it now follow that subsequent to the tyrant's demise it becomes the duty of the remaining stamp collectors not to lose interest in their stamp collecting so as not to hand the tyrant a posthumous victory? Isn't there all the difference in the world between exterminating persons who wish to be stamp collectors just because they wish to be stamp collectors and the right of individuals or groups to lose interest in something they no longer wish to remain interested in? Would it be a posthumous victory for the tyrant were stamp collecting to disappear from the world as long as this disappearance is due, not to force, but to free choice? I cannot see why, if I am a secular, non-believing Jew, it is incumbent upon me to preserve Judaism because Hitler wished to destroy it.[59]

Secular Jews were not false when they announced their nonbelief because "as Jews, they are in the service of God in spite of their convictions," Wyschogrod argued.[60] Furthermore, to cast the Holocaust as an event unlike any event in the history of humanity, and then construct a theology based upon it, distorted Judaism (and history) because it sought to find affirmation where it could never be found. Wyschogrod asserted:

> Finally, I do not think that Judaism can be given a new hold on life by means of Auschwitz. For me, the Holocaust was a totally destructive event which makes my remaining a Jew infinitely more difficult than it has ever been. I can only marvel at Fackenheim's effort to extract a positive result from the Holocaust, a kind of negative, natural theology with the survival of the people rather than the existence of God, as the conclusion.[61]

On the left wing of Jewish theology Steven Schwarzschild also found Fackenheim's arguments on behalf of Jewish survival disastrous for Judaism. Judaism was a religion primarily conceived around commitments to peace and justice.[62] Jews could not choose to do violence as an expression of Judaism, Schwarzschild argued. He said in 1967 that "whatever casuists and theologians and philosophers and ethicists may say about Jewish theory with respect to violence, one thing I think is absolutely indisputable: namely, that two thousand solid years of *actual* Jewish history—and the hell with all the theorizing—is quite *unqualifiedly* de facto the most extraordinary exemplification of persistent practiced pacifism in the history of the human race (with the possible exception of what the American Negro community has been doing in this country in the last ten years)."[63]

Nor did the radical challenge posed by Auschwitz alter or refute a theology of Jewish survival conceived around fundamental *opposition* to violence. Already early in 1965 Schwarzschild observed that when confronted with violence, and when asked to react to it, humanity had to "decide early in the game what the outermost boundaries are of permissible and feasible action" in light of "the reality of the threat of becoming involved in barbarism and blasphemy." After Auschwitz this meant that "we are confirmed in our hearts that in the face of ultimate evil—brutality and ruthlessness—a man is not allowed to make the slightest compromise, for whatever reason: because he hopes to save himself, because he fancies that he may save others, or because he hopes that he and others will be saved by marginal, temporary concessions." To exist in a post-Auschwitz universe meant to resist always and forever all temptations to commit violence: "Ultimate evil is an irrepressible power which, having once been joined in tactical alliance, sucks you into itself beyond the hope of moral extrication." This did not mean that Jews had first to allow themselves to be killed rather than kill. But it did mean that there were the strictest limits on the right to do violence under Jewish law. In Vietnam, for instance, it was clear to Schwarzschild already in 1965 that U.S. military force had sailed plainly past those limits. Accordingly, he reached these conclusions: "If the Vietnamese wish to live under some form of communism, we have neither the right, nor in the long-run the means, to stop them."[64] There would only be a possibility to achieve victory when there was the willingness to accept defeat. As Schwarzschild had stated in a paper at the National Interreligious Conference on Peace, held in Washington, D.C. on March 16, 1966:

> Because the God of the religious man is the root of all radicalism, the religious man himself is bound to be radical in every respect, including in his insistence on peace. In specific terms, it is clear that, even as the civil-rights movement demands justice, all of it, here and now, and in all ways, so the peace movement demands peace, only peace, immediately, everywhere, in the methods of operation as well as with respect to the goal.[65]

Schwarzschild dismissed categorically all mounting pressures from influential figures like Rubenstein or Fackenheim to welcome both the practical responsibilities that came with Jewish power and the new-found obligation to place Jewish survival at the core of Jewish social thought. By contrast, Schwarzschild maintained an unwavering commitment to the ideal pursuit of justice and peace, and he consequently rejected Zionism as a necessary component of Jewish survival after Auschwitz. Schwarzschild found in Zionism the seeds of Judaism's undoing; this iconoclastic thesis only grew in intensity after the Israeli victory in June 1967. (Not surprisingly, and as one commentator has written, Schwarzschild was "well known, in fact notorious, for being the only Jewish theologian of stature in our day to maintain a consistent, radical, and *Jewish* critique of Zionism.")[66] This Jewish obligation to resist Zionism went back to the Holocaust. "What can we learn about how we are to survive from what we did survive?" Schwarzschild asked in 1968. For one thing, and in a way not too dissimilar from Michael Wyschogrod, Schwarzschild argued that it was tremendously dangerous for Jews to argue that God somehow ordained Israel to triumph in warfare. Yet this was what happened in June 1967 when the Israeli victory "produced an immensely aggravated danger of pseudo-faith and pseudo-messianism." After years in which rabbis and other Jewish leaders had been complaining about lack of interest in religious life among their congregants, Schwarzschild was deeply disturbed to find American Jews suddenly, in the wake of the Israeli victory, embracing their religious faith as never before (and even seeking justification for that victory in the Talmud). Schwarzschild wrote: "I confess with great sadness, that I see a dominant note of rampant self-assertiveness and self-righteousness in world Jewry, which may be compared with the ideology of those against whom Jeremiah prophesied, who thought that their strength lay in their own arms and in alliances with foreign, pagan powers." This behavior blasphemed the memories of the Jews who died in the Holocaust, Schwarzschild said, because it turned survival into "the yardstick of tactical or ethical worth." There had been no dishonor to die in Auschwitz or Warsaw because "the world had turned into hell and no longer had a place for decent human beings," nor could it imaginably be a disgrace to have been one of the "more than five million who did not, as it happens, resort to guns, knives, stones, and fire." Yet the popular post-Holocaust view was that the imperatives of survival superseded all other Jewish ethics, and this meant inevitably that Jews would engage in relentless military actions "which victimize other human beings and result in unending conflict and eventual defeat." Even if this was not so, and Israel could forever stave off its Arab opponents, Schwarzschild wrote, "what human, spiritual and moral price would we have to pay for it." He continued:

> I always remember that when my son was less than ten years old he came home from a summer in an Israeli children's camp and said that his chief impression was of barbed wire all over the country. The transvaluation of all Jewish values which has already seriously set in in Israeli and world Jewry should soon completely overwhelm us. The problem of our Jewish generation and of our children is whether we can live with the ethics and politics of the persecuted, having, in some ways, ceased to be the persecuted. I implore you and me and all of us not to prove Nietzsche to have been right—that morality is the rationalization of the weak.[67]

Only a very few vocal American Jewish leaders actively linked their antiwar sentiments to radical critiques of Israeli military actions. To do this, as Balfour Brickner wrote in 1970, as a self-identified Zionist committed to left-wing causes, was to find oneself living "in a special sort of exile." Yet it was critical, Brickner said, for Jews to challenge an emerging and "particularly disgusting" impulse within the American Jewish community to back Israeli military action at all costs. "How can we take seriously their call for free speech in every other facet of American life when they themselves deny it?" Brickner asked, and (in reference to the Six-Day War) added sorrowfully: "It may sound strange but it might have been better for Israel had the Palestinians won" because an Arab victory "would have made it possible for Israel, American Jews and the world to discount their inflammatory rhetoric about driving Israel into the sea."[68]

Another rabbi who openly voiced anger at the American Jewish community's general stand on U.S. and Israeli militarism was Arnold Jacob Wolf. After the National Guard shot and killed four antiwar demonstrators at Kent State University in Ohio (three of whom were Jewish), Wolf marveled in distress at how irrelevant a Jewish identity had become for so many young American Jews. But it could hardly come as a surprise that young Jews did not care about Judaism, remarked Wolf, for if "the great, empty congregations and the dying, endlessly self-protecting organizations have nothing to say about Cambodia and Kent State they have nothing to say." Jewish communal life had become a life ruled by fear and cowardice, Wolf continued, a life bound "so tightly and so unthinkingly to our perception of the Israeli cause that we have no *koah* left for our own Jewish kids fighting the draft, standing up to the guns and finally bleeding in the streets—alone." Jews had to oppose Israeli and U.S. war-mongers alike or face the consequences, Wolf wrote. And Wolf concluded with a statement that could be interpreted as a direct response to Richard Rubenstein (whom Wolf had known well as a rabbinical student) and his call for Jewish power: "American Jews who separate themselves from their own blood children in order to look more respectable or to become more powerful will end up neither respectable nor powerful."[69]

It would be a considerable understatement to say that these radical positions were denounced and dismissed. More typically, they were simply ignored as beyond the pale. Yet *Jewish Spectator* editor Trude Weiss-Rosmarin did trouble in 1969 to write a letter in reaction to Schwarzschild's opinions, wondering whether he really meant

> to suggest that the government of Israel should have waited for the UAR's air force to shower Tel Aviv, Jerusalem and Haifa with napalm rather than have the Israeli Air Force destroy the Arab planes before they could take off for their genocidal mission proclaimed by President Nasser? Is inaction in the face of mortal danger God's will? Or is such inaction reliance upon a miracle which is expressly forbidden (*ein somkhin al hanes*, Pesahim, 64b)?[70]

By the early 1970s, and in large part as a result of a Jewish triumphalism on exhibit in the wake of the Six-Day War, or so argued Steven Schwarzschild, American Jewry now existed in

> an almost entirely undemocratic community; it repels and expels most significant elements intellectually, ethically, and politically liberal within that community; it brings the *de facto* policies of that community increasingly in line with the "enlightened self-interest" of the dominant socio-economic powers; and it creates an American Judaism which Israelis rightly know to be abysmally inauthentic and an Israeli Judaism which American Jews rightly sense to be wildly distorted and debased.

In agreement with Brickner, Schwarzschild also observed how a "heavy wet blanket of conformism is being lowered over dissenters in Israel and here." The time had come to reflect on how this state of affairs developed both in the United States and Israel. Schwarzschild wrote:

> One over-all cause can easily be determined: until very recently Jews wanted things that they did not have and had, therefore, to try to wrest from the powers that be—emancipation, social and political security, and national existence; now we have by and large attained to these desiderata in the Western world and Israel, and we want to protect and keep them. "Protect and keep" are the watchwords of the *status quo*. The year 1967 coagulated various developments leading up to this point, and that year can, therefore, symbolize the real beginning of this new historical period in Jewish history. Barring catastrophic changes, it is a period that can be expected to last a long time.[71]

THE LIMITS OF SELF-SACRIFICE

By the end of the sixties and into the early seventies there were increasingly melodramatic attempts to ridicule or shame out of existence the prophetic tradition of social action identified most closely with the Union of American Hebrew Congregations. Prophetic Judaism, labeled misguided and anachronistic, also came under assault as a rejection of authentic Jewish values. Richard Rubenstein became a leader in the attacks on the same liberal Jewish values he had championed just a few years earlier. As he had argued in Israel, Rubenstein repeated time and again that it was nothing more than "a pathetic dream to believe that any social order can exist without some measure of domination and power." It was a fact American blacks understood all too well, and black militants articulated their (often violent) programs in light of it. Yet many American Jewish leaders voiced a prophetic theology that cast the realities of domination in solely moral terms. Such noble views amounted to little more than evasions of actual circumstances.

Citing Konrad Lorenz's studies, which linked humans to rats in the ability to slaughter their own species, Rubenstein insisted human beings were naturally prone to violence, and it was foolhardy to pretend otherwise. "More Jews would probably have survived Hitler had Europe's Jews been politically more realistic," Rubenstein argued, and it mattered not at all that today Jews appeared middle class and successful in society because—as in the past—they still lacked "real power." For American Jews to cling to "the good or the moral position" resulted almost inevitably in continued powerlessness—and this threatened Jewish security. "As paradoxical as it may seem," Rubenstein had written in May 1968, two months before the Rehovoth conference, "the Negro is potentially more secure than the Jew." This was precisely because the former tended to see his situation "realistically," while American Jews seldom did. Rubenstein elaborated:

> Jews constitute a highly visible minority near the top of the economic ladder without real power. As such they arouse envy. They are disliked. They can be easily displaced. This has happened elsewhere. It can happen here. Furthermore, the American Jew lacks the disruptive power which makes a measure of violence a real option for the Negro. American Jews are by training and disposition incapable of utilizing violence to gain a social objective. The Negro knows that he has great power to disrupt the normal functioning of American urban society. If he utilizes this capacity intelligently, he can extract important concessions from the White community.

Unable or unwilling to set aside its rose-tinted vision of humanity, the American Jewish community inevitably became "the victim of its own moral indignation and social myopia," and it would continue to deny itself a measure of real security, Rubenstein predicted, until it was willing to abandon entirely a "rhetoric of morality, the language of powerlessness."[72]

Poet and essayist Judd L. Teller, a consultant for the Synagogue Council of America, also argued that liberal values had long clashed with the imperatives of Jewish survival. He astutely observed that "ever since the French revolution," liberal and radical movements, in their universalizing tendencies, had "intermittently been distressed that the Jews insist on classifying themselves as a people" and had often viewed "Jewish peoplehood" as "an unrepentant presence, a historical mishap." But he turned quickly from this insight to draw other kinds of conclusions. Liberalism's readiness to betray Jews became a stark reality when German Jews "were being dragged back into the medieval ghetto along the route that ended in Auschwitz" and

"American Jews turned for support to the liberals and radicals who, they discovered, although anti-fascist, were divided on Nazi policy towards Jews." Now in the postwar period, American Jews allowed themselves to be deceived once more by the lures of liberal values; arriving comfortably in the middle class, and seeking "to keep the ethnic profile low," they kept "the Prophetic posture high." Teller contended forcefully that "during the two decades of the civil rights struggle in the courts and legislatures which preceded the Black revolution, the Jewish Establishment often confused . . . the Black's bleeding as its own stigmata." Blacks' current angry and proud rejection of Jewish paternalism, in Teller's opinion, "should have taught Jews that excessive, indeed possessive, involvement in another people's struggle is bound to have pathological consequences for all concerned." Teller was disturbed by those Jewish leaders who expressed "public apprehension that the Jewish community was turning inwards, away from larger concerns" and continued to announce that their civil rights activism was "an acting-out of the Jewish prophetic tradition." This, in his view, was just more self-deception that could, as had happened before, and recently, lead directly to tragedy. With mocking wit, Teller appealed to antiliberal resentments within the American Jewish community.

> The term "prophetic Judaism" was first put into circulation by the early Reform rabbis in Germany, and was their warrant for housebreaking Judaism for the acculturated upper class and its social satellites by spaying it of its richest traditions and ethnic vigor. Furthermore, the term provided the acculturated Jew with the conceit that his obscene pursuit of social acceptance by his Christian peers had a divinely-preordained higher purpose. But for differences of time and environment, such has been, universally, the "prophetic" Judaism of this class of Jew. The "prophetic Jew" gravitates, in politics, to the liberal wing of his country's Establishment, while his children sometimes turn from the parental bourgeois environment, because of its social limitations on the Jew, to Populism or more formal radical doctrines, a process which produced Leon Trotsky and Rosa Luxemburg. It also fathered the Russian Jewish radicals who, in 1881, were persuaded that the pogroms of that year had constructive purpose as a prelude to Revolution, as well as the young Jews on the American campus today who similarly empathize with Black Panther anti-Semitism and with Al-Fatah.[73]

These kinds of arguments made a decided impression on Jewish spokespersons still committed to the ethics of Jewish social action. By the later 1960s it was scarcely possible to speak in an uncomplicated way about the direct relationship between Judaism and justice. This did not mean that followers of prophetic Judaism folded up their tents and quit. But it did mean that they began to grasp that the terms of debate over the politics of American Jewish identities were undergoing sharp and rapid transformation in a rightward direction and that appeals to moral righteousness sprinkled with quotations from the Talmud now sounded more like fuddy-duddy pedantry and less like valid ethical wisdom. Teller's analysis also tapped into populist middle-class resentments—and in many ways this was characteristic of the more aggressive and popular antiliberal attacks—through the association between prophetic Judaism and an exalted economic status. These values simply did not reflect the more mundane aspirations for a down payment on a house in a safe Jewish suburb. In other words, or so the antiliberal argument went, Jewish liberals were hypocritical elitists who pronounced from on high (that is, from Westchester County, Forest Hills, and Great Neck) as to what all those plebeian Jews in less splendiferous social surroundings should believe and how they should act. And it was often the local rabbi who came typically to stand in for all that was wrong with this activist interpretation of Judaism.

To some extent, this analysis was nothing if not paradoxical, especially since the vast majority of rabbis were hardly radical firebrands during this era. Indeed, those rabbis who did articulate commitments to social action—though not in the caricatured way Teller suggests—often complained about the rabbinical community's political quiescence. As Richard G. Hirsch, a Reform rabbi and self-described "social actionik," wrote in 1968, the "plain truth is that among our scholars there is still too much blatant indifference and even outright opposition to the necessity of Jewish social action, to its purposes and its methods." Yet Hirsch's belief that if "social action is a fulfillment of Jewish ethics, then it is also an instruction for motivating study of Judaism" appeared likely to have sounded chimerical to many, even at the time.[74]

Indicatively, furthermore, Hirsch eventually adjusted his own political philosophy in recognition of the charges that it was old-fashioned and not sufficiently responsive to particularist Jewish concerns. This meant, in part, the subtle renunciation of past liberal-left alliances. "The Reform Jewish 'social actionicks' should not be categorized with the 'New Left' any more than all Orthodox Jews should be categorized as members of the Jewish Defense League," Hirsch said in a July 1971 meeting in Israel between kibbutz members and representatives of the Central Conference of American Rabbis. More important, it also meant a thorough reevaluation of Jewish liberalism.

Now Hirsch implied (much as had Rubenstein) that the American Jewish liberal was a naive ingenue who inhabited a "social stance [which] is not conditioned by political power or responsibility," and was therefore often "governed by pristine absolutes without sufficient consideration of pragmatic realities." When Jewish liberals got fired up about an injustice somewhere in the world, they were "involved in the process of protesting government action or pressuring for government action in which no direct Jewish stake, interest or risk is involved." Such was not the case in Israel, Hirsch added, because Israeli Jews understood the machinations of real power. They had to "make daily decisions affecting their own survival, the conduct of war and the treatment of minorities." This meant, Hirsch argued, that in Israel Jews "who exercise power must give adequate consideration to the real as well as the ideal."[75] No doubt intended as a shift towards moderation and balance aimed at maintaining the credibility of Jewish social action, Hirsch's concessions also sounded defensive and ambivalent. That assaults on prophetic Judaism as an obsolete program resulted in a political realignment by some progressive rabbis provided paradoxical (if inadvertent) proof that Jewish liberalism had been in desperate need of ideological upgrade in the first place.

This is not to single Richard Hirsch out for slipping away from the prophetic tradition. Andre Ungar, who had written so movingly of the rabbis who had joined the civil rights movement in the South in 1963, also came to question what social activism and Judaism really had to do with one another. "Mississippi Freedom Schools and the Peace Corps and Vista are splendid ethical action projects, wholly in the mood of Amos and Akiba," wrote Ungar in 1969, "but how many of the Jewish youngsters involved were led to them by Jewish *religious* concerns?"[76] Even Avraham Schenker, who had taken an early Zionist stand against the Vietnam War, could in 1969 only argue for social activism through a negative construction: "What is clear is that an affirmative involvement with Israel and Judaism does not preclude identification with the attitudes, actions and thinking of the New Left."[77] It was becoming harder and harder to articulate persuasive reasons why Jewishness mandated liberal social values. On the other hand, it was becoming easier to say that it did not. As Rubenstein wrote late in 1971, and not without good cause, terms like *liberal* and *conservative* might really no longer apply to the American Jewish condition—if they ever did. There had, he contended, never been a genuine alliance of Jews with liberal-left values. Instead, and as Judd Teller also argued, Rubenstein said the "more fundamental issue" in Jewish political life was "the bitter class conflict that lurks beneath the facade of Jewish communal unity." Jewish liberals tended to be wealthier than conservative Jews, who tended to be more middle class. The reason Jewish liberals liked to parade their liberalism was because they were "apparently more interested in maintaining their position of relative privilege *vis à vis* the WASP élite than in defending the interests of their middle-class co-religionists."[78] Such argumentation was becoming an almost impossible position to challenge within the narrowing terms of discussion in the American Jewish community.

Pressures also came from the right wing of the Jewish religious leadership, above and beyond the popular grassroots appeal of the Jewish Defense League. Influential as well was a small group of rabbis and intellectuals clustered around a right-wing Jewish journal begun in 1968. From the start, *Ideas: A Journal of Contemporary Jewish Thought* celebrated and fostered a more extreme rightward turn in American Jewish political life. Its contributors opposed any "preferential treatment" for minorities, supported the Vietnam War, argued for the enforcement of law-and-order policies, and decried as whimpering the liberal values of many Reform rabbis. American Jewish liberals were seen typically as morally bankrupt, politically doctrinaire, and contemptuous of real Jewish needs and traditional Jewish ethics. As contributing editor Jakob J. Petuchowski, a Reform rabbi and professor of Jewish theology at Hebrew Union College in Cincinnati, put it, when they defended social programs to alleviate poverty, liberal Jews disgraced the memory of hard-working and impoverished first-generation Jews at the turn of the century. Those immigrant Jews had been "poor and destitute," wrote Petuchowski with near mythic rapture, yet "those recent ancestors of ours did not riot," they "did not murder," they "did not loot, and they did not burn." Nowadays Jewish liberals, consumed by guilt because they had made it up the economic ladder, argued that "not only are we to submit meekly and without protest to the kind of changes which would adversely affect our position" but also we "are actually being asked to take an active part in bringing those changes about, to sacrifice ourselves for the benefit of others."[79] This abject behavior could never be labeled appropriately Jewish because Jewish law placed strict limits on self-sacrifice, Petuchowski said. Jews never willingly contributed to their own destruction. In contemporary terms, the limits on Jewish self-sacrifice translated into specific political positions, for instance, a principled opposition to "compulsory busing of school children to make sure of racially balanced schools—with all that this implies in terms of increased violence and lower academic standards."[80] No clearheaded Jew could ever consent knowingly to such a scenario, Petuchowski believed.

The group centered around *Ideas* also attracted rabbis with formerly strong ties to liberal causes. One of the associate editors, for example, was Seymour Siegel, who in the pages of the journal (and elsewhere) furthered his denunciation of liberalism. According to Siegel, liberals often allowed themselves to be led by abstract principle while they ignored specific fact. After Auschwitz, Siegel argued, this could not be permitted to happen. Jews could never fall prey again to the lure "of schemes for social betterment that take no notice of reality, and of the tendency to set aside law because the lawbreaker means well."[81] In practical terms, among other things, and like Petuchowski, what this meant was support for de facto segregation on the grounds that genuine integration was an unattainable goal. Thus, and while "theoretically, integration is a good thing," it was "also clear that forced integration through establishing racial quotas and busing only tends to re-segregate the schools." For their own good, Jews had to recognize that authentic Jewish values were in strict opposition to utopianism. And finally, utopianism was potentially dangerous to Jewish survival. "Men who promise a heaven on earth usually succeed in creating a hell on earth," concluded Siegel ominously, adding that in all meaningful respects "Jewish teachings are contrary to liberal ideology."[82] Thus, it would come as no surprise when Rabbi Siegel accepted an invitation to recite a prayer at the second inauguration of President Richard M. Nixon on Saturday, January 20, 1973. In order to assure that he did not violate the Sabbath, Siegel stayed at a motel within walking distance of the inaugural site at the Capitol.

5 "If There Was Dirty Linen, It Had to Be Washed": Jews for Urban Justice and Radical Judaism

As responsible Jews: We feel the unique responsibility not only to articulate the moral imperatives of Judaism but the compelling need to translate these words into actions which will stimulate change in our community. . . . Our purpose is to breathe new life and meaning into such words as mitzvah (moral imperative), tzedek (justice) and hesed (loving-kindness).
—Jews for Urban Justice: Principles and Goals, 1968

JEWS FOR URBAN JUSTICE

The story of Jews for Urban Justice, a strongly Jewish-identified New Left group based in the metropolitan Washington, D.C. area, has been written out of the history books. Its existence and the several projects in which it was involved are discussed minimally or not at all in accounts of New Left activities of the 1960s and in histories of postwar American Jewry. Nor does it merit more than fleeting mention in the far fewer texts on the decade's radical Jewish movement—and this despite the fact that JUJ was the first radical Jewish group of the 1960s. At the time, however, the challenges posed to established Judaism and Jewishness by this small intentional community of radical New Left Jews were taken quite seriously. As mainstream Jewish leaders were understood to be retreating from the tradition of prophetic Judaism, here was a group of young Jews who struggled to refuse the dichotomous choices available to them, and in so doing they evoked not only rage but also ambivalence and self-reflection. Moreover, JUJ was hardly an isolated phenomenon. From the group's inception in 1967 onward, and increasingly after 1969, JUJ gained not only notoriety but growing numbers of adherents as well, both through the leadership role it played within the National Jewish Organizing Project, which had affiliates across the United States, and through the heightened visibility of its activities after JUJ organized the first and second Passover Freedom Seders, held in the District of Columbia in April of 1969 and 1970. The seders gained remarkable media attention both for their incorporation of black liberation concerns into the Haggadah and for their interracial attendance. The text of the radical Haggadah sold tens of thousands of copies nationwide. Above all, JUJ was taken seriously not least because it articulated, in especially passionate terms, yearnings that were much more widely felt and with which mainstream Jewish leaders were struggling as well.

Increasingly in the course of the 1960s, American Jewish commentators with otherwise profoundly differing political and religious perspectives concurred that something urgently needed to be done about what they perceived to be the superficiality of much mainstream daily Jewish life. Country club–style synagogues (usually including recreation facilities, a Hebrew school, and meeting and game rooms) proliferated in the rapidly growing suburbs. These synagogues would have been complete, as poet and essayist Judd Teller would bitingly observe in 1968, if they could also find an occasional moment to ponder matters of faith.[1] Religious observance, however, as many rabbis and sociologists noted, was not really a core activity at these "shuls with pools and schools," which only filled on the High Holy Days, while weekly Sabbath services drew scant participation. As historian Edward Shapiro would summarize the trends, "The raison d'être of Sabbath morning services was providing a suitable religious setting so that families could celebrate the Bar Mitzvahs of their thirteen-year-old sons," and synagogues were fast becoming little more than "Bar Mitzvah factories."[2] Even the intensive growth of Jewish identification after the Six-Day War would still be seen by many as not much more than a spiritually vapid "checkbook Zionism" whose emotional connection to Judaism as a religion was vicarious, attenuated, and inauthentic. "The suburban synagogue is bad theater," Rabbi Arthur Hertzberg would tell a conference of the National Council of Jewish Women in 1970. He added, "Jewish youngsters find that it has too much identification with the caterer and not enough with those Judaic ethics and values that are supposed to give answers to contemporary problems."[3] It was not obvious at the time how best to address the crisis of disaffection from Judaism.

The case study of Jews for Urban Justice and its critics offers broader insights into the now forgotten complexities of interaction between generations of Jews, between members of the Jewish establishment and the radical community, and between liberal-minded religious leaders and New Left–affiliated political activists. Among other things, what the intricacies of this local story reveal is that the traditional establishment was not at all confident that its versions of Judaism and Jewishness were right. There was a genuine sense that new answers were needed if young people were not to drift away entirely from their heritage. Moreover, establishment leaders were initially uncertain how best to respond to charges that Judaism mandated social justice action. Meanwhile, the story of JUJ also reminds us that the late sixties turn among many American Jews toward deepened religious commitment and ethnic affiliation was in part initiated and nurtured by young leftist Jews who, far from withdrawing from black justice concerns, actually reinvented their Jewish identities in the context of ongoing cross-racial activism. The point for these young radical Jews was neither to advance yet again the liberal impulse toward universalism nor turn only toward particularist concerns but, rather, precisely to refuse such choices and instead dedicate themselves as Jews to the project of "multi-particularism."[4]

DIRTY LINEN

Early activism of Jews for Urban Justice addressed what it identified as the indifference of the local Jewish community to racial injustice in the metropolitan Washington area. It all began in the summer of 1966, when a small group of open housing activists set up a picket line in front of Buckingham Apartments, a "whites only" building just outside Washington. Organized by an antisegregationist group known as ACCESS (Action Coordinating Committee to End Segregation in the Suburbs), the activists had conducted similar pickets for more than a year throughout the metropolitan area. Most landlords, interestingly, agreed to meet with ACCESS to discuss open housing practices. However, in this particular instance, Allie Freed, the owner of Buckingham Apartments, would not budge, and when ACCESS turned to her rabbi to ask him to mediate a meeting with her, he insisted "that the business practices of his congregants were no concern of his."[5] Shocked by this, eight Jewish members of ACCESS leafleted at Washington Hebrew Congregation (Reform), Freed's synagogue, on Yom Kippur 1966. (Washington Hebrew Congregation was one of the most prestigious synagogues in the capital, and a key symbol of the Jewish community for non-Jewish Washingtonians.) The leaflet named Freed and outlined her "whites only" housing practices, and noted that the rabbi had declined to get involved. The leaflet read in part:

> We are here today because we feel that individuals do *not* have to wait for a law to pass before they choose to do something that is morally right. We have chosen the Washington Hebrew Congregation because the Rabbi has chosen to remain silent and we as individuals, as human beings, and as Jews, are ashamed![6]

Predictably, congregants were disgusted that the Jewish members of ACCESS were, as they put it, "ruining the High Holy Day services," and in the weeks that followed, ACCESS was asked by leaders of Washington's Jewish community not to "wash out dirty linen in public."[7]

The Jewish members of ACCESS who organized the synagogue vigil were well-prepared for these unsympathetic reactions. It was not the first time ACCESS and the Jewish community had sparred over the (still entirely legal) "whites only" policies of many Washington area apartment buildings. Isaac Franck, executive vice president of the Jewish Community Council of Greater Washington, had already broached publicly that he considered ACCESS guilty of antisemitism because it chose only to picket segregated apartment houses with Jewish landlords. Mike Tabor, an ACCESS organizer who had previously been chairman of the Prince George's County (Maryland) chapter of Congress of Racial Equality (CORE), denied Franck's accusations. Tabor indicated that the choice of landlords was not deliberate, rather, ACCESS members "had each been individually disturbed by the fact that every segregationist we picketed against turned out to be Jewish." This response did nothing to appease Franck, who remained convinced that ACCESS picket lines at houses owned by Jews proved the group's anti-Jewish prejudice.[8]

However, despite the hostility, individual Jewish community leaders, as ACCESS activist Sharon Rose later reported, also requested that ACCESS work together with them to advance the antisegregationist cause. ACCESS agreed; consequently, several Jewish members of the group joined the local chapters of the Anti-Defamation League, American Jewish Committee, and the American Jewish Congress. In addition, Tabor was invited to attend the meetings of the Urban Affairs Committee of the Jewish Community Council of Greater Washington. For the duration of the next year, Jewish ACCESS activists tried to work more within the system, attempting to get each Jewish organization to go formally on record as being "opposed to the practices of slumlords and segregationists amongst its own constituency."[9] However, each organization ACCESS approached declined to do this; the argument was that business ethics had nothing to do with Jewish identity.

Consequently, a year later, for Yom Kippur 1967, Jewish members of ACCESS gathered once more in front of the Washington Hebrew Congregation, with an even more forceful leaflet condemning rationalizations in the face of racist practices, and calling on congregants to take "this Day of Atonement" seriously. Each and every racist act, the leaflet argued, inevitably "kill[ed] a part of our integrity . . . chop[ped] away part of our souls." And in a clear allusion to the Holocaust, the leaflet asked each congregant to consider: "Have *you* discriminated against another human being? Have *you* remained silent? Have *you* 'just followed orders'?"[10] The reaction from community leaders was blistering. Jason R. Silverman, regional director of the Anti-Defamation League, reacted furiously that he considered the Yom Kippur demonstration "a profanation—for to engage in such activity on this day is a violation not only of all religious ethics but prostitutes the very purpose you profess to serve." Silverman accused ACCESS of hypocrisy and false virtue, and concluded that "despite your 'pious' protestations, to the contrary, you and those associated with you in this ill-advised venture are more interested in deliberate harassment and notoriety than in achieving dignity and harmony in our community."[11] In short, the demonstrators twisted the meaning of a High Holy Day to serve their own political ends; this merely revealed as *inauthentic* any claim that such action represented Judaism's most important moral values.

I TAKE STRONG EXCEPTION AND OBJECTION TO THIS GROUP OF SELF-RIGHTEOUS PEOPLE

It was indeed this outraged letter from Silverman that finally prompted the Jews active in ACCESS to "begin to take their Jewishness more seriously." A response to Silverman was signed by sixteen people who said they were planning to organize a group "which will tentatively be called 'Jews for Urban Justice' " as a means of "involving Jews more directly in community activity." Reaching for the first time into theological considerations and Jewish communal traditions as justifications for their actions, and underscoring the premeditated and openly debated nature of the decision to protest at the synagogue a second time, the reply to Silverman read in part:

> We don't really think that Yom Kippur or any other holy day is inappropriate for protest and discussion. . . . Amos, on the New Year, very bluntly denounced a tyrannical king, the rich parasitic nobility, the unscrupulous merchants, the accommodating rabbis, and the false prophets. Communal reaction to this was not very good! . . . Rabbi David Einhorn in 1861 attacked the institution of slavery from his Baltimore pulpit and was forced to flee to Philadelphia after his life was threatened.
>
> In discussing what action to take this year on Yom Kippur, many possibilities confronted us. Not the least of these—which incidentally might better have satisfied your definition of harassment and "notoriety"—would have been to march into the Washington Hebrew Congregation and demand that

> the Torah not be read until our opinion was heard. (This is perfectly traditional and was done in European congregations whenever individuals felt that they were victims of injustice or that an immoral act had been committed by the rabbi and leadership of the congregation.) Neither did we invite the press, TV, radio, nor set up a picket line or block the entrance to the Temple or chain ourselves to the Temple doors.[12]

Those individuals who began Jews for Urban Justice were primarily young professionals, several of whom had worked with New Left organizations like CORE, the Student Nonviolent Coordinating Committee (SNCC), and Students for a Democratic Society (SDS) as well as local antipoverty groups. Their personal and religious experiences varied greatly. One member, Arno Winard, was a survivor of Auschwitz; he had come from a Hasidic background. Another early member, Arnold Sternberg, was a Zionist and a veteran of Israel's War of Independence in 1947. Tabor had belonged to an Orthodox congregation before moving to the Washington area from New York but now considered himself a Conservative Jew. Nearly all felt that their experiences with organized Judaism failed to satisfy a hunger for spiritual or political meaningfulness.

The group's initial order of business was to survey the 140 Jewish groups and organizations in the Washington area on matters related to social injustice. On May 22, 1968, at a press conference held at the headquarters of the Union of American Hebrew Congregations, JUJ officially issued its forty-page "Report on Social Action and the Jewish Community: A Study Conducted Feb.-March 1968 on the Greater Washington, D.C. Jewish Community Leadership's Attitudes Toward Involvement in Social Action." The report concluded that those Jewish representatives interviewed reflected an astounding degree of indifference to social inequities. For instance, only two synagogues (of nearly three dozen) in the Washington area planned any activities that addressed problems associated with urban poverty. Announcing that its findings had been reached "in as objective and unbiased a manner as possible," the report recommended the following actions be taken by Washington's Jewish community: a council of synagogue social action committees be formed, the Jewish Community Council hire a full-time staff officer to work on urban problems, the Board of Jewish Education develop curricula "to educate their constituency on the problems of the urban crisis," and the Orthodox rabbinate "reevaluate" its philosophical opposition to social action projects sponsored by its congregations. But nothing received greater attention than the recommendation that rabbis and Jewish communal leaders tackle directly "the issue of dishonest and discriminatory practices among members of their own congregations."[13] This served as the trip wire that set off alarms among the local Jewish leadership.

Although some Jewish community leaders acknowledged that the JUJ survey highlighted a few valuable points concerning a lack of local Jewish participation in social justice concerns, the overwhelming professional reaction was sharply negative. Brant Coopersmith, area director for the American Jewish Committee, declared: "I take strong exception and objection to this group of self-righteous people."[14] Rabbi Eugene J. Lipman of Temple Sinai, a prominent liberal with a national reputation for social activism, denounced the JUJ survey as "methodologically ridiculous" and "a lot of paper based on vastly insufficient data." Lipman added: "The problem is, this is a very dangerous business. Who's playing God here? Who sets the standard? . . . These young people think it's easy to tell a good Jew from a bad Jew."[15] And Bernard Mehlman, another activist liberal and the only rabbi willing to sponsor JUJ meetings at his temple, offered a scathing indictment of the group in a letter to *Jewish Week*, the widely read Jewish newspaper for the Washington metropolitan area. Citing his authority as someone who had sought to cooperate with these young Jewish radicals, Mehlman now spoke of his "serious concern" at the recent actions taken by "my friends in JUJ." Mehlman struck a rather paternal tone when he wrote:

> When a group seeks to be an integral part of the Jewish community it must be willing to submit itself to the "discipline" of the Jewish community. The first rule of such communal "discipline" it seems to me, is the realization that the hurt and the detriment of the Jewish community are not publicly and actively sought after. This first rule, which serves as a guideline for preservation of the integrity of the Jewish community, is that we do not use methods which bring disrepute to our community until all the possible means within the Jewish community have been exhausted. In short, the old cliche about not washing one's dirty laundry in public is standard operating procedure.

Finally, and although Mehlman's letter condemned the JUJ survey as symptomatic of "a kind of Jewish self-hate, an illness afflicting our people too long," it concluded on a more hopeful note, urging JUJ "to have a 'heshbon ha-nefesh' (a soul-reckoning)" and to return to Temple Micah for their next meeting so that all could contemplate the words of the prophet Isaiah: "Come let us reason together."[16]

The reaction of JUJ to these attacks and pleas for conciliation was to pump up the pressure on the established Jewish community. As Tabor recounted the early attacks on JUJ:

> The main theme of the criticism was not that we were necessarily wrong in our accusation, but that we had discussed it openly. And we had "singled out" the Jewish community. I think now that some of their criticisms were valid. But other things were involved. We had usurped the leadership. . . . up until now, they'd been calling the shots. All of a sudden, along comes this group of young upstarts and broadcasts "dirty linen" to the public. Jews are not supposed to stand out. Jews are not reactionaries. Nor are they radicals. "Jews are like everyone else, only more so." Right? Security was a primary concern for people who still had a "ghetto mentality."
>
> But it was all wrong we felt. Why should Jews appear faultless? Dissent was rampant in the Catholic church. The black community was in turmoil. Why shouldn't we also discuss our problems openly? If there was dirty linen, it had to be washed. And hung up to dry. And if no one else was going to do it, we would.[17]

NEVER IN MY MIND HAD I SEEN ANYTHING JEWISH ASSOCIATED WITH SIGNIFICANT RADICAL ACTIVITY

As far as JUJ was concerned, a struggle for the soul of Washington's Jewish community was on. In the summer of 1968, JUJ organized several actions designed to heighten Jewish awareness of urban poverty and racial inequality. When the group learned, for example, that the Jewish Community Center director had rejected a request that the center's showers be made available to representatives of the Poor People's Campaign (initiated by Martin Luther King Jr. as a nonviolent movement whose aim was to clog the capital with masses of disinherited Americans until Congress funded a jobs program or a guaranteed yearly income), JUJ said they would "physically seize" the center if it did not open its doors to the poor. But the JCC—which was then located in the heart of downtown—remained closed to the public. To force the issue, JUJ members declared that early evening was the time for *mincha* (traditional afternoon service) and they demanded the right to *daven* (pray) inside the building. Faced with the threat of a "*daven*-in," the building was opened immediately to the public. Arthur Waskow, a fellow at the Institute for Policy Studies in Washington, D.C., who was participating in a JUJ protest for the first time, said that this demand to pray as a means to advance a social protest was like nothing he had ever experienced in his life as a New Leftist of Jewish background. Although Waskow had by this point written books on both nuclear disarmament and civil disobedience: "Never in my mind had I seen anything Jewish associated with significant radical activity."[18] He also later wrote of how "this crazy piece of Jewish tradition, boiling up out of the unconscious and the irrational, could fuse itself with the politics I understood; that my focus as a radical on direct action for life against or around the deadly institutions could find its way against or around in such an utterly Jewish path—this stunned me."[19] It proved to be only the merest of beginnings.

Other actions that merged religion and politics quickly followed. All through the remainder of 1968 and into 1969, JUJ organized and participated in numerous protests. When the Poor People's Campaign came to the city on June 19, 1968, JUJ provided several thousand kosher sandwiches for the marchers and marched along with signs quoting the Torah on welfare.[20] The group lobbied against the Jewish Community Center's intention to sell the downtown JCC building "to the highest bidder" in order to raise funds for a new building in the Maryland suburbs; instead, JUJ asked that the building be donated for socially "appropriate" uses.[21] JUJ also set up an informal but well-attended Monday evening discussion series; initial topics included "The Moral Dilemma of the Jew Over the War in Vietnam" and "The Need for a More Differentiated Jewish Community."[22]

Significantly, moreover, although JUJ had first made its name through a politics of confrontation, it frequently worked together with liberal and progressive groups within the Jewish community. For instance, also in the summer of 1968, JUJ established a workshop for Camp Moshava in Annapolis, Maryland, sponsored by Habonim, the youth movement of the Labor Zionists of America. The workshop took Jewish children on "an exhausting ten hour marathon 'sight-seeing tour' " through the African American communities of Washington, D.C. Among other things, the tour visited a museum of black history and culture (where the Jewish curator compared Zionism to black nationalism) and met with black militants. As Tabor would write, "To our surprise, a few of the young people later remarked that they had never really talked with black people before, outside of colored maids they knew in Silver Spring or Bethesda."[23] Such outreach to Jewish youth resulted in the group finding itself in the middle of a Jewish generational gap—understood to be offering positive Jewish values to Jewish kids who felt they were not getting them from parents or traditional Jewish sources. Indeed, JUJ received numerous invitations that summer to speak at local synagogues and social organizations on matters relating to Jewish youth and radical activism. Group members were not surprised to find parents in the audience unsympathetic. But JUJ certainly was more amazed when some people approached them privately afterward. "The parents and leaders [who came to hear JUJ speak] knew the high Jewish education drop-out rate," Tabor wrote in 1972. "They knew they were losing their children. And we were, in a way, their sons and daughters. . . . No matter where we spoke, no matter how hostile the audience was, invariably a few mothers and fathers would quietly come up to us and sometimes plead to put their children on our mailing list. This increased as the years went on."[24]

In the fall and winter of 1968 Jews for Urban Justice continued to attract new members, even as it expanded its list of activities and concerns. During the "anti-inaugural" of Richard Nixon in January 1969, for instance, the group sponsored a workshop aimed at addressing ways to "restructure the Jewish community by radical injection of Judaic ethics."[25] Additionally, the group organized a semiweekly Talmud class, led by Rabbi Harold White, Hillel director at American University.

The group's central political action at that time was an ongoing effort to organize the Jewish community in Washington to take part in the national boycott of California grapes, especially urging rabbis not to use California grapes in their congregational *sukkahs*.[26] In particular, JUJ pressured Joseph B. Danzansky, president of the D.C.-based Giant Food supermarket chain, to remove California grapes from his stores' shelves, citing the Talmudic principle of *oshek* (the fruit of exploited labor was not lawful food for eating). JUJ circulated a leaflet with Danzansky's home address and telephone number and demonstrated at Danzansky's home and at his synagogue, Adas Israel; JUJ also threatened to pour blood on the stores' grapes and the money in the cash registers.[27] When California grapes subsequently disappeared from Giant's shelves, Giant representatives insisted that this had nothing to do with JUJ protests and vowed that California grapes would be back in the stores when they were once again in season.[28] However, at around this same time the Boston Board of Rabbis ruled to boycott California grapes because of Talmudic law. As one JUJ member indicated later: "When that word trickled down to Washington, the reaction of JUJ was relief and disbelief, puzzlement and joy. The Talmud could speak on the issue of the grape strike? Then surely JUJ's vague hunch and hope had been correct, and Judaism was real when it came to politics and to the issues that young Jews cared about."[29] A year later, when the grape pickers' strike was successfully settled, it was clear that the political protests in support of the farm workers had been absolutely essential to the success of the strike, for eventually "hundreds of synagogues and temples across the nation refused to use nonunion grapes for sacramental wine or for the decoration of the suka, the booth which is usually adorned with fruits and vegetables during the Jewish Festival of Tabernacles."[30]

In the months and years that followed, JUJ projects reflected a significant shift in the group's self-understanding and political analysis. As Waskow put it, "From then on, JUJ changed more and more speedily from a group of tentatively Jewish young radicals to a group of radically committed Jews who leaped over their own immediate past, leaped over the conservatism of their Americanized Jewish upbringing, by appealing to the many strands of intransigent radicalism woven into the older Jewish tradition."[31] Specifically, in part as a result of a group retreat in March of 1969, and in part as a response to the hostility it was receiving from the established Jewish leadership, JUJ made known that it would no longer single out Jewish individuals or institutions for censure. Although it would still especially emphasize Jewish institutions in its actions (because "usually the power of Jews to effect change will be greater if they focus on Jewish institutions"), the point would be to focus on those institutions that "cooperate with . . . larger, usually non-Jewish" "immoral structures of American society." As the draft for "Criteria for Action by JUJ" from 1969 made clear: "The project must make explicit . . . that Jewish institutions are not the major enemy."[32]

NEXT YEAR IN A WORLD OF FREEDOM!

The first decisive turning point for the group came on April 4, 1969, when Jews for Urban Justice received national condemnation—and acclaim—for its project to fuse Judaism and New Left radical politics. That evening, which was the third night of Passover and the first anniversary of the assassination of Martin Luther King Jr., JUJ sponsored the first Freedom Seder in the basement of Lincoln Temple, an African American church, near the center of Washington, D.C. (A church was chosen because no local synagogue was available on a Friday evening.) A well-publicized event, invitations contained a timely quotation selected to address all those devastated by the King assassination, the outraged riots that erupted in over one hundred cities in the days that followed it (the most terrible of which arguably occurred in the several blocks surrounding Lincoln Temple), and the tragic collapse of a nonviolent interracial civil rights agenda: "This is the bread of affliction which our fathers ate in the land of Egypt / All who are hungry—Let them come & partake / All who are in need—Let them come and celebrate the Passover / This year we are slaves / Next year we shall be free men" (figure 5.1).[33] JUJ arranged for special invitations to be sent "by name" to "the Jewish merchants and landlords in the black community [in Washington] who seem in particular need of recalling the message of their tradition."[34] (There is no record of whether any of these individuals accepted these personal invitations to attend.)

The Freedom Seder drew a large and diverse crowd from the metropolitan Washington area (although some participants traveled from as far away as New York). When JUJ member Rabbi Harold White began the Sabbath service, almost eight hundred people had gathered. When the service ended, the crowd moved to the basement where tables had been set with a traditional seder plate alongside copies of a new Haggadah. Here the Freedom Seder was co-officiated by the Reverend Dr. Channing Phillips, senior minister of Lincoln Temple and the first African American nominated for the U.S. presidency, and Rabbi Balfour Brickner of the Union of American Hebrew Congregations. Jewish families from the suburbs and Jews with liberal or social activist backgrounds came to hear how radical politics might be expressed in a Haggadah, but black militants and others in the black community as well as hippies (who wore stocking caps as yarmulkes) and a small contingent of Yeshiva students were also in attendance. All broke matzoh together. While the local newspaper, *Jewish Week*, declined to report on the event (although it did include an item beforehand to announce it), journalists from *Hadassah Magazine*, *Washington Post*, *Village Voice*, *Jewish Liberation Journal*, and the Jewish Student Press Service all attended the seder as well, while the popular New Left monthly journal *Ramparts* had already arranged to publish the text of the radical Haggadah that same month. Additionally, the New York Pacifica radio station, WBAI, was set up to broadcast the proceedings live and the Canadian Broadcasting Company was on hand to film the evening for a television documentary. This highly unconventional ceremony then opened as Waskow selected a young girl (rather than a boy) to ask the first of four traditional questions: "Why is this night different from all others?" Thus, it was clear from the outset that this night *was* different—not just from other nights, but from all other Passover seders as well.

The aims of the radical Haggadah were simple enough. It sought to renew the relevance of a traditional Passover message commemorating the exodus of the Jews from slavery in ancient Egypt. It sought consciously to universalize the twin themes of liberation from oppression and "the issue of violence in the struggle for freedom" for the contemporary historical moment. Waskow, au-

FREEDOM SEDER

Friday evening April 4, 1969

8:00 p.m.

LINCOLN TEMPLE

11th and R STREETS, N. W.

Rabbi Harold White Will Conduct Sabbath Services Rabbi Balfour Brickner, The Reverend Channing Phillips, and Father Philip Berrigan Will Participate in the reading of **THE FREEDOM SEDER: A NEW HAGGADAH FOR PASSOVER,** By Dr. Arthur I. Waskow

Sponsoredby . . .

Jews For Urban Justice

Susan Pagash-965-5724 — Sharon Rose-244-6752

R.S.V.P.

FIGURE 5.1 An invitation to the first Freedom Seder, held on April 4, 1969. Courtesy of Michael Tabor.

thor of the radical Haggadah, defended these aims by maintaining that the revision of tradition had always been an essential aspect of Judaism. In true JUJ style, Waskow moralized fearlessly, contending that only by updating the Haggadah could participants eliminate "the hypocrisy of finding the violence of liberation glorious in history but appalling in the streets."[35]

The radical Haggadah included a meditation on the historic struggle of the Jewish people for survival, for "in every generation there are some who rise up against us, to annihilate us." Addressing the Holocaust, Waskow focused on the armed resistance to Hitler, and quoted Emmanuel Ringelblum on life in the Warsaw Ghetto. Waskow wrote: "May we remember and honor tonight and at every Passover the bleak and hopeless courage of those who during the week of Passover 1943 began the Ghetto Uprising in Warsaw." Yet, as its many critics would soon claim, the radical Haggadah did not linger long on Jewish history or Jewish subjects. However, as Waskow put it, that had been the whole point. The goal had been to "develop the liturgy in ways that asserted the liberation of the Jewish people *alongside* the liberation of the other peoples—not theirs as against ours, or ours as against theirs." So there were references to "our prophets, our rabbis, and our shoftim—men like Micah who spoke the word of God directly to the kings and the people, men like Hillel who worked out the law of justice in daily life, and revolutionary leaders or 'judges' like Gideon," and these references appeared with (and were in fact far outnumbered by) quotations from "the *shofet* Jefferson, that revolutionary judge and leader," "the *shofet* Nat Turner," "the rabbi Thoreau" (defending the violent deeds of radical abolitionist John Brown), and "the *shofet* Eldridge Cleaver (who has gone into exile as Moses did)."[36] In short, the Haggadah was an extended acknowledgment (or apologia, if one was hostile to its precepts) that revolutions for justice were seldom bloodless.

For those who attended the Freedom Seder, and even for those who objected to aspects of the Haggadah, it was reportedly an extraordinary—if lengthy—evening, ending after several hours with the singing of "We Shall Overcome" and shouts of "Liberation now! Next year in a world of freedom!"[37] For those who experienced it at first hand, the idealism expressed by the Freedom Seder was a radical affirmation of faith many considered impossible to find in organized Judaism. As one couple would write in response to the harsh criticisms the event immediately began to receive from within the Jewish community:

> One of the most remarkable aspects of the Freedom Seder has been ignored by most commentators, and this was the pride of so many of the Jews in at-

tendance, particularly the younger ones. As we looked around us, we saw these young people wearing yarmulkes and singing Hebrew with a spirit indicating that they had some special message to share with the world. Here is the kind of pride that will keep Judaism strong in a changing world.[38]

Or as Mike Tabor would recall of that night, "All the meaningless, drab, dull, synthetic, assimilationist veneer was, for an evening it seemed, wiped away."[39]

It is important to recognize that the radical Haggadah was not an endorsement of violence to achieve justice; it noted that the "freedom we seek is a freedom from blood as well as a freedom from tyrants." Instead, the Haggadah was a document suffused with inspiration and fervor, even while it was perhaps rather unclear on how a transformation of the world into a better place might actually come about. In short, it was a utopian statement—intent more on sparking discussions, shoring up hopes, and inciting righteousness—and not a precise program for action. As the evening drew to a close, these representative words were read aloud:

Brothers and sisters, we have been remembering our slavery and our liberation. But just as it was we, not our ancestors only, who were liberated in Egypt, so it was we, not our ancestors only, who live in slavery. Our slavery is not over, and our liberation is not complete. The task of liberation is long, and it is work that we ourselves must do. As the Talmud tells us, we like Moses may not live to complete the task; but neither may we refrain from beginning. We are about to eat; may our dinner give us strength for the work ahead! We are about to drink; may our wine give us joy for the work ahead!

Waskow made clear that he hoped the Freedom Seder might be taken as one possible way "to assert a unity—in the form of a Haggadah—between the historic imperatives of Jewish liberation and the urgency of today's black rebellion."[40] He also said that he hoped that the Haggadah would not be seen as a "final act. It is still an experiment so far as we are concerned, and we hope that anyone who wants to use it will himself feel free to experiment with it."[41]

Boosted by the enthusiasms and passions surrounding the Freedom Seder, delegates from Jews for Urban Justice met with more than three dozen other Jewish activist leaders (like Todd Gitlin and Stanley Aronowitz) that same weekend in Radnor, Pennsylvania "to lay the groundwork for the formation of a radical Jewish movement throughout the United States." Organized by JUJ, the meeting was attended also by individuals and delegations "from New York, San Francisco, Oakland, Los Angeles, Cincinnati, Philadelphia, Madison, Hanover, and Cambridge. Some were socialist radicals, some Zionist radicals, women's liberation radicals, intellectual radicals, and some were not very radical at all. In age they ranged from 17 to the mid-thirties, the majority in their middle twenties."[42] Citing the difficulty of organizing Jewish youth on the left within the framework of Jewish concerns, conference members discussed ways to reach out to all sectors of the Jewish community. Even though JUJ members were challenged by other radicals at Radnor for their seeming single-minded preoccupation with Jewishness and Judaism, what emerged from the conference was a decision to form the National Jewish Organizing Project (NJOP) whose objectives mirrored JUJ's own positions on the inherent link between social activism and prophetic Judaism.[43]

The draft statement for NJOP read in part:

> The authors of injustice and oppression in America are not Jewish. But as in Egypt, until Moses and Aaron began to organize; as in Babylon; as in the Roman Empire; as even under Hitler—some of our people have collaborated. For the sake of a mess of pottage, they have abandoned their birthright in the Prophets. They have been given permission to survive and prosper as Jews—if they will stop believing and practicing Judaism. And some of them have agreed. We do not see them as our enemies, but we do believe they must stop collaborating. Jewish businessmen must not buy grapes from farmers who exploit their hired labor; Jewish organizations must not lend money to banks that oppress Black people; Jewish political leaders must not serve the military-industrial complex. We must speak prophetically to them and to all our people, demanding that those who have gathered power within the Jewish community use their power not to uphold the injustice of the American Babylon—but to end it.[44]

One crucial point was the decisive inversion the NJOP formulated of mainstream associations between assimilation and New Left activism. Far from demonstrating its departure from the faith and community of its elders by advancing New Left causes, NJOP assumed that it was the self-preserving status quo–accommodating members of the older generation who were the assimilated and indeed self-destructive ones. Despite this important reversal, the NJOP philosophy was nonetheless also in effect caught on the horns of a paradoxical dilemma: Like JUJ before it, it sought both to avoid tactics which might shame or humiliate the Jewish community, even while it advocated making individual Jews and institutions aware when they functioned as collaborators for social injustice.

HEAR OUR SINS

This ostensibly revised political stance was soon put dramatically to the test—and the points about assimilation elaborated—on June 15, 1969, when the multimillion dollar suburban Maryland Jewish Community Center complex held a gala dedication ceremony to mark its official opening. The special guest of honor was Republican vice president (and former Maryland governor) Spiro Agnew. Deeply appalled by the ostentatious facilities set far away from an urban center, and doubly disturbed that Agnew had been invited to speak, JUJ quickly mobilized its most outrageous action. Gathering in a parking lot two blocks from the community center, where people parked their cars and boarded buses which would take them to the festivities, JUJ members distributed a poem/leaflet that read:

THIS IS THE BUS TO AUSCHWITZ.
At the other end is a building for the destruction of the Jewish people—showers, baths, and all.
Think twice before you get on.
It's a soft Auschwitz, of course.
They won't be stripping your bodies and gassing your lungs. They'll just be stripping your Judaism and gassing your minds.
There's an Olympic swimming pool and a microscopic library. Is that likely to create Jews? The Jews of scholarship?
There's plush—you wouldn't dream there was a poor man for 60 miles in any direction. Is that likely to create Jews—the Jews of the prophets and the kibbutz?
There's a membership list already closed on the day it opens. Is that likely to create Jews—the Jews of the Chasidic communities?

The owners of the Jewish Community Center are not interested in creating Jews.
They want to create conformists.
They worship Power, not God—Baal, not Adonai.
But power is not our God.
Conformity is not our God.
If you get on the bus to Auschwitz, better recite what the Jews of Auschwitz

recited before they died: Shema Yisrael, Adonai Elohanu, Adonai Echad.
Hear, O Israel, the Lord Our God, the Lord is *ONE*.
Remember that.
Don't die.
Resist dying.
The Lord is *ONE*.[45]

As Holocaust survivor and JUJ member Arno Winard distributed these leaflets in the parking lot, he listened to the military band perform for the gathering crowds and began to weep. Winard swore that the tunes the band played were the same music he had heard when he emerged from a freight car and marched through the gates of Auschwitz.[46]

Again in July of 1969, JUJ clashed with the mainstream Washington Jewish leadership over the appropriateness of linking Judaism to political action. That month the group sponsored a Tisha B'Av (Ninth of Av) religious service on the steps of the U.S. Capitol as part of a vigil to commemorate the destruction of the Temple in Jerusalem and to protest the proposed Anti-Ballistic Missile System (ABM). The idea for the service had originated from a reading of Robert Gordis's *Judaism for the Modern Age* on the meaning of Tisha B'av, and it was the first time a formal Jewish service to protest a political issue had ever been held at the Capitol. Invitations had been sent to all Jewish members of Congress. The vigil drew more than one hundred people; Rabbi Harold White, to the accompaniment of guitar and oboe, read selections from the book of Lamentations that "emphasized the character of false prophecy in Jeremiah's time, namely that of a false sense of security. . . . A parallel to the contemporary scene was made by individuals who spoke about the false sense of security which will be provided by the ABM systems if passed by Congress."[47] In addition, the vigil included a litany based on the book of Amos written by JUJ member Fran Schreiberg. It read in part:

Reader:
Thus saith the Lord,
For three transgressions of the United States;
Yea, for four, I will not reverse the judgment of doom:
Because they preached falsely of security through military escalation
And oppressed the poor in allocating resources
And alienated the youth with false promises of peace in Vietnam.
Congregation:
I will devour the buildings of this fair city

Tumble into ruins the false economy on which the country stands.
For the sake of all my people
Reader:
Hear this word, you contented cow in mink's clothing;
That dwell in the fat pieces of Suburbia
That oppress the poor, that crush the needy;
That say unto your husbands: get riches,
That we may feast in splendor and ride in limousines;
Look into your hearts; seek, and ye shall find.[48]

The Tisha B'av actions of JUJ continued the next day when members of the group joined a picket line at the Soviet Embassy organized by the Jewish Community Council to protest on behalf of civil rights for Soviet Jewry. Since the JCC picket was a few hundred feet from the embassy (in accordance with a District of Columbia ordinance), JUJ members decided to break the law and march directly to the front of the embassy. They carried signs that read "End Racism Here, End Racism There," "Jews = Revolution / USA & USSR = Counter-Revolution," and "Free [Soviet Jew] Kochubievsky *and* [court-martialed Jewish antiwar activist army captain] Howard Levy." The JUJ position was that it was cowardice both to obey district laws (that rendered the protest ineffectual) and to draw false distinctions between Jewish oppression in the U.S. and USSR. Several JUJ members were arrested for this protest. As Fran Schreiberg would summarize this event, it resulted in "renewed attention (though even more deeply puzzled) from Jews who don't understand how JUJ can be *both* radical and Jewish—indeed, twice as Jewish because it's radical, and twice as radical because it's Jewish."[49]

A major turning point came in September 1969, in the wake of a sermon on social justice that Waskow had given on Kol Nidre night at the Tifereth Israel Congregation, a Conservative synagogue located in an integrated neighborhood and attracting an increasingly liberal membership. Among other things, Waskow had asked those present to participate in a modern-day confession of sins, and that they also pledge themselves to affirm social justice. Waskow read to the assembly:

O Lord our God, King of the Universe!
Hear our sins that we have sinned together, in unholy union.
We have sinned by killing other human beings—
By paying soldiers to burn Vietnamese babies alive—
without forcing our rulers to stop the war machine;

> By sending 40,000 of our sons to be killed in an illegal war—
> *without forcing our rulers to stop the war machine*;
> By using chemical products that poison the air and give people cancer—ourselves and our families included—
> *without forcing our rulers to change these products*;
> By creating and using a medical system that condemns Black babies to die at twice the rate of white and Jewish babies—
> *without forcing our rulers to change the medical system.*[50]

Within a short time there were disturbances in the synagogue, which involved shouts and scuffles in the audience. Someone cried out, "Kill the Arabs, kill them!" and someone else yelled, "I *paid* for this synagogue, and it's never going to happen in this synagogue again!" Then several people rushed toward Waskow, while several JUJ members moved forward to protect him from a threat of physical harm. Someone pulled the plug on the sound system, leaving Waskow "bellowing out the prayer at the top of his voice to drown out the protestations of the synagogue financier and other objectors."[51] The situation, as one eye-witness later recounted, became "very close to a mob scene."[52] Order was eventually restored. In response to these events, the synagogue established a Special Committee on Kol Nidre Night to investigate the "offended feelings, protests, harsh words and commotion" of the service.[53] The committee's report concluded that neither Waskow nor JUJ had precipitated the disturbances that evening.

A QUEER AND UN-JEWISH KIND OF HOLINESS

In reaction to the Freedom Seder, the "Bus to Auschwitz" protest, and the Kol Nidre incident, the pages of the influential local *Jewish Week* repeatedly published letters to the editor attacking Jews for Urban Justice. In response to the Freedom Seder, one letter writer stated that "Waskow (and his group) embodies the saddest traits of the Jewish intellectual who finds strength in tearing away at 'the establishment' while offering nothing constructive in the way of ideas or suggestions," while another opined that by "replacing the old Haggadah with a new one we cut ourself off from the inspiration of past glory." A third writer outlined what he found most alarming about the Freedom Seder. "We often see how certain Jews, ignorant of and alienated from historical Judaism, find it necessary to seek some gimmick by which to join the non-Jewish community in a so-called 'meaningful' way."

Furthermore, he declared that members of Jews for Urban Justice deserved "a tour de force in gimmickery" for sponsoring the event, which, he suggested, they had hosted as a means to compensate for lost manhood. The writer went on to offer a memorable sequence of rhetorical associations that blurred white racist ideology and supposed Jewish ethics, while strategically presenting Waskow as the one who was condescending to African Americans:

> This oddity, with its bizarre guide-book written by Arthur I. Waskow, accomplishes in one fell swoop three significant, if unintended, objectives: 1) it shows how big-hearted some Jews can be—inviting culturally-impoverished black people to share in what is nonchalantly acknowledged as a millenia-old Jewish festival of freedom; 2) it demonstrates the superiority of young Jewish men who can rewrite the traditional Haggadah text so cleverly, over black young men whose literary forte seems to lie more in the handling of four-letter words; and 3) It indulges the "Jewish mother" syndrome of the J.U.J., characterized by a compulsive showering of smothering attention on innocent victims, with or without an invitation. The essential humiliation to Negro participants in this charade could hardly be more complete if Waskow were to read his piece in blackface with a mammy accent.[54]

After the June protest at the JCC dedication ceremony in Maryland, yet another critic (who said he had formerly defended the group for its emphasis on "burning urban problems") now declared that JUJ had succeeded only in "offend[ing] many innocent people in our community and alienat[ing] friendly supporters." JUJ's decision to "compare the new Jewish Community Center with Auschwitz" was "obscene, profane and insane," the writer added: "The memory of Auschwitz will remain sanctified in Jewish experience and not even the self-appointed JUJs of Washington may tamper with it loosely."[55] Likewise, after the Kol Nidre debacle that September, a local Washington resident wrote that JUJ were "alleged Jews" and "enemies from our own ranks." They were, he added, "sick self-haters, who protest all injustices, except those committed against Jews," while another writer labeled Arthur Waskow "a local 'Portnoy' [who] saw fit to mock and disrupt the recent Kol Nidre service with a litany of self-abasement and self-hatred." Yet another letter charged it was imperative for the Jewish community to band together and reject "Jewish ranting revolutionaries bent on adding their Orwellian drivel to the anti-Jewish attacks of the Far Right and the Far Left."[56]

However, most official local communal spokespersons did not issue formal public declarations criticizing Jews for Urban Justice. The exception to this general rule came from Rabbi Harry J. Kaufman, president of the Rabbinical Council of Greater Washington (Orthodox), in the wake of the Tisha B'av vigil. Kaufman, who had participated in the Monday evening discussion series sponsored by JUJ, now denounced the group.[57] In a statement to the press, Rabbi Kaufman called the JUJ vigil a "bizarre pseudo-religious happening" and an example of "sensational posturing and self deluding exploitation of our hallowed traditions by the pretentiousness of Civil Rights Seder Circuses and Tisha B'av tune-ins." Kaufman also said: "Tisha B'av is most decidedly not a tool for political dilettantism and hackneyed gimmickery, but a sad and sacred instrument for the total communion of the Jew with his historic reality and existential truth, whose place above all else is in the Synagogue."[58]

The harshest and most prominent attack on JUJ and the Freedom Seder's radical Haggadah came from a nonlocal source: Rabbi Emil Fackenheim. Writing in *Hadassah Magazine*, Fackenheim found the Haggadah had appallingly demeaned the memory of the Shoah. Since Fackenheim had written in 1960 that all efforts to turn Passover into an ecumenical festival of freedom would be misguided, these criticisms were hardly surprising now that he had the actual experience before him. Fackenheim wrote:

> Surely the author, Arthur Waskow, is right in claiming the right to "innovate" in his telling of the ancient tale. Surely he is right as well in his wish to "universalize." . . . But, alas, misgivings concerning the radicalism of the Radical Haggadah are aroused by its very preface. . . . No mention is made of invitations sent to non-Jewish leaders, white and black, to remind them of *their* tradition (Christian or humanist) which forbids them to keep silent when it is asserted that, so far as Jews are concerned, Hitler was right. Nor are we told of invitations sent to the ambassadors of Soviet Russia, Poland or Iraq to accuse them, respectively, of the repression of Jewish culture, of reviving anti-Semitic persecution of the pitiful remnants of a once-great community and of outright murder of Jews for no reason other than their Jewishness. We wonder: what universalism can this be which ignores oppression when Jews are victims? And what radicalism?

Furthermore, according to Fackenheim, the Freedom Seder was in direct lineage with the "anti-Zionism and anti-Jewishness on the so-called New Left." Waskow's Haggadah also shamefully "renders the Nazi holocaust innocuous by making it safely past and by classing it with other, quite different tragedies." In short, Fackenheim saw the Haggadah as

> either the product of craven cowardice unworthy of any radical, which seeks goodwill on the Left at any price, or else, if its radicalism is to be taken seriously, it denies to Jews alone in the name of Judaism the right to rise against their revilers and persecuters; it demands that Jews show a queer and un-Jewish kind of holiness which falls short but little of suicide.[59]

THE VIETNAM WAR IS AN UNJUST WAR IN THE TALMUDIC SENSE

Jews for Urban Justice stayed on the offensive against the public criticisms it endured. For instance, the September 1969 issue of *Jewish Urban Guerrilla* included an official JUJ response to Rabbi Kaufman's attack. It asked "why a Jewish 'community' paper should go out of its way to help one Jew pillory others." The statement maintained that Kaufman's message was "ironic from an Orthodox Rabbi who is concerned with preserving Judaism." Written by Fran Schreiberg on behalf of JUJ, the statement continued:

> The message that I read is saying—if you won't practice Judaism as I see it, go away. This I must stress, is not only the message of the Orthodox Rabbi. This message is coming from the whole Jewish community in Washington, D.C. It says to me: don't assimilate, marry within the Jewish faith, but don't rock the boat, and if you can't do things our way—don't do them. I ask: what are you afraid of?
>
> . . . In our everyday lives, we are confronted with such atrocities as the Vietnam War, the A.B.M., the alienation of youth and minority groups from the American way of life (death), the dissatisfaction (too often silent) of our parents with the spiritually empty lives they are programmed to lead as middle-class Jews—if that is what we are confronted with, and if we see that as a contradiction of Judaism, and further see the hypocrisy of the Jewish institutions that remain SILENT—WE MUST SPEAK OUT.[60]

Privately, however, these criticisms appear to have prompted considerable soul searching on the part of many JUJ members. Recalling the JCC demonstration, Mike Tabor acknowledged that several JUJ people wondered whether they had taken things too far. Had "This Is the Bus to Auschwitz" been "too harsh," and was "the memory of Auschwitz too sacred for it to be profaned in this way?" Tabor wrote:

> Perhaps so, we thought later. But our indignation blinded us to any other path. We were saddened and maybe a bit ashamed at the confused reaction of the older people who came. "Auschwitz, gas chambers . . . what are they talking about! This is America, not Germany!" But to the masses of the people there, we were just ruining their good day. Spoiling their fun. The time when they came to dedicate their mausoleum. Why did we hate Jewish people so much? Why were we always doing things like this? A bunch of kooks and sick people . . . that's what we were.[61]

So why did local Jewish leaders mainly refrain from joining in on making public critiques of the group? There were three overlapping reasons. First, the participation of Balfour Brickner, a popular and charismatic figure within the UAHC, worked to legitimate the Freedom Seder—at least initially—and softened hostility to the event, especially among those more liberal Jews affiliated with Reform Judaism. Brickner's participation also contested the position that the radical Haggadah was an anti-Jewish document, suggesting instead that it fell well within the bounds of a text grappling authentically with the contested contours of what constituted a valid Jewish identity. Second of all, the ongoing struggle within the Jewish community over the social justice issues JUJ addressed meant that there was at least a tentative willingness not to attack JUJ tactics if the stated goals of the group seemed valid. As one sympathetic letter writer to *Jewish Week* wrote in October of 1969, perhaps Arthur Waskow deserved more credit for his outspokenness, especially since Jewish spokespersons typically had "been silent—and too often, active—partners in Christian America's degradation and exploitation of black people."[62] Thus, given that there was an ongoing intra-Jewish controversy in Washington about how to react to the actions taken by JUJ, public criticisms remained for a time kept in check. Furthermore, there was also continued cooperation between JUJ and mainstream Jewish leaders around issues relating to Jewish education, especially for young people. Still, and third of all, the hesitancy of most Jewish leaders to take a stand against JUJ had to do with the mounting Jewish presence in the antiwar movement that summer and fall, and the degree to which radical and liberal forces found common ground in an opposition to U.S. military policies in Vietnam.

The antiwar protests scheduled for the autumn of 1969 brought various elements of the Washington Jewish community together for a unified political agenda like seldom before. The second Vietnam Moratorium demonstration in mid-November, coordinated by both the Vietnam Moratorium Committee and the more left-leaning New Mobilization Committee to End the War in Vietnam (New Mobe), turned out to be massive, attended by at least a half million protesters. JUJ took a leadership role in organizing the local Jewish community's participation, and readily agreed to work alongside liberal Jewish leaders and organizations. Strikingly, this meant that less than a month after the Kol Nidre disturbance at Tifereth Israel Congregation, JUJ members convened there again to confer with rabbinic and community leaders to discuss how they might all work together to mobilize for the moratorium. Rabbi Bernard Mehlman, who had criticized JUJ publicly after the group's social action survey, now co-sponsored a gathering with JUJ, bringing more than two dozen prominent area leaders together. Although the meeting began with a verbal clash between Isaac Franck and Arthur Waskow over Waskow's statement calling for immediate withdrawal of all American troops from Southeast Asia, the meeting did result in the establishment of a peace committee to oversee Jewish participation in the second moratorium.

However, and citing concerns that Jews for Urban Justice's active participation would frighten away more moderate Jewish supporters of the moratorium, establishment leaders cautioned JUJ to play only a more minor role in moratorium and New Mobe activities geared to the Jewish community. The group heeded no such advice. Instead, and with the integral assistance of the National Jewish Organizing Project, JUJ members were instrumental in setting up the New Mobe–affiliated Jewish Movement Center (in a Methodist church because no Jewish facilities were made available). The center became the organizational base for numerous religious and political activities, among them an Orthodox minyan followed by a communal dinner and a Sabbath service whose emphasis was peace. The Oneg Sabbath was also to have featured a panel discussion on "Jewish Tradition, the War and the Draft," to be conducted by Arthur Waskow and representatives from the Jewish Peace Fellowship and the New York Havurah (though the discussion was interrupted by reports of violent clashes between police and demonstrators in nearby Dupont Circle). In addition, NJOP-affiliated activists joined the thirty-eight-hour March Against Death, where forty thousand demonstrators carried placards with the names of an American soldier killed in Vietnam or a destroyed Vietnamese village in a procession to the Capitol. When the march concluded, several dozen Jewish students held an impromptu memorial service where kaddish was said for the war dead.[63]

Throughout the moratorium weekend, members of JUJ worked with the National Jewish Organizing Project to press the position that U.S. military policies in Vietnam were in direct conflict with Judaism. As Mike Tabor put it at the time, "The Vietnam war is an unjust war in the Talmudic sense."[64] JUJ members assisted with a full slate of Jewish-themed activities that included workshops on "Havurah, Community, & Counter-Institutions," "The Jewish Community and Racism," and "Alternatives to Zionist Organizing in the Diaspora"; a screening of the CBC documentary film about the first Freedom Seder; and *Tikun Hatzot* (midnight prayers). The most memorable event, however, occurred on Sunday morning, November 16, when approximately 150 Jewish radicals gathered in front of the White House to sing Jewish peace songs, burn a paper golden calf, smash war toys, and sound the *shofarot* (rams' horns) as a national call to fast for peace on the next Moratorium Day, scheduled for December 12 (which was also the last day of Hanukkah).[65] All told, more than six hundred young Jews from across the nation participated in the NJOP- and JUJ-sponsored activities.[66]

These activities were not met with universal support from Jewish establishment leaders. Perhaps most striking in light of his long and prominent commitment to Jewish social activism, Albert Vorspan, director of the Commission on Social Action of Reform Judaism of the UAHC, castigated the Jewish radicals in the wake of the moratorium. In an impassioned letter Vorspan wrote:

> The raised golden calf, the burning of dollar bills as a way of exorcising the dybbuk of capitalism, the stomping on the golden calf, the Kaddish to Ho Chi Minh, the Black Panther sloganeering, the sentimental romance about the "Hebrew slaves who rebelled against the Pharaohs" (meaning the race riots of last year)—you may see this as courageous and radical and iconoclastic as hell. I see it as a melange of sloppy thinking, adolescent romance of violence, cheap revolutionary politics, bad taste, arrogant self-righteousness with respect to other people's views and sensibilities and exploitation of Judaism and Jewish symbols to advance a pre-ordained New Left point of view.[67]

Yet the general sentiment in the Washington Jewish community was quite supportive of the antiwar agenda.[68] Although the Jewish Community Council had decided against a formal endorsement of the antiwar demonstration, its president, Seymour D. Wolf, had urged all local synagogues and their members to offer housing to Jewish demonstrators and noted afterward that "the response was heartwarming and gave us reason to feel proud."[69]

Local Hillel foundations and the National B'nai B'rith headquarters organized housing as well; several area synagogues also held prayer services for peace.[70] After the weekend was over, it was clear, as the *Jewish Week* reported, that "thousands of Jews joined the massive anti-war demonstrations Saturday while others attended special services and teach-ins at congregations. The crowd represented the largest-scale Jewish participation in any mass demonstration here, exceeding the participation in the 1963 Civil rights march."[71] A member of the Jewish Community Council particularly marveled at the "special feeling" it gave her to see the active Jewish student participation in the moratorium: "It was emotionally overwhelming to see the outpouring of kids. For me it was like a culture shock." Speaking with evident pride, Rabbi Oscar Groner, longtime staff member of the B'nai B'rith Hillel Foundation, added: "We became a unit as of last week. . . . In one afternoon we created a beautiful thing, a true unity of students and the organized Jewish community."[72]

Groner's faith in the radical Jewish movement was indicative of the inroads it was making also within the mainstream Jewish leadership. Nor was Groner's support for this movement short-lived; in early summer 1971, he would write approvingly of radical Jews: "However volatile their dissatisfactions with the organized Jewish community, they are a far cry from being 'alienated' Jews. And they are very much the tip of an iceberg, more and more reflecting the sentiments and a new Jewish consciousness among many of the silent Jewish majority on the campus. They are, in my experience, a source of Jewish community strength."[73] The small irony here—at least so far as Jews for Urban Justice was concerned—is that, even as Groner's rousing endorsement of a radical Jewish movement was published, the Washington group that effectively began the movement found itself in the process of dissolving.

WHY IS IT JEWISH . . . ?

Yet, for a time, and certainly through the year 1970 and into the early months of 1971, even close observers of the Washington Jewish community might not have been aware that the leading local radical group was experiencing increasingly divisive internal tensions. For, as far as its public profile was concerned, JUJ appeared to be flourishing. Its high-profile actions linking Judaism to leftism continued unabated. For instance, one major project JUJ completed early in 1970 was an investigation into where the Jewish institutions in the metropolitan area invested their monies; this was undertaken with the aim of pressuring Jewish individuals and organizations not to do business with banks that engaged in unfair or discriminatory savings and loan practices and encouraging banks to democratize their lending practices. Among other things, JUJ argued that "we . . . must remember that he who befriends the poor lends to the Lord. The Talmud emphasizes that the Jew has the same obligation in lending to the poor as in giving charity to them. In fact, the Talmud states that lending without interest to a poor man is *more* worthy than charity."[74]

In February 1970 JUJ executive director Sharon Rose took part in a hunger strike for nearly two weeks as part of a vigil sponsored by the Fellowship of Reconciliation and Clergy and Laymen Concerned About Vietnam (CALCAV), a group whose national co-leader was Rabbi Abraham Joshua Heschel.[75] In April JUJ members traveled to Cornell University to hold a Freedom Seder where Father Daniel Berrigan, a former Cornell chaplain who had gone underground to avoid a jail sentence for nonviolent destruction of draft records, made a dramatic appearance. They also conducted a seder at Battery Park near Wall Street in Manhattan, where they leafleted against "the Rockefeller Empire." And finally, a Freedom Seder attended by eight hundred people was held in the cafeteria of the University Center at George Washington University. Rock music, poetry, dancing, and the symbolic burning of a dollar bill punctuated the event.[76] The GWU seder concluded when more than two hundred people announced, with reference to the U.S. and the USSR, "a plague on both your houses." First they marched to the White House where they spilled blood and released rats, frogs, and roaches on the front lawn; White House secret service agents amused the crowd as they hurried around to round up the small creatures. An attempt then to release the same nine plagues (the plague of death to first-born sons being omitted) at the Soviet embassy was prevented by a blockade of several dozen local police. A JUJ press statement about the event said its intention was to protest "against the repression of our brothers and sisters by the Pharaohs of both countries." It continued: "In Amerika, those who speak out against the genocide of the Vietnamese people and against racist exploitation at home, are jailed by the government and murdered by its agents. In the Soviet Union, those who wish to openly practice traditional religion are harassed and jailed."[77]

Although JUJ was clear and forceful in its commitment to the rights of Soviet Jewry, and persistently refused to see any inconsistencies between advocating the rights of American blacks, the Vietnamese, and Soviet Jews (instead continually linking these causes), its relationship to Israel was a source of far greater private agony. In the fall of 1970, and after long deliberation, JUJ issued its first public statement on the Middle East situation, noting that any statement faced an "untenable position" because those "dissenting from any view that implies complete support for Israel are labeled 'anti-semites,' while others who are critical but not willing to endorse an 'anti-Zionist' line find themselves being called 'imperialistic' and 'reactionary.' " The statement said JUJ was "a group which is neither anti-Zionist nor 'pro-Fatah,' yet is constantly working with the Jewish & left community." The group outlined its position by advancing five basic points:

1. Self-determination for the Palestinian people.
2. Self-determination for the Israeli people.
3. No Israeli intervention in Arab struggles.
4. No U.S. or Soviet intervention in Arab struggles.
5. We are opposed to all acts of genocide.[78]

As Tabor later observed, these positions "differed little from the stand many radical Zionist groups adopted. Sometimes their criticisms [of Israel] were even more severe than ours."[79] Nonetheless, even JUJ members' attempt to offer a seemingly balanced position well within the spectrum of opinions offered by radical Zionist groups would soon come back to haunt them.

At around the same time, JUJ members also began to become more fully aware of their group's cultural and political roots in the Jewish Labor Bund. Founded in 1897 in Vilna, and soon thereafter an influential political force throughout Yiddish-speaking Eastern Europe, the Bund was most especially popular in Poland during the 1920s and 1930s. Dedicated to democratic socialism (as opposed to communism) and to secularism, the Bund championed *Yiddishkayt* as a cultural alternative to Zionism. It contended that the Zionist call to uproot and move to Palestine as a means of asserting Jewish identity was tragically misguided. Instead, Bundists heralded the principle of *doykeyt* (or "here-ness"), urging Jews to transform the societies in which they already lived. Additionally, as David P. Shuldiner has documented, Bundists at the turn of the twentieth century were revising the Haggadah for Passover to reflect the spirit of their radical ideology.[80] Thus, the Freedom Seder, not to mention almost every action JUJ had ever undertaken, stood in a historical lineage traceable to the Bund. But this rediscovery also prompted other more troubling reflections. JUJ members wondered why the Bundist heritage seemed "so carefully kept from us? Why was it hidden? Shame over the fact that we haven't always been a well-to-do middle class people? Or that we

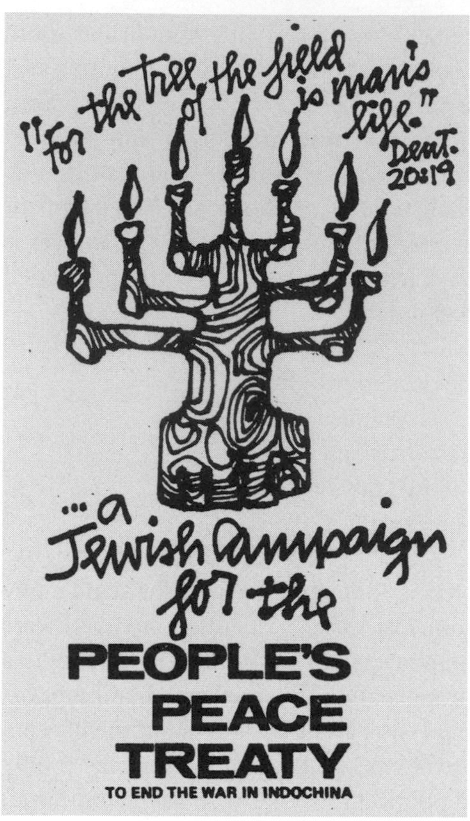

FIGURE 5.2
"A Jewish Campaign for the People's Peace Treaty to End the War in Indochina." Illustration accompanying an essay on the "Trees for Viet Nam" project that originally appeared in *American Report* 1, no. 32 (May 21, 1971). *American Report* was a publication of Clergy and Laymen Concerned About Vietnam (CALCAV).

haven't always been fighters modeled after the Israelis? Yiddish, I was told by a friend who had a strict Reform upbringing, was 'the language of our degradation,' something that's best forgotten. But it was part of our history. Again, the specter of Jewish shame hovers over people trying to 'make it' in America, the promised land."[81]

Finally, though, even as its members were beginning to look backward, the group was unraveling. In what may have been the group's last major project, JUJ sponsored the Jewish Campaign for the People's Peace Treaty, issuing a statement in March 1971 (figure 5.2). In answer to the question "Why is it *Jewish* to be against the war?" the statement continued:

> The most important fact about being Jewish is that Jews ought not to *separate* religious and ethical commitments, on the one hand, from politics or everyday life on the other. *Jewishness at its best is a whole life process*, and the war is part of our daily lives. (For example, all of us pay for it through taxes

> even if we speak out against it.) So if we're committed to being Jewish, then dealing with the war is part of being Jewish—we can't just feel we're Jewish on Yom Kippur.
>
> Admittedly, this is Jewishness *at its best*—not the way we have often practiced it in America. But we think the separation between being "Jewish"—that's for Yom Kippur—and being "people"—that's for all the rest of the time—is one of the reasons our lives are so empty.

Among others, the statement was signed by Balfour Brickner, Shlomo Carlebach, Paul Cowan, Everett Gendler, Abraham Heschel, Bill Novak, Sharon Rose, Steven Schwarzschild, and Mike Tabor.[82]

ONE OF THE REASONS OUR LIVES ARE SO EMPTY

Yet the third and final phase in the history of Jews for Urban Justice had also begun with the events surrounding the Vietnam Moratorium/New Mobe of November 13–16, 1969. In the days and weeks that followed, several members of JUJ had begun talking about the possibility of living together in a political collective. As part of an effort to establish an ongoing feeling of community, the regular Friday night and Saturday morning services were becoming the group's central focus each week; as Waskow described it, these services were

> held not in the rigid rows of suburban synagogues, but in the crowded circle of a living room, by people sitting on cushions on the floor. Services in which our liturgy treated Buber and Fromm and Heschel as seriously as our forefathers' liturgy treated Maimonides in *Yigdal*. Services that women took part in as freely and joyously as men. Services of singing and dancing.[83]

Consequently, the fusion of religion and politics gradually gave way to more attention on Judaism and less on radical activism. Indeed, as Shabbat increased in significance for the group, individuals who sought a venue to pursue radical politics began to leave the group, while others more interested in reconnecting to their Judaism continued to join. Yet some longtime JUJ members did not see this new emphasis as a loss of political intensity, but rather a redefinition of it; as Waskow put it, "Those of us who had been 'political' but had been cut off from the 'religious' tradition began to understand the 'political' dimension of the Shabbat as foretaste of the Messianic Age—Shabbat as a present moment of the future revolution."[84]

In the fall of 1970 and into the early months of 1971, leading members of Jews for Urban Justice began to explore the possibility of establishing a Jewish countercultural center in Washington, D.C. Robert Agus, a lawyer and son of a prominent Baltimore rabbi, sought funding for such a center from the director of the local Jewish Social Service Agency, stating that the center's purpose would be to provide outreach to alienated Jewish youth, and especially those with drug-related problems. In their rather carefully phrased funding proposal, Rob Agus and Paul Ruttkay (both JUJ members) stated that, although white American youth usually did not suffer from "physical repression," "nearly all of us suffer feelings of guilt, loneliness, inadequacy, etc. that prevent us from fully facing ourselves and asserting control of our lives." Young Jews, moreover, "who want to develop and live a truly Jewish communal existence" experienced "an extra degree of alienation from the present system and its culture." Consequently, Agus and Ruttkay hoped to establish a community center "based on the values of cooperation, sharing, and love that would work toward individual development within a communal context . . . a place where the evolutionary process of developing the new Halacha could begin."[85] A board member of the agency agreed to pursue this possibility, and other local organizations (like the American Jewish Committee) also expressed interest in supporting such an project.

In February of 1971 the Fabrangen Jewish Free Culture Center (*Fabrangen* is Yiddish for "a coming together") received an initial six-month grant of fifteen thousand dollars from the United Jewish Appeal (despite objections from the local Jewish Community Council). As one organizer of the center summarized it—with a hint of sarcasm—when "UJA [United Jewish Appeal] Washington first funded *Fabrangen*, it had a vision of a steady procession of Jewish drug users throwing away their needles under the salutary influence of Jewish culture."[86] Fabrangen opened a coffee house that quickly began to sponsor several popular cultural activities such as poetry readings and a speaker series. The center also offered courses in topics such as Jewish rituals and modern Jewish literature. And on Friday nights the center hosted a Kabbalat Shabbat (a mystically inspired service to usher in the Sabbath); a smaller group returned for Saturday morning service and Torah study.

But the UJA grant had come with strings attached, primarily the result of several years of soured and mutually suspicious relations between the local Jewish establishment and JUJ. Most specifically, it was a condition of the grant that Jews for Urban Justice could not hold its meetings at Fabrangen, and the grant was also conditional on the fact that neither Sharon Rose nor

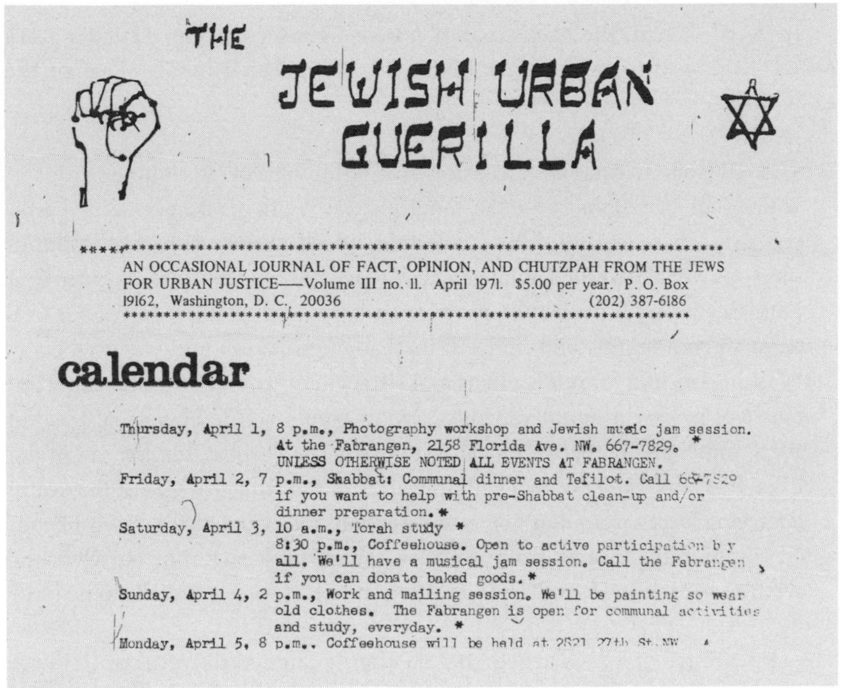

THE JEWISH URBAN GUERILLA

AN OCCASIONAL JOURNAL OF FACT, OPINION, AND CHUTZPAH FROM THE JEWS FOR URBAN JUSTICE—Volume III no. 11. April 1971. $5.00 per year. P. O. Box 19162, Washington, D. C. 20036 (202) 387-6186

calendar

Thursday, April 1, 8 p.m., Photography workshop and Jewish music jam session. At the Fabrangen, 2158 Florida Ave. NW. 667-7829. *
UNLESS OTHERWISE NOTED ALL EVENTS AT FABRANGEN.

Friday, April 2, 7 p.m., Shabbat: Communal dinner and Tefilot. Call 667-7829 if you want to help with pre-Shabbat clean-up and/or dinner preparation. *

Saturday, April 3, 10 a.m., Torah study *
8:30 p.m., Coffeehouse. Open to active participation by all. We'll have a musical jam session. Call the Fabrangen if you can donate baked goods. *

Sunday, April 4, 2 p.m., Work and mailing session. We'll be painting so wear old clothes. The Fabrangen is open for communal activities and study, everyday. *

Monday, April 5, 8 p.m., Coffeehouse will be held at 2821 27th St. NW

FIG. 5.3 Masthead for *Jewish Urban Guerilla* 3, no. 2 (April 1971). The JUJ calendar routinely announced events at Fabrangen. Courtesy of Michael Tabor.

Mike Tabor would be centrally involved in the organizational leadership of Fabrangen (though both were initial members). Still, and at the same time, there was an understanding that other members of JUJ would be centrally involved in the new center's planning as well as that JUJ and Fabrangen were closely affiliated. This was reflected in the fact that the JUJ newsletter, *Jewish Urban Guerrilla*, listed Fabrangen events alongside JUJ activities; it was also evident in that Fabrangen initially functioned as one primary place where JUJ found new members (figure 5.3). But the UJA conditions also caused tensions—right at the outset—as to what precisely the connection between the cultural center and JUJ really was—or ought to be. As Tabor put it, "Most of the people accepted that *Fabrangen* was the non-political part of JUJ," even while others merely felt that "JUJ had now become the *Fabrangen*."[87] In fact, however, the actual relationship between the center and the radical group was far from settled.

In April of 1971, the back page of *Jewish Urban Guerrilla* carried a story called "Proposal for a Summer Living-Working Experiment." Part of the essay read:

> The JUJ Collective has been working on developing a living community for itself and for other Jews in the Washington area. We have taken on several projects which have expanded the possibilities of self-liberation through community—one has been the Fabrangen, a new Jewish counter-culture center near Dupont Circle. . . . In an attempt to expand even further liberation of our lives through community, both for JUJ, the Fabrangen Community and others in Washington, and for our brothers and sisters in other cities, we are taking initial steps to have a summer living-working experiment to liberate, at least for the summer and perhaps afterwards, not only the Shabbat, but the rest of our lives. It is conceived not as a withdrawal from the struggles against the death-decreeing forces around us but as the creation of an example of a truly liberated community life-style, from which we can draw strength for ourselves and serve as an example for others in resisting the death forces, and affirming life.[88]

The appearance of a *JUG* article that so closely aligned the aims of JUJ with Fabrangen was cause for serious concern, especially for Rob Agus, who had worked hard to negotiate the initial six-month grant with the local United Jewish Appeal. Agus and others in Fabrangen felt that a continued close association with JUJ would give UJA reason to suspend their funding. What resulted were accusations from radical members of JUJ that Fabrangen had been co-opted by the same Jewish establishment it had previously been so willing to challenge—all because the UJA dangled the carrot of money. Also in April 1971, as the mood in JUJ and Fabrangen shifted further from radical politics, Sharon Rose quit JUJ and became active in a new (and more politically anti-Zionist) collective, the Middle East Research and Information Project (MERIP). This resignation effectively left Tabor isolated in the view that radical political activity was the central reason for JUJ's continued existence.

In May of 1971 Tabor decided to write the remaining three dozen individuals still loosely affiliated with Jews for Urban Justice, stating that the group's difficulties with Fabrangen illustrated how much a political commitment to "the universal" had waned. Summarizing his feelings at the time, Tabor later wrote:

> Had we become so involved in our own problems that now we too were forgetting the second part of Hillel's message ["If I am only for myself, what am

> I"]? People seemed more interested in gossip, ego-trips, and escapism. I said exactly what I felt about the split that was becoming more & more tense each day. At the end of the letter, I suggested that JUJ be abolished.[89]

While nearly all still involved with JUJ thought the group ought to continue—also because of a perception that Fabrangen provided an unsatisfactory alternative—JUJ met only twice more before Tabor finally and officially disbanded the group in July 1971, when it became clear that there was little will to pursue a radical Jewishness dedicated centrally to political activism.

WHEN EL FATAH GOES TO SHUL!

Interestingly, at the same time, Fabrangen was experiencing its own internal splits. While the center's statement of purpose focused on the needs of disaffected Jewish youth, in its first six months Fabrangen did not undertake a single major program in this area. Rather, the center's clientele was primarily young Jewish professionals who wished to participate in, "as has been disparagingly remarked, nothing but 'a hip shul,'" where "services are accompanied by a guitar, but which in essence has the same concerns as Establishment synagogues." A smaller group, however, pushed for Fabrangen "to provide a total environment—a kind of urban kibbutz."[90] This minority of members hoped the center would pursue a "more activist and challenging" role in the community, and see "the parameter of a Jewish identity [as] larger than a narrowly defined religion."[91] Finally, and ironically perhaps—given that the center was largely an outgrowth of JUJ—there were tensions at Fabrangen over the proper relationship between Judaism and political activism. Should Fabrangen sponsor and pursue political activism? Or should it see the "primary imperative of the [Jewish] tradition as developing a Halachic community—a community which observes *Shabbat* and the holidays and the rhythm of Jewish life, and which tries to come to terms with *Halacha* as a system," while avoiding an immediate role in radical politics and activism?[92]

While all this was going on inside Fabrangen, UJA determined it would only decide whether to refund the center after a committee thoroughly investigated charges that Fabrangen fostered anti-Israeli ideas and was a front for Jews for Urban Justice. At a July 1971 meeting held to hear testimony on Fabrangen, many in the community who opposed refunding the center "felt that it was sufficient merely to prove that Arthur Waskow was associated with Fabrangen to render it unfit for UJA support."[93] However, the UJA committee concluded that Waskow and Tabor represented minority voices at the center, and its final report recommended refunding.

This decision encountered outraged reactions from the Jewish Community Council, which had opposed funding in the first place, as well as those now convinced that Fabrangen organizers were militant anti-Zionists. In the short period of time after the committee submitted its recommendation that Fabrangen be refunded, but before UJA met to make its final decision, the local *Jewish Week* published a front-page story that was the most extreme smearing of Jews for Urban Justice ever to appear in print (made even more bittersweet since the group no longer existed largely because of its tensions with Fabrangen). Written by "Bertram Jonas" (a rumored pseudonym for editor and publisher, Philip Hochstein), "When El Fatah Goes to Shul!" appeared alongside a prominent photograph of a grinning Waskow. It served up a host of almost libelous accusations—naming Tabor as "leader of the pro-Arab Jews for Urban Justice," Rose as an anti-Zionist who wished "to make common cause with a radical wing of the Arab terrorists," and Waskow as urging "the overthrow of existing society because, in his opinion, it frustrates Jewish living." It listed these three as key organizers of Fabrangen. The article cited a Sabbath service at Fabrangen held on July 19, 1971, that had functioned as an event "utilized to drum up support for [a] subsequent demonstration at the Arab Information Center in Washington in behalf of Arab terrorists who were then being routed by King Hussein's forces." It charged that the Middle East Research and Information Project was "a supporter of the Arab terrorist movement" and that since MERIP had at one time used "the same Post Office Box number" as JUJ, this proved beyond a doubt that it was merely one of JUJ's "various organizational fronts." And the banner headline for the article cast the matter in terms intended to be as inflammatory as possible: "Establishment-financed New Leftists succeed in becoming divisive issue in Jewish communities across nation as they politicize religious rites."[94]

As far as the United Jewish Appeal was concerned, the *Jewish Week* article left it little choice how to proceed, and its decision was swift and unequivocal. The UJA overturned the recommendation of its own advisory committee and voted against refunding Fabrangen. A bitter letter war followed in the pages of *Jewish Week*, but it had no impact on the UJA decision. Instead of the thirty thousand dollars that the committee had recommended for Fabrangen, or the twelve-thousand-dollar-a-year subsidy that had been reported as a likely compromise (given the controversy surrounding the larger proposed sum), the UJA voted to suspend funding entirely. A wide spectrum of representa-

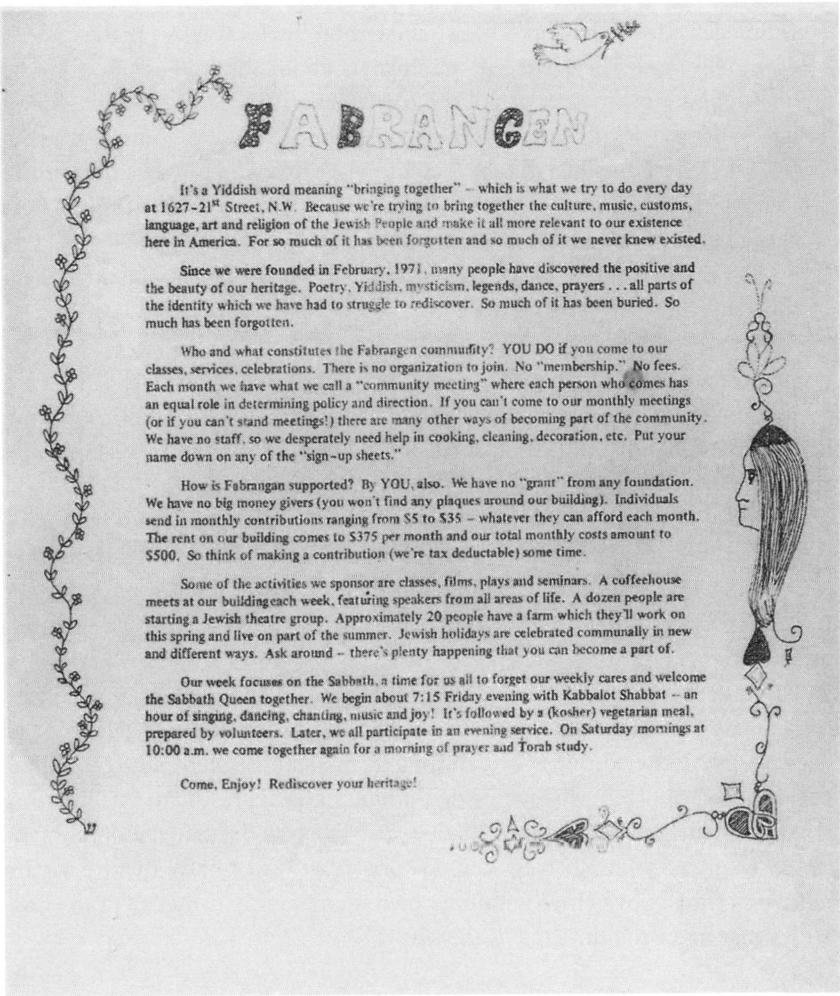

FABRANGEN

It's a Yiddish word meaning "bringing together" -- which is what we try to do every day at 1627-21st Street, N.W. Because we're trying to bring together the culture, music, customs, language, art and religion of the Jewish People and make it all more relevant to our existence here in America. For so much of it has been forgotten and so much of it we never knew existed.

Since we were founded in February, 1971, many people have discovered the positive and the beauty of our heritage. Poetry, Yiddish, mysticism, legends, dance, prayers . . . all parts of the identity which we have had to struggle to rediscover. So much of it has been buried. So much has been forgotten.

Who and what constitutes the Fabrangen community? YOU DO if you come to our classes, services, celebrations. There is no organization to join. No "membership." No fees. Each month we have what we call a "community meeting" where each person who comes has an equal role in determining policy and direction. If you can't come to our monthly meetings (or if you can't stand meetings!) there are many other ways of becoming part of the community. We have no staff, so we desperately need help in cooking, cleaning, decoration, etc. Put your name down on any of the "sign-up sheets."

How is Fabrangan supported? By YOU, also. We have no "grant" from any foundation. We have no big money givers (you won't find any plaques around our building). Individuals send in monthly contributions ranging from $5 to $35 -- whatever they can afford each month. The rent on our building comes to $375 per month and our total monthly costs amount to $500. So think of making a contribution (we're tax deductable) some time.

Some of the activities we sponsor are classes, films, plays and seminars. A coffeehouse meets at our buildingeach week, featuring speakers from all areas of life. A dozen people are starting a Jewish theatre group. Approximately 20 people have a farm which they'll work on this spring and live on part of the summer. Jewish holidays are celebrated communally in new and different ways. Ask around -- there's plenty happening that you can become a part of.

Our week focuses on the Sabbath, a time for us all to forget our weekly cares and welcome the Sabbath Queen together. We begin about 7:15 Friday evening with Kabbalot Shabbat -- an hour of singing, dancing, chanting, music and joy! It's followed by a (kosher) vegetarian meal, prepared by volunteers. Later, we all participate in an evening service. On Saturday mornings at 10:00 a.m. we come together again for a morning of prayer and Torah study.

Come, Enjoy! Rediscover your heritage!

FIG. 5.4 An early flyer for the Fabrangen Jewish Free Culture Center in Washington, D.C. Courtesy of Michael Tabor.

tives in the Jewish community—including a local representative of the Radical Zionist Alliance as well as the editor of the nationally distributed weekly newspaper, *Jewish Post and Opinion*—condemned *Jewish Week*'s handling of the controversy.[95] Notably, even a former adversary of JUJ, Rabbi Eugene Lipman of Temple Sinai, now sharply criticized the UJA's decision, calling it "a cop-out and a serious one." Lipman wrote:

> Fabrangen's funds have not been renewed by the local UJA for the coming year. Why not? There were no complaints about the staff. There were no questions about whether or not the place met a real need in Washington. It did. What was wrong? Some of the people who went there, some of the people who led discussions there, some of the people who taught groups there were politically radical—THE RADICAL LEFT! Even worse, sentiments were alleged to have been expressed against the state of Israel.
>
> So we who trumpet freedom of dissent and who despise repression—have done just that.

Lipman concluded: "I do not expect every young Jew who enters the Fabrangen or the Jewish Center or Temple Sinai to have a mechanized brain which believes and spouts only some line in order for us to care about him and to provide him with the facilities and services he needs."[96] For Tabor, meanwhile, who was now a regular columnist for *Jewish Post and Opinion*, the matter was yet another example of how the Jewish communal leadership was willing to engage in "modern 'red-baiting' " (which "often takes the form of labeling someone 'pro-Arab' ") to "insure [the] writing off of an individual or organization."[97]

Fabrangen survived. It was even strengthened as a result of the debacles with *Jewish Week* and the United Jewish Appeal over funding (figure 5.4). Perhaps ironically, the loss of funding from establishment sources rallied Fabrangen supporters who set aside a lingering ill will over the debilitating infighting with Jews for Urban Justice. But JUJ was definitively defunct—a closed chapter in Jewish New Left history. It proved finally to be a victim more of a shift in priorities within its own membership rather than the hostilities that had been directed against it.

SELF-ABASEMENT MASQUERADING AS AN EXPRESSION OF SELF-AFFIRMATION

In February 1971, *Commentary* published the epitaph for the radical Jewish movement. Gathered under the heading, "Revolutionism and the Jews," this group of essays collectively said in print about the American Jewish New Left "what no non-Jew could say without being thought prejudiced," or so gushed William F. Buckley approvingly in a *National Review* editorial.[98] Buckley was certainly perceptive, for in this issue of *Commentary* not just secular New Left Jews but also Jewish-identified New Leftists were attacked in the nastiest terms.

Professor Walter Laqueur, for example, of the Institute of Contemporary History in London, made fun of Jewish-identified New Leftists' habit of professing "that they 'identify strongly with Israel although not necessarily with her politics.'" From an Israeli point of view, he asserted, "the American-Jewish radical represents the Diaspora Jew *par excellence*: immature, irresponsible, tormented with sundry imaginary problems . . . restless, neurotic, faddish." Laqueur styled himself amused that American Jewish radicals could not handle the "discipline" of a kibbutz, and came back from visits to Israel "declaring that the kibbutz is not radical enough" and eager to return to the "more glamorous struggle for liberation" as practiced in the U.S. Naming Jews for Urban Justice directly, as well as like-minded organizations in Berkeley, Ann Arbor, and Somerville, Massachusetts, Laqueur also asserted that the "doctrines" of these groups "betray strange and contradictory ideological influences." In his opinion, furthermore, "Jewish radicalism in America is, of course, a form of assimilation." And he declared that

> the hope that young radicals of this generation will again become "good Jews" is a slender one, comparable perhaps with the hope of a psychoanalyst for the recovery of a patient with a weak ego structure or a serious intellectual deficiency. Individuals may rediscover their Jewish identity and consciousness, but a catastrophe of the magnitude of Nazism would be needed to effect a mass reconversion of people so far removed from Judaism.[99]

In his contribution Nathan Glazer too invoked Nazism. Clarifying at length that "because so many intellectuals are Jews (even if most Jews are not intellectuals)," Glazer was concerned that Jews might be blamed for the trends of the recent past. Glazer found in the "potential conflict between the intellectuals and 'Middle America,' and therefore for Jews because of their prominence among the intellectuals" a forbidding "parallel between Weimar and America" that "cannot be dismissed." After all, Glazer warned, Hitler had successfully blamed "the moral 'degeneration' of Germany on the influence of the Jews" and now in America a "potential backlash" represented the "greatest single danger to Jews in the next ten years." It would be very easy, Glazer warned, for those in "the hinterland" to blame Jews for the strength of the antiwar movement, the prevalence of pornography and marijuana smoking, and the recent overthrow of "the traditional restraints—on sexual behavior, on antiauthoritarian behavior, on violent behavior in certain settings." But in his conclusion Glazer turned, as had Laqueur, to questions of psychology. Aligning himself with "those of us concerned with Jewish interests," Glazer argued strongly that radical Jews were displaying "anti-Jewish tendencies" and "the sticky phenomenon known as 'self-hatred.'"[100]

Robert Alter, professor of Hebrew and comparative literature at the University of California at Berkeley, had even more to say about self-hatred. In his contribution, and in a spirit similar to Fackenheim, Alter took careful aim specifically at those Jewish radicals who drew on religious tradition to advance their political aims. Alter's indictment of radical Jews focused on NJOP, which he accused of "that most dangerous form of intellectual promiscuity, the melodramatization of politics," and above all on Waskow's radical Haggadah, which he characterized as "surely the most bizarre instance of the tyranny of politics over religion among radical Jews." Alter described Waskow's work as "offensively shrill," "profoundly un-Jewish," and "so clearly the crude political rape of a religious tradition." Yet he was most concerned not only to contest radical Jews' claim to be building authentically on Jewish tradition but to identify their efforts expressly with self-hatred as well. Alter was appalled by what he saw as Waskow's "self-effacement before black militancy," not least because of "all peoples in a world that has lived through Auschwitz, Jews ought to be the last to accept mindlessly the propagandistic black-militant usage of 'genocide.' " Strongly offended by "the renunciation of Jewish ties made in the name of a higher Judaism," Alter also announced that "Waskow's Haggadah is in a very literal psychological sense a perversion because it is a document of self-loathing and self-abasement masquerading as an expression of self-affirmation."[101]

Yet *Commentary* editor Norman Podhoretz found Alter to be too kind. Podhoretz thought the support given by "Balfour Brickner and other prominent rabbis" to Waskow's Freedom Seder to be "most disgraceful." Praising Alter and his "careful analysis" of the radical Haggadah in his editor's column introducing the issue, Podhoretz found Alter's points about "self-loathing and self-abasement" to be "a touch too gentle to do justice to the truly abominable case at hand." Podhoretz, for his part, preferred to take "a lead from Mr. Laqueur's suggestive observation that New Left radicalism is for American Jews a form of assimilationism." To say Waskow and his ilk were self-hating was to miss the severity of the danger they posed. In Podhoretz's view Waskow was guilty not just of self-hatred but of "the sin of anti-Semitism." The Jewish radical, to Podhoretz's mind, was not pathetic but "wicked."[102]

On the whole, these are the analyses of Jews in the New Left that have stuck. The differences in nuance exemplified by the various critics of the New Left propounding their views in this issue of *Commentary* have set the terms of debate for the subsequent decades. By the mid-seventies a comprehensive essay on the radical Jewish youth movement in *Encyclopedia Judaica Year Book* concluded simply that Waskow's radical Haggadah had been "a fascinating instance of the tyranny of politics over religion (to use Robert Alter's term) among certain radical Jews."[103] By the early 1980s, open season on Jews in the New Left reached an apogee in *Roots of Radicalism* by Stanley Rothman and S. Robert Lichter. This psychohistorical critique found Jewish mothers largely to blame. Militant causes, especially black ones, attracted Jewish boys "who had always had doubts about their masculinity and their sexuality" and who "may have felt that they could finally express both masculine aggression and sexuality freely because they were part of a powerful 'revolutionary' group. More than that," Rothman and Lichter concluded, in such groups Jewish boys "could recapture the polymorphous perversity of childhood."[104]

These are not developments that could have been anticipated in the late 1960s in Washington, D.C. Brant Coopersmith may have found JUJ to be offensively self-righteous, but he, like most other leaders of the mainstream Jewish community in the metropolitan area, took its challenge to heart. The story of JUJ and its critics is a tangled and complex one with no easy heroes or heroines; both sides got personal, sometimes in disturbing ways. But what a charting of the intra-Jewish conflicts provoked by JUJ makes clear is just how unsettled relations between religion, politics, and ethnic identification were felt to be for a time; the meaning of both Judaism and Jewishness was seen by almost all participants in the controversies as rightly in the process of reformulation and revitalization.

6 "We Are Coming Home": New Left Jews and Radical Zionism

We are coming home. To Brooklyn. Those of us who have moved away and forgotten our birthplace, and those of us who still live here and always dreamed of getting out. We have been running away too long, cutting ourselves off from our roots too long, and it has stunted us. We are coming home to Brooklyn to live, to love, to begin building a new world, and to be Jewish.

—Brooklyn Bridge Collective, 1971

THE FEDERATION IS GUILTY OF ANTI-SEMITISM

In November 1969 a group of young radical Jews took over the Jewish Federation-Council in Los Angeles, affixing two hundred mezuzahs to the doors in the building, dramatically symbolizing what they saw as the Federation-Council's indifference to Jewish educational, spiritual, and cultural concerns.[1] Also in November, a group of three hundred protesters calling themselves Concerned Jewish Students gathered in Boston to picket at the national convention of the Council of Jewish Federations and Welfare Funds (CJF). The CJF was responsible for the coordination of priorities for over two hundred Jewish charities in the U.S. and Canada. Having threatened to disrupt a dinner meeting, the group was finally granted permission to address the convention. Speaking for the group, Hillel Levine, a twenty-three-year-old Harvard graduate and Conservative rabbi, told those in attendance: "You might dismiss us as children of our times, bored with the battle of the campus and looking for a new stage upon which to play our childish pranks of doubtful morality." Such, however, he went on to assure his listeners, was not the case. The protesters were most concerned about the funding choices being made by Jewish federations across the country. Rather than give the bulk of their money to nonsectarian institutions like hospitals or Jewish Community Centers, which served the wider non-Jewish community as well, federations should instead invest far more in Jewish education and in other activities and institutions that "are vital to the survival and development of the American Jewish Community." In addition, the protesters called for the founding of a "National Committee for Developing Jewish Identity." They also expressed regret that "the Federation allocates money to Jewish War Veterans, but nothing to the Jewish Peace Fellowship."[2] And in February 1970, in guerrilla theatrical style, the Radical Jewish Union at Columbia University organized an exorcism of the dybbuk "that we presumed was existent in Judge Julius Hoffman," the presiding (Jewish) judge at the Chicago Eight conspiracy trial (where several Jewish defendants, including Abbie Hoffman and Jerry Rubin, faced charges that they had crossed state lines with the intent to incite a riot at the Democratic National Convention in 1968). As one participant in the exorcism of the dybbuk in Judge Hoffman wryly put it afterward: "I take it there wasn't one because his behavior hasn't changed that much."[3]

As these diverse examples suggest, the turn from the 1960s to the 1970s witnessed a new insurgency among Jewish youth that could not easily be fit into conventional political categories. The young activists vehemently rejected the assimilationism they saw in their parents' generation. Yet there were also remarkable echoes between the young people's demands and the growing insistence among many older establishment leaders that Jewish organizations' finances should go to the benefit of specifically Jewish causes, and that Jewish youth education should be made a priority. The new youth activists also shared with an increasing number of their elders an intensified dedication to Israel and to the cause of Soviet Jewry. At the same time, however, there was some overlap—in personnel and in attitude—between the membership of New Left–linked Jewish organizations and this new phenomenon of specifically Jewish youth activism. Many of the new activists, for example, were fiercely opposed to U.S. involvement in Vietnam; many also shared with the New Left a hostility to materialism and so-called plastic culture. But there were also profound tensions between Jewish youth activists and the New Left. Although—or perhaps precisely because—they stood astride many conventional divisions within the American Jewish community, the new Jewish activists were absolutely essential to the revitalization of American Jewish ethnic identity. Borrowing from the civil rights, black militant, and antiwar movements, they contributed to the community not only a new revolutionary style but also wholly new conceptions of religious commitment, Zionism, and a distinctly American brand of Jewish pride.

An indicative case of combining New Left tactics with the goal of meeting Jewish communal needs more effectively came in April 1970 when eighty young Jews "liberated" the offices of the Federation of Jewish Philanthropies in New York, taking over the switchboard and blocking entrances. Members of several area Jewish youth and radical groups participated, including the Ad Hoc Committee for Jewish Education of Yeshiva University, Habonim, the New York Havurah, the Jewish Cultural Foundation of New York University, the Jewish Liberation Project, the Jewish Peace Fellowship, the Radical Jewish Union of Columbia University, the Students Struggle for Soviet Jewry, and Yavneh, as well as several rabbinical students. Although approximately half left the building when threatened with arrest, forty-five people refused to leave, demanding an immediate meeting with the board of trustees to discuss the allocation of federation funds and stating that the federation was "no longer serving the Jewish community, but serving hospitals which are not Jewish and YMHA's in non-Jewish neighborhoods."[4] The protesters asked that the federation guarantee quality Jewish education in the city, finance a foundation to aid youth projects, underwrite Jewish cultural endeavors, and contribute ten thousand dollars to an April 26 Exodus March for Soviet Jewry. The federation rejected the protesters' demands, asked them to leave and, when they refused, called the cops. As police arrested the forty-five protesters (who quickly became known as the "Federation 45"), charging them with criminal trespass, some sang "Am Yisrael Chai" (Israel lives), while others shouted, "Let them arrest us studying Rambam" and, even, "The federation is guilty of anti-Semitism." Another student protester reportedly said, "If our brothers in the Soviet Union can lay down their lives for what they believe in, we can risk a little stay at the police station." Significantly, furthermore, despite the intergenerational conflict represented by the action, the Federation 45 also got strong support from prominent older Jewish leaders of the most varied political allegiances. In the wake of this well-publicized protest, writer Elie Wiesel, Rabbis Emanuel Rackman, Norman Lamm, Haskel Lookstein (all Orthodox), and Professor Eugene Borowitz (Reform), among others, issued a statement calling on the federation to withdraw criminal trespass charges against the arrested activists and requesting that the federation "reconsider its priorities and meet its obligations to Jewish youth and education."[5]

I AM A JEW IN A SYNAGOGUE

Over and over again, activists not only adopted a physically confrontational style but also expressly emphasized their own Jewishness as a weapon against members of the Jewish establishment perceived to be too accommodationist to gentile society. This happened both when the issues at stake were the priorities of Jewish communal organizations and in quite different situations when the matter at hand was the perceived abrogation of proper Jewish values. On May 29, 1970, for example, Rabbi A. Bruce Goldman, now director of the Institute for Creative Jewish Living, along with Victor Levin, a Columbia University graduate student, and Anne Rosen, a Barnard student, got arrested on charges that they had disrupted Friday night services at Temple Emanu-El, the largest Reform synagogue in the world. As members of the Radical Jewish Union of Columbia University (RJU), their appearance at the temple had been expected; the RJU had disrupted services two weeks earlier, when Goldman was arrested a first time. Both disruptions had come after Rabbi Nathan A. Perilman denied RJU a request to speak to the congregation during services about the peace movement and the "shameful war in Indo-China." (The temple had withdrawn from the Union of American Hebrew Congregations in 1967 after statements from UAHC president, Rabbi Maurice Eisendrath, that demanded the U.S. cease its bombing campaign against North Vietnam "without conditions" and declared American Jews were part of the white backlash opposed to civil rights legislation.)[6] After Perilman's decision, the RJU announced its intention to interrupt Friday services until the rabbi changed his position. Thus, on May 29, the protesters returned, again led by Rabbi Goldman, who entered the temple's sanctuary shouting, "Remember Kent State University." Once inside, Rosen successfully climbed over a railing between a row of pews and the bimah (podium) and managed to get to the microphone, where she was met by plainclothes police disguised as ushers. While they dragged her from the pulpit, Rosen shouted, "I am a Jew in a synagogue. How can you arrest me?" But it was Goldman the police wanted most; rather remarkably, he now faced charges of disrupting a worship service, which—if he were to be convicted—could result in a four-year prison term.[7]

The Radical Jewish Union responded to these arrests by soliciting signatures for a petition in defense of the actions taken by Goldman and the two students. Signed by Jews for Urban Justice and the National Jewish Organizing Project as well, and (in a manner reminiscent of many JUJ declarations) mixing assertions about religion with Holocaust references, the RJU statement read in part:

> Temple Emanu-el's refusal to allow students to speak during the service about the war and repression was a blatant breach of sacred Jewish tradition. . . . The obligation of every Jew to speak out against injustice is a priority higher than any consideration of decorum. . . . American Jews have long been vocal in op-

> posing oppression of Soviet Jewry. Yet, paradoxically, when these same Jews speak out against war and repression in the U.S. they are arrested as criminals by their fellow Jews. . . . Temple Emanu-el's action is very reminiscent of the *Judenrat* of Nazi Germany.[8]

The Radical Jewish Union did in fact achieve its immediate aim. In June 1970, after the petition, signed by a number of rabbis across the country, said the students should be allowed to speak at the service, RJU announced it was canceling plans for further protests at Temple Emanu-El because it had reached an accord with temple officials "that further constructive conversations will take place between the two groups on matters of mutual concern, focusing on the Jewish response to pressing social and political issues of our time, such as war, poverty, racism and political repression." Furthermore, temple officials asked the district attorney to drop charges against the three protesters. But the district attorney refused to oblige, insisting the case go to trial because "this is not a private matter." After several postponements, and requests by Goldman that the New York Board of Rabbis convene a Beth Din (rabbinical court) to hear the case, Rosen accepted a guilty plea to the lesser charge of disorderly conduct and received a suspended sentence. (Goldman and Levin refused to plead guilty, and it would only be in November 1971 that a New York City criminal court would finally dismiss the charges against them.)[9]

Meanwhile, those who protested against Jewish federations across the country also began to see at least nominal progress in the allocation of funds for experimental Jewish student programs. This may have been especially true when it came to the funding of cooperative religious youth residences called *havurot* (sing., *havurah*; Hebrew for "fellowships").[10] For example, in June 1970 the Oakland Jewish Welfare Federation provided funding for a *havurah* for students at the Berkeley campus. Additionally, at the same time, the Cleveland Jewish Community Federation allocated monies for "new and innovative programs at college campuses in northeast Ohio," while federations in Portland, Oregon, and Baltimore, Maryland, were also extending their funding in ways designed to involve young people more deeply in Jewish communal affairs.[11]

NORTH AMERICAN JEWS ARE A MARGINAL PEOPLE

Yet these responses by Jewish philanthropic agencies were often interpreted as inadequate by Jewish radicals. Over and over again, Jewish rad-

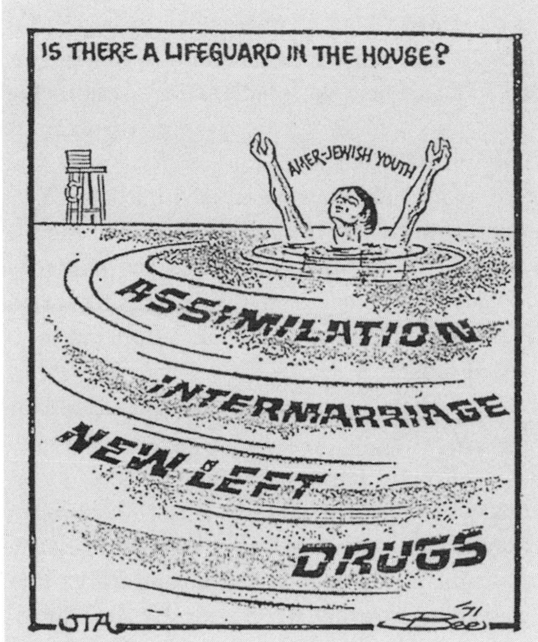

FIGURE 6.1
"Is There a Lifeguard in the House?" (1971) by political cartoonist Noah Bee. Bee's work was syndicated weekly across the United States and Canada by the Jewish Telegraphic Agency. Courtesy of Marion Bee, Carmi Bee, and Sharon Herman.

ical student newspapers took aim at the Jewish establishment in their editorials. Many in the older generation worried that young Jews were being drawn away from the community by the lures of secularization and assimilation (figure 6.1). Yet here were youth activists trying to reconstitute the community. What these young people wanted was *more* Judaism, rather than less. The perceived vacuity of mainstream synagogues and the incoherence of the messages sent to the young were major targets. *Bagolah*, a socialist-Zionist newspaper based at the University of Illinois–Chicago, for instance, wrote in 1970:

> Our task is to explain patiently to the unconscious masses of Jewish youth the national character of Judaism. Our task is to attempt to undo the horrors that have been perpetrated in the name of Jewish education; educating young Jews into an American historical consciousness that leads inevitably to complete assimilation. Our task is to confront "Jewish leaders" militantly with the full consequences of their contradictory policies: pious efforts to battle assimilation and equally pious efforts to further remake the Jewish community into a model of liberal bourgeois America.[12]

Likewise, as Jewish student radical Mike Masch lamented in early 1972 for *Hayom*, the newspaper published by the Philadelphia Union of Jewish Students: "No one gave us a real Judaism that we could accept or reject. We know that the plastic synagogues our parents go to are no more than haunted echo chambers of a once vibrant past. But that past is so long gone that most of us cannot even conceive of a living, meaningful Jewish existence."[13]

If what was required was the revolutionary awakening of radical Zionist consciousness, then this process was set officially in motion in February 1970 at Camp Ramah in Palmer, Massachusetts, where Jewish students from seventy-five campuses in the United States, Canada, and Israel gathered for a two-day conference, "Jewish Radicalism: A Search for a Renewed Zionist Ideology." Among those groups in attendance were ACIID (A Call for Insight Into Israeli Dilemmas) from Washington University, St. Louis, the Jewish Liberation Coalition of Providence, the Jewish Liberation Project of New York, the Student Zionist Organization of Montreal, the Boston Jewish Activist League, and the University of Michigan Coalition of Jewish Students. Voicing "total rejection of the assimilationist position and strong affirmation of the need for a liberation movement for the Jewish people," a caucus of conference members drafted the founding manifesto of the Radical Zionist Alliance. It read in part:

> North American Jews are a marginal people in a society of economic, political, and cultural oppression. The Jewish community has adopted a tradition of ignoring its own needs, and has structured itself in an undemocratic manner, geared toward assimilation and disappearance as a functioning nation. We call for the liberation of the Jewish people and the restructuring of our people's existence in such a way as to facilitate self-determination and development of our own institutions so as to control our destiny as a nation.[14]

As this document suggests, radical Zionism was not so much a movement developed in backlash against Black Power, as rather a movement modeled on Black Power and conceived as parallel to it. The movement saw Jews as suffering profound oppression within the United States—an oppression made all the more insidious by its invisibility. It was also in this spirit that Itzhak Epstein, for example, a founding member of the Jewish Liberation Project in New York and a former member of the Students for a Democratic Society, wrote in 1969—with mixed metaphoric intensity—that given the way American Jews live in "an assimilationist community whose establishment is trying to pass us off for whites, it is our primary function to create a radical national consciousness" and thereby "avoid becoming pawns of the white power structure when the polarization reaches its logical conclusion, the barricades are erected, and the boom is lowered."[15] And it was in a related vein that Hillel Levine, a member of the Havurat Shalom Community Seminary in Somerville, Massachusetts, and the main spokesperson for the protesters at the 1969 National Convention of the Council of Jewish Federations and Welfare Funds, drew on the inspiration offered by Black Power in order to justify a Jewish liberation movement. As Levine told *Newsweek*: "The black awakening reminded us that the melting pot was a fool's fantasy, and that racial and religious differences are legitimate. For many of us, this means turning our concerns inwards toward the Jewish community."[16]

Occasionally, radical Zionists and New Left Jews worked together, and it is crucial not to overstate what might appear in retrospect like insurmountable differences within the radical Jewish youth movement. The shared passionate objection to U.S. military involvement in the Vietnam War was one key example. One remarkable instance of collective radical Jewish action occurred at a November 1969 rally in which members of Washington, D.C.'s Radical Zionist Alliance demonstrated together with the local non-Zionist activist group, Jews for Urban Justice, in front of Marine Corps headquarters. They were protesting the Marine Corps' antisemitic treatment of a recruit named David Handler, who had been discharged for medical reasons. Handler had, as one report put it, suffered "a breakdown which the two groups charged was the result of his being treated like a concentration camp inmate" at boot camp on Parris Island, South Carolina. Charging that one drill instructor had incessantly badgered and ridiculed Handler, calling him "Jew boy" and "bagel," and that another drill instructor had painted the Star of David on Handler's forehead, the demonstrators "wore Stars of David on their foreheads and carried signs reading, 'No Viet Cong Ever Called Me Bagel.' "[17] Here, then, was a potent guerrilla street theater protest performed in nonsectarian Jewish outrage and solidarity, even while it once more showed the radical Jewish youth movement's self-conscious adaptation of a black militant antiwar slogan (in this case, the famously defiant remark "No Viet Cong ever called me nigger," made by black heavyweight champion Muhammad Ali when he refused on religious grounds to be inducted into the U.S. military).

For radical Zionists, however, the inherent failure of most New Left Jews to grasp their proper self-interests as Jews *and* as members of an oppressed group remained a major obstacle en route to the liberation of all Jewish people. Indeed, as an editor for *Achdut*, a Brooklyn-based journal for Jewish high school students, stated categorically in early 1971: "No people have suffered as much as the Jews. It is that simple."[18] This opinion was characteristic, and it often overlapped with a bitter disdain for New Left Jews perceived as still generally indifferent to the specific oppression of Jews. Furthermore, this supposed indifference was typically interpreted as a sure sign either of those New Left Jews' own assimilationist mentality and/or as a sign of the damage done by their parents' assimilationism.

One important contribution to this line of analysis came from Jonathan Braun, editor of the *Flame*, an influential newspaper published by the Jewish Student Union at City College of New York. Braun's essay provided a classic example of radical Zionists' ability to rival their elders in the intensity of their assault on New Left–affiliated Jews while simultaneously managing to blame assimilated parents for making the New Left appealing. In 1970 Braun unleashed his scorn on those "assimilation-minded, Establishment Jews" whose "Bagels & Lox Judaism" was running rampant in the American Jewish suburbs. This fact resulted in young Jews who were "the products of a protestantized, Borscht-Belt Judaism (a hollow model based on the interpretations of Jewish law by wedding and bar-mitzvah caterers)," and who consequently "have left Miami and Queens Boulevard to build communes in the American wilderness, publish nihilist newspapers in the East Village, cut sugar cane in Cuba, and in some extreme cases, run obstacle courses in Arab terrorist training camps." Thus, even while "well-meaning, middle class parents who so terribly wanted their Cathy and Eric to be 100% Americans, are puzzled," Braun observed that it was hardly a coincidence that young Cathy and Eric—denied full access to their Jewish heritage—were now raising their "clenched fists before the pop-poster ghost of Che Guevara."[19]

BE A REVOLUTIONARY IN ZION

Central to the conflicts between the New Left and radical Zionists were attitudes about Israel. The leftist Israeli writer Amos Kenan spoke for many in the radical Zionist movement when he argued that Jews who offered support to a "parasitic" American New Left had chosen sides with "those who seek to annihilate us," an act "beyond corruption—it is complicity in murder." For Kenan, and his writings were widely distributed and debated in U.S. Jewish radical circles, New Left Jews might argue that they sought to make a revolution, but they were "obviously incapable" of genuine sacrifice and certainly would never pay "a more honorable price for a different ideal" than the one paid by the six million Jews killed by Nazism. Above all, according to Kenan, left-wing American Jews romantically "seeking their heroes among men who fought for an agrarian revolution" in some underdeveloped nation would do better to recognize their own people's roots in the Third World, and their ancestral link to "the natives of the under-developed Middle East."[20]

For many radical Zionists, the struggle for Jewish liberation was inseparable from Israeli survival. Jewish life in America, moreover, was a life in exile (*galut*), and thus a life of perpetual contradiction. They angrily mocked "checkbook Zionists" whose devotion to Israel amounted only to an annual monetary contribution or a brief tourist visit. By contrast, these Jewish radicals identified their commitment to Israeli survival as at the core of what it meant to be a Jew in the Diaspora. As Chava Katz, a founder of the Radical Zionist Alliance and a self-defined "fiery Zionist," put it in 1970: "To talk about being pro- or anti-Israel is like saying, 'Are you pro or against yourself?' "[21] Indeed, most who stood at the forefront of the radical Zionist movement (like Katz herself) would soon turn their words into deeds and emigrate to Israel to make real their dream of a socialist Israeli state.

And yet it was precisely Kenan's insight about Jews' Third World roots that allowed many radical Zionists to stake out a position that in some ways also adapted New Left perspectives for Zionist ends. As one member of the Jewish Radical Community in Los Angeles bluntly put the matter in 1969: "Taken as a whole, Judaism is more of a Middle Eastern culture than a European one." And to recognize this historical and geopolitical reality was to empower Jewish radicals finally to abandon the "humiliation of being a Jew in America," and to enable them to

> now enjoy a natural affinity towards Israel (and still remain critical of her policies, if they wish) and thereby enjoy a *natural* affinity with the Third World. They have seen that they themselves, as Jews in America, are an oppressed people. Just as the Blacks and the Mexicans must move toward self-education, solidarity, and a sense of group dignity, so must the Jew, in his own way, not aping the militant Black.[22]

It can come as little surprise, then, that there emerged a popular slogan among radical Zionists dramatized by a stark photograph of an Israeli soldier, rifle and rounds of ammunition strapped to his back: "Be a revolutionary in Zion and a Zionist in the revolution" (figure 6.2).[23] That this "revolutionary in Zion" bore an unmistakable resemblance to a Third World freedom fighter was no coincidence.

FIGURE 6.2 "Be a Revolutionary in Zion and a Zionist in the Revolution" appeared in *Hayom* 1, no. 2 (May 1971). *Hayom* was a publication of the Philadelphia Union of Jewish Students.

JEWS ARE TERRIFIED OF ASSERTING THEIR POWER

Yet not all expressions of radical Zionist ideology concerned Israel. Aviva Cantor Zuckoff, editor of the New York–based *Jewish Liberation Journal*, was an early and influential spokesperson for the concerns of the radical Zionist movement in the U.S. In her manifesto-style essay, "Oppression of Amerika's Jews," published in 1970, Zuckoff offered her own searing indictment of the Jewish establishment, most especially how it was "programmed to be the surrogate of the ruling elite in doing its dirty work of helping to keep down other oppressed groups." As both this line of analysis and the *k* in "Amerika" indicate, Zuckoff's perspective had more than a little in common with the ideas advocated by Jews for Urban Justice. But Zuckoff's ultimate message also bore more than a passing resemblance to the notions about the need for power that Richard Rubenstein was advancing as well. Taking a long view, Zuckoff found how Jews had historically been "constantly forced into the dangerous position of being trapped between the peasants and the nobles, the ruling elite and other oppressed groups. In this role of oppressor surrogate, and otherwise, the Jew functions as society's 'lightening rod' for absorbing and deflecting the rage of oppressed groups that might otherwise be turned on the ruling elite." This strategy deliberately kept Jews apart from other oppressed minorities, and allowed "the oppressing elite" to "divide-and-rule" those in its domain. Furthermore, Jews had historically been subdued into a psychologically submissive state, Zuckoff argued, through a "passivity conditioning" exacted by a ruling elite that kept "the Jews paralyzed by fear for their own survival and unable to think beyond it." As far as Zuckoff could tell, this pattern of passivity was still very much in evidence at the present time:

> Jews are taught not to "antagonize the goyim"; do not provoke them by asserting your rights. Never give cause for criticism. "Nice" is a favorite word in the Jewish lexicon. A "nice Jewish boy" is non-aggressive and non-assertive with the goyim. . . . Whenever a Jew deviates from the prescribed non-assertiveness, i.e., asserts himself as much as a goy would, he is put down as "pushy" (the equivalent of "uppity" for blacks and "non-feminine" for women) in order to intimidate him into returning to the previous passive posture.

The disastrous end result of this conditioning, Zuckoff then argued, was an historic inability on the part of Jews and Jewish groups to stand up on behalf of other Jews because "it is not considered kosher for a Jewish organization to fight only for Jews."[24] It was a pattern that had to be broken if an authentic Jewish liberation movement stood the slightest chance of success.

Zuckoff focused much of her analysis on the group therapy American Jews needed desperately to do on themselves. And to make her point as plain as possible, she invoked both African American militancy and the lessons of the Holocaust to dramatize her argument about the ongoing dysfunctional relationship Jews still had toward political or social power:

> Try to imagine, if you can, a group of Jews demanding reparations from the Church or some other oppressive institution, for 2,000 years of oppression. Of course it's a complete wild fantasy. We wouldn't do it, we would tell ourselves we're above all that. The truth is, Jews are terrified of asserting their power in this manner. One of the main roots of so much Jewish antagonism to the black power movement is Jews' jealousy of blacks for not being afraid to do this . . .
>
> Jewish defenselessness is among the most dehumanizing aspects of the oppression of Jews—and the most dangerous. For it is precisely this defenselessness that provokes and encourages attack. Jews will not riot and the goyim count on this. We do not know what would have happened had German Jews rioted against Hitler before or just when he came to power; but we do know the Nazis counted on the fact that they would not do so.[25]

Although here she clearly revived and reinforced the deeply problematic cliché of Jewish passivity in 1930s Germany in order to underscore her point, much of Zuckoff's analysis hinged on the chronic phobias of American Jewish existence.[26] She assaulted a Jewish "compulsion to achieve" as well as a Jewish craving for acceptance ("Jews are constantly looking to the goyim for approval; the main question always is 'what will the goyim say?' "). She labeled as repulsive all attempts by "assimilationist Jews" to "try to over-compensate for their differences" in the "hope that by doing this they will not only 'pass', but that the outer [assimilated] personality will become, by force of habit, the inner personality." And—in a manner not unlike Jonathan Braun's analysis in the *Flame* —she lambasted the Jewish community's "fantastic cultural and spiritual poverty (which drives its children to embrace Zen, astrology, drugs, left sectarianism, encounter groups, Scientology, psychoanalysis and so on)." The painful consequences of Jewish assimilation were everywhere in evidence, wrote Zuckoff. One had only to note how so many young Jews were "constantly falling in love with other peoples' countries, societies and struggles," and were going "beyond their goyish comrades in denouncing Israel or parroting a particular group's line (even if it's antisemitic) to say, in effect, " 'Look Ma (or Mao), I'm a radical.' " Finally, Zuckoff pleaded for American Jews to cease "internaliz[ing] the oppressors' hostility and mythology," and to stop denying the "Jewish gut feelings" of an authentic Jewishness:

> It is a tragedy that Jewish emotionalism and expressiveness, one of the really healthy and positive characteristics of our tradition, has been so put down that we are intimidated into repressing them, particularly among goyim—and embarrassed when a Jew is emotional. . . . Jews are kept powerless by being taught to feel guilty about being together. Brain-washed into believing that the warm feeling of concern Jews feel for each other is "chauvinistic" and that the freeness Jews experience only in each others' company is "racist," Jews will always try to refute that most terrible of all terrible accusations: Jews are "clannish." Never do they stop to think, hey what's so bad about being clannish?[27]

Zuckoff's summary statement encapsulated many of the key elements of the radical Zionist position in particularly stark terms. One of the most important contributions had to do with her willingness to raise matters involving communal and individual shame. Both through her historical analysis of Jews' vulnerable role as surrogates for the gentile elites' "dirty work" and through her emphasis on painful psychological problems, Zuckoff worked to make the otherwise invisible contours of Jewish oppression and self-oppression visible. Again, however, although she presented herself as a critic of the generation of her elders, there was also considerable overlap between her position and that of the critics of New Left Jews in such venues as *Commentary*. Indeed, it is not surprising that Robert Alter, in his 1971 *Commentary* essay debunking the Freedom Seder, approvingly cited radical Zionist Jews for their defenses of particularism and "clannishness" and praised radical Zionists for being among those few "young Jews for whom the generations to come will not have to blush."[28]

UP AGAINST THE WAILING WALL

Yet while previous incarnations of Jewish antiliberals had stressed the incommensurability of the African American and Jewish experiences and/or even (as Rubenstein did) articulated the notion that blacks would not be able to learn from Jews because of the psychological dysfunctionality pervasive in the black community, radical Zionists made quite a different claim. For them, it was Jews (and not only New Left Jews) whose psyches were horribly disfigured and blacks who showed the way to self-acceptance, self-renewal, and pride in group distinctiveness. Elaborating on this perspective sometimes involved taking a strong stand against black militancy or against those New Left Jews perceived to be subservient to it. But usually radical Zionists engaged in a kind of double move, which reflected some anger at blacks and more at New Left Jews but also borrowed heavily from Black Power motifs. Far from only contrasting black militancy with Jewish passivity, as Zuckoff had, increasing numbers of radical Zionists insisted that Jews could be as militant as blacks.

Early in 1969, for example, Jack Nusan Porter, then a graduate student at Northwestern University, pointed out that in the wake of the Six-Day War and the subsequent conversion of many Jewish New Leftists to the Israeli cause, the days of servility to the "blackman" were clearly over. This conversion was even more strongly evident in the departures from the New Left occasioned by the demand of the nationalist Black Caucus put forward at the National Conference for New Politics (held in Chicago three months after the Six-Day War). The caucus insisted that Israel be condemned for conducting an "imperialistic Zionist" war, and although the resolution included the qualifying rider that "this condemnation does not imply anti-Semitism," many Jewish participants walked out of the convention and renounced their New Leftism. Porter also analyzed the disgust of many New Left Jews at the overt antisemitism of some SNCC publications. Although warning that Jews should not confuse "anti-white for anti-Semitic sentiments" and calling for "dialogue" and "confrontation" with SNCC over its attacks both on Israel and American Jews, Porter concluded his essay with the summary observation that "the 'New Jew,' with new respect and pride, will not allow another Kristal Nacht."[29]

Along different but related lines, also in 1969, and emphasizing more the parallel possibilities for blacks and Jews, M. Jay Rosenberg, a student at the State University of New York at Albany, stated that radical Zionism condemned any Jew who remained in the New Left as behaving like "today's Uncle Tom." The New Left Jew, in Rosenberg's view, was someone who "scrapes along . . . ashamed of his identity," an "aspiring WASP." Using the common radical Zionist epithet for the Jewish equivalent of an "Uncle Tom"—"Uncle Jake"—but referring to members of his own generation rather than older Jewish establishment figures, Rosenberg elaborated upon his image of "our *Uncle Toms* (let's call them 'Uncle Jakes')":

> He joins black nationalist groups, not as a Jew but as a white man. . . . He does not understand that his relevance to the black struggle is as a Jew and a fellow victim of endless white exploitation. He can comprehend the black struggle but only in the context of his own. His involvement in these black nationalist organizations make him a living lie. Blacks don't need his white leadership and they don't want it. The sad fact is that the Jewish Tom is an inevitable product of American civilization. But it is time that he realize that he, not today's black, is the invisible man; he, like yesterday's Negro, wanders in a no man's land.

Rosenberg's essay summed up what he saw as the unavoidable choice facing him as a Jew and also as a radical:

> Black nationalism and Jewish nationalism will exist concurrently. To accept one you must accept the other. The black is America's Jew; a common fight must be waged. And yet when some black spokesman tells us we are poisoning his children's minds, when he calls us kikes, we must see him for what he is. Then he is just another goy using the Jew, the available and accepted victim, as scapegoat. That's the way it must be. We shall scrape for no one.
>
> And thus from this point on, I shall join no movement that does not accept and support my people's struggle. If I must choose between the Jewish cause and a "progressive" anti-Israel SDS, I shall choose the Jewish cause. If the barricades are erected, I will fight as a Jew.

Rosenberg too held back history's trump card to the end. He concluded with an impassioned assault—it verged on a threat—against those young Jews "who are so trapped in your Long Island split level childhood that you can't see straight": "In the aftermath of the crematoriums, you are flippant. After Auschwitz, you are embarrassed. Thirty years after the holocaust, you have learned nothing and forgotten everything. *Ghetto Jew*, you'd better do some fast thinking."[30]

Yet another twist on these various motifs came in Tsvi Bisk's essay, "Uncle Jake, Come Home!" published in May 1969 in the *Jewish Liberation Journal*'s founding issue. Bisk was, as the paper noted, "a young Philadelphian-born Jew who has settled in Israel." Bisk, like Zuckoff, saw a lot of psychological sickness in American Jewry and called for "a healthy solution." Like Kenan, he emphasized Israel's difference from "the West," stressing especially the "utopian" possibilities of the kibbutz and workers' cooperatives, and the contrast between them and the West's "massive urban concentrations [, which] have caused an alienation that is almost endemic." But calling for aliyah was not his only recommendation. Bisk considered "Black-Jewish relations in America" another matter of foremost concern for Jews, and his suggested remedy was for "the total disengagement of the Jewish and Black peoples." In terms oddly reminiscent of those used by Jews for Urban Justice, Bisk argued that some Jews' roles as slumlords or merchants in black communities were "a socio-political embarrassment to the Jewish people" and a "chronic source of public dishonor." But he also departed dramatically from JUJ aims when he called not just for "the ending of Jewish financial interests in the Black ghetto"—and especially "the ending of the employment of Black maids by Jewish housewives" (because "one cannot entertain a dignified relationship with another who is on his hands and knees scrubbing one's floor")—but also for "the removal of Jewish teachers and social workers from the Black ghetto" and "the ending of all Jewish contributions to the Black revolution."[31]

Unlike many ex-liberals such as Norman Podhoretz or Richard Rubenstein, then, Bisk was not only scathing in his indictment of "Jewish participation in civil rights" (which he believed was "caused as much by Jewish anxiety as by any objective loyalty to a greater social ethic") but eager as well "to purify Jewish society and make it a beacon of morality (a 'light to the Gentiles' if you will)." He too invoked Nazism; Bisk argued that if the Jewish community did not self-purify "we will have done to ourselves what all the Hitlers and Hamans couldn't do to us—we will have committed national suicide." But he found "fighting other peoples' battles" an inexcusable and indeed "degrading" exercise. Bisk saw the emergence of Black Power both as an inadvertently fortuitous development for Jews, and—in this way like Rosenberg—wished Jewish activists would model themselves on it. Particularly disdainful of the sort of Jew who "rejects vociferous Jewish pride in Jewish history and Jewish accomplishments . . . as manifestations of the Ghetto neurosis while, in the same breath, he defends the similar claims of the Black nationalists as a necessary purging of the collective inferiority complex of the Black after centuries of persecution (it never occurring to him that the same justification may be used in a Jewish context)," Bisk also suggested that "Black nationalism may have saved Jewish identity in the U.S. by removing the route of escape (participation in Black causes) from the radical Jew and by making ethnic identity once again fashionable in the U.S."[32]

...WARSAW
On April 19, 1943, the night
of the first Passover Seder, the
Warsaw Ghetto uprising began.
Resistance then.
Resistance Now.

FIGURE 6.3
" . . . Warsaw" appeared in *Hakahal* 1, no. 2 (March-April 1972). *Hakahal* was a publication of the Minnesota Jewish Student Services in Minneapolis.

Zuckoff, Porter, Rosenberg, and Bisk were not alone in turning both to Nazism and to the symbolism of black militancy as sources of moral outrage and inspiration; radical Zionists did so recurrently. Many of the illustrations in the radical Zionist press, in fact, merged elements of both reference points. Thus, for example, one illustration widely reproduced in 1971 and 1972 contained the image of a fist raised in protest under the single word "WARSAW." The text below the image read: "On April 19, 1943, the night of the first Passover Seder, the Warsaw Ghetto uprising began. Resistance then. Resistance Now." The point was clearly to tie a certain version of Holocaust consciousness to the need for Jewish resistance to oppression in the early 1970s present. Yet the fist was black and raised in the familiar Black Power salute. Meanwhile, the attached shackle and chain evoked slavery and thus—though presumably the slavery alluded to was Jewish slavery under Nazism—suggested another black-Jewish parallel (figure 6.3). In a related vein, the masthead of *Bagolah* (Hebrew for "in exile"), the newspaper published by the Jewish Student Press Collective in Skokie, Illinois, also included chains as well as the raised fist—albeit this time white—with the number

FIGURE 6.4 The masthead for *Bagolah* 1, no. 1 (1970), published by the Jewish Student Press Collective in Skokie, Illinois.

six million written across it (figure 6.4).Another adaptation of American black culture (or readaptation, one might say, of the biblical story of Moses) was evident in the frequent use of the slogan "Let My People Go" for the cause of Soviet Jewry. Sometimes the slogan stood on its own, as in the caption to a drawing of various Soviet Jews printed in the *People*, a Jewish student newspaper at the University of Oklahoma (figure 6.5). But in one case (printed in *Hayom*, the Philadephia Jewish student newspaper, in 1971) the words of the African American spiritual were actually rewritten to make the song relevant for the situation of Soviet Jewry, even as the image of the outstretched hand was evocative also of some Holocaust imagery (figure 6.6).[33] Finally, there was another image widely reprinted in the radical Jewish press, a photograph of a man in Orthodox clothing before the Wailing Wall in Jerusalem. Modifying the prevalent black militant phrase "up against the wall" (even as no other evident connection to blackness was being made), the caption informed the reader, "Thirty years ago his back was up against another kind of wall." Of course the wall from thirty years earlier would have been a Nazi-patrolled ghetto wall, and the clear implication was that any perspective one might wish to take on the situation in Israel needed to keep the fact of the Holocaust firmly, respectfully, and foremost in mind (figure 6.7).

FIGURE 6.5 "Let My People Go!" appeared in the *People* 1, no. 2 (September 27, 1971). The *People* was published by members of the University of Oklahoma Jewish Community.

FIGURE 6.6 "Let My People Go!" appeared in *Hayom* 1, no. 2 (May 1971).

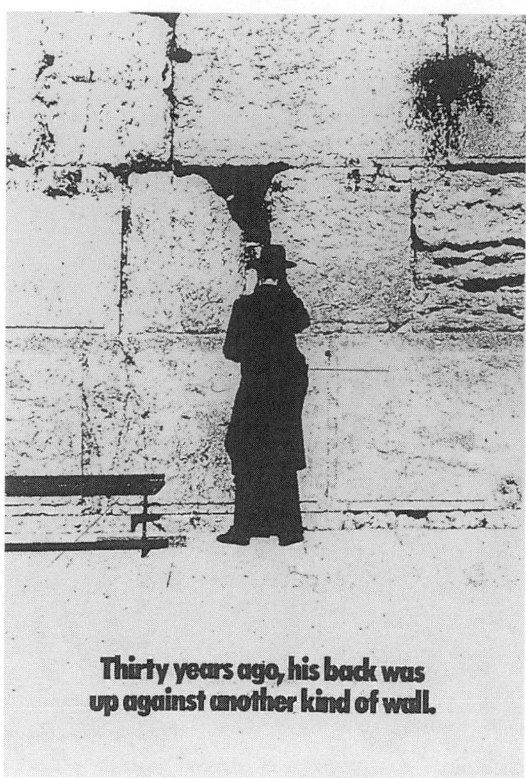

FIGURE. 6.7
"Thirty years ago, his back was up against another kind of wall" appeared in *Bagolah* 1, no. 1 (1970).

NO NUTS

Radical Zionist sentiments bringing references to the Holocaust and to black militancy together in creative ways found further visual expression in the work of illustrator Jerry Kirschen. Beginning in 1969, Kirschen produced cartoons for the *Jewish Liberation Journal*, though they appeared in virtually every other radical Jewish student newspaper in the U.S. as well, because of their syndication by the newly founded Jewish Student Press Service.[34] Like other radical Zionists, and developing his own spin on the "up against the wall" theme, Kirschen was disgusted with the Jewish liberal and leftist traditions of philanthropic giving and marching on behalf of others, and mercilessly skewered craven assimilationism. In "Up Against the Wall, Shmucks," Kirschen closely echoed the kind of threatening tone adopted also by M. Jay Rosenberg: "Comes the revolution and, we regret to inform you, there are a few of our 'brothers' that we'll have to learn to live without" (figure 6.8). In

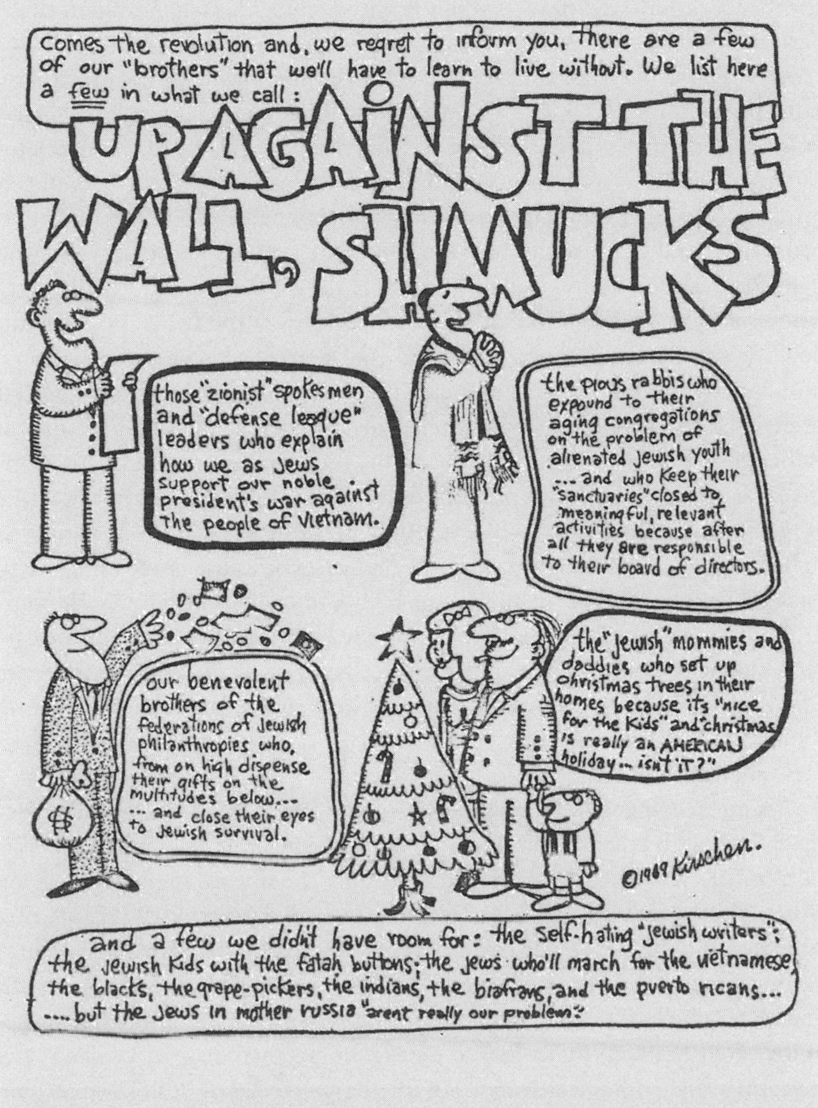

FIGURE 6.8 "Up Against the Wall, Shmucks" appeared in *Jewish Liberation Journal* no. 5 (November–December 1969). Courtesy of Yaakov Kirschen.

another cartoon, "and now . . . the Pig City Follies," Kirschen unflatteringly parodied several American Jewish types in a stream of doggerel verses. One verse, which came from the mouths of three little pigs with demonstration signs proclaiming, "U.S. Out of Asia Now," "Free the Panthers," and "Stop Pollution," read as follows: "We're the marching liberals / and we march for all the others / but we're much, too much too busy / for the causes of our brothers." Another verse cut even closer to the bone: "I'm a pompous, righteous leader and I look with sharp disdain at the activists for Soviet Jews who fight for freedom. Oh we looked away in Hitler's time and ignored the ones who cried. . . . Cause to march and shout and raise the fist is too undignified." It was surely also not incidental that Kirschen favored pig imagery, both because pork is not kosher meat and because of the black and New Left preference for denigrating policemen and those who upheld establishment values as "pigs." Significantly, however, the frame cartoon "Calling All Zionists" was cropped away by a number of the student newspapers in which the "Pig City Follies" appeared—one can only presume because it was perceived to be basically insulting toward radical Zionists who chose *not* to emigrate to Israel. The tension around aliyah ran high within the radical Zionist community; clearly Kirschen was here taking the hard line. For as the frame cartoon character put it, after asking rhetorically, "Will all the ZIONISTS please stand up?": "WRONG! Cause if your still here in Amerika . . . you aint no Zionist! . . . you're a shmuck."[35] (True to his convictions, Kirschen moved permanently to Israel in 1973.)

Also in keeping with the pig motif, "Uncle Jake's Fun Time Proudly Presents the Jewish Liberal Quiz," a cartoon from 1969, offered a standard radical Zionist view when it compared favorably the liberation struggle of the North Vietnamese with the situation of Israelis (while explicitly comparing Al Fatah, the militant Palestinian organization, with fascists). It also, once again, expounded on the similarities between an "Uncle Tom" and a "Jewish liberal": "Which of these gentlemen is aware that there are immediate causes that are more important than the needs of his own people? Which is the traitorous pig?" Identical bubbles with the single word "Oink" emerging from both men's mouths gave a big hint (figure 6.9).

In Kirschen's judgment there could be no such thing as too much commitment to Zionism. As such, and rather also in the spirit of Rosenberg's manifesto, Kirschen's cartoons exhibited a strong flavor both of machismo and "tough Jew" bravado, qualities already readily available in the male-dominated New Left, but now woven seamlessly together with a new post-1967 image of the avenging and militant Jewish man who was not inciden-

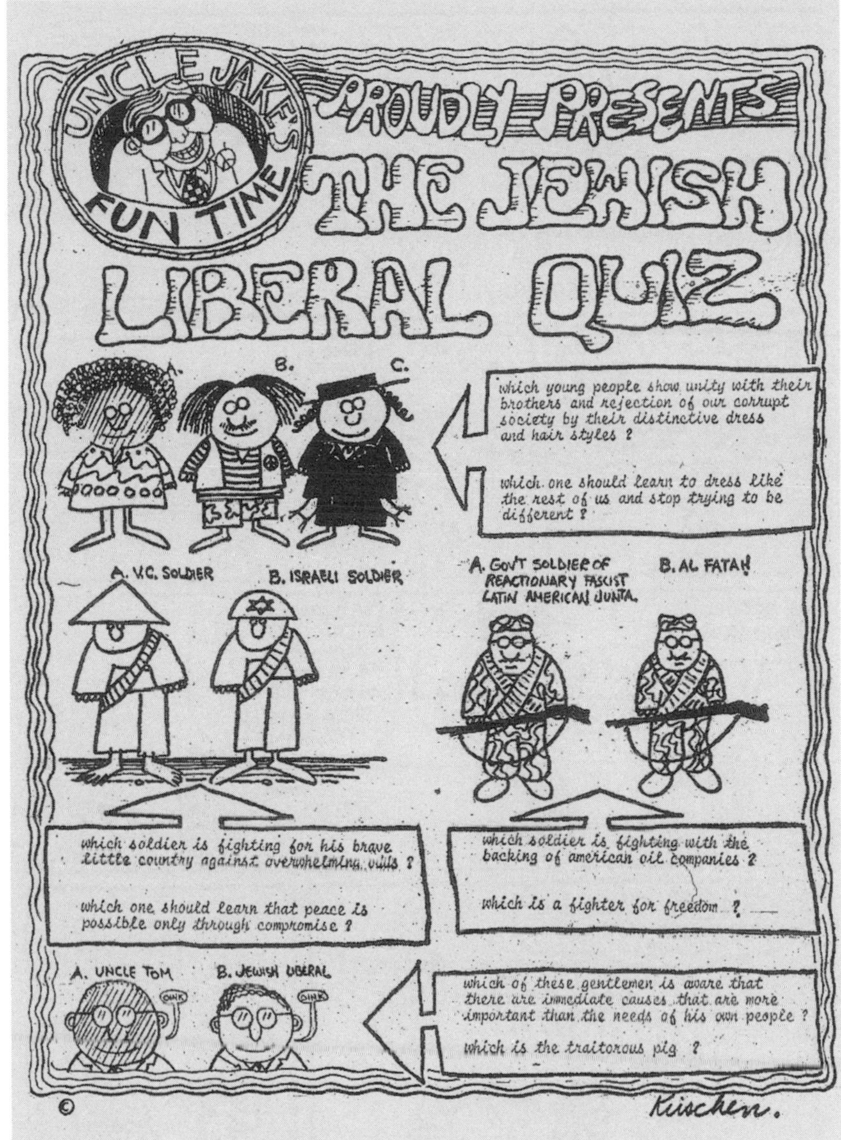

FIGURE 6.9 "Uncle Jake's Fun Time Proudly Presents the Jewish Liberal Quiz" appeared in *Hayom* 2, no. 2 (October 1971). Courtesy of Yaakov Kirschen.

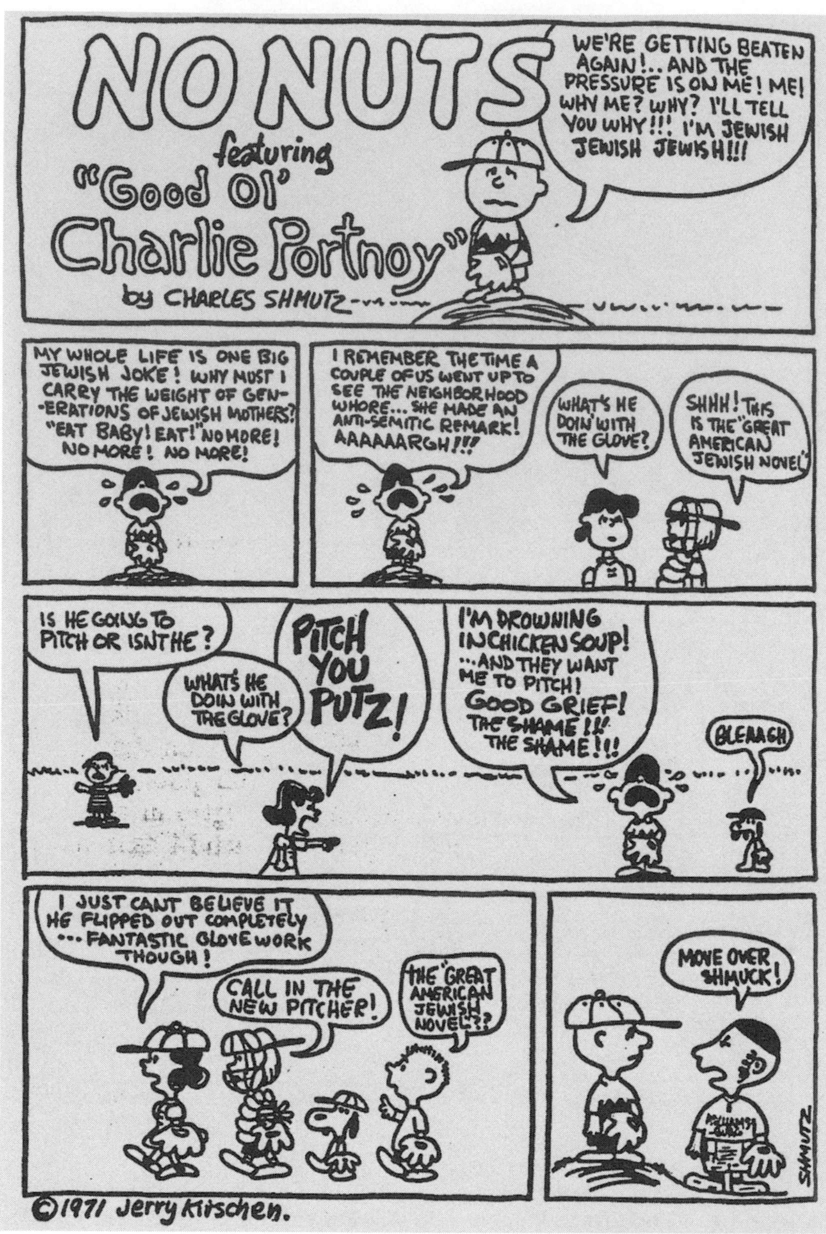

FIGURE 6.10 "No Nuts" (1971) appeared in *Jewish Radicalism*, edited by Jack Nusan Porter and Peter Dreier. Courtesy of Yaakov Kirschen.

FIGURE 6.11 "On the Problems Inherent in Making a Small Donation to a Revolutionary Cause" (1970) appeared in *Jewish Radicalism*, edited by Jack Nusan Porter and Peter Dreier. Courtesy of Yaakov Kirschen.

tally directly linked to Jewish Orthodoxy. It was a deliberately aggressive image, and a strongly self-conscious one, diametrically opposed to the neurotic, meek, and frail Jews who (in various guises) frequented the sixties work of filmmaker Woody Allen or novelist Philip Roth, among others.[36] In short, gone but not forgotten was the psychoanalytic wet dream of a schlemiel, Roth's Alexander Portnoy—a figure Kirschen savagely mocked in a classic piece from 1971 done in the style of "Peanuts," with Charlie Brown renamed Charlie Portnoy in a cartoon Kirschen entitled "No Nuts" (figure 6.10). Indeed, some of Kirschen's most effective and powerful work made unsubtle use of the emerging idea that any American Jewish man who was *not* a militant Zionist suffered either from psychological unwellness, sexual loserdom, hopeless self-effacement, or all of the above. It was, to say the least, a crude but provocative wake-up call for a new and headstrong movement in search of young recruits for the Zionist revolution.

In one especially memorable 1970 cartoon entitled "On the Problems Inherent in Making a Small Donation to a Revolutionary Cause," Kirschen imagined a dialogue between a proud and assertive black militant and a flip and unfunny Jewish New Leftist (figure 6.11). In many respects it served as a parable for a new generation of young radical Jews who sought to reconcile the historic legacy of Jewish support for black civil rights activism with the assertion of a distinctively Jewish struggle for ethnic identity. With the language of serious Holocaust consciousness brilliantly here put into the mouth of the black militant, Kirschen succinctly presented once again the analysis that New Left Jews were as lame as the jokes they told—both pathetic and self-hating. In short, Kirschen believed, as did many radical Zionists, that the New Left Jew could learn a lot from the black militant (if he would only listen) about the healthful symbiotic link necessary between one's ethnic consciousness and one's political identity. Kirschen's parable made clear how it was the self-aware and proud black who must finally be the one to spell out for the clueless and self-negating Jew that the urge to repress ethnic loyalties—or swap them for an emotional (or monetary) investment in blackness—constituted something shameful, even traitorous.

EVERY JEW A .22

Radical Zionist Jews often addressed the theme of shame as they contrasted their own post-Holocaust Jewish identity against either a New Left Jew, on the one hand, or an assimilated Jewish establishment member, on the other. Shame and shaming also operated as tactics in many actions taken by young radical Zionists in their protests against mainstream Jewish organizations. For instance, when Yossi Klein, editor in chief of the Brooklyn-based *Achdut*, joined nearly one hundred others to take over the offices of Hadassah, the Women's Zionist Organization of America, in April 1971, he did so to demonstrate against what Klein felt was Hadassah's lip service to the Zionist cause. Remarking on Hadassah's habitual indifference to the plight of Soviet Jews, Klein asked disparagingly, "How serious can Hadassah's efforts be if they have yet to appoint a full-time Soviet Jewry co-ordinator, when their administrative budget alone is one million dollars annually?" And of Hadassah's attempt to argue that its Zionism meant a sole focus on Israel, Klein bitterly asserted: "When adherence to Zionism is used as an excuse to negate one's responsibility to fellow Jews—Zionists, no less—then the very ideal of Zionism has been perverted." As Klein understood it, Hadassah's "do-nothing" hesitancy to direct money and time to save Soviet Jewish lives left a void only the Jewish Defense League (JDL) appeared courageously willing to fill. Klein wrote:

> The longer American Jewry procrastinates, the more enticing JDL becomes to me. I haven't joined JDL yet, because I honestly believe that the effect of massive peaceful protests exceeds the results of isolated acts of violence, which can be easily dismissed as the work of a "fringe element." Only the Jewish organizations can mount the offensive that they have time and again pledged themselves to. But if the organizations continue to stagnate, I will have no other choice.
>
> Then I shall be, as the Establishment contemptuously calls them, one of "Kahane's boys." And we will all know who is to blame.[37]

Klein's response to Hadassah was indicative; the pull to become one of "Kahane's boys" (and cease merely to be just a "Nice Irving," as Meir Kahane derisively labeled the stereotypically meek Jewish guy) became strong for many young radical Zionists.[38] For the Jewish Defense League was a group unashamed to act, and it did so precisely as a means to undo the image of the passive Jew. Interestingly, as several documents by radical Zionists suggest, much of what the JDL articulated was often difficult to distinguish from radical Zionist philosophies.

Like much radical Zionism, JDL philosophy placed the inability of American Jews to confront the legacy of the Holocaust at the core of what was wrong with the community. And also like much radical Zionist thinking, the JDL articulated that the spiritual sickness of American Jewish identity lay precisely in a reflexive inability to defend itself against aggression. Using language that would have been familiar to any young radical Jew, JDL writing emphasized both the need to love Jewishness and the connectedness of all Jewish people: "The pain of a Jew, wherever he may be, is our pain. The joy of a Jew, wherever he may be, is our joy." In a militant extension of, but also rebuke to, Aviva Zuckoff's analysis of Jewish passivity, the JDL turned the phrase "*it is not a Jewish tenet to turn the other cheek*" into a call to arms. Its early 1970s pamphlet, *The Jewish Defense League: Principles and Philosophies*, evoked images reminiscent of those put forward years earlier by Norman Podhoretz, but was far more explicit in a self-stated (at least rhetorical) urge also to inflict pain:

> The Jew, with his persistent image of weakness, unwillingness and inability to fight back is open to constant physical attacks on the part of non-Jews. A youngster wearing a skull cap and returning from a Yeshiva is fair game. Jews walking in a park or playing ball in a playground are open to attacks. Such things must be met in the one way that we have found to be the effective one—a feeling on the part of the attacker that he stands an excellent chance of being severely beaten himself. . . . The knowledge that Jews are no longer "patsies" will go a long way to eliminate the readiness of certain groups to feast on the Jew.[39]

In fact, so far as Kahane was concerned, the notion that Jews did not know how to defend themselves was an antisemitic stereotype that had little basis in Jewish history. It was a false image "as obscene as it is untrue," and yet "it persists and it must be answered. The true story must be told."[40] It was this story of authentic Jewish values mandating that Jews militantly defend themselves that Kahane said he intended to resuscitate after a near-death experience in "the snake pits of assimilation and alienation."[41] As Kahane put it in 1968 in "A Small Voice," the regular column he contributed to the *Jewish Press*, a Brooklyn-based Orthodox newspaper:

> Vandals attack a Yeshiva—let that Yeshiva attack the vandals. Should a gang bloody a Jew, let a Jewish group go looking for the gang. This is the way of pride—not evil pride, but the pride of nation, of kinship. . . . There are those who will protest: This is not the Jewish way. And yet since when has it been a Mitzvah to be punished and beaten? Since when is it a Kiddush HaShem (Sanctification of G-d) to be spat upon and smeared with vegetables? It is not a Kiddush HaShem, it is quite the opposite. It is a disgrace to the pride of our people, our G-d.[42]

Begun officially by Meir Kahane and two close friends in May 1968 on a Sabbath afternoon in a Brooklyn synagogue, the Jewish Defense League was conceived initially (like other Jewish radical groups of its day) as a necessary grassroots alternative to a Jewish establishment insensitive to Jewish communal needs. Kahane was an Orthodox rabbi and associate editor of the *Jewish Press*. For Kahane, along with Bertram Zweibon and Morty Dolinsky, who had first met at a militant Zionist summer camp several years earlier, this meant primarily taking steps to counter antisemitic violence directed at their working-class Brooklyn Jewish community. It was far from Kahane's first political venture—he had been active (some believed too active) for years—and in 1967 the *Jewish Press* ran an ad urging readers to contact Kahane so they could join the National Liberation Front for Soviet Jewry under the words "Fellow Jews! Stand Up & Fight NOW! Your brother's blood calls out to you from the Soviet land. . . . THE TIME HAS COME FOR ACTION. Will you join the fight? We can, we must, we will free our Russian brethren!"[43]

The new organization, initially known as the Jewish Defense Corps, adopted more explicit tactics. "JEWISH SURVIVAL!" ran a large banner headline for an early Jewish Defense Corps ad in a July 1968 edition of the *Jewish Press*. The ad continued:

* Anti-Semitism is exploding in the United States.
* Revolutionary leftist groups—hostile to Israel and Jewishness—are capturing young people's minds and destroying law and order.
* Right wing extremism is growing at an alarming rate.
* Anti-Semitic Black racists are battling for control of cities.
* America is being divided and the democratic fabric ripped apart.
* Your child or loved one is a target.

"ARE YOU WILLING TO STAND UP FOR DEMOCRACY AND JEWISH SURVIVAL?" the ad rhetorically demanded.[44] Attached was a coupon with a box number that requested a ten-dollar donation for membership. At the same time, front-page *Jewish Press* articles by Kahane (some ghostwritten) profiled deepening threats to Jewish communal survival.[45] Kahane's tactics were consistently inflammatory. For instance, before the September 1968 strikes by the—largely Jewish—New York City teachers' union over school decentralization and community control, a June 1968 *Jewish Press* headline read: "Racist Leaflets in N.Y. Schools Warn White Teachers to Leave." The article by Kahane informed readers that "New York schools throughout the city have been flooded with blatantly anti-Semitic leaflets. The leaflets, once again, betray signs of Arab financial support." The article conspiratorially continued: "Despite the fact that the leaflets appeared throughout the city, none of the New York newspapers carried anything about them. The JEWISH PRESS received the information from the Jewish Defense Corps and private sources."[46] As historian Shlomo Russ has noted: "In this manner, Kahane fully exploited his position in the paper, advocating and justifying JDL's actions."[47] The synergy between advertisement and news item got the message out especially effectively. And that message was, as one early member of the group summarized it, "Jews have to stick together to protect themselves."[48]

In its early days the Jewish Defense League also found influential Orthodox supporters willing to assist with fund raising. Rabbi Emanuel Rackman, then Provost of Yeshiva University, brought JDL speakers to Yeshiva University, and introduced Kahane to wealthy members of the Fifth Avenue Synagogue, where Rackman served as rabbi. As Shlomo Russ has written, this friendship proved a major financial boon for Kahane:

> Kahane had his first successful parlor meeting at the home of one of Rackman's members. "Through it he got money in the tens of thousands from sympathetic people," Rackman said. "He must have raised $50,000 or more." Alfred Joffe and Joseph Gruss, who heads his own investment company on Broad Street, were among those introduced to Kahane by Rackman and they contributed to the League. "Gruss's contributions were a kind of insurance money," Rackman recalled. "He said that if his grandchildren wouldn't be Jewish at least he would be causing others to have Jewish grandchildren."[49]

With both blunt language and paramilitary tactics, the JDL quickly gained national notoriety. One especially prominent confrontation began when former SNCC leader James Forman attracted considerable media attention in May 1969 after he interrupted a service at New York's Riverside Church to present what he called a Black Manifesto. In this manifesto Forman demanded that the white Christian churches pay black Americans a half billion dollars as reparations for their role in perpetuating centuries of African American exploitation. It was, to be sure, a shocking demand, and one that Forman proceeded to make that month at several other churches in the New York area.[50] He then announced he would also deliver his demand for "reparations" at Temple Emanu-El during its Friday night service. The Jewish Defense League countered that if Forman attempted to set foot in the temple,

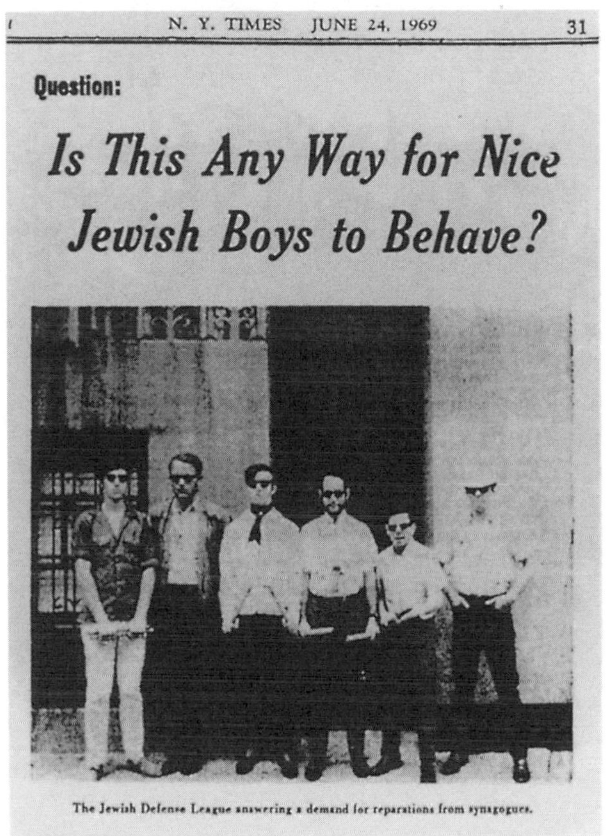

N. Y. TIMES JUNE 24, 1969 31

Question:

Is This Any Way for Nice Jewish Boys to Behave?

The Jewish Defense League answering a demand for reparations from synagogues.

FIGURE 6.12 "Is This Any Way for Nice Jewish Boys to Behave?" appeared initially as an advertisement in the *New York Times*. It was also reprinted and distributed by the Jewish Defense League as part of a publicity packet.

they would "break both his arms and legs." As it happens, forty JDL members carrying bicycle chains, baseball bats, and lead pipes congregated in front of Temple Emanu-El on the appointed Friday evening; they were met by numerous members of the press—Forman himself was a no-show. (Notably Rabbi Nathan A. Perilman, who conducted the Friday service, deplored the JDL's unsolicited invitation to "defend" his temple, and said that Forman would have been permitted to read his demands once the worship ended.)[51] Soon after the JDL demonstration and the extensive media coverage it received, a photograph of JDL men wielding their lead pipes outside the temple

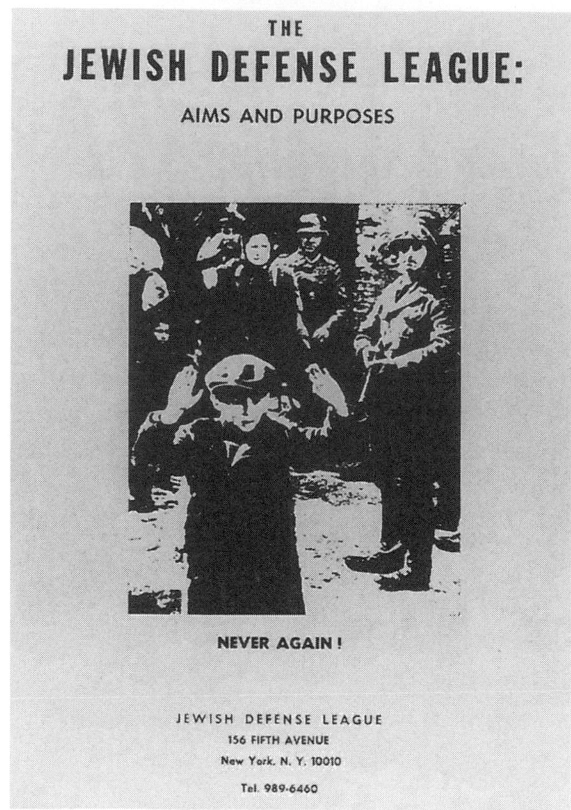

FIGURE 6.13 "Never Again!" was the cover for a Jewish Defense League pamphlet distributed in the early 1970s.

became the centerpiece for what was possibly the Jewish Defense League's most controversial recruitment tool: a large *New York Times* advertisement that appeared in June 1969 (figure 6.12). The ad's caption asked, "Is This Any Way for Nice Jewish Boys to Behave?" The answer was provided:

> Maybe. Maybe there are times when there is no other way to get across to the extremist that the Jew is not quite the patsy some think he is.
>
> Maybe there is only one way to get across a clear response to people who threaten seizure of synagogues and extortion of money. Maybe nice Jewish boys do not always get through to people who threaten to carry teachers out in pine boxes and to burn down merchants' stores.
>
> Maybe some people and organizations are too nice. Maybe in times of crisis Jewish boys should not be that nice. Maybe—just maybe—nice people build their road to Auschwitz.[52]

Juxtaposing the presumed rampant antisemitism of African Americans with a macho Holocaust consciousness became the major mode in JDL discourse. Liberal Jewish leaders who attempted to denounce JDL tactics as inflammatory and racist, and worked to turn back JDL "tough guy" invocations of the Holocaust with a morally indignant rhetoric of their own, often found themselves the object of considerable counterattack from within the Jewish community. For instance, when Rabbi Maurice N. Eisendrath, president of the Union of American Hebrew Congregations, stated publicly in response to the Forman incident that the JDL demonstration was "no less offensive and, in essence, no different from whites carrying robes and hoods . . . standing in front of burning crosses," he afterward "received the largest volume of hate mail from Jews he had ever experienced in a long and controversial career." It began to appear as if Kahane's argument that "men like James Forman . . . unfortunately understood the language of bats and chains far more clearly than sermons by Rabbi Eisendrath" had struck a strong populist Jewish chord.[53]

"Never Again" was the JDL's most memorable rallying cry, a slogan that rapidly achieved tremendous emotional and political resonance throughout the American Jewish community in the final years of the sixties and the early seventies (figure 6.13). Here (one more time) was a radically reinterpreted lesson of the Holocaust for the American Jewish community—and (one more time) one articulated in complex relationship to African American activism. Along with the slogan "Never Again," the JDL promoted a siege mentality to go with its call for Jewish paramilitary training. It advocated that all Jews learn martial arts like karate and judo and that all Jewish children enroll in rifle associations. Indeed, in the late summer of 1971, the JDL would launch the "Every Jew a .22 Campaign" which involved the distribution of a .22 caliber rifle to any Jew who requested one (for only a nominal fee). Announcements for the campaign promised: "You will receive a rifle, ammunition, siddur [the volume containing the daily prayers], yarmulka, and 'Every Jew a .22' button."[54] The sole way to win respect, Kahane argued over and over, was to show a willingness *and* an ability to fight for it. In a 1971 radio address, Kahane explained the philosophy of "Never Again" with these words:

> Never again means that we have had it in the concept of being beaten and not hitting back. No one will respect us, and no one will in the end love us, if we don't respect ourselves. . . . I have often said that when I've had contact with anti-Semitic groups—that it's got to be man to man. If it's not man to man,

> if you're not willing to have it on a man to man basis, then it again will be pig to pig, but never again will it be man to pig with us the pig.[55]

Here was a message of Jewish pride fully conscious of its debt—however paradoxical it might have sounded—to the Black Pride model promoted by the Black Panther Party. Nor were JDL members bothered by the seeming ideological contradictions in their appropriation of the black militant style. To the contrary, as one JDL woman said, explaining why she no longer straightened her naturally curly hair: "I used to straighten it because it seemed animal-like, but now it's a question of Jewish identity not to . . . that happened to blacks when they got their movement." Along similar lines, another JDL member, drawing both on the example of black militancy and the memories of Nazism, described his own commitment to the militant Zionist movement this way:

> The government, made up of WASPS, is willing to throw Jews to the dogs to save themselves. The Jew must make an intense militant effort just like the blacks did, or he'll be pushed out like in Europe in the 20s and 30s. Life will become impossible for Jews—politically, socially, and eventually physically.[56]

Such analogies to black consciousness, spun in a newly Jewish militant direction, intensified the JDL's popular appeal, as it quickly enlisted an estimated six thousand young Jews during the spring and summer of 1969 and made efforts to organize a national membership as well. Nor can this number properly begin to count those American Jews who found the rhetoric of the Jewish Defense League inspiring, even while they may have hesitated to support its willingness to provoke racial conflict or its vigilantism.

Thus, although in varying degrees, to be sure, the (religious and overtly right-wing) JDL and the (often more secular and certainly more politically eclectic) radical Zionist youth movement nonetheless found themselves on the same side of several emotionally charged issues related to "Jewish self-interest." They both demonstrated on behalf of Soviet Jewry, and often also protested anti-Israel demonstrations together with their own counter-demonstrations. They both ridiculed and condemned Jews in the New Left for their support of black militancy and described the Jewish New Left's anti-Zionism as little more than thinly disguised self-hatred and internalized antisemitism. And they both made clear their disdain for an ineffectual Jewish liberal establishment whose typical member, as Rabbi Kahane repeatedly liked to say, "almost always comes from . . . Scarsdale or some other rich suburb," adding apocalyptically that Jewish liberal complacency "could mean destruction for the country and the Jews."[57] On the other hand, neither movement was above making requests for financial support from those same Jewish liberals; in 1969, for example, the JDL demanded one hundred thousand dollars from Jewish organizations so it could build a stronger paramilitary operation—a request promptly labeled "chutzpah" and denied.[58] Radical Zionists, through their sit-ins at the Federation of Jewish Philanthropies and elsewhere, made similar financial demands.

It is therefore not surprising that Rabbi Kahane successfully courted students in the radical Zionist movement. In a widely distributed 1971 interview with Zvi Lowenthal and Jonathan Braun for the *Flame* of City College, Kahane observed how he felt "very close in many ways to the Radical Zionist Alliance and to the Jewish Liberation Project," and noted that he admired the "sincerity" of these groups.[59] For their part, important voices within the radical Zionist movement responded often by staunchly backing the JDL, even as they downplayed (or ignored entirely) Kahane's white racism, rabid anticommunism, and unconditional support for President Nixon's military policy in Vietnam. For example, Jonathan Goldin, a member of the Radical Jewish Union in Boston, in early 1970 wrote with evident pleasure that "the spreading of the Jewish Defense League, which has chapters in almost every large American city" represented "a substantial and growing mobilization of the Jewish community. It's about time!" It should no longer be possible, Goldin added, for any antisemitic group or nation "to make us invisible, just as Ralph Ellison pointed out white society was trying to do to black people."[60] Likewise, echoing Kahane's own words, Steven Gurner, a student at Northwestern University, speculated in early 1971 that had "more of the Jews of Europe been willing to defend themselves, millions might not be lying in the unmarked graves of Buchenwald, Bergen-Belsen, and Auschwitz." In pure tough-Jew fashion, Gurner noted that it "must always be with great regret that one is forced to take a human life, but it is a greater sin to submit willingly to murder than to kill in self-defense."[61] And Jack Nusan Porter, who had emerged as a key figure in the Jewish student activist movement, acknowledged in 1971 that he too had participated in a JDL-sponsored stinkbomb attack on the Omsk Siberian Dancers' show in Chicago. Porter also published an "open letter" in a publication of the North American Jewish Students' Network urging Jewish radicals to join forces with their "Jewish brothers and sisters of the JDL." Even after Porter recanted his JDL affiliation, he added almost wistfully: "I only wish that a group was around that dove-tailed left-wing ideology and militant activism."[62]

Despite their at times overlapping ideological positions—or perhaps because of them—more than a few radical Zionists also expressed distress at JDL ideology. Reasons for this disaffection with the JDL were numerous. For Steve Cohen, a graduate student at Harvard University, JDL ideology was misguided because it "sets the focus on what 'they' are doing to us rather than on what we might do to transform ourselves." Cohen felt that this error in thinking was glaringly apparent in the group's appropriation of the Holocaust for a political message summarized by the slogan "Never Again." So far as Cohen was concerned, "Never Again" was "a reminder that everything in Jewish experience is compared by the JDL to the holocaust," which made of "the six million a political pawn in every controversy." Cohen asked, "What can one say except to recognize this view as obscenity?"[63] Meanwhile, a rather different critique came from a Radical Zionist Alliance member who said during a pro-Israel demonstration in 1971: "Those anti-Israel people just don't understand. They don't understand. . . . But what I don't understand is how did we get to be on the same side of the street as the JDL. They're just like the Black Panthers."[64]

Many radical Zionists who opposed the JDL pointed out its reactionary support (in the name of Israeli security) for the Vietnam War, while they also denounced the JDL for "its abuse of power as a tactic" and its "persecution of other peoples as a goal."[65] In this way, and again uncomfortably for some, such criticisms from radical Jews mirrored much of the hostile reception given the JDL by the same establishment Jewish organizations these radicals also opposed; for instance, the National Jewish Community Relations Advisory Council, which represented almost a hundred local and national communal agencies and groups, had similarly condemned the JDL "as destructive of public order and contributory to divisiveness and terror."[66] Rather uneasily, this was not a simple matter where the enemy of an enemy became a friend. According to a *Newsweek* poll conducted in early 1971, one out of every four American Jews voiced either complete or qualified approval for JDL activities; support was higher among less affluent Jews.[67] At around the same time, an unpublished study conducted by the American Jewish Congress of its members found that more than one in three supported JDL tactics.[68] It would appear that the radical Zionist movement as well remained divided over how to respond to the emotional anti-elitist appeal of the JDL.

While he did not tag his analysis as designed "for Jewish men only" (and a small contingent of Jewish women did also learn karate alongside JDL men in the group's boot-camp style training grounds), when Kahane spoke and wrote about revitalizing Jewish pride—something he did on a nearly obsessive basis—what he above all meant was pride in being *a Jewish man.* "The JDL was the id of American Jewish men," Aviva Cantor (formerly Zuckoff) would pithily observe many years afterward.[69] In a manner of speaking, the allure represented by the JDL went still further than that. As facetious and odd as this might sound, the JDL might actually be best understood as the original Jewish men's group—organized around a therapeutic model that encouraged Jewish men and boys to let go of their insecurities and their hang-ups and get in closer touch with their feelings *as men.* Although it has not been much discussed in subsequent years, Kahane was a genuine master at exploiting these latent anxieties about the grassroots content of American Jewish masculinity.

ISRAEL ÜBER ALLES

Keeping the populist appeal of the JDL and its fetishistic infatuation with militarism in mind may make the highly irreverent expressions of some anti-Zionist Jewish radicals more comprehensible. For while nearly every radical Jew shared a wholesale distrust of liberal Jewish politics and established Jewish organizations, not all concluded that radical Zionism was the answer. At the opposite far end of the spectrum, at least in Zionist terms, might have been Paul Krassner's loopy San Francisco-based periodical, the *Realist*, an anarchistic—if distinctly Jewish—stepchild of a Beat Generation personified best by abrasive stand-up comedian Lenny Bruce. For instance, never at a loss for words (or images), the *Realist* dared to run a cartoon in the immediate wake of the Six-Day War that openly ridiculed Zionist triumphalism. The cartoon pictured a parade of Orthodox Jews marching through a Bavarian village. They carried two placards: the first had a Star of David; the second read "Israel Über Alles" (figure 6.14). Another cartoon in the *Realist*, however, targeted assimilationism—but it did so also by tweaking the sensibilities of those who treated allusions to Nazism and the Holocaust reverentially. "You don't have to be Jewish to enjoy Levy's real Jewish rye" was an advertising blockbuster in the late sixties—various members of different ethnic groups (blacks, Italians, Irish, etc.) would be pictured eating rye bread with this slogan as a caption (figure 6.15). Yet the *Realist* had a more thoughtful message of its own, which anyone at the time would have been able to decode. What the *Realist* was satirizing here was not only (though also) consumer capitalism and a pandering oh-so-eager-to-please sell-out kind of Jewishness. The cartoon very specifically was taking a stab at the hypocrisy of the Jewish executives at Doyle Dane Bernbach (the premier advertising agency in the country) responsible for creating the Levy's ad campaign. For it was well-known in the sixties that DDB founder Bill Bernbach had also developed what was perhaps the most famous and successful ad campaign of the decade—turning Germany's Volkswagen beetle into the countercultural "love bug." That the Volkswagen had been the quintessential "Nazi car" was no secret; the company had profited greatly under Nazism through its use of slave labor.[70]

In a similar spirit as Krassner's, Yippie leaders Abbie Hoffman and Jerry Rubin promulgated a radical Jewish political style with a heavy emphasis on guerrilla theater. For instance, at their conspiracy trial in Chicago, Hoffman in particular found ample opportunity to ridicule and insult the Jewish judge, whose name happened also to be Hoffman. "Your name is synonymous with Adolf Hitler in the world today!" Abbie Hoffman shouted at Judge Julius Hoffman. Abbie Hoffmann also loudly charged that the trial represented a *shande fur de goyim* (or an embarrassment of Jews before the gentiles). As the Boston-area Jewish community newspaper *Genesis 2* satirized the intergenerational encounter, "Hoffman-Hoffman: Who is a Jew?" (figure 6.16). Meanwhile, co-defendant Rubin liked to provoke other Jews by announcing: "If Moses were alive today, he'd be an Arab guerrilla."[71]

Anti-Zionist radical Jews frequently noted that American Jewishness suffered from a close association with right-wing Zionism. Many of these commentators were far more earnest than Krassner, Hoffman, or Rubin. For instance, Ed Richer, a commentator for the *Los Angeles Free Press*, acknowledged in 1970 that while "global anti-Semitism for the past 2,000 years" had "apparently coerced many Jews into habitual identification with accomplished seats of power, as against emerging, decolonizing areas," this represented a terribly unfortunate interpretation of history's lessons. Richer also found that as a result of "a preference that is marked with racist zealotry and panic," Zionism had "become increasingly rightist, rigid, and racist as it becomes increasingly a client of American Empire." Richer observed warily: "Those of us in America with Jewish personal histories must do everything in our power to create a leftwing vision for the post-American Jewish citizen of the world, a vision that might prevent Israel from becoming another Vietnam."[72]

Along related lines, a self-described "nice Jewish girl" (who turned out to be JUJ member Sharon Rose) wrote anonymously in 1970, in the alternative Atlanta paper the *Great Speckled Bird*, how a visit to Israel as a teenager several years earlier to live on a kibbutz had sealed her fate as an anti-Zionist. Whereas she remembered she had "dug the whole scene" at the kibbutz, she also found herself asking "embarrassing questions": "Why are all the dock

FIGURE 6.14 "Israel Über Alles" appeared appeared in the *Realist* 75 (June 1967). Courtesy of the Labadie Collection, the University of Michigan.

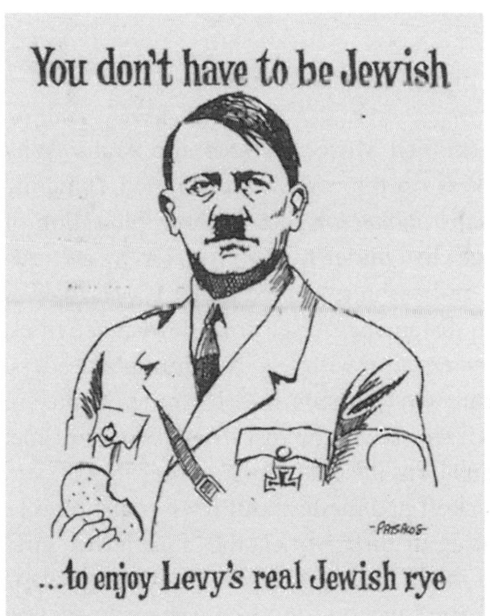

FIG. 6.15
"You don't have to be Jewish . . . " appeared in the *Realist* 86 (February 1969). Courtesy of the Labadie Collection, the University of Michigan.

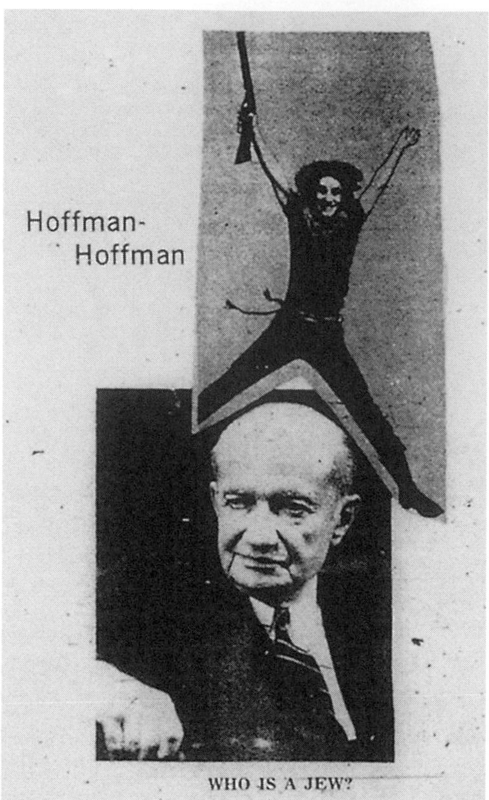

FIGURE 6.16
"Hoffman-Hoffman: Who Is a Jew?" appeared in *Genesis 2*, March 20, 1970.

workers and other laborers dark-skinned Moroccan Jews and Arabs? Why are all the ditch-diggers and workers on the roads dark-skinned Yemenite Jews and Arabs? Why do the socialist *kibbutzim* join in the exploitation of this labor? Why do the Arab villages live under military rule? Why are crucial civil rights denied Palestinian Arabs who remained under Israeli rule?"[73]

Returning to the U.S., far from distancing herself from Jewish activities, she over and over again sought conversation with Jewish communal leaders. She tried to explain to them "about why so many Jewish young people are rejecting a brand of religion that is irrelevant to the real struggles of our time, and what the community might do about it." And among other things (and similar to the arguments Aviva Zuckoff had made about Jews' tragic roles as "surrogate of the ruling elite in doing its dirty work") the "nice Jewish girl" tried to talk about what she called the " 'Jewish rung' on the economic ladder that is the Amerikan system." She suggested (and here she echoed Tsvi

Bisk) that the Jewish community could assist not only others but also itself if it were to "help Jewish merchants get out of Black ghettoes, and to see to it that there are no Jewish slumlords and segregationists"—because "as long as that ladder exists, those who oppress the people on the rungs below them will be equally oppressed by those on the rungs above them." Remarkably, moreover, and despite these perspectives on American domestic politics, "a dialogue of sorts, strained and tenuous as it may be, is often established." But then there would always come that "inevitable moment when someone in the room asks: 'And what is your position on Israel?' "[74]

The "nice Jewish girl" tried to explain what was problematic about the question.

> Now that question is a trap, because the person who asks it recognizes only two possible positions: the position he or she attributes (equally) to *El Fat'h* and all the Arab states (namely, that "all the Jews will be pushed into the sea"), and the position he or she views as the only "Jewish" position (namely, the rigid, militaristic, morally and tactically indefensible stance of the present Israeli regime).
>
> The very inevitability of that question and the fact that it admits of only two responses lie at the heart of what is wrong with our system. A rich cultural heritage based on a prophetic religious tradition has been largely forfeited to the Amerikan melting pot, to be replaced by an uneasy, guilt-ridden quasi-loyalty to a foreign state. It is a blind loyalty—one which forces Amerikan "Zionists" into the absurd positions of favoring disestablishmentarian religious liberty here, while defending the existence of a theocracy in the Middle East, of attesting to the survival of the Jewish people through two millenia of "dispersion" from their homeland, while denying the existence and rights of the Palestinian people after their twenty-five years or less as refugees.

And she further asked:

> From what does this uncritical loyalty of "Zionists" in Amerika stem? (I put the word in quotes to indicate that the people to whom I refer actually have no serious desire or intention to emigrate to Israel.) When pushed, most of the same people admit that their "Zionism" is based on a real fear that Amerika could produce another wave of anti-Semitism from which they could take refuge in the Jewish state. That this fear is real, however, is no reason to allow it to go unchallenged. For the "refuge" theory is a dangerous self-delusion.

> The Amerikan system does show every sign of becoming expert at genocide. Unless we stop it now, there will no piece of real estate far enough away, no cave deep enough in the earth, to protect any of us. Organizing to help stop that genocide requires that we ally ourselves with brothers and sisters in the Black community who are organizing to prevent a race war in this country, and against whom the repression has already begun to be unleashed. Let us criticize them whenever they attempt to use anti-Semitism as a tool for organizing, but let us not allow *that* to put us in the position of defending unequivocally the foreign policy of any government.[75]

In short, as these excerpts indicate, it *was* imaginable to refuse the dichotomous options generally available at the turn from the 1960s to the 1970s. It was possible—if just barely—to question the equations being made between fidelity to Judaism and loyalty to a particular type of Zionism, and to elaborate a vision of possible—even necessary—ongoing cooperation with black activists without masochism or self-hatred.

WE WILL NOT BE FORCED TO CHOOSE

One further example of a non-Zionist revolutionary Jewish approach existed around the collective known as Brooklyn Bridge, which published several issues of an eponymous newspaper in 1971–72 (figure 6.17). *Brooklyn Bridge* too pursued a form of radical activism whose aims it considered as much an expression of "Jewishly" concerns as those advanced by the radical Zionist movement. Striking out against "the assimilationist mentality of Amerika," which has "robbed us of our past, and substituted a collection of false myths and stereotypes that have cut deeply into our self respect" and resulted in "intense self hatred," *Brooklyn Bridge* evolved an analysis that, on one level, echoed the explicitly Zionist-identified *Jewish Liberation Journal*. "We are pawns," *Brooklyn Bridge* declaimed, "perfectly poised to absorb the rage of the ghetto's colonized minorities, and the contempt of the powerful above us." Additionally, and also like much radical Zionist rhetoric, the Brooklyn Bridge Collective identified Jews as a minority people whose "ethnic origin, culture, language, and religious tradition stem from the Middle East."[76] Here, however, common cause with radical Zionism abruptly ended.

Indeed, *Brooklyn Bridge* took the opportunity to accuse radical Zionist groups of attacking Jewish organizations (like the Federation of Jewish Philanthropies) just to guilt them into providing financial support. According to *Brooklyn Bridge*, this tactic was crude hypocrisy:

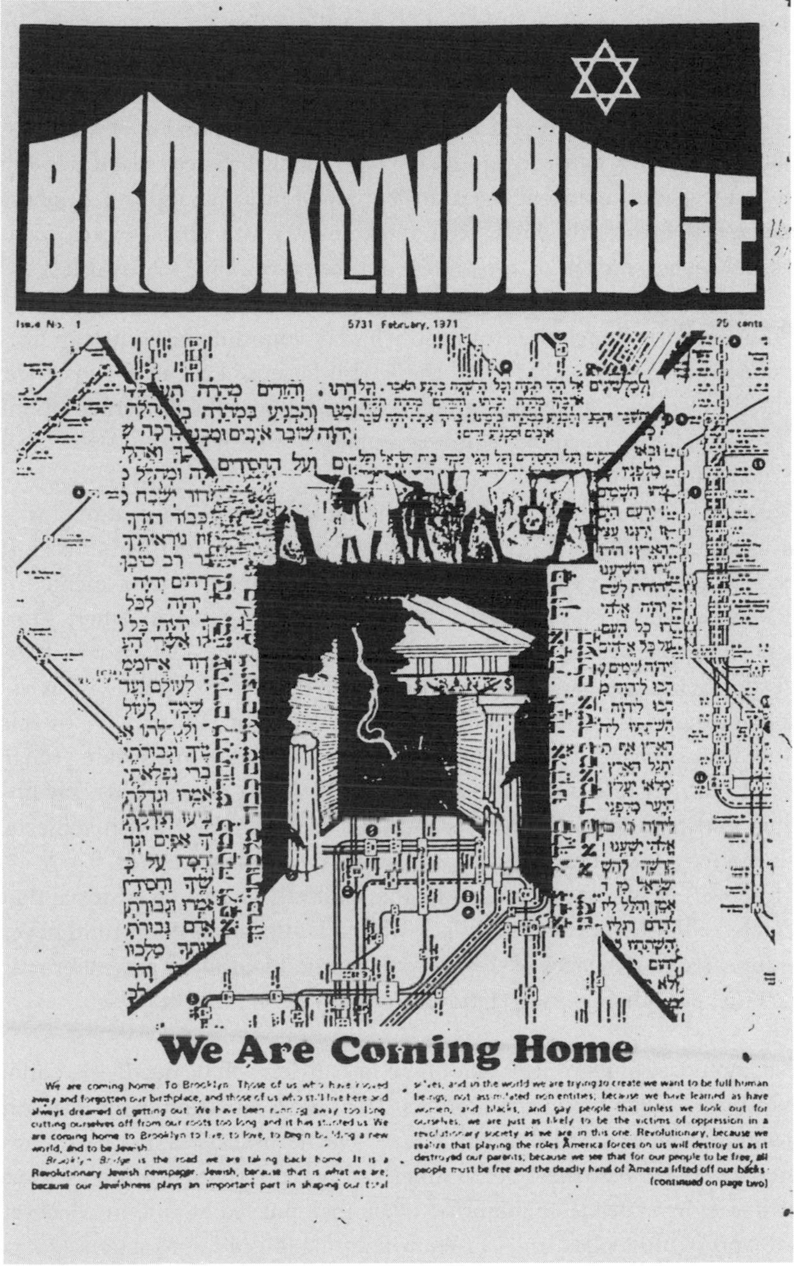

BROOKLYN BRIDGE

Issue No. 1 | 5731 February, 1971 | 25 cents

We Are Coming Home

We are coming home. To Brooklyn. Those of us who have moved away and forgotten our birthplace, and those of us who still live here and always dreamed of getting out. We have been running away too long, cutting ourselves off from our roots too long, and it has stunted us. We are coming home to Brooklyn to live, to love, to begin building a new world, and to be Jewish.

Brooklyn Bridge is the road we are taking back home. It is a Revolutionary Jewish newspaper. Jewish, because that is what we are, because our Jewishness plays an important part in shaping our total selves, and in the world we are trying to create we want to be full human beings, not assimilated non entities; because we have learned as have women, and blacks, and gay people that unless we look out for ourselves, we are just as likely to be the victims of oppression in a revolutionary society as we are in this one. Revolutionary, because we realize that playing the roles America forces on us will destroy us as it destroyed our parents; because we see that for our people to be free, all people must be free and the deadly hand of America lifted off our backs

(continued on page two)

FIGURE 6.17 "We Are Coming Home" was the cover for *Brooklyn Bridge* 1, no. 1 (February 1971).

> It is not possible to ride two horses at the same time. That is a stunt worthy only of a circus. The people running these organizations are not fools. They don't *give* away money and they don't allow themselves to be ripped-off. They are always trying to co-opt any critical Jewish voice that arises. And if they can't co-opt that voice they either try to shut it off, or, failing that, deny that it is Jewish or that it speaks for anyone but a small group of malcontents. And they have managed to provide the young Jews of this country with a hand-picked "radical" leadership who are all, consciously or otherwise, willing to play ball.[77]

Nor did *Brooklyn Bridge* shy from intra-Jewish communal critiques, pointedly denouncing Meir Kahane and the Jewish Defense League, for instance, for their "misguided analysis," which, "while supposedly concerned about the Jewish plight, is in actuality assimilating the Jew into traditional Amerikan racism."[78]

Brooklyn Bridge did not only depart dramatically from conventional wisdom by accusing the JDL, of all groups, of advancing assimilationism. It hearkened back to an earlier version of prophetic Judaism and merged it with New Left and post–New Left concerns. "The ruling class in America oppresses all people," as an editorial in the Brooklyn Bridge Collective's inaugural editorial in 1971 had already announced. "As Jews we carry a vision rising out of our tradition of a radical and inclusive social justice."[79] In this spirit of inclusion and solidarity *Brooklyn Bridge* attended to a striking range of social, cultural, and political issues, among them women's rights, gay liberation, and antiwar resistance, in addition to specifically Jewish subjects, like Brooklyn's Jewish history or examinations of the Jewish poor.

Moreover, in 1972 the Brooklyn Bridge Collective wrote an editorial that articulated a kind of idealistic and nonwhite identification that would never have appeared in the pages of the *Jewish Liberation Journal* or any other radical Zionist periodical—and yet *also* articulated strong Jewish pride:

> We know that our strongest allies here in Babylon will be our Black, Latin, Asian, and Indian sisters and brothers. They, as we, are fighting for their self determination as national minorities. . . . Our Jewishness cannot be accommodated to the barbarism of the Amerikan system; a system which views us as one more expendable minority, to be manipulated at will, in whatever ways prove most expedient. . . . We will not be forced to prove ourselves as heavier-than-thou revolutionaries, or allow others to tell us that to gain acceptance in the movement, we must first renounce our past, and denounce our people as irrelevant fools and oppressors. We are part of the movement.

> We are one with our people. We will not be forced to choose . . . It is time to recognize the existence of a revolutionary Jewish movement in Amerika. People who have no past can have no future.[80]

And one particularly powerful image in the same issue directly linked memories of the Shoah to African American oppression. A poster-size spread read: "Kaddish—For Our Sisters and Brothers who fought and died in Warsaw and Attica" (figure 6.18). Prominent in the poster was a photograph of a demonstration against the actions taken by Governor Nelson Rockefeller of New York to quell the uprising at Attica State Prison in September 1971. Rockefeller authorized the violent retaking of Attica by the National Guard; consequently, forty-three people were killed—all but one by gunfire from the National Guard. And after the National Guard regained control of the prison, numerous African American inmates were tortured by vindictive prison guards. In the photograph, beside a sign of Malcolm X (with the single word "Remember" repeated), there was a second sign that read:

> **HITLER had OVENS**
> **NIXON has NAPALM**
> **ROCKY has GUNS.**

Handwritten beside the photograph was a Hebrew text from the *Yizkor* service, when a traditional Jewish prayer for the martyred dead is spoken. Thus, and emphatically, *Brooklyn Bridge* directly connected the Jewish heroes of the Warsaw Ghetto uprising with the African American dead and tortured victims of the Attica prison uprising, and it memorialized them all in equal (and equally religious and equally Jewish) terms. The excerpted Hebrew prayer read in part:

> May God remember the souls of the holy and pure ones who were
> killed, murdered, slaughtered, burned, drowned, and strangled . . .
> May their souls be bound in the bond of light together with the souls of
> Abraham, Isaac, and Jacob, Sarah, Rebecca, Rachel, and Leah.[81]

What these many diverse examples of late 1960s/early 1970s radical Jewishness—from Jews for Urban Justice to the Jewish Defense League, from radical Zionism to such non-Zionist but nonetheless fiercely Jewish experiments as the Brooklyn Bridge Collective—make clear is that there was no obvious way to know what it was in Judaism and Jewishness that was most

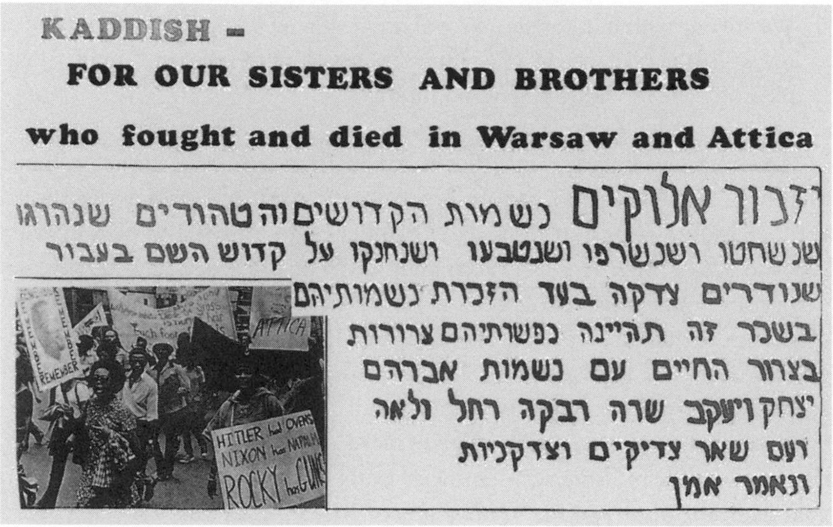
KADDISH -
FOR OUR SISTERS AND BROTHERS
who fought and died in Warsaw and Attica
יזכור אלוקים נשמות הקדושים והטהורים שנהרגו
שנשחטו ושנשרפו ושנטבעו ושנחנקו על קדוש השם בעבור
שנודרים צדקה בעד הזכרת נשמותיהם
בשכר זה תהיינה נפשותיהם צרורות
בצרור החיים עם נשמות אברהם
יצחק ויעקב שרה רבקה רחל ולאה
ועם שאר צדיקים וצדקניות
ונאמר אמן
ATTICA
HITLER had OVENS
NIXON has NAPALM
ROCKY has GUNS

FIGURE. 6.18 "Kaddish" appeared in *Brooklyn Bridge* 1, no. 4 (June 1972).

worth cherishing, and that there was, in short, more than one way to come home. How it is that so many aspects of each of these strands of American Jewishness have been lost from collective memory is a question that remains open. The seventies were to become, as Steven Schwarzschild had warned, a time of strong pressures for American Jews to conform with the least liberating and least empowering impulses emanating from the sixties. However, as the next chapter will show, in the realm of personal politics, of sexuality and gender relations, the seventies would be a time not just of some of the most intense efforts to shore up conservative and unapologetically repressive attitudes with reference both to Jewish religious tradition and the lessons of Nazism. The seventies would as well be a time when the combination of Jewish pride and countercultural impulses represented by both Zionist and non-Zionist young Jewish radicals would find fullest expression in feminist and gay and lesbian Jewish liberation movements. Far from breaking with Judaism and the Jewish community, these new movements would become fundamental to rescuing and renewing both.

7 "Are You Against the Jewish Family?" Debating the Sexual Revolution

The youth problem among American Jews is not pot, it's not radicalism, it's that we don't have enough of them.
—Milton Himmelfarb, 1972

THE AMERICAN JEWISH FAMILY IS IN TROUBLE

Beginning in the early 1970s the tone of discussion about the purportedly perilous state of the American Jewish family became noticeably overwrought. It was almost as if, having decided to turn inward and attend to personal concerns more than activism on behalf of others, the mainstream Jewish community was as disturbed by the state of affairs on the home front as it had been by developments on city streets or overseas. In 1971 Brandeis professor Jacob Cohen declared in his speech, "New Sexuality in America," at a meeting of the university's Women's Committee that "an unprecedented pagan, sense-ridden civilization has come into being in this country," one in which "there are no taboos, no inhibitions, no restraint." These were disturbing trends, Dr. Cohen said, and they were damaging the "incomparable moral conscience of the Jew, his emphasis on moral restraint—that is what a Jew is." Thus, Cohen concluded, there was only one moral option: "At this moment, it is time for Judaism to say, 'NO!'"[1]

Clearly, however, the overwhelming evidence suggested that many Jews were not heeding such calls. In a survey published in 1971 by the National Jewish Welfare Board, for instance, executives of Jewish federations and community centers in over thirty cities said they considered the "social pathology in Jewish families" and "drug abuse among Jewish youth" among the most important areas of concern for the contemporary Jewish community.[2] Also in the early 1970s, there was an outpouring of concern about Jewish girls' sexuality in particular. In 1971, for instance, Reform rabbi Stanley Brav of Cincinnati bemoaned the fact that the young brides he married were seldom virgins any longer, and he criticized those parents who considered themselves "liberal-minded and wise" when they encouraged their daughters to take birth control pills. Brav commented that "I cannot help but think of the ancient biblical injunction: 'Profane not your daughter to make her into a prostitute, lest the land fall into harlotry, and become full of lewdness.' "[3] In 1972 Conservative rabbi Jack Segal of Houston made news with a study of hundreds of Jewish female college students in the Southwest, concluding that almost 75 percent were sexually active by the time they were twenty-two. Finding that those with "maximal attachment to Judaism" were less likely to engage in premarital activity, Segal's own recommendation was for parents to begin working on their children in the formative years: "I honestly believe in the old proverb, 'The family that prays together stays together.' The time to implant ethical principles in your children is—when they are children. A good way to start is by you yourselves practicing strong devotion to your religion."[4] However, in its editorial response to Segal's survey, the *Jewish Post and Opinion* waxed philosophical, noting how it had been "well known" for a long time that "Jewish males never abided" by the "sex morality that Jews of today have been taught is the Jewish way." What was newsworthy was that now "our girls have largely abandoned" those teachings.[5]

Yet other commentators found both men and women, parents and children, to blame for lost moral moorings. In 1972, for example, at a national B'nai B'rith conference held in New York, a Brooklyn College sociologist cautioned that the American Jewish family was in dire straits, the result of climbing rates of infidelity, intermarriage, divorce, drug addiction, and "sexual liberalism" among middle-class Jews; Dr. Melvin Verbit warned that these factors taken together were currently trapping the Jewish family in "a vicious circle" where a "weakened Jewish family leads to a weakened Jewish identity, which leads to a weakened Jewish family."[6] Along related lines, after attending a similar conference in 1973 on problems confronting the Jewish family (sponsored by the American Jewish Committee and B'nai B'rith), prominent Orthodox rabbi Emanuel Rackman contended that "one could almost say that the Jewish family contained within itself the seeds of its own destruction." In Rackman's analysis, the present-day Jewish family had historically "sought to achieve within itself the democratic ideals of equality and freedom," but the move toward democracy and permissiveness in the family had now gone too far. Today the Jewish father was "abdicating his role as the symbol of authority," and now "the husband and father played his role so poorly that many a family disintegrated and many who contributed to the general culture were alienated from the Jewish family, the Jewish people, and the Jewish heritage." Patriarchal authority must be reasserted, Rackman sharply announced, and Jewish children "must be made to appreciate the fact that beyond a certain point their autonomous behavior constitutes treason to the family and must end in exclusion."[7] Meanwhile, and emphasizing completely different aspects of the crisis, Rabbi Robert J. Marx, director of the New York Federation of Reform Synagogues, bluntly told the 1973 annual assembly of delegates: "We see men and women who cannot cope with their loneliness: we see married people who cannot stand one another and single people who cannot stand themselves."[8]

Not all diagnoses were so dire. In 1974, for instance, a Long Island rabbi likened Jewish family life to a water supply in a drought. He acknowledged that "the American Jewish family is in trouble," but added: "Obviously, the Jewish family—for all its current deficiencies—has great reservoirs of strength on which it still draws. It is worth underscoring this fact and stressing that for all that ails our homes, much is still wholesome, still healthy and still hopeful."[9] Yet most observers continued to strike more pessimistic notes. As a Conservative New Jersey rabbi wearily concluded in 1975, the Jewish family should now be classified as an "endangered species."[10]

The sources of danger to the Jewish family were apparently multiple. In the growing cacophony of nervousness-promoting statistics and pronouncements, every commentator made a different argument about what was wrong and what should be done. Once again, Jews blamed each other across the divides of ideology, theology, and generation and now also fought over the increasingly thematized barriers of gender. Matters seemingly unrelated to each other—such as abortion and mixed marriage, gay sex and parenting, or sexy attire and feminist demands—got lumped together with impunity, as spokespeople for different constituencies strove to communicate their concerns with maximum emotional intensity and rhetorical persuasiveness. The only area of agreement was that the state of crisis was becoming unbearably acute.

This chapter analyzes the volatile conflicts among American Jews in the seventies over various aspects of the sexual revolution: movements for gay and lesbian liberation, birth control and abortion, rising rates of intermarriage, declining birthrates, and the rise of feminism. Dominating the debates of the 1970s was an obsession with the Jewish family, with the difficulties Jewish men and women were having being happy with each other, and with the purported need for Jews to make more babies. The argument that the appropriate response to the Holocaust was heightened Jewish reproductivity became pervasive in the 1970s, and the argument was not without antifeminist and antigay implications. And yet it is also striking how rapidly this Holocaust lesson was adopted within some Jewish feminist and lesbian and gay perspectives. The evidence from the seventies shows just how defensively embattled movements for gender justice and sexual liberation were from their very beginnings. In every area of concern relating to sex or family life, a remarkable number of commentators across the denominational spectrum defended male and heterosexual privileges and castigated those who were working to transform sexual and familial ethics in progressive directions. Yet the evidence also suggests just how powerfully the movements for gender justice and sexual liberation contributed to the renewal and strengthening of the American Jewish community.

WHY NOT TRY TO MAKE YOUR HOME A HAPPIER PLACE?

As recently as 1967 an Orthodox guidebook, *The Road to Responsible Jewish Adulthood*, was able to declare self-confidently that "the Jewish family has long been a model of harmony, love and stability; the envy of the entire world. The very social evils that tend to disrupt and destroy modern society, such as divorce, prostitution, adultery, wife-beating, or juvenile delinquency, are almost unknown among unassimilated, traditional Jews."[11] But, already only a year later, this ability to boast about the differences between observant and nonobservant Jewish family life—and indeed even between Jewish and non-Jewish family life—was being severely challenged by a growing awareness that those differences were dissolving.

An indicative text was Dr. Morris Mandel's 1968 book, *How to Be Married—and Happy*. Mandel was a psychiatrist whose marriage and sex advice column, "Problems in Human Emotions," appeared regularly in the *Jewish Press*, a weekly Orthodox paper in Brooklyn. Although advancing a manifestly Orthodox perspective, Mandel's book was designed to reach a much broader Jewish audience; Mandel counted among the most popular and influential of Jewish sex advice givers writing at the time.[12] *How to Be Married—and Happy* interspersed letters from his seemingly inexhaustible supply of troubled *Jewish Press* readers with Mandel's own pithy responses, introduced by brief impressionistic essays on a range of topical subjects like "Marriage Is No Eternal Honeymoon," "Guerilla Tactics in Marital Disputes," and "Who Says: Sex Is Not Important?" Throughout, Mandel emphasized the seriousness of tensions between men and women; he made little effort to prettify or minimize how difficult things had become for the contemporary couple. In his view, as women eschewed their traditional obligations to housework and childcare—and sought to become their partner's equal in all things—men were transformed gradually into "the neglected sex." Now that the father's former "prestige" as "commander-in-chief" had been so "weakened" by the new "emancipated woman," the father had become little more than "the errand-boy of the family." This had led to "weak family structures, and disorganized family life." The man had too often become nothing more than "a 'bit' player" in his own home, a minor character "who makes an entrance on the stage from time to time to recite his lines he feels he is expected to say," but someone with precious little authority or control over his—or his own family's—destiny.[13]

According to Dr. Mandel, these tragic developments were not inevitable. Men *allowed* them to happen; husbands did it to themselves. As a typical husband fell into his typical "over-stuffed chair" in the evening to salvage "a few minutes of peace before the tranquilizing effect of the television screen," this average guy "did not object too strongly" when his wife and kids relegated him to a role as "non-voting member" in his own household. The result was a complete mess, Mandel concluded, but the situation was not insoluble. The prescription for this disease was easy, even if it was a hard medicine to take. Mandel wrote:

> It is time that we put the father back as the much revered head of the family. Of course, this will take some motivating and doing. He will have to be wooed back to his former position. His ego will have to be rebuilt, but back he must go! When he will finally return to his paternal throne, the family will benefit and society (the family of families) will improve.[14]

Thus, in a crucial chapter, "How to Preserve Your Husband," Dr. Mandel's book spelled out its rescue and recovery operation for the debilitated American man. Women should abandon their "dreamy romantic unreal world" and accept that the "reality of marriage" could never emulate the "distorted picture" found on television and the movies, and, above all, they should cease all "nagging, belittling, by constant criticism" of the men in their lives. In return, Dr. Mandel wrote at another point, women also did require a little nurturing. "All that she really longs for is to be praised a little, appreciated a little, loved a little, and even pitied a little," Mandel confided to his male readers, adding cheerfully: "It isn't such a tremendous order to fill!"[15]

However, women readers often found Mandel's upbeat advice that working to restore Jewish patriarchy was the answer to their woes hard to reconcile with their own experiences. Both married and unmarried women wrote letters to the *Jewish Press* describing lives full of quiet desperation. "My husband gets more distant all the time," said one woman married twelve years. "There are days on end that he doesn't exchange a single sentence with me. . . . I am trapped and see no way out."[16] Another married woman sadly wrote that when "it comes to affection," her husband "has so much to learn it is almost pitiful."[17] A third woman wondered how it had happened that the man she married two years before who had "adored me and always let me know how he felt" was "so different now. It's at a point where I just don't have an answer." She explained her dilemma: "Practically every day he screams at me. No matter what I do, he screams. I've asked him a thousand times to TALK to me, NOT SCREAM, but he doesn't care—he just screams."[18] Meanwhile, an unmarried woman wrote that there was something "wrong with men today," stating that "you wouldn't believe the names I've been called for refusing the overtures of some men."[19]

Nor were men any happier about women. A father wrote to Dr. Mandel to mourn how his son was currently "dating a non-Jewish divorce [*sic*], with a small child," and said that his son had "no interest any longer in Jewish girls" because he thought that "every Jewish girl he ever took out, played him for a sucker."[20] A husband wrote to say that his wife "has me bulldozed. . . . It has come to a point where I am actually afraid of crossing her in any area."[21] And an unmarried man wrote to say that all he wanted was "a normal life, a Jewish life; a life with a woman who knows what love, devotion, kindness, understanding, and compassion are, a woman who will help erase a tear, turn depression into laughter and happiness." Rather remarkably, his letter continued:

> If only wives knew how to welcome their husbands home when returning from work. Yes, why not a kiss? A warm embrace? A sweet Shalom? A carefully prepared dinner? . . . If this way of married life was practiced, there would be no broken homes, no runaway children who cannot identify with parents or religion, no young drug addicts, no intermarriages.[22]

Yet a sampling of Mandel's responses indicates clearly that in his view women bore primary responsibility for the lousy relations between the sexes. Of course, Mandel did say to the man whose wife had him "bulldozed": "Don't hide! Don't cower! SPEAK UP! Who knows! If you will, she might sit up and take notice!"[23] Yet if men's task was to stand up for themselves, then women's role was to stand by their men. In response to the woman whose husband ignored her, Mandel posed this question: "Why not try to make your home a happier place?"[24] To the woman whose husband screamed at her, Mandel counseled that she work harder to "fall in love with your husband all over again, and get him to fall in love with you."[25] To the woman whose husband did not express affection, Mandel counseled: "Don't verbally kill your husband; try instead to preserve him. Show him that you love him and believe in him. Don't belittle his plans with sarcastic comments.... Make him feel important and that he is the most important person in your life. You cannot build a man up by knocking him down."[26] In short, men were repeatedly represented (by *both* men and women) as vulnerable, insecure, and emotionally anemic creatures; women, on the other hand, were seen as too often unwilling to donate the lifeblood required to keep those men alive.

IF THERE IS A CHOICE IT SHOULD BE HETEROSEXUAL MARRIAGE

Amidst so many awful announcements about familial life and heterosexual relations, the homophobia of leading Jewish spokespersons during these years was blunt, unapologetic, and frequently extreme. For instance, Louis M. Epstein's classic study, *Sex Laws and Customs in Judaism*, reissued in 1967, said that Jewish tradition considered homosexuality "an evil practice." Epstein wrote: "In the Bible and the Talmud sodomy and buggery are treated as similar sex crimes, and the assumption is that the one like the other had its origins in the licentiousness of the heathen Canaanites." It was a "form of sex perversion," not dissimilar in kind from "copulation with beasts," and the penalty for it was death, unless the crime was sodomy with a minor—the punishment for this lesser offense was flagellation. Lesbian sexual activity was also condemned in Jewish tradition, although not so severely as gay male sex. It was considered "an unseemly, immoral act, which Maimonides advises should be disciplined by flagellation, declaring also that women known to be addicted to this vice should be excluded from the company of decent women."[27] Basically there was no wiggle room whatsoever for the traditionalist when it came to gay sex.

Despite traditional strictures, and beginning in 1972, gay synagogues were established in several major U.S. cities. Nonetheless, receptiveness to the idea of openly gay rabbis remained nearly nonexistent in the 1970s. In 1971, when

Jean Herschaft published a series of articles on "Jews, Judaism and Homosexuality" for the *Jewish Post and Opinion*, Rabbi Balfour Brickner (himself a supporter of the ordination of gay rabbis) informed Herschaft in an interview that although there was certainly a closeted contingent within the American rabbinate, and he personally knew of a dozen Reform rabbis who were gay, "none have openly declared," and "none will under current conditions." Another supporter of gay ordination, Rabbi A. Bruce Goldman, who now served as chaplain for the Radical Jewish Union at Columbia University and who had been asked to serve as rabbi for a gay synagogue in Brooklyn (he declined), agreed that "it would be suicidal to openly declare [oneself as a gay rabbi] in the repressive Jewish establishment as it exists."[28] In 1977, when he was interviewed for *Gaysweek*, an anonymous closeted gay rabbi noted that although he knew of "several dozen" other gay rabbis, "many of them married, representing the Reform, Conservative and Orthodox movements," "as far as I know, no rabbi ordained by a recognized seminary has come out."[29] Yet this reality hardly led to a movement for the reform of Jewish antigay policies.

The inheritors of the traditionalist position did not believe for a moment that their absolutism required revision in light of a new and more tolerant moral climate. To the contrary, and most prominently, Yeshiva University professor Rabbi Norman Lamm, an influential proponent of Modern Orthodoxy, repeatedly lamented what he saw as an incipient tendency in some religious circles to doubt that homosexuality required moral condemnation. In 1968 Lamm said this tendency merely demonstrated how the "much heralded 'sexual revolution' of our times has finally infiltrated the very bastions of official morality in our Western world." Disturbed by statements of tolerance issued by American, British, German, and Swedish Protestant church leaders—a phenomena he could only see as evidence of a Christian return to "pre-Judaic" paganism—Lamm compared homosexuality to incest and polygamy and argued that for those "Jews who retain their first loyalty to Judaism and Halachah, rather than to the newest canons of contemporary liberation," there was no question that gay sex—both male and female—was "abominable, and can never be legitimized in the eyes of Judaism." Acknowledging that it was possible for Judaism to view the homosexual not as evil, but rather as someone "trapped by this dreadful disease, suffering the loneliness, the humiliation, and the social ostracism to which such individuals are condemned by their unfortunate tendencies," Lamm powerfully argued that an authentic Jewish view could never accept the "current campaign in this country and in Europe to declare homosexuality a matter of personal taste within the range of normality."[30] Nor did Lamm tone down his arguments in subsequent years. In 1974, for example, Lamm reiterated that "the Torah condemns homosexuality as *to'evah*, an abomination," though he also added that he did "not find any warrant in the Jewish tradition for insisting on prison sentences for homosexuals." His reasoning here, however, was that "sending a homosexual to prison" has "rightly been compared to sending an alcoholic to a distillery." Because he did not believe it should be treated as a criminal offense, Lamm was understood as adopting a moderate Orthodox stance toward homosexuality. However, as for recent developments in the Jewish gay community to establish gay synagogues, Lamm was unequivocal:

> Certainly, there must be no acceptance of separate Jewish homosexual societies, such as—or especially—synagogues set aside as homosexual congregations. . . . To assent to the organization of separate "gay" groups under Jewish auspices makes no more sense, Jewishly, than to suffer the formation of synagogues that cater exclusively to idol worshipers, adulterers, gossipers, tax evaders, or Sabbath violaters. Indeed, it makes less sense, because it provides, under religious auspices, a ready-made clientele from which the homosexual can more easily choose his partners.[31]

Crucially, also important non-Orthodox commentators felt nothing good would result if the Jewish community legitimated homosexual relationships. For Professor Fritz A. Rothschild of the Jewish Theological Seminary (Conservative), it was an open-and-shut issue, since it was clear to him that homosexuals as a group "are ill."[32] For Reform rabbi Eugene Borowitz, the matter was not quite so clear; in a lecture, "Why Marry," delivered at the University of Pennsylvania Hillel Foundation in late 1971, Borowitz focused on the importance of heterosexual union in the Jewish tradition. The heterosexual investment in familialism was central to the survival of the Jewish people, and in his view gay people did not—indeed could not—share that investment. Borowitz said, "Judaism is not a religion of the present. It is future oriented. That is why parents go nutty over kids. It is directed toward the coming of the Messiah. It is the only way to insure that Jews will be around waiting for the Messiah." In addition, Borowitz expressed his sincere reservations about the morality of gay marriage, advising that "in Judaism, if there is a choice it should be heterosexual marriage because it involves you with the path of the generations."[33] In 1982, in his summary meditations on "the hydra-headed monster of assimilation" and his critique of the ways "all the phenomena we associate with the 'sexual revolution' generally have the effect of reducing procreation," respected Conservative rabbi Robert Gordis expressed concern that Jews were "richly represented in all the statistical categories that are effectively reducing the birth rate." Gordis not only called on women to recognize their own "indestructible need" for "home, mate, and family" and insisted that "each Jewish couple must see in larger families a command of our age." He also called attention to the statistical category of "homosexuals" and noted as a "disquieting" fact that "these millions of men and women have elected to withdraw from the procreative process."[34]

Other influential communal spokespeople also often acted dismissive toward homosexuality on the grounds of its purported threat to procreativity. A notable example came from sociologist and prominent Jewish communal leader Earl Raab. Writing for the *San Francisco Jewish Bulletin* in 1972, Raab observed that there appeared to be a goodly number of Jewish homosexuals these days. He noted how gay Jews "sought out the official Jewish community and warned them that the Jewish community had too long ignored the problem." With regard to these pleas, Raab worried over Jewish groups, like the Board of Rabbis of Northern California, that had "voted to support the legalization of any private sexual act between consenting adults, including those now forbidden by law." But were Jews really taking into consideration what the consequences of such benevolent liberal gestures might be? Given their potential impact on the future of Jewish survival, Raab expressed sharp skepticism:

> Homosexuality, as a concept is by its nature antithetical to the idea of children, to the idea of continuity, and finally to the concern about future generations. But a society is a social invention one of whose very purposes is to be concerned about continuity and future generations. Under those circumstances—while a civilized society can be humane towards homosexuals, can it be neutral on the subject of homosexuality? Is sexual orientation really a matter of indifference to human society?

Thus, Raab questioned, if the Jewish community embraced its queers, what might happen next? Who would protect Jewish children? "Should society invite homosexuals into the schools to expound on their philosophies?" Raab asked rhetorically. Raab reminded his readers that past civilizations like "the late Romans and Greeks" which had "practiced homosexuality 'on a grand scale' " had rapidly self-destructed. And he also alluded to the Third Reich: "Whether as cause or symptom, a narcissistic lack of concern with the future generations of humanity may be the link between homosexuality as an 'alternative life style,' and the decline of certain civilizations. See fashionable Berlin of the 1930's."[35] Strikingly, this comment left unclear whether Raab was referring to the phantasmagoric image of the queer Nazi or whether Raab meant to remind readers that Weimar Germany had seen the heyday of a Jewish-led homosexual rights movement. Other commentators also agreed that to grant homosexual rights opened a veritable Pandora's box of social problems. As the esteemed Jewish sociologist and philosopher Will Herberg had put it in 1969, the critical moment had arrived for all good heterosexuals to stand up to the growing gay menace because the recently increasing tolerance of gayness reflected "some of the most ominous aspects of mid-twentieth century Western decadence." Making "the case for heterosexuality" as "a death-defying act," Herberg insisted that "it is clear that heterosexuality, with its drive for sexual union" represented what was "natural," and that the family, with "its unshakable solidity, stability, and substance" was "the foundation of society."[36]

As late as 1990, when the Central Council of American Rabbis (Reform) finally approved a policy statement urging that gay and lesbian rabbis be permitted to serve their congregations openly, the Ad Hoc Committee that formulated the statement still felt obligated to add a paragraph that reinforced heterosexuality as a norm. The passage read:

> In Jewish tradition heterosexual, monogamous, procreative marriage is the ideal human relationship for the perpetuation of the species, covenantal fulfillment and the preservation of the Jewish people. While acknowledging that there are other human relationships which possess ethical and spiritual value and that there are some people for whom heterosexual, monogamous, procreative marriage is not a viable option or possibility, the majority of the committee reaffirms unequivocally the centrality of this ideal and its special status in kiddushin. To the extent that sexual orientation is a matter of choice, the majority of the committee affirms that heterosexuality is the only appropriate Jewish choice for fulfilling one's obligations.[37]

IT IS PARTICULARLY REPREHENSIBLE FOR JEWISH GROUPS TO PROMOTE ABORTION

However, although homophobia transcended denominational divides, so far as Orthodox rabbis were concerned, assimilated and liberal Jews deserved the bulk of the blame for the sexual and emotional sicknesses rampaging through the Jewish community. They said so in no uncertain terms.

In 1971, for example, Orthodox rabbi Chaim Dov Keller, affiliated with the right-wing movement Agudath Israel, described the decline of U.S. society this way: "We are witnessing the disintegration of the Protestant work ethic and the tearing aside of the thin veneer of Puritan morality which had covered the pagan core of our society." In Keller's view, this was a "world of violence and obscenity, drug abuse, promiscuity and an unrelenting pursuit of material possessions and pleasures" in which "restraint and self discipline are being tossed aside with such rapidity that we find it increasingly difficult to cope with the atmosphere of everyday life. We are surrounded—even engulfed—by waves of obscenity and pornography. We are told that the woman who has many children is polluting the environment while the abortionist is performing a great humanitarian service." The trouble was, moreover, that "unfortunately great numbers of our fellow-Jews have lost their bearings and have been set adrift" as a result of "the efforts of almost two centuries of Reform and assimilation." Keller was especially disturbed that "there is a plethora of leagues and congresses and committees all speaking in the name of Jews and Judaism in support of the legalization of abortions and of the relaxation of the laws which could limit pornography." And—citing the case of the Jewish legislator whose vote had been decisive in passing New York's landmark bill legalizing abortion a year earlier—Keller estimated that "in the State of New York, as of today, close to one hundred thousand human lives have been snuffed out before they had a chance to see the light of day, all in the name of Jewish liberalism."[38] Although a leading spokesperson for Modern Orthodoxy, and certainly no member of Agudath Israel, Rabbi Rackman made related points, noting curtly in 1975 how "the abortion mills are making it almost impossible to get Jewish children for adoption and many Jewish childless couples are being denied the joys of family life. Jewish liberals are the friends of humanity but one wonders how helpful they are to Jewish survival."[39]

Abortion in fact became a major topic for Orthodox leaders. This was so not least because of the (accurate) assessment that most American Jews strongly supported abortion rights.[40] Orthodox rabbis across the spectrum of Orthodoxy were especially incensed that Reform and Conservative rabbis said Jewish law permitted abortions. By contrast, Rabbi Joseph Karasick, president of the Union of Orthodox Jewish Congregations of America, asserted that "the Bible itself, the Talmud, and our religious codes are quite explicit in rejecting wanton interference with pregnancy and birth." In the wake of the passage of the New York law legalizing abortion, Karasick stated that

> the increasing permissiveness in this area is but another indication of a deep-seated moral decay which seems to gnaw on the vitals of our society. We seem to live for gratification and not for responsibility. . . . The very fiber of our society is fatally weakened by lending the cloak of legality to such hedonistic tendencies.[41]

An appeal in 1972 to legislators from the Rabbinical Council of America, representing nine hundred Modern Orthodox rabbis, categorically stated that legalized abortion was "murder." It also noted: "No woman is the final arbiter about the disposition of her body and the embryonic human life that flourishes therein."[42] Orthodox rabbi J. David Bleich, a major halakhic authority, also testified in 1973 to a Senate subcommittee considering an anti-abortion constitutional amendment to overturn *Roe v. Wade*: "Abortion is not a private matter between a woman and her physician. . . . It impinges on the most fundamental right of a third party—the unborn baby's right to life."[43] In these moments Orthodox Jewish and Roman Catholic leaders came to sound virtually indistinguishable from one another (and in fact they made common cause in seeking to reverse pro-abortion legislation). But the most frequent argument put forward had to do with the threat abortion posed to Jewish survival. As Rackman's remarks suggested, there was particular concern that the legal availability of abortion would diminish Jewish adoption rates, already affected by the widespread use of contraceptive pills.[44] By 1972, for example, the largest Jewish adoption agency in the United States disclosed that it had placed nearly three hundred infants in 1967–68, but it anticipated that it would place no more than sixty babies in 1971–72. This meant that Jewish couples who hoped to adopt faced sharp declines in the numbers of available babies, a fact commentators directly linked to the liberalizing of abortion laws.[45]

Nor did Orthodox leaders hesitate to invoke the Holocaust in making their anti-abortion case. Most influentially, Rabbi Walter S. Wurzburger, first vice president of the Rabbinical Council of America, told a conference sponsored by the Federation of Jewish Philanthropies of New York in 1973 that "having lost one-third of our population in the Holocaust and lacking sufficient population to settle the land of Israel—the Jewish community does not reproduce itself adequately."[46] By early 1976, Rabbi Wurzburger stepped up his attack and expressly condemned the liberal stand of Reform leaders toward abortion as "insensitive to the injurious effects on Jewish survival which permissive abortion represents." Wurzburger added: "It is particularly reprehensible for Jewish groups to promote abortion in light of the fact that the Jews have not yet replaced the holocaust losses and in light of the fact that Israel needs more population desperately and yet has an alarming rate of abortion."[47]

Meanwhile, and despite the widespread support for legal abortion rights among the non-Orthodox, acute concern about Jews' waning population was a shared focus for all denominations in the early and middle 1970s. A slew of disturbing statistics and facts related to American Jews' future prospects were publicized and debated with increasing fervor and much mutual monitoring. Concerns about Jewish numbers were raised whenever discussion turned to divorce rates or to Jewish married couples' birth control practices. However, no single domestic issue at the end of the sixties and through the 1970s seemed to galvanize the ire and anxiety of the American Jewish community more profoundly than reports over the rising rate of intermarriage.

THE GREAT BUGABOO

The idea that the Jewish family was under threat from intermarriage was in itself nothing new. Already in 1958, for instance, Rabbi David Kirshenbaum laid the blame for this trend on the parents. Kirshenbaum observed how Jewish parents neglected "basic Jewish content and traditions," which led children to feel absolutely no compunction about choosing non-Jews to marry. The rabbi imagined this monologue spoken by a Jewish young person to his or her parent: "What is the difference? What is wrong? . . . I love her. She (or he) is the same as I. Religion? You are not religious and neither are his (or her) parents. This is what you told me. What is all the fuss about?' "[48] Kirshenbaum could have had no idea how prescient his analysis would shortly come to be.

"Intermarriage," wrote Mike Tabor in a 1973 column for the *Jewish Post and Opinion*, "is the great bugaboo of Jewish life today."[49] And indeed it was. Prompting Tabor's observation was the decision early in 1973 by the Synagogue Council of America, the Rabbinical Assembly of America (Conservative), the Commission on Interfaith Activities of the Union of American Hebrew Congregations (Reform), and the Union of Orthodox Jewish Congregations of America to condemn a half-hour CBS sitcom (about a wealthy Irish Catholic woman married to a working-class Jewish cab driver) for condoning—even glorifying—intermarriages. Some (like the New York Metropolitan Region of the United Synagogue of America) passed a resolution calling for CBS to "remove the show from the air immediately." Corporations whose commercials appeared during the program, *Bridget Loves Bernie* (whose ratings were quite respectable and whose estimated audience was thirty-five million viewers each Saturday night), were also threatened that their products would be subject to a national boycott if they failed to drop commercial sponsorship of the program. Additionally, the Pacific Association of Reform Rabbis asserted that the show frequently made "flippant, undignified and incorrect portrayals of Jewish belief and practice," while Rabbi Balfour Brickner, director of the UAHC Commission on Interfaith Activities, charged angrily that *Bridget Loves Bernie* "treats intermarriage in a cavalier, cute, condoning fashion, and deals with its inevitable problems as though they're instantly, easily solvable."[50] The most extreme reaction, however, came from the Jewish Defense League member who made several telephone calls to the show's producer, Ralph Riskin, in which he allegedly threatened Riskin's life.[51] This comedy was no laughing matter.

Of course, some in the Jewish community were less disturbed by a sitcom and more upset that Jewish groups appeared willing to behave like cultural vigilantes out to censor a television program. These individuals found it ludicrous—even pathetic—that a comedy show about intermarriage could cause such a fuss. As one observer facetiously inquired: "Can my co-religionists believe that boycotting the products of *Bridget Loves Bernie* sponsors will illuminate the spiritual values of Judaism for our young people? Can they believe that every young person who sees the show is going to shack up with the first non-Jew he sees?"[52] However, and although the network did not acknowledge that it was bowing to public pressure, despite efforts by the program's representatives to stem criticism by stating that they planned to minimize the show's emphasis on ethnic humor, CBS announced in April of that year that the show would not be renewed for the network's fall schedule.[53] Marc H. Tanenbaum, director of the American Jewish Committee's interreligious affairs department, hailed the show's cancellation as "a commendable action entirely consistent with the FCC's regulation requiring that programs must be 'in the public interest.' "[54] And so ended the short fictional romance of *Bridget Loves Bernie*.

Yet it was hardly the end of real-life fears over intermarriage within the Jewish community. As Tabor reported, "Many Jews point to intermarriage and rabbis who perform them as the main reason for the decay of Judaism in this country."[55] And a writer for *Jewish Week* noted as fact in 1973 that

> a sense of great urgency if not of panic marks all sectors of American Judaism—Orthodox, Conservative and Reform—as studies continue to show a sharp upward trend in intermarriage. . . . The greatest number of American

> rabbis share in the alarm; only those who officiate at mixed marriages poo-pooh it and the dire prediction that unless the trend is reversed, it will mean the end of the American Jewish community.[56]

Efforts on the part of the American Catholic bishops to ease restrictions on mixed marriages from the Christian side were met with ambivalence by Rabbi Armond E. Cohen, professor of pastoral psychiatry at the Jewish Theological Seminary, who applauded this display of "genuine tolerance" among Christians but was concerned that such leniency "may result in staggering losses to the Jewish people."[57] With somewhat more humor, Rabbi Arthur Hertzberg, in his new role as president of the American Jewish Congress, declared in a 1973 interview that "the American Jew wakes up in the morning with two worries. He turns on the radio for any news of Israel. What are those crazy Israelis doing now? Before he shaves, the worry is gnawing him: Was my daughter sleeping with a goy on the college campus last night?" Despite the joke, Hertzberg was serious about the danger of Jewish "evaporation," and was summarized as declaring it to be "the No. 1 problem of American Jewry."[58]

Concern over intermarriage (and "interdating") ran so high by the early seventies that the ultra-Orthodox *Jewish Observer* suggested that a flourishing of Judaic studies programs at over 185 university campuses in the United States could actually be contributing to these difficulties. Quoting a professor who said that "many non-Jews who were dating Jews were taking courses in Judaic studies to understand the faith of their fellow students better," a *Jewish Observer* article concluded warily: "Providing a stronger sense of Jewish identity—*for whom*?"[59] Commentators also did not shy away from threatening young people with the prediction that mixed marriages were bound for unhappiness. A 1969 illustration by political cartoonist Noah Bee, for example, widely distributed through the Jewish Telegraphic Agency, captured beautifully the view that a mixed marriage was built on a "shaky foundation" (figure 7.1).Or, as JTS professor Armond E. Cohen put it, "interfaith romance and marriage" only resulted in "trauma and heartache."[60] But even the prospect of intermarried happiness was considered unacceptable by many. As the primer *How to Stop an Intermarriage: A Practical Guide for Parents* (1976) categorically stated, it was simply wrong to accept the view that "as long as they are happy" an intermarriage might be okay, since a parent

> certainly would not say the same thing if their child was "happy" being a drug addict, a thief, or a homosexual. In such instances they would realize their responsibility to do everything within their power to effect a change. . . . A par-

FIG. 7.1 "Mixed Marriages" (1969) by syndicated cartoonist Noah Bee. Courtesy of Marion Bee, Carmi Bee, and Sharon Herman.

> ent who loves his child and appreciates the deep personal hurt that can come through intermarriage will not sit back—under any pretext—and allow his child to ruin his life.[61]

Deep concern over intermarriage was also cogently voiced in an advertisement (to promote Jewish day school education) often reprinted in Jewish periodicals during the mid-1970s under a banner headline (that symbolically got lighter and faded away as it went along): "IF YOU'RE JEWISH CHANCES ARE YOUR GRANDCHILDREN WON'T BE." The text below then continued in equally provocative language:

> That's right. Plain and simple: an ever-increasing rate of intermarriage, assimilation, alienation from Judaism; and, a lack of Jewish education is resulting in a decline of American Jewry.
>
> Current trends indicate that in a matter of time there will be no American Jewry to speak of.
>
> Finish. No more. . . . No Jewish faith. No Jewish culture. No Jewish beliefs. And no Jewish life experiences.[62]

Or, as Rabbi Isaac Trainin of New York's Federation of Jewish Philanthropies predicted at the B'nai B'rith triennial convention in 1971 in a formulation that would become standard rhetorical fare for years thereafter: "We are likely to lose more Jews through intermarriage and assimilation in the decades to come, than we have already lost through the pogrom and the holocaust."[63]

Interestingly, however, despite such high rhetorical drama, actual evidence that the children of intermarriages were becoming non-Jewish was entirely contradictory. In fact, although in some earlier and more anecdotal accounts it had been suggested that approximately 70 percent of the children of intermarried couples were lost to Judaism, the first comprehensive study released by the Council of Jewish Federations and Welfare Funds in 1973 reported that a "large majority of intermarried couples are bringing up their children and educating them as Jewish."[64] Nonetheless, this small bit of comfort did little to stem fears about Jewish survival. This became increasingly true as higher and higher rates of intermarriage—and concomitant concerns over assimilation, alienation, and the state of parent-child relations—got linked also to further pieces of a disturbing puzzle over what was going wrong with the American Jewish family.[65]

For one thing, divorce statistics for Jews were now climbing considerably. Early in the decade, it had still been possible for national divorce rates to be used, as Rabbi Allen S. Maller had noted in 1972 upon a review of California statistics, to contrast intermarriages unfavorably with the relative stability of Jewish marriages, because "the divorce rate for Jewish-Gentile marriages is at least three to four times as high as Jewish marriages."[66] But within a very short time, this argument appeared impossible to sustain, as observers began to suspect that Jewish marriages did not have a higher success rate than non-Jewish marriages or intermarriages. As one rabbi attempted to exhort his Miami congregation in 1975: "Jewish wives and husbands, look at yourselves! You are not supposed to be like everyone else."[67] Yet in the same year, there were reports that failed marriages were a pronounced problem even for the Orthodox, as for instance the number of divorce cases granted by the Orthodox rabbinical court (Beth Din) in New York skyrocketed.[68] And by the end of the decade, observers felt that because American Jewish divorce rates "had risen dramatically in recent years," it was very possible that they approximated the general divorce rate.[69] Thus, as in so many other areas of American life, Jews were becoming very much like everyone else.

No topic, however, was more frequently linked with the crisis of rising intermarriage than the issue of falling Jewish fertility. As sociologist Marshall Sklare noted in 1970, it was the one-two punch of the combination that especially frightened him: "To put the case baldly, there is no surplus Jewish population to cushion the impact of mixed marriage."[70] Particularly in light of the growing popularity of the ZPG (Zero Population Growth) movement—a movement dedicated to stabilizing world population figures in an effort to slow a depletion of global resources and prevent widespread starvation, and one that proposed every couple have no more than two children—American Jewish commentators struggled to explain why Jews should not participate. Very few Jewish leaders felt comfortable pointing out—as, for example, Balfour Brickner did—that it was unconscionable for Jews to expect others to restrain their reproductivity while Jews were enjoined to have more babies.[71]

Most Jewish leaders felt Jews should be exempt from ZPG. Almost every Jewish periodical of note weighed in on the subject, and in the emerging concatenation of admonitions directed at the American Jewish community—as Conservative rabbi Asher Bar-Zev summarized the trends in 1976—the majority of commentators found everything wrong with the Jewish family to be interrelated: Because of "Jewish contraceptive expertise, delay in marriage, the favorable attitude of Jewish women and most Jewish physicians (92%!) to abortion on demand, and high and increasing rates of mixed marriages, assimilation and divorce, all of which operate upon the relatively small number of Jews in the world (about .4 of 1% of the total world population)," there were "disastrous implications," and "we have been warned that for Jews ZPG is tantamount to total annihilation within two generations." Like Brickner, Bar-Zev was uncomfortable with Jewish self-exemption. His own recommendation was to reverse Jews' traditional reluctance to missionize among gentiles and instead encourage Jews to work for conversion to Judaism among "young, idealistic, intelligent and morally committed individuals." Like several other commentators of the time who felt that "Jews by choice" often made excellent Jews, he reminded his readers that "*the essence of Judaism is not necessarily genetic but rather intellectual, moral and emotional*" and that "Jews have survived as a group not because of numbers but because of a commitment to certain spiritual values."[72] However, this was not the prevalent view. More typical was the Reform rabbi in Florida who received national media coverage when he wrote in 1976 that the implications of the sexual revolution for the Jewish community were "catastrophic" because the "net result" was "a decline in the number of marriages, the delaying of marriages, the decline in families with children, the mingling of people of different religious faiths, and a surging stream of people who use each other as long as the situation permits." His pessimistic conclusion was that "all of these facts together are disastrous for the prospect of the continuation of the Jewish people and the Jewish faith."[73]

BE FRUITFUL AND MULTIPLY

Despite (or because of?) most American Jews' support for birth control and abortion rights and comfort with many aspects of the sexual revolution, a broadening range of observers—both women and men—from across the denominations argued ever more emphatically that Jewish women were just not grasping how critical it was that they have more Jewish children. As one rabbi, "a family life specialist," put it in 1972: "I'll still tell the Jewish couples I marry the teachings of the commandment 'be fruitful and multiply' and that Jewish parents must have two children to replace themselves."[74] Others, like University of Michigan psychology professor Elizabeth Douvan, described the concern about the future of American Jews in more clinical terms: "Increased education of women, together with the improvement in contraceptive methods, is leading to negative population growth, and this may well prove a dilemma for a minority group concerned with questions of continuity, identity, and the preservation of its ethnic and religious heritage."[75] The general meaning, however, was basically the same: in order for American Jews to survive, more Jewish women needed to procreate—and more often. In 1974 Rabbi Sol Roth, president of the New York Board of Rabbis, identified the low American Jewish birth rate of the previous three decades as a "Holocaust-size loss" and announced that while he was "not saying whether or not I oppose zero population growth for the rest of the human family," he firmly believed that "three children should be the minimum number for Jewish families. . . . But the larger the better."[76] Also in 1974 a writer in *Reconstructionist* noted that the threat facing Jewish survival due to an "all-time low" fertility rate, while "not the result of local pogroms, massive extermination campaigns by Nazis or Communists, or even inter-marriage," could have the same "ultimate effects" as these "within only one or two generations."[77] Along related lines, in 1975 Norman Lamm stressed that while world population control was a "moral imperative," the Jewish situation required special consideration. "Jews are a disappearing species," Lamm stated, "and should be treated no worse than the kangaroo and the bald eagle." He therefore recommended that each married Jewish woman have four or five children.[78] Indeed, even the typically liberal-minded Central Conference of American Rabbis (Reform) released a statement after its annual convention in 1977 that urged Jewish families "to have at least two or three children" because "there are simply not enough of us to be assured of survival in succeeding generations."[79]

The rallying cry for American Jewish women to bear ever larger numbers of Jewish children found its most aggressive and persistent standard-bearer in *Commentary*'s contributing editor and director of information and research services for the American Jewish Committee, Milton Himmelfarb. No one worked harder, longer, or more passionately than Himmelfarb to advance the view that Jews needed urgently to up their numbers. Already in 1963 Himmelfarb addressed the dire consequences of low Jewish fertility and cited the especially unfortunate attitudes of the Reform and Conservative rabbinate on the subject:

> The rabbis, more than anyone else, are worried about our survival, but they seem to prefer not to know that we are failing to reproduce ourselves. When they do turn their attention to Jewish fertility, it is to invoke the support of Jewish tradition or law for birth control. There are famous Reform and Conservative responsa of that kind, and recently a well-known rabbi felt it necessary to say the same things again—as if we needed the encouragement. Some years before Hitler came to power, the doom of the German Jews had already been pronounced. Their birth rate was so low by the 1920's, the ratio of old to young so high, and intermarriage so common, that only an impossible average of 7 children in every German Jewish family could reverse the trend to extinction. We are more fortunate. To pass from minus to plus all we need is to raise the number of children in the average Jewish family to something like 2.5 or 3—not a great rise, but a rise nevertheless. If the rabbis wanted us to have more children, would they make a point of telling us that Jewish law favors birth control?[80]

By the 1970s Himmelfarb became even more devoted to the cause of raising Jewish fertility rates. For instance, in 1972 Himmelfarb voiced fears over the fact that the American Jewish community was greying; he noted the median American Jewish age of thirty-seven, compared to a national average of twenty-eight. This meant a pool of older Jewish women, which translated into fewer children. Speaking to the Cleveland chapter of the National Conference of Jewish Communal Service, Himmelfarb observed that American Jews were marrying less—and later—and that this too meant Jewish women had a shorter child-bearing period. "We're the only group whose population has declined in the past 30 years," he said. Citing the words of the Babylonian rabbis "to be fruitful and multiply," Himmelfarb cautioned that "without Jews in numbers there can be no Jewish community; without Jewish people there can be no Judaism." This father of seven authoritatively concluded: "The central problem confronting Jews is the need for more rather than fewer children."[81] In a scathingly sarcastic passage in his 1973 book, *The Jews of Modernity*, Himmelfarb contrasted "prophetic Jews . . . cheerfully volunteering for sterilization" and advocating ZPG with "parochial, fleshly Jews" who knew that what Jews needed was "not ZPG but MPG—Maximum Population Growth."[82] And at a Conference on Population and Intergroup Relations held in 1975, Himmelfarb noted that the issue of Jewish fertility rates was "a question of simple math." He explained:

> If I'm going to lose 33 percent and I start with three, I end up with two, which is the same number as my wife and I. But if I start with two and lose 33 percent, for every thousand couples, or two thousand adults, with a 33 percent loss rate and a modal two-child family, in one generation you'll be down to something like 1,300, in the next generation down to fewer than 900, and in the next down to fewer than 600.[83]

Even more pointedly, at a 1975 seminar sponsored by the Women's League for Conservative Judaism, held at the Jewish Theological Seminary, Himmelfarb stated that there was no doubt the survival of Judaism depended above all on young Jewish women breeding more children. He surmised that the widespread use of birth control by Jewish women meant that there were an estimated two million fewer Jews in the United States than there would be otherwise. Lamenting that the Jewish woman had become a "contraceptive virtuoso" (a term he ascribed to Marshall Sklare), Himmelfarb concluded that so much disinterest in having children on the part of so many Jewish women posed a "greater threat to the future of the Jewish people than intermarriage."[84] Sex was a necessary good, Himmelfarb implied, but the wrong kind of sex, the nonprocreative kind (and there was altogether too much of that) was of no help in the crusade to lift those all-important Jewish fertility rates.

For some antifeminists like Helen Cohen, whose advice column appeared regularly in the nationally distributed *Jewish Post and Opinion*, Jewish women's disinterest in procreation was a nasty side effect of the sexual revolution. "Whatever the world situation, in this spacious, prosperous land," Cohen wrote in 1973, "there is still room for many more babies, yet our population is on a steep downhill course." Remarking on the legalization of abortion rights, Cohen recalled (with overt nostalgia) that once upon a time "the community, including our Jewish community, accepted the fact that when a wife was with child, it was God's will. Didn't the Bible say, 'Be fruitful and multiply?' Contraceptives themselves were discussed in shameful whispers. A husband approached the drug counter with embarrassed reluctance to make such a purchase."[85] Times were different now, and even Blu Greenberg, an Orthodox lecturer whose views on women's rights were sometimes aligned with the nascent feminist impulse within Orthodoxy, saw fit to express her public disapproval. Greenberg told the biennial convention of the American Jewish Congress National Women's Division in 1977: "For the rest of the world, ZPG—zero population growth—is a wonderful thing. For the Jewish people, in view of the huge losses our people have suffered in our own lifetime, it is a form of suicide, a kind of death wish." A mother of five children herself, Greenberg suggested a solution: "Starting a family 10 years earlier would add a new generation of Jews every 30 years."[86] Or, as one participant at the 1973 women's conference organized by the Jewish Students' Network, an affiliate of the World Union of Jewish Students, told a reporter: "We cannot afford zero population growth."[87]

Sometimes, though, these concerns about procreation and the desire to perpetuate Jewish families were put by Jewish women in more intimate—even anguished—terms. One moving example was a piece that appeared in the *National Jewish Monthly* in 1978. As Diane Levenberg, the author of " 'Either I'm Neurotic or I Haven't Found the Right One Yet': Growing Up to Be 30, Single, Female and Jewish," said also of herself: "Here we are, 30ish, alone, Jewish, wanting children, a home and a husband. Scylla: no children ever—a very un-Jewish way of looking at the meaning of life. Charybdis: becoming a statistic—one of the fifty percent who divorce." What followed were several interviews with Jewish women who felt much the same way. "Oddly enough, *havurot* militate against marriage," argued Marilyn, who had been in the havurah movement for years. "What's scary for everyone—single and married—is that many 'model couples' have disrupted their marriages. Helping these couples through their periods of stress is a *mitzva*. But it doesn't encourage the rest of us to risk that kind of pain and enmity. So we remain frightened, single and lonely." Other women complained that there were simply not enough "good men" for the more numerous good women. "In the last ten years," explained Deborah, "women have been trying to control what overpowers them. We're not walking around any more like 1950s zombies, choked by our Peter Pan collars, wondering why we're unhappy. . . . A lot of men still find us too threatening to live with." As Deborah put it, one man she had been involved with "needed a mother, a mistress and a madonna. We broke up after six months." Yet Deborah still sought to be married—and married to a Jewish man: "Imagine cooking three-course *Shabbos* meals for just one person. It's depressing. And marriage and family without Judaism feels sterile." Deborah summarized eloquently the emotional cul-de-sac in which many heterosexual and single Jewish women of her generation felt they found themselves. As Levenberg poignantly phrased it, asking not only for herself: "Wasn't there even one tattered *mentsch* left who might come walking into our lives bringing comfort, some love, and the promise of procreation?"[88]

And yet male observers continued impatiently to exhort these same young Jewish women to hurry up and bear as many children as soon as possible. A relatively extreme case was Conservative rabbi William Berman, executive director of the Jewish Population Regeneration Union (a name chosen because the acronym PRU puns in Hebrew on the traditional commandment *P'ru ur'vu*, meaning, "Be fruitful and multiply"). As reported in 1976 by the Jewish Telegraphic Agency, Rabbi Berman was summarized as saying that the "American and Israeli Jewish communities are experiencing a 'demographic disaster' which may well constitute the greatest threat to Jewish survival since the Nazi holocaust: an appallingly low Jewish birth rate." The report went on to quote Berman:

> To maintain its numbers, any group must average 2.5 children per family; the Jewish birth rate, however, is estimated at 1.5 per family. Coupled with an intermarriage rate of 40 per cent in the U.S., a dismal picture emerges. Sociologists maintain that if the present birth-intermarriage rate continues, American Jewry will be reduced to a paltry remnant within four generations . . . with the present rate of decline calculated at more than 100,000 per year.

Berman also noted drily that "self-elimination of Jewry will do virtually nothing to alleviate the world's overpopulation problem."[89] Yet in the context of what Levenberg and the unmarried Jewish women she knew were feeling and experiencing, Berman's elaborations sounded clueless, callous, and almost cruel. Here was a classic instance of a gendered failure to communicate.

FUN IN THE BEDROOM IS THE JEWISH VIEW

Jewish scholars routinely agreed that Judaism was anything but puritanical when it came to sex. They also routinely asserted—a not inconsequential point in view of the emerging feminist movement and its complaints about men's behavior in bed and men's insufficient attention to women's pleasure—that Jewish tradition was especially respectful of women's sexuality. Both the Torah's and the Talmud's attitudes toward sexuality, it was argued, resisted any interpretation that Jewish women (that is, *married* Jewish women) received any less pleasure from sex than they wished or that they could possibly be second-class citizens in the bedroom. Indeed, a close look at Torah and Talmud suggested that women should have *more* fun than men. A man might choose "to deny *himself* that pleasure," wrote Rabbi David Feldman in *Birth Control in Jewish Law* (1968), his authoritative study of Jewish law and its views on sexuality, but "if a man took a vow to deny his wife the pleasure of marital intercourse, his vow is automatically null and void; he cannot vow against what the Torah requires of him."[90] In a 1973 talk Feldman elaborated this point; he was quoted as saying that in the Talmud "it is recognized that the woman has the stronger sex need," and that—so far as Jewish law was concerned—the "traditional view is that anything goes in the privacy of the bedroom provided that what goes on meets with the approval of the wife."[91] With a sexual heritage like this, who needed to be liberated?

Certainly, as already noted, some Jewish commentators objected to the society-wide liberalization trends. Remarking on the new shamelessness in sexual relations, for example, Rabbi Levi A. Olan, CCAR past president, lamented at a meeting of the American Jewish Committee in 1971 that "the trouble with pre-marital sex is that it is exploitation of each other, often without care."[92] Or as advice columnist (and opponent of premarital sex) Helen Cohen observed in 1973, liberated sex really amounted to nothing but "a lonely, de-humanizing ego-shattering treadmill going nowhere," a "depressing" spectacle that degraded women, while it gratified the casual whims of unfeeling men for whom "sex becomes a bore and the long line of females become faces that pass in the night."[93] But the far more popular strategy was to present the Jewish people as quite simply centuries ahead of the times.

Whether Reform, Conservative, or Orthodox, rabbis concurred that Jews appeared to have little need for sexual liberation, since Judaism was a tradition already liberated in its attitudes toward sexuality. For instance, Reform rabbi Roland B. Gittelsohn was held to argue that Jewish tradition "values women's rights for sexual gratification" and that "Judaism has never been repressive with regard to its sexual mores."[94] Conservative rabbi Robert Gordis stated that Jewish tradition "recognized female sexuality long before the advent of modern psychology" and also that Judaism "regards it not merely as permissible but as mandatory for a man and his wife to derive pleasure from the sexual act."[95] Nor did Orthodox rabbi Walter Wurzburger find reason to differ on these points, noting, "Jewish law imposes upon the husband the responsibility for conjugal relations designed to provide sexual satisfaction for his wife. This Mitzvah must be performed even under circumstances when there is no possibility that intercourse might result in pregnancy."[96] And Norman Lamm, although highly critical of the "much heralded 'sexual revolution' of the present decade" (which he saw as "nothing more than plain, old-fashioned libertinism" growing "out of a sense of exasperation and despair" and that really, in his view, hid an unconscious "sex-negating outlook" inherited in Western culture from Christianity), emphasized with pride that it was traditional Jews who got the balance right. In his influential guide, *A Hedge of Roses: Jewish Insights Into Marriage and Married Life*, first published in 1966 (but soon reprinted several times as well as being translated into Spanish and Hebrew), Lamm noted that

> the Jewish family, traditionally, may not have been overly demonstrative in expressing affection outwardly. Yet love was ever-present, the bedrock of the home, as solid and reliable as the ancient and sacred tradition from which the character of our people is hewn. Squeamishness never allowed the sexual nature of this marital love to be overlooked or minimized; modesty never permitted it to be vulgarized and dishonored.

"Sexual comradeship," in Lamm's view, "is an intrinsic good," and the message of Torah was that "sexual communion is considered a legal right of the wife, no less than the food and clothing her husband is required to provide for her."[97] Or, as a 1973 *Jewish Post and Opinion* headline declared: "Fun in the Bedroom Is the Jewish View." The text went on to quote Reform rabbi Eugene Borowitz: "I don't know about you, but to relax and learn to enjoy ourselves more fits in with my Jewishness." Indeed, Borowitz went on to say, with a touch of Jewish chauvinism, that "the so-called 'new morality' may be new to the Christian community, but is, in its major points, a restatement of Jewish tradition."[98] Thus, rabbis and other spokespersons who could agree on little else agreed here: Judaism was good for heterosexual sex and heterosexual sex was good for Judaism. Not only was the sexual revolution a redundancy so far as Jewish tradition was concerned, but in Borowitz and others one could even detect the slightly strutting inference that Jewish sex was just possibly more exciting than gentile sex. And this too was due in no small part to the special kind of respect Jewish women received from Jewish men in the bedroom. So what was the problem?

THE THOUGHT OF SHORTS IN SHUL IS BAD ENOUGH

The problem was not only (though also) the pervasive atmosphere of overt sexism in American society—innocently saucy and insidious at once, and evident, for example, in the unabashed pandering to any straight Jewish male's potentially roving eye in the 1973 National Airlines "Kosher tours to Miami" ads. "Fly me," said the ethnically unidentifiable smiling blonde (figure 7.2). The main problem was Jewish men's incoherent and sometimes ugly attitudes toward Jewish women's sexuality. For despite the plethora of high-minded and even self-congratulatory pronouncements available in Jewish scholarship and the Jewish press on both the ubiquity and moral legitimacy of women's pleasure, a far more contradictory popular discourse circulated in the community. One strand emphasized the special sexual desirability of the Jewish woman—notwithstanding her other failings. Appearing on the David Susskind television show in 1970, for instance, comedian Mel Brooks not only highlighted Jewish women's mercenary use of their own sexuality ("If you meet a Jewish girl and shake her hand, that's dinner. . . . If God forbid anything filthy should happen amongst you, that's marriage. . . . They do expect a lot for a little fooling around") but also suggested that ultimately they deserved whatever they wanted because Jewish women were in fact "terrific in bed."[99]

Another strand, however, cited the sexual allure of Jewish women precisely as the reason why all potential feminist incursions into roles traditionally reserved for men must be resisted. Men were slaves to the rhythm, Mortimer Ostow, chairman of the Department of Pastoral Psychology at Jewish Theological Seminary, indicated in 1974, observing that

> there is the problem of sexual arousal, consciously or unconsciously, by women performing on the *bimah*. In our society it is generally true that men

FIGURE 7.2
This advertisement for National Airlines appeared in *Jewish Week*, May 31–June 6, 1973.

> are far more readily aroused by an attractive woman than women are by an attractive man. That being the case, a woman appearing as a central figure in a religious service is likely to distract some of the male worshippers from a reverent attitude and encourage erotic fantasies.[100]

Others were not even talking about feminism but merely voicing their own unreflected blend of misogyny and concupiscence. Acting as the guardian of traditional standards of modesty within Judaism, for instance, one Conservative rabbi in New Jersey banned hot pants and see-through blouses from his temple. To justify his prohibition, the rabbi noted that "the thought of shorts in shul is bad enough," but that anything called "hot pants" had to be unacceptable for worship. Actually revealing more about where his own head was, he explained:

> I possess an aesthetic sense. It is this which is both violated and exalted when I see someone in "hot pants." When an older woman with thick thighs, or as we used to call them in our day, "pulkahs," wears "hot pants," my aesthetic sense is violated. On the other hand, if a younger person wears "hot pants," and wears them well, they are extremely aesthetic. My aesthetic sense is appreciative. But this appreciation in no way dovetails with the purpose for which we came to services, i.e. to pray.[101]

Yet the most pervasive tendency was plainly to label Jewish women *undesirable* love objects. Such views were aired, for instance, in "an inexpert, inexact, and yet interesting survey about the Jewish American Princess" conducted by the *Jewish Post and Opinion* in early 1975. The newspaper acknowledged that the Jewish American Princess stereotype might be unfair, but "at the same time it contains some truth like a third-hand story relayed on the telephone." Defining a JAP, respondents to the survey offered the following: " 'A spoiled girl. She feels everything's coming to her.' . . . 'Today's royalty or JAP feels entitled to privileges without earning them or being qualified.' . . . 'She's afraid to be genuine and down to earth. She is primed to be a controlling manipulative wife and mother.' "[102] As scholars David Biale, Aviva Cantor, and Riv-Ellen Prell, among others, have thoughtfully documented, the demeaning stereotype of the JAP involved not only her avid pursuit of material possessions but also the view that she was (contra Brooks) a seductress who was far from terrific in bed—someone in fact rather abnormally stifled and repressed. Even the liberal journal *Moment* jumped on this particular bandwagon when it reported anecdotally in 1976—and without the slightest sense that it might be contributing problematically to negative views of Jewish women's sexuality—that Jewish men turned out to be frequent customers at a Manhattan massage parlor. Why? "The Jewish guys love it because they don't get it at home," one (gentile) masseuse said about oral sex. "One of my customers told me that it took him two years to get his wife to do it. I think they must have a very straight, clean sex life."[103]

Such insults about Jewish women's sexual unresponsiveness found primary expression through awful jokes that got repeated wherever Jewish men and women happened to congregate. "How do you keep a JAP from having sex? Marry her." Or: "What's the definition of a Jewish nymphomaniac? A woman who makes love once a year." Or: "How do you give a JAP an orgasm? Scream, 'Charge it to Daddy.' " Or: "Why does a Jewish woman make love with her eyes closed? Because she can't stand to see anyone else having a good time." And so on. In a 1977 issue of the newly founded Jewish feminist journal *Lilith*, Susan Weidman Schneider speculated that these jokes "reflect Jewish men's uneasiness about their relationships with Jewish women." She went on to argue, among other things, that for Jewish men the "alleged [Jewish] female disinterest in sex" was frequently getting "used as one rationalization for intermarriage and assimilation. ('I'd like to marry a Jewish woman, but they're just no good in bed.') Making it with non-Jewish women is some men's way of entering mainstream America." She also proposed that the jokes might be a way for Jewish men to express their own unacknowledged anti-Jewish feelings "under a mask of misogyny." Yet Schneider appeared to concede as well that there might be an uncomfortable truth to these stereotypes about the bad sex Jewish women were having with Jewish men, even as she forcefully turned the tables on the men: "If we're unresponsive, it means unresponsive to *them*."[104] In *Jewish and Female* (1984) Schneider again returned to the puzzle of what it was that squelched Jewish women's sexual pleasure with the Jewish men in their lives:

> The tradition, and the language of the Bible and post-Biblical writings, tell us that sex (in marriage) is a mitzvah, a pleasure, has divine sanction and divine presence, and is as important for women as for men. Reality suggests that sex for many women is something less than this ideal. At a Jewish feminist conference in the seventies, following a session in which women discussed their attitudes about sex, Rabbi Laura Geller gave what observers called a "glowing report" on Jewish attitudes towards women's sexuality. One participant turned to Geller after her presentation and asked: "If the tradition is so positive about our sexuality, why are Jewish women so screwed up?"

Schneider herself was not sure where exactly the difficulty resided, but after tracking through various possibilities, she ultimately suggested that since Jewish women did not share Christian women's "theologically inspired guilt about sex," the reason "Jewish women may hold themselves back from their partners (consciously or not)" was "because of *anger*."[105]

And, it was becoming clear, there was plenty of anger, both about the resistance to women's demands for greater equality and participation in communal and religious life and about the impossible contradictory expectations placed upon Jewish women. Women's efforts to enter the rabbinate were subjected to malicious mockery.[106] Leading communal spokespersons declared that allowing women to play roles that were formerly restricted to men would only weaken Judaism.[107] Feminists were warned that they would never find a husband.[108] And at a conference sponsored in 1973 by the American Jewish

Committee and B'nai B'rith on "The Role of Jewish Women in Strengthening the Jewish Family," participants elaborately praised the mother's role in purveying Judaism to children, openly lamented that "the woman committed to a career is not likely to have more than 1.2 children," and proposed that Jewish women be encouraged "to withdraw from other activities."[109]

For many Jewish women's rights activists it was terribly painful, as religious studies scholar Judith Plaskow said in her address to the 1973 National Jewish Women's Conference in New York, "that the Jewish community will not let us, as feminists, feel at home in it."[110] Or, as Orthodox feminist Rachel Adler acerbically noted the same year, although there had been an edict forbidding polygamy back in 1000 C.E., "the problem is that very little has been done since then to ameliorate the position of Jewish women in observant Jewish society."[111] Meanwhile, as Conservative feminist Paula Hyman observed—after thoroughly researching the reality of past Jewish family life and the ubiquity and longevity of the phenomenon of the working mother in it—the 1970s rhetoric enjoining women to stay home so that Judaism might be preserved would not succeed in causing women to leave their jobs but only in making working mothers "angry and guilty," feeling "that their community is not supportive of them."[112] And as religious studies scholar Susannah Heschel summarized it, feminism, emerging as it did during a "period of retrenchment, was not viewed as a movement for equal rights, like the Civil Rights Movement or the Free Soviet Jewry Movement of the 1960s. Rather, feminism was perceived as a threat to Jewish survival, a danger to be opposed rather than a cause to be supported."[113] As Jewish New Leftists were accused of internalized antisemitism, so too were Jewish feminists. Paula Hyman opened an essay on Jewish women in 1972 with the observation that "it has become fashionable in certain circles to label the more outspoken, and most often young, critics of Jewish life as self-haters. When those critics are women, and their critique a feminist one, they can be written off as doubly self-hating."[114]

NOWHERE DO THEY TALK ABOUT HOW A WOMAN MIGHT FEEL

One of the first manifestos for Jewish feminism appeared in the New Left Jewish journal *Brooklyn Bridge* in February of 1971. The authors railed at the "double bind" in which Jewish women were caught: "We are expected to grow up assimilating the American image of 'femininity'—soft, dependent, self-effacing, blonde, straight-haired, slim, long-legged—and at the same time be the 'womanly' bulwark of our people against the destruction of our culture." In their view the nasty stereotypes continually fastened onto Jewish women above all served to manipulate them: if women were strong and self-sacrificing for the sake of their families, they were maligned with the "ridiculous and disgusting" image of the "Jewish mother"; if they were strong vis-à-vis men, other images were mobilized: "We've been called 'Jewish princess' and 'castrating bitch,' by the rest of the world and by our own men loud and clear." Being obligated to negotiate the ensuing tightrope act kept women in their proper place: "Jewish men demand that their women be intellectual sex-objects. So Jewish families push their daughters to get a good education. The real purpose is not to be forgotten however. While PhD's do make Jewish parents proud of their daughters, the universities are recognized as hunting-grounds for making a 'good' marriage. Grandchildren assure the race."[115] Along related lines, in "The Oppression of the Jewish Woman," her important 1973 manifesto published in *Response*, radical Zionist and *Lilith* cofounder Aviva Cantor Zuckoff proposed that Jewish men were working through their own ambivalence about their Americanization via Jewish women: "A lot of tension exists between Jewish men and women because Jewish men want women who are both useful and independent like their mothers and, at the same time, helpless and dependent as they perceive non-Jewish women to be. Jewish women have gotten enough double messages to cause anyone to be neurotic."[116] Or, as Gloria Averbuch put it in *Lilith*, "the stereotype of the naggy Jewish Mother is an invention of jealous, insecure men. . . . Having become acquainted with numerous American Jewish men and their various complexes which they blame on Jewish women, I have only one thing to say to them or to any others like them who may seek my advice or affection: 'This Jewish Mother doesn't live here anymore!' "[117] Early volumes of *Lilith*, as well as special issues of *Davka* and *Response* dedicated to the Jewish women's movement, were filled with like-minded testimonials that both expressed Jewish feminists' yearning to be full and respected members of the Jewish community and provided extensive evidence of Jewish male boorishness.

Jewish feminists were especially incensed by so much guilt-inducing talk that they accept an urgent obligation to bear more (and more) babies. Some were so angered that the Holocaust became a key weapon in their rhetorical arsenal against Jewish men. In her keynote address at the 1975 conference sponsored by the Jewish Feminist Organization of Metropolitan New York, for instance, Aviva Cantor Zuckoff hauled forth once more the prevailing shibboleth of Jewish passivity in the face of Nazism to underscore her rage. As *Jewish Week* reporter Elenore Lester characterized the talk, it was a "most scathing attack" on the Jewish male establishment. According to Lester's summary:

> Mrs. Zuckoff traced the history of Jewish family life back to the fall of the second temple and said women had always worked both in the home and outside it as "enablers—that is, to enable men to do their thing, which was study." She admitted that this served its function in sustaining the Jewish people, but claimed that today men wanted women to continue in that role although men had long ago forsaken their own responsibilities to Jewish life. She went so far as to accuse the "establishment" of doing nothing to prevent the Holocaust and now asking women to have five or six children to make up for the lost one-third of the Jewish people.[118]

Likewise, in an interview published in *Lilith*, Zionist and feminist Phyllis Chesler aired her dismay at the burgeoning communal obsession with Jewish familialism. Noting that many women as well as men were hostile to feminism, she told of her encounters with "wives of Establishment Jews . . . organized into relatively powerless but status-granting organizations": A "chorus of Babel erupts: 'Do you hate men? Are you a communist, an atheist, don't you know which side the bread is buttered on?' Or more darkly, 'Are you against the Jewish family?' " Meditating on both the past and the present, Chesler went on to wonder how much "the traditional Jewish family and the Jewish religion were able to do against the threat of Nazism. If indeed this social vehicle—without a state and without land—is what counts for Jews, then why did it fail for the Jewish masses during the Holocaust? And if it failed because at its very heart is a grave fault, then we have to be open to looking for more viable means of survival." Pointing out as well that "there's nothing funny about the pain felt and caused when women are consigned to powerlessness," Chesler reiterated the points other feminists made about the impossible-to-meet demands placed on Jewish women: "Has the Jewish family been able to eliminate wife-beating, wife abandonment, female depression, sexual frigidity, insecurity and a pathological degree of female dependency and self-sacrifice for men and small children? Has the Jewish family been able to . . . understand the enormous burden and unfortunate consequences of being responsible for keeping a family together—and for then being blamed as a castrating 'matriarch,' a Spider Lady, a vindictive and bitchy 'human cleaning machine'? A butt of Jewish male comics? Of mother-in-law jokes, Jewish Mother jokes, Jewish Princess jokes?"[119] The implied answers to these questions, clearly, were No, No, No, and No.

Meanwhile, some Jewish feminists found ways besides an egregious use of the Holocaust to sting Jewish men. For instance, feminist playwright Susan Dworkin, writing in 1975 in the first issue of *Moment*, joked that so much was wrong with Jewish male attitudes toward Jewish women these days that "intermarriage begins to look good." In fact, Dworkin added, "no marriage at all begins to look good."[120] And in 1976 Jewish feminist Mary Gendler also tried to put matters in more moderate terms: "I feel that what the Population Regeneration Union (PRU) is asking shows a lack of respect for the woman, for the child and for the family. To be blunt, they are asking Jewish women to become baby machines, hatching . . . as many kids as possible for the political benefit of the community. Nowhere do they talk about how a woman might feel using her body in this way."[121] But once references to the Holocaust were introduced into the contentious dispute over Jewish familialism, it appeared inescapable that individuals on both sides would seek in the Holocaust support for their own arguments.

One of the few to examine critically the strategies of pro-fertility advocates rather than simply reverse them was *Lilith* contributor Shirley Frank. In one passage in her 1977 critique of the Jewish fertility debates, Frank first quoted Milton Himmelfarb from *Commentary* in 1961 and then provided her own analysis. Himmelfarb had written: "Where does a Jew's obligations lie? Should he absent him from paternity awhile, for the good of the human race? Or should he be of good courage, and play the man for his people?" Frank then commented: "One hardly dares to wonder what 'play the man' means in this context. It seems clear, however, that man is making decisions about his paternity quite as if he were a self-fertilizing flower." Frank also observed how "the present downward trend in population growth is constantly associated with the Holocaust—as if those who are failing to reproduce in sufficient numbers are somehow collaborating with Hitler. Commentators quote Emil Fackenheim's powerful statement, 'Jews are forbidden to grant posthumous victories to Hitler.' " She added:

> The fact remains that we cannot replace the Holocaust victims, and any attempt to equate the unborn with Jews who were murdered is an insult to the martyrs' memories—for surely we define those six million Jewish lives in terms more significant than their numbers alone. Moreover, those who urge women to breed more babies for the sake of increasing the Jewish population are strangely, indeed shockingly, echoing Hitler's exhortation of German women to breed more babies for the Fatherland.[122]

While in earlier years Nathan Glazer and Robert Alter had castigated Jewish liberals and leftists for applying the term *genocide* too loosely to the treatment of African Americans, Frank was now at pains to point out that it was the pro-fertility activists who used the term *genocide* with "abandon to describe what we are supposedly doing to ourselves." Frank's overarching argument was that although pro-fertility activists carefully avoided attacking feminism directly (instead either taking vague jabs at "hedonism" or claiming that work outside the home—especially if it was part-time—was fully reconcilable with more motherhood), it was not by chance that the campaign to raise Jewish numbers escalated just as the community felt the first tentative stirrings of a Jewish feminist movement. Could it really be only coincidence, Frank asked, that as Jewish women began to demand a greater role in both Jewish communal and religious life, a chorus of Jewish men were now "loudly hitting the old 'barefoot and pregnant' motif as if our very lives depended on it?" Moreover, and strikingly, Frank insisted in conclusion that while the pro-fertility rhetoric "depresses and disgusts me," it did so "not so much because I am a feminist, but because I am a Jew. I am deeply ashamed at the idea of Judaism sinking to a level where we are scrounging around for every warm body we can get."[123]

THEIR OPPOSITION IS AS LOYAL AS OPPOSITION CAN BE

Despite the many reasons for rage, one of the most notable aspects of the Jewish feminist movement and the Jewish gay and lesbian movements was their investment in making themselves a more significant part of the larger Jewish community, rather than breaking from it. As Susan Dworkin phrased it with respect to Jewish feminists already in 1975: "Their opposition is as loyal as opposition can be."[124] Notable Jewish leaders of the women's movement testified how their feminism became *the* path by which they reconnected with their Judaism.[125] Numerous autobiographical statements published in the 1970s confirm these assessments, even as they also speak of the often excruciatingly conflicting pulls caused by the longing to be both fully Jewish *and* feminist.[126] Similarly, experiential reports by Jewish lesbian and gay activists frequently expressed the view that finding oneself as a Jew and joyfully accepting one's sexual identity were not just mutually complementary but often fundamentally inextricable processes. As the writer Lev Raphael, for example, put it, "Coming out as a Jew ultimately made it possible for me to come out as a gay man and then work at uniting the two identities."[127]

Precisely these activists' devotion to the Jewish community and to Judaism and/or Zionism made the community's rejection all the more anguishing. In an interview published in *Lilith*, lesbian feminist Batya Bauman spoke of her sadness at the fact that she was comfortable announcing her Jewishness in ethnically mixed lesbian groups but unable to "express my lesbian identity in the mainstream Jewish community. I don't believe there would be the same appreciation of who I am." Disturbed to find that the Jewish denominations lagged behind "some segments of the Church" in "making efforts to come to terms with their hitherto pejorative attitudes about homosexuality," she said: "I find it painful that the Jewish community, often at the forefront of liberal causes, has not as yet risen to this particular challenge, even as Jews count significantly in the emerging homosexual community." The mainstream Jewish community's response was all the more unfortunate in view of the strength of so many Jewish gays' and lesbians' dedication to Judaism. Describing services at Beth Simchat Torah, the gay synagogue in New York, for instance, Bauman noted that "it is hard to find another congregation of people with more intense and knowledgeable Jewish expression and devotion to Judaism and to each other; a number of Jewish scholars belong to BST and the scholarly level of the *divrei* (discussion of) *Torah* is unique among synagogues. The spirit of the Ongei Shabbat can only be compared with that of young Zionist movement kids. Such singing, such dancing! Such love!" Bauman predicted that "the various Jewish counter-cultures will save Judaism from its present slide into obsolescence."[128] Many commentators have since confirmed Bauman's prediction. But as her own experiences and those of many others showed, the transition was a rocky one, and fiercely resisted by those hostile to homosexuality and feminism.

In an atmosphere of tremendous searching for a meaningful renewal of Jewish communal and religious life—a search in which heterosexual feminists and gay men and lesbians were urgently and often successfully participating—it was doubly devastating to be told that one's desires ran counter to the very essence of Jewish survival. The power of the argument that a properly respectful response to the fact of the Holocaust was to strengthen Jewish family life and make more Jewish babies was one to which not only heterosexual feminists but also gays and lesbians clearly felt they had to be responsive. For example, confirming the sense conveyed by Zuckoff, Chesler, Frank, and others that Jewish women experienced the pro-familialist and pro-fertility version of Holocaust consciousness as an especially sensitive issue for Jewish feminism, one with which they had to come to terms, Susan Dworkin too commented on Jewish women's "mighty effort to right the historic Jewish population deficit": "No one inherits the Holocaust as pointedly as the Jewish wife. . . . The Jewish feminist is the only feminist who is told, by mentors who are feminists too, that the abortion option is not for her."[129]

Along related lines, one of the most noteworthy aspects of Jewish lesbian and gay writings from the 1970s and 1980s is the evident pressure the authors felt to make the case that—as Barry Alan Mehler put it in one of the first openly gay statements to appear in a mainstream Jewish venue—"Homosexuality is not responsible for the disintegration of Jewish family values." Mehler's essay, "Gay Jews," published in a 1977 issue of *Moment*, also confirmed Batya Bauman's point that it was hardly a simple matter to "come out" as a gay Jew. Mehler, who had come out in 1972 after four years of marriage (and former dreams of becoming a rabbi), reflected on the historic hatred and distrust of gayness in the Jewish community and summarized Judaism's view toward his sexual identity:

> In short, homophobia is built into Jewish tradition: homosexuality is unnatural, an abomination to God and nature; it has its origins in the fall of humanity through the serpent in the Garden of Eden; it is one of the essential differences between the Jew and the non-Jew and is associated with idol worship; finally, it does not lead to procreation.

Indicatively, moreover, Mehler not only felt the need to reiterate the obvious point that "homosexuality is a natural occurring phenomenon among Jews" but also included the not exactly factually correct but emotionally dramatic claim that the "first gay liberation movement began in Auschwitz, where 250,000 homosexuals died."[130] Bauman, too, tellingly included comments on the Third Reich in her interview for *Lilith*: "There are probably few Jews who ever heard of the pink triangle patch which the Nazis forced known homosexuals to wear, identifying them and leading them to the same crematoria as Jews. We were consumed together in the fires of the Holocaust and were united in our ashes."[131]

It is crucial to stress that these statements were made in a climate where some Jewish communal leaders said the Holocaust had nothing to do with gay history. This view was exemplified by the public comments of Connecticut rabbi Issac Avigdor. In response to gay activists' requests to have homosexual victims of Nazism recognized along with other victims in a proposed Holocaust memorial to be built in West Hartford, Avigdor declared categorically in 1978 that "homosexuality is a sin in the Biblical sense. I am not out to fight homosexuals but I won't insult the Jewish people by placing them in the same monument as with the homosexuals."[132] This kind of pronouncement provides a valuable historical context for the comments of the aforementioned closeted rabbi interviewed in *Gaysweek* in 1977. In that interview the rabbi sought to reclaim the earlier way to understand the lessons of the Holocaust so prevalent among left-liberals in the 1950s and early 1960s: the view that to learn "from the oppression of our Jewish people, particularly during the Holocaust" meant to "remember what it's like to be the underdog." From this point of view, those who were able to see that "the fight for gay rights is the same fight Jews have always championed . . . are the Jews who haven't assimilated, who keep the real faith. I don't think it's a coincidence," he added, "that a rather large percentage of activists in the gay and women's movements are Jews."[133]

The durability of homophobic prejudices, and the ongoing urgency of responding vigorously to them, remained evident as well in a late 1980s pamphlet put out by the progressive alliance New Jewish Agenda, "Coming Out, Coming Home: Lesbian and Gay Jews and the Jewish Community." The pamphlet not only elaborated parallels between the painful histories of Jews and homosexuals (among them the pressure to "pass" and the difficulties of confronting prejudice) but also noted that "Nazi Germany was the most extreme example of a society that used both groups as scapegoats; the fact that homosexuals went to the gas chambers along with Jews has only recently received attention from historians." Moreover, and again indicatively, the pamphlet devoted considerable attention to the ubiquitous concerns about Jewish survival and Jewish family values. It summarily observed that "since the Holocaust, we as Jews feel an intensified responsibility to raise Jewish children and transmit Jewish culture." Reminding readers that "Jewish leaders sometimes use the pretext that 'lesbians and gay men don't have children' to exclude them from communal life," the pamphlet not only stated the important caveat that "many lesbians and gay men *are* parents" but also elaborated further that "many more Jewish lesbians and gay men are actively nurturing future generations of Jews—as teachers, as aunts and uncles, as youth group leaders, and in many other capacities. We need many hearts to 'parent' our younger generations, and to pass on Jewish values." It continued cautiously: "Whether or not lesbian and gay Jews have children of their own, welcoming them into the Jewish community can only enrich its texture. We as a community must attend to issues of quality of Jewish life, not merely quantity. At the same time, we must take care not to exclude Jews even as we express concern about our numbers."[134] The pamphlet, in short, provided inadvertent but powerful evidence of the ascendance of conservative arguments and of the ways in which within the American Jewish community familialist and survivalist rhetoric had come to acquire the status of self-evident and uncontested common sense.

Yet the years of struggle and tremendous intracommunal conflict that eventually led to demonstrative gains for Jewish feminist and lesbian and gay activists are more seldom acknowledged than those advances themselves. By the 1980s, historian Edward Shapiro concluded in 1992, "Much of the Jewish feminist agenda had been achieved."[135] Indeed, Charles Silberman was able to argue matter-of-factly in 1985 that "in the long run the energy being released by the Jewish women's movement is likely to provide the most important source of religious renewal."[136] It took somewhat longer for lesbian and gay activists' concerns to gain formal recognition, but the 1990s saw considerable progress on these fronts as well, especially in Reform and Reconstructionist circles. In the year 2000 the Reform movement formally declared that it would support rabbis who officiated at gay and lesbian unions. Historians of postwar American Jewry now frequently and genially integrate the centrality of feminist activism, and sometimes also of lesbian and gay activism, into their discussions of the religious and communal revitalization of the 1970s and 1980s. But what is more customarily sidestepped in the extant mainstream accounts is the initial atmosphere of disdain and hostility that made those activist movements a necessity in the first place. Little mention is made of how extraordinarily arduous it was to make the case that (as Susannah Heschel phrased it in her anthology on Jewish feminism) "Judaism can belong to all who desire it."[137]

8 "If We Really Care About Israel": Breira and the Limits of Dissent

Are we, in the end, one people?
—Arnold Jacob Wolf, 1977

THE CASE OF BREIRA

In the aftermath of the Yom Kippur War in October 1973, *Response* editor Bill Novak publicly announced his decision to quit Havurat Shalom in Somerville, Massachusetts because he felt group members' reaction to the war had been inadequate. Dismayed that the spiritual side of the havurah resulted in members "remaining ignorant of or uninterested in the physical aspects of their Jewish commitment," Novak found his own "frantic worries during the Yom Kippur war made little sense to those around me" in the havurah. Unable any longer to sustain (what he saw as) the false "dichotomy" between the spiritual inward turning encouraged by the havurah and the real-world obligation of committed Jews also to address political issues, and centrally concerned with Israeli vulnerability, Novak moved promptly to help establish a new American Jewish group dedicated to the view that the Israeli government must immediately begin to do more to pursue prospects for a lasting peace with the Palestinian people.[1]

Calling itself Breira: A Project of Concern in Diaspora-Israel Relations, the group announced (as national chairperson, Rabbi Arnold Jacob Wolf, would later put it) that the name "betokened our desire for an alternative (*breira* in Hebrew) to the intransigence of *both* the PLO and the several governments of Israel. We proposed what has come to be known as the two-state solution, now more than ever the chief possibility for a peaceful, long-term resolution of the Middle East conflict."[2] There were also more subtle but no less significant reasons for choosing the name. Bill Novak explained:

> Breira is Hebrew for "alternative," but in Hebrew the word has much richer connotations than in English. For years Israelis have used the phrase *ein breira*—there is no alternative—to explain their situation, their attitude, and, increasingly, the policies of their government. Over time, the phrase has acquired more and more of a kind of official usage, to the point where, like the American notion of "national security," *ein breira* is sometimes used indiscriminately and reflexively as a defense of the status quo. Calling a Jewish organization "Breira" was a challenge to that usage. (It was also a comment about the importance of Israel and the Hebrew language, a point which seems to have been discounted by most observers.)[3]

In its first public statement from December 1973, Breira called for Israel "to make territorial concessions" and "recognize the legitimacy of the national aspirations of the Palestinians," but it insisted both that the purpose was "achieving a lasting peace" and that its effort to involve itself in Israeli affairs was inspired by "the idealism and thought of many early Zionists with whom we identify." Significantly, moreover, the statement emphasized not only the mutual responsibility of Israeli and Diaspora Jews to one another but pinpointed specifically the domestic U.S. atmosphere discouraging debate. As its founding statement went on to emphasize, "*This is the reason we join together now—we deplore those pressures in American Jewish life which make open discussion of these and other vital issues virtually synonymous with heresy.*"[4] Within a year Breira was a national membership organization with an impressive list of supporters, including approximately one hundred Reform and Conservative rabbis. Also among its members were such respected American Jewish writers and intellectuals as Steven M. Cohen, Paul Cowan, Arthur Green, Irving Howe, Paula Hyman, Jack Nusan Porter, Henry Schwarzschild, and Milton Viorst.

Breira survived four tumultuous years. Its proposals on Israeli-Diaspora Jewish relations and Palestinian nationalism generated fierce international debate over the limits of public dissent and conflict in Jewish communal life, and virtually every major American Jewish organization took a public stand on the group and what it advocated. Despite its prominence, however, Breira is routinely ignored in histories of postwar American Jewry; otherwise comprehensive studies like Edward Shapiro's *A Time for Healing: American Jewry*

Since World War II (1992) and Jack Wertheimer's *A People Divided: Judaism in Contemporary America* (1993) do not mention the group. When Breira is acknowledged, as in the work of Daniel Elazar, it is summarily dismissed as self-evidently having emerged from "the far peripheries" of the Jewish community, without "any standing with the mainstream."[5] Even a more balanced commentator like Chaim Waxman, in his brief discussion of Breira in *America's Jews in Transition* (1983), found reason to doubt whether Breira "was, first and foremost, a Jewish organization dedicated to the well-being of Jews and Jewish communities both in Israel and throughout the world."[6] Only in the scholarship of political scientist Marla Brettschneider have Breira and its legacies received more sympathetic treatment. Describing the intracommunal attacks that crushed Breira as a "tragedy," Brettschneider wrote in 1996:

> The case of Breira is all the more poignant when we realize the particular way in which the silencing of Breira was a tremendous loss to our community and to the movement toward deep struggle with a peace process in the Israeli-Arab and Israeli-Palestinian conflicts. Twenty years later, Breira's calls for a reevaluation of American Jewish self-conception and priorities, a revitalization of American Jewish culture and communal life, and its responsibility in [the] world Jewish community are still the cries from a community in crisis.[7]

Such contradictory evaluations of the group's relative importance (or lack thereof) remain in place to this day. To a remarkable degree Breira is simply forgotten, despite the fact that (as historian Jacques Kornberg predicted already in 1978) its brief life and ungentle end "may turn out to have been a watershed in contemporary American Jewish life."[8] Evaluating Breira's significance, and reconstructing the history of an organization that—in its day—provoked such widespread debate, requires first taking a closer look at the war of October 1973, the ideological tensions that preceded it and shaped responses to it, and the Jewish communal conflicts that resulted within both Israeli society and the United States in its wake.

THE YOM KIPPUR WAR

On October 6, 1973, Egyptian and Syrian armies staged a full-scale military assault against Israeli positions along two fronts: the Suez Canal and the Golan Heights. The Syrian aim was to overwhelm and destroy Israeli Defense Forces (IDF) and reach the Jordan River, retaking territories occupied by Israel since June 1967. Likewise, the Egyptian strategy was to cross the Suez Canal and recapture the Sinai Peninsula also taken by Israeli troops in the Six-Day War. Despite detailed surveillance of Arab military operational plans, and despite a widespread general perception that war was pending, Israeli intelligence was caught completely off guard by the simultaneous Arab offensives against outnumbered Israeli divisions. The initial consequences of this ill-preparedness proved almost catastrophic, a state of affairs exacerbated by the fact that war had begun on Yom Kippur, the most solemn of all Jewish holidays, and consequently many Israeli soldiers were in synagogue when the urgent call went out for them to rejoin their units.

"The Arab aim in launching the war," wrote Israeli historian Avi Shlaim, "was to break the political deadlock and to provoke an international crisis that would force the superpowers to intervene and put pressure on Israel to withdraw from the territories it had captured in June 1967."[9] Additionally, there was the pernicious factor of shame; Egyptians and Syrians wished to wipe away the deep sense of humiliation left by their stunning defeat in 1967. Israelis (and most especially Prime Minister Golda Meir) treated Arab military and political ineptitude as a given, and they reveled in the idea that any Arab military offensive would only reconfirm Israeli invincibility. As Foreign Minister Abba Eban, a dove who had criticized such jingoistic smugness, later described this prewar mood: "The rhetoric of 1973 is almost inconceivable. Opinion passed from sobriety to self-confidence and from self-confidence to fantasy, reaching a somewhat absurd level in 1973."[10] Yet for most Israeli leaders the view that prevailed was that Arabs were losers; in effect, they actively courted the very belligerence they soon found themselves shocked to encounter.

For a matter of several terrifying days, Egyptian and Syrian forces maintained a startling military advantage on both the northern and southern fronts. The Israeli command scrambled to catch up with developments it had so badly misinterpreted. There were indications that Prime Minister Meir, in consultation with Defense Minister Moshe Dayan, may have authorized the arming of Israeli missiles with nuclear warheads; however, it has also been reported that Israel threatened nuclear deployment only to hasten the delivery of crucial U.S. weapons resupplies.[11] As the crisis worsened, the Soviet Union flew huge amounts of military materials to resupply Egyptian and Syrian troops; the military airlift from the United States to Israeli forces was even greater. Once U.S. materials—including desperately needed aircraft—began to arrive, Arab forces lost their initiative, and the Israeli counteroffensive began to have its desired results.

By the end of October, when an effective cease-fire was finally in place, Israel had once again prevailed on the battlefield. Yet the country's postwar mood was utterly dissimilar from the mood after the war in 1967. Traveling to Israel in late November, I. L. Kenen, the influential director of the American Israel Public Affairs Committee (AIPAC), wrote: "Visitors to Israel are startled by the depths of her depression."[12] Or as Israeli historian Benny Morris would conclude with more than a quarter century of hindsight, the Yom Kippur War "had given Israel a stinging slap in the face."[13] Unsurprisingly, there was an immediate wave of mass demonstrations (staged by many embittered reservists) against Meir and Dayan, charging that they were personally accountable for the more than two thousand Israeli soldiers killed. Although the report of a national commission in April 1974 would formally exonerate Meir and Dayan of these accusations, continued protests nonetheless compelled the prime minister to resign. When Yitzhak Rabin was selected new head of state, Dayan was also excluded from his minister post.

The Yom Kippur War intensified ideological differences within Israeli society that would prove tremendously difficult to reconcile. Already in the wake of the Six-Day War, a nascent Israeli peace movement had questioned whether permanent Israeli occupation of the West Bank and Gaza Strip would only perpetuate regional conflict and warfare. After the 1967 war Israel had placed under its authority the world's largest Palestinian population; with no small irony Israel's military triumph had revitalized the dormant cause of Palestinian nationalism even as it transformed that cause into a domestic problem. The civil rights (or lack thereof) of more than one million Palestinian inhabitants under Israeli military rule in the occupied territories became a looming concern for intellectuals and activists mainly affiliated with the Israeli left. For Israeli leftists, and arguably for more moderate elements of the population as well, "the earthquake" (as many Israelis derisively called the Yom Kippur War) underscored that no lasting peace could be achieved without an exchange of land.

At the same time, and also since 1967, an ultranationalist movement within Israel sought to establish Jewish squatter settlements in the occupied territories. Some in the settler movement, like many members of the Movement for the Whole Land of Israel, were secularists convinced that Israeli security dictated that the captured territories never be returned. However, most in the settler movement were religious Zionists who identified the 1967 victory as a messianic call to embrace Biblical land (notably Judea and Samaria) as part of a "Greater Israel." Affiliated with the National Religious Party (NRP), and then by 1974 with the newly established umbrella organization Gush

Emunim (Bloc of the Faithful), these religious fundamentalists sought to redeem the ancient land of Israel through Jewish annexation; when necessary, Arab inhabitants were evicted to achieve this goal identified as divinely ordained. The settlement movement commenced already in the immediate aftermath of the 1967 war; although their actions were often unauthorized and illegal, the settlers received either direct government assistance (like military protection or expropriated state-owned land) or tacit government approval. By the end of 1973 there were nearly four dozen settlements altogether in the West Bank, the Gaza Strip, the Sinai Peninsula, and the Golan. By 1977 the number of settlements had risen to more than seventy.[14] Although Prime Minister Rabin opposed the settlements, support for the settlers from within his coalition prevented his administration from doing anything substantive to stop them.

MYTHS AND FACTS

In the several years after June 1967 ideological divisions with respect to the Israeli-Arab conflict deepened among American Jews as well. Speaking for the hawks in his popular AIPAC pamphlet *Myths and Facts* (1970), I. L. Kenen angrily critiqued those anti-Israeli forces who sought to "rewrite history" when they "create and glamorize a 'Palestine Arab Nation,' which, they contend, was exiled by an aggressive Israel."[15] The pamphlet—which sold more than 225,000 copies—also spelled out how Israeli annexation of the occupied territories was both militarily imperative and historically justifiable.

The 1974 edition of *Myths and Facts*, released in February of that year, made plain that for Syria and Egypt the October war "was not merely a war to recover territory lost in 1967" but a direct attack against "Israel's existence." It further argued: "Arab propaganda is sustained by a double moral standard. What is right for the Arab states is wrong for Israel. It is right for Arabs to mobilize Moslems all over the world to stand up for Arab nationalism and against Israel. It is wrong for Jewish nationalism to win the support of Jews." Statements like "Israel mistreats and discriminates against her Arab citizens," or "A UN commission has repeatedly condemned Israel's treatment of Arabs within the occupied territories" were debunked as myths spun by "propaganda mills in Arab countries."[16] Already in the immediate wake of the Six-Day War, the 1967 edition of *Myths and Facts* (released two months after the war) had announced its own "answer" to the Middle East crisis. On the one hand, Palestinian nationalism had no basis in history: "Palestine was never a separate Arab state," but "Jews have lived in Eretz Israel since the days of Abraham, about 2000 B.C." On the other hand, the best plan for managing the problem of displaced Palestinians was to resettle them in neighboring Arab nations (like Iraq) "where there is ample room and where they would live among their own people."[17]

By contrast, in the years following the Six-Day War American Jews identified as doves saw hopes for a peaceful resolution to the Middle East crisis as residing principally in recognizing the demands of Palestinian nationalists. For instance, as Don Peretz, a professor of political science at the State University of New York at Binghamton, opened his paper at the Annual Conference of the American Academic Association for Peace in the Middle East held in Philadelphia in February 1970:

> My purpose is neither to praise nor to bury Palestinian Arab nationalism but to explain why I think an awareness and understanding of it is essential to peace in the Middle East. Without such attention the movement will certainly continue to be a major source of conflict. Although there are many who would like to dominate, to destroy or to deny it, the Palestinian Arab national movement seems to have become autonomous of any local or outside force.

Peretz further observed that "it would be a disservice to the quest for peace in the Middle East to dismiss the new Palestinian nationalism as a transitory phenomenon that will disappear after a few retaliatory raids."[18] At the same conference Labor Zionist Marie Syrkin primarily agreed with Peretz's assessment, concluding in her paper that the "most reasonable solution" to the Middle East crisis

> is the proposal to set up a Palestine entity on the West Bank and the East Bank of the Jordan. . . . Such a Palestinian state could serve to satisfy newborn Palestinian nationalism and in conditions of peace prosper economically in partnership with Israel. The emergence of such a state would mean compromises for both parties to the conflict. Israel, regardless of victory, would have to accept the narrow confines of its much amputated state, and the Arabs would have to come to terms with the reality of Israel.[19]

New peace groups in Israel like the student organization SIACH (New Israeli Left) and in the U.S. like CONAME (Committee on New Alternatives in the Middle East, based in New York) adopted largely comparable positions.

Also during these years, a number of leading liberal American Zionists voiced frustration with the intransigence of official Israeli policy towards the

Palestinians—and simultaneously began to articulate distress at the constraints on dissent within the American Jewish community. For instance, in a 1970 essay, "My Zionist Dilemmas," long-time UAHC activist Balfour Brickner declared that "I love the State of Israel but I cannot stand some of the tactics of its supporters." Brickner confessed that he agreed "with those radical Jewish youth who talk about the necessity of Israel's recognizing the Palestinians." Yet he spelled out as well what he saw as "the cruelest paradox": that although "Israelis, despite their emergency, freely debate what attitude to take to the Palestinians, in America merely to raise the issue is to risk being branded a heretic or an enemy of the Jews."[20] Along different but related lines, Joachim Prinz, now affiliated with Americans for Progressive Israel—Hashomer Hatzair, the socialist Zionist group long committed to a binational state, in 1970 blasted the rise of a "kind of fanatical and ritualistic Orthodoxy in Israel" whose goal of "religious dictatorship . . . has made Israel a country that does not believe in religious liberty." Addressing the annual convention of the Rabbinical Assembly (Conservative), Prinz too, like Brickner, alluded to the felt sense that American Jews should not criticize Israel. Prinz indeed recommended "*a continuation of such self-imposed discipline*." However, he also cautioned that "the fact that we are silent in public does not and ought not to convey the notion to Israel that there are not many thoughtful American Jews—and for that matter, Jews in other countries as well—who do not always share the views expressed in public utterances by leaders of Israel." Prinz added that "the time has come for Israel to embark upon a new and dramatic peace offensive. . . . I am not talking about empty gestures and homiletics. I am talking about concrete proposals and concrete assurances. I am talking about an attempt on the part of Israel to assure the world that *shalom* really means peace."[21] Here, then, were members of an older American Zionist guard with strong memories of a domestically liberal-left form of American Zionism; after all, in the fifties and early sixties that form of Zionism with which Prinz and Brickner had been closely identified had promoted the cause of antiracist activism in the Jewish community. But since the later sixties, the content and meaning of Zionism was shifting rightward.

For younger liberal-left and leftist activists who came Jewishly of age in the post-1967 moment, there appeared little in American Zionism worth rescuing. Opposed to the new rightist tendencies of American Zionism, and seemingly unaware of Zionism's diverse earlier incarnations, some younger radicals categorically defined Zionism per se as part of the problem, not part of a solution. For instance, UC-Berkeley graduate student Michael Lerner stated in 1969 that American Zionists "are hypocrites—and this realization is what shapes young Jews' consciousness on all Zionist questions. The real misfortune is to the people of Israel who, whatever their problems, ought not to be shackled with the responsibility for the corruption of the American Zionists." Consequently, Lerner organized the Committee for a Progressive Middle East, based in Berkeley, "to provide an alternative to the reactionary Zionism of the Jewish community on the one hand and the somewhat mindless reaction of many young Jews against Israel on the other."[22] Even more dramatically, Barry Rubin, foreign editor of the weekly socialist newspaper, the *Guardian*, argued during a 1972 discussion attended by several radicals (both Jewish and non-Jewish) on the future of the Palestinian struggle organized by the Middle East Research and Information Project (MERIP) in Washington, D.C., that

> our problem—one of our problems—is that there's been a recent revival of Zionist ideology in the United States, which I think is purposely aimed not only to give aid and support to Israel but also to attempt to make people—especially Jews in this country—accept a racist, reactionary ideology which also will turn them against the American Left. . . . And what we have to do, both as American leftists and especially those of us who are Jewish, is to start waging a really strong ideological struggle against Zionism in the Jewish community.

And Rubin concluded: "I think it would be good to have Jews actively campaigning in favor of Palestinian needs. It immediately breaks up the myth combining Judaism and Zionism."[23]

Yet the overwhelming tone taken by mainstream American Jewish commentators during these years toward the cause of Palestinian nationalism, or toward those Jewish leftists and liberals who chose to advance that cause or to condemn the new forms of American Zionism, was adversarial, if not outright hostile. Some, like Brandeis professor Ben Halpern, questioned the very authenticity of Palestinian identity. Halpern not only saw the notion of "Palestinian national personality" as a "weapon in the war to eliminate Israel" but also argued that "Palestinian Arab nationalism often gives the impression of a tactical expedient rather than an end in itself" and suggested that "all the protestations that Palestinian Arabs . . . can preserve a deeply-felt national identity only in Palestine seem contrived and quite provisional."[24] Others, like Harvard professor Seymour Martin Lipset, pondered why radical Jews so routinely appeared to embrace the Palestinian cause; he found his answer in those radicals' unhappy childhoods. In an oft-cited 1969 essay in *Encounter*, "'The Socialism of Fools': The Left, the Jews and Israel," Lipset argued that because young Jewish leftists had most customarily been raised in assimilated Jewish families they now "exhibit familiar forms of Jewish self-hatred, of so-called 'Jewish anti-Semitism,' of the sort which were widespread within the Left before the Nazi holocaust and the creation of the State of Israel. Self-hatred," Lipset added, "is becoming a major problem for the American Jewish community." It was evident to Lipset that as part of their rebellion against their parents Jewish leftists supported the Palestinian cause as a bizarre form of transference; they embraced the view of "American Jewish life as essentially immoral and hypocritical, and not a few of them extend this view to Israel's relations with Arabs. Israel, in effect, seems to be behaving like their parents."[25] So far as the leftist Jew was concerned, Lipset concluded, the real mistake Israel had made in the Six-Day War was win.

Even commentators with ongoing sympathy for New Leftism nonetheless registered laments for what they perceived as the movement's increasingly blunt anti-Israeli sentiments. For instance, in 1971 the popular New Left journal *Ramparts* published a lengthy internal critique of the New Left precisely for taking a "knee-jerk approach to the Middle East and the question of Jewish nationalism." Written by Sol Stern—a contributing editor of *Ramparts* and an activist who had participated in the Free Speech movement at Berkeley—"My Jewish Problem—and Ours" noted "perplexing developments" in the New Left, which "shattered for me the unspoken assumptions that there was no conflict between being a Jew and a radical." Stern wrote,

> Jewish national consciousness now is being portrayed as incompatible with revolutionary internationalism. The images of the contestants in the Middle East conflict have been reversed from what they were in 1948, and the truce between Marxism and Zionism has been shattered. Now it is the Arab side that has the aura of being a national liberation struggle and a people's war, with the attention of the international left being focused on the Palestinian guerrillas, not on the reactionary Arab governments.[26]

With less mournfulness and more anger, radical Zionist M. Jay Rosenberg also detailed how contradictory challenges confronted Jews in the New Left:

> What we say is this: We are radicals. We actively oppose the war in Vietnam. We support the black liberation movement as we endorse all genuine movements of liberation. And thus, first and foremost, we support our own. We will march with our brothers on the left. We will support them.

> But when they call for the death of Israel, when they acquiesce in plans for the liquidation of the Jewish state, we then have no choice but to fight them. We shall denounce anti-Semitism whether it emanates from the right or the left. There is no such thing as "progressive" anti-Semitism. And we shall not allow the "revolutionaries" to escape our indictment of racism by claiming that they are "anti-Zionist but not anti-Semitic." If they can reconcile themselves to the existence of every nation on the planet but Israel, if they call for revolution in every country but only death for Israel, then they are clearly against the Jewish people. One may call them what he will.[27]

In short, the years after 1967 saw increased internal dissent among Jews involved in the radical American movements for social change, as well as greater polarization between leftist Jews and the Jewish mainstream. While some American Jewish radicals continued to articulate views honed on the left wing of the antiwar movement, applying a New Left critique of American imperialism in Vietnam to Israeli military rule of Palestinians on the West Bank, for instance, more often than not, Jewish radicals were hesitant to fall so quickly into line with an analysis that appeared increasingly to align them—at least ideologically—with Israel's sworn enemies.

ALTERNATIVE

In the immediate aftermath of the Yom Kippur War, then, an alliance of diverse members of the American Jewish community—among them liberal Conservative and Reform rabbis, left-leaning and moderate intellectuals, and young Jewish radicals and students in the Jewish counterculture—joined together to establish Breira. One purpose of this new left-center alliance was to reverse the growing ideological polarization within the American Jewish community; for many this also meant organizing a formal challenge to right-wing Zionists both in Israel and the United States. A second aim was to provide public forums where contentious topics like Palestinian nationalism, the Jewish settler movement, and the rise of Gush Emunim could be engaged in open debate. A third objective was to bring together liberal communal leaders of an older generation (many of whom had also been active in civil rights and antiwar protest) with members of the Jewish counterculture and Jewish radical movements around matters of shared urgency. One indirect goal, then, was to address a decade of sharp intergenerational divisions within the American Jewish community. Furthermore, and also reflective of a post-sixties commitment to lessen sectarian conflict, the coalition brought together secularist and religious—as well as Zionist and non-Zionist—elements. (Critics would later also contend that the group embraced anti-Zionist views, but this is more arguable.) Finally, though not least of all, the strong presence of women within the coalition reflected feminism's recent powerful impact on nearly every dimension of American Jewish communal existence.

In a relatively short time Breira appeared well on its way to becoming precisely what its founders intended: a sort of dovish alternative both to the mainstream American Israel Public Affairs Committee and to the more militant right-wing religious Zionism of the Jewish Defense League or Gush Emunim. Unsurprisingly, given its profile and the surge of grassroots communal disillusionment with the status quo of Israeli-Palestinian relations after the October war, Breira gained often enthusiastic endorsements from at least six overlapping quarters. First, it found support from socialist Zionist groups, especially Hashomer Hatzair and its allied organization, Americans for a Progressive Israel—both of which had been active for decades.[28] Second, Breira quickly attracted dozens of rabbis dismayed by the rightward drift both in the U.S. and Israel; notable among these were Eugene Borowitz, Balfour Brickner, Everett Gendler, Robert Gordis, Richard Levy, and Joachim Prinz.[29] Third, Breira drew considerable support from numerous Hillel Foundations across the U.S. While they would later be mocked as "incubators of Breira," Hillels across the country indeed proved remarkably receptive to this new peace initiative; at least eight Hillel directors (including those at UCLA, Dartmouth, Carnegie-Mellon, Adelphi, Temple, and Yale) served on Breira's advisory committee. Fourth, Breira also concretized aims emerging out of the larger and more amorphous phenomenon known as the radical Jewish youth movement. Already early in 1973, at Rutgers University's Hillel, a conference of Jewish student activists initially raised the idea for a group that would provide an alternative to establishment Jewish communal views on Zionism as well as Israeli military policies and attitudes toward Palestinians. Many, though not all, of these activists were themselves radical Zionists, such as those involved with the Jewish Liberation Project in New York.[30] The fifth strand of support for Breira, and possibly the most influential, came from the havurah movement; the New York Havurah and Fabrangen in Washington, D.C., proved particularly helpful. (The New York Havurah, for instance, contributed its small office space where Breira began publishing a newsletter, *interChange*, in September 1975.)

Finally, and crucially in terms of how the intracommunal controversy over Breira's actual intentions would later explode, the group's staff and advisory committee also included individuals that had prior affiliations with American Jewish peace organizations on the New Left. These included several peace activists closely associated with the Jewish Peace Fellowship (like Rabbi Gendler), CONAME (like Bob Loeb, Don Peretz, John Ruskay, Allan Solomonow, and Arthur Waskow), and MERIP (like Barry Rubin), all of whom later joined Breira or wrote for its newsletter and several of whom assumed important roles in the group's operations. Waskow, for example, had already in 1970 proposed that Jewish Israeli security depended on encouraging the establishment of an independent Palestinian state and that American Jews had an obligation to advocate and help make this possible.[31] Many members of Breira shared this general outlook.

Yet what remains most striking about Breira, as Jacques Kornberg observed as early as 1978, is that despite the prominent participation of radical Jews within it the organization's official platform "hardly constitutes a call to the barricades."[32] Breira did *not* position itself as "out there" on the New Left. On the contrary, Breira also sought deliberately to gain moderate—and even neoconservative—support; as Breira executive director Bob Loeb said: "We are a coalition which is not predicated at all on a left-right debate."[33] And the group did successfully draw prominent Jewish academics and communal spokespersons like Nathan Glazer, Charles S. Liebman, Jacob Neusner, and Michael Wyschogrod into its circle of sympathizers. This is hardly surprising, given that, as Bill Novak would point out, "the members of Breira had all the right credentials: they had been involved all their lives with Jewish schools, Jewish youth groups, seminaries, summer camps, programs in Israel, Jewish publications, and the like."[34] Moreover, Breira both consistently asserted its own loyalty to Zionism and persistently made arguments very much in the spirit of traditional Jewish liberalism. For example, and not coincidentally given many of Breira's roots in the Jewish antiracist activism of the early sixties, a Breira statement from 1975 openly reinvoked the language of that era, merging the gesture toward an earlier form of Holocaust consciousness with the new concern about limits on dissent in the U.S.:

> Our immediate and overriding concern is peace in the Middle East. Our concern grows out of our love and respect for the people and the land of Israel as well as our understanding that the continuity of Jewish life in the Diaspora is inextricably linked to the existence of Israel.
>
> We are not innocent bystanders. If we share the anxieties about Israel's policies, we have the responsibility to say so. If we detect mistakes which

> might have catastrophic consequences, we must not ignore or swallow our concern. . . . For the sake of Zion, we shall not be silent.[35]

Thus Breira represented a dissenting Jewish voice, but it was a voice that saw itself coming, as one Breira publication put it, "from within the mainstream of the American Jewish community and from a more moderate perspective" than the "extreme" views one heard from groups like the Jewish Defense League (which were considered to be outside the mainstream).[36] This distinction needs to be kept in mind in view of how swiftly the terms of debate surrounding the group would eventually shift. Its members understood—and expected—that going public with American Jewish criticism of Israeli policies toward the Palestinians would generate debate and controversy. But it is safe to say that Breira members could in no way have anticipated the intense barrage of assaults the group would ultimately provoke.

IF WE REALLY CARE ABOUT ISRAEL

Jewish communal and professional response to Breira went through three phases. The first phase was the longest; it lasted almost three years from late 1973 until mid-1976. During this time there was a widespread sense that although Breira was raising unpleasant issues, these issues were important and indeed a segment of the American Jewish community agreed with Breira's positions. The nationally distributed *Jewish Post and Opinion*, for instance, thoroughly covered Breira's policy statements, and its editorials on the group acknowledged that the group's views were causing conflict, but held that intracommunal debate only benefited the American Jewish community. "Actually, we seem to need to learn all over again that differences of opinion, even those strongly held, are healthy," stated a *Jewish Post and Opinion* editorial from 1974.[37] Yet the *Jewish Post and Opinion* had long maintained a liberal editorial policy, and would be expected to embrace a new peace initiative like Breira.

On the other hand, a more indicative communal bellwether might be the Washington, D.C. area newspaper, *Jewish Week*. Again, it too remained remarkably evenhanded in its coverage of Breira. This was notable not least because a *Jewish Week* editorial from 1971 had seen fit to upbraid American Jews who publicly dissented from Israeli official policies, going so far as to argue that there was "no place for them in the American Jewish community" because their actions "can and do help to undermine Israel's cause before the American people."[38] It was notable as well because *Jewish Week* editor

Philip Hochstein had a notorious track record of red-baiting radical Jews; this seemed to go double for anything involving local radical Jewish leader Arthur Waskow. As discussed in chapter 5, Hochstein had been instrumental in the smear campaign that aborted local United Jewish Appeal funding of Fabrangen—almost solely because Waskow was associated with it. Additionally, *Jewish Week* carried a regular column by right-wing commentator I. L. Kenen, director of AIPAC, on media coverage of Middle East issues. In short, Hochstein would have been well-informed on Breira and what it stood for and could easily have undermined it from the very outset.

Despite this history of Jewish antileftism, *Jewish Week* found nothing too objectionable about Breira. When Breira opposed the "Rally Against Terror" on November 4, 1974, organized by the Conference of Presidents of Major American Jewish Organizations to protest the appearance of PLO leader Yasir Arafat at the U.N., a *Jewish Week* editorial did opine that "Israel's refusal to negotiate with a murderous band that openly avows the aim of destroying Israel must be upheld." Yet its handling of Breira was more conciliatory, even conceding Breira might have a point when it charged that "perhaps Israel erred during the long years since the war of 1967 in not having done more to promote" dialogue with the Palestinians (though adding quickly that "it is misleading to suggest that the option is now open.")[39] More significant, though, in terms of getting the word out to the Washington Jewish community, is that (until early 1976) *Jewish Week* repeatedly reported statements by local Breira spokesperson Rabbi David Saperstein, associate director of the Religious Action Center of the Union of American Hebrew Congregations. More than once, Saperstein was also provided a column where he could rebut the views of American Jewish hawks on the Middle East conflict. Against Herbert A. Fierst, chairman of the Washington chapter of the American Jewish Committee, whose concern for Israel (he said) obligated him to support increased U.S. defense spending, Saperstein wrote, "If we really care about Israel, let us not give into any kind of blackmail on the question of the Jewish community's support for the military budget."[40] And when Wolf I. Blitzer, who edited *Myths and Facts* (1976) for *Near East Report*, argued that "as American Jews, I am sure that we can find better things to do than tell Israelis what is—or what isn't—in their best national security interests," Saperstein queried, "Are we going to stand up and say to the American people, you can be for national rights of the Palestinians and be strong supporters of Israel, or, by our silence, are we going to force Americans to choose between support of Israel and support of the Palestinians just because Israeli policy at this moment make the two seem incompatible?"[41] Given a self-consciousness over how such debates within Washington's Jewish communal leadership might likely also influence members of Congress, *Jewish Week*'s balanced handling of Breira and what it advocated becomes that much more striking.

Throughout this initial phase Breira continued to publicize its positions, refine its arguments, and expand its national membership. It sponsored lectures by leading American Jewish commentators, like *Jewish Spectator* editor Trude Weiss-Rosmarin, as well as Israeli doves, like Mattiyahu Peled, a retired Israeli Defense Forces major general. It published a collection of essays by Israeli doves and regularly invited Israeli intellectuals in the peace movement to write for its monthly newsletter, *interChange*; these contributions called for direct negotiations with the Palestine Liberation Organization, advocated the formation of a self-determining Palestinian state, and criticized the settlement movement and Gush Emunim. In January 1976 *interChange* reported in a fashion clearly intended to sound ominous that Gush Emunim "is sending a delegation to the United States where they expect to find great support from members of the Conference of Presidents of Major American Jewish Organizations, the United Jewish Appeal, and the Israel Bonds. One of their most prominent supporters here is Rabbi Fabian Schonfeld, leader of a wealthy congregation in Queens and President of the Rabbinical Council of America."[42] While such reports on Gush Emunim in *interChange* were strictly factual, there was no doubt that they also sought to reinforce who was speaking from outside the mainstream of Jewish communal life—and who from within it. Repeatedly, then, Breira sought (with no small degree of initial success) to lay claim to the center of American Jewish political discourse on the Middle East and thereby reverse a rightward swing of the ideological pendulum underway at least since 1967.

U.S. JEWS BEGINNING TO GO PUBLIC IN CRITICISM OF ISRAEL

During Passover week in 1976 Gush Emunim organized a march of more than thirty thousand supporters through the West Bank. The march resulted in clashes in which one Arab was killed and several were injured by Israeli security forces. This fatal confrontation, taken together with the death of six Arab Israelis in the Galilee area, prompted the Breira executive board to draft an "Open Letter to Israel's Leaders." Dated April 7, 1976, it read in part:

> We are grieved by the tragic events of the past weeks in the occupied West Bank and within Israel proper. . . . Police action, even when justified, will not

> end growing Arab civil resistance to the Israeli government's plan for the expropriation of Arab and Jewish land in the Galilee, nor will it end growing frustration in the captured territories over Israel's nine year occupation. Rigorous suppression of Arab dissent serves only to strengthen Arab nationalism and to weaken faith in Israeli and Jewish commitment to the human and national rights on which Israeli society was founded and is maintained.[43]

With the distribution of this April 7 letter to leading Israeli government officials, the second phase in the Breira controversy commenced. On May 3 the *Washington Post* ran a headline that read: "U.S. Jews Beginning to Go Public in Criticism of Israel." Breira was named as a group calling on Israel to "turn its occupied territories on the West Bank into a separate Arab state and pull back to its 1967 boundaries." This, the *Post* added, "is a proposal argued widely in Israel, but rarely heard in this country, where criticism of what Israel does has come to be equated with an attack on Israel's existence." The article quoted Breira members Joachim Prinz and Balfour Brickner as well as outspoken Orthodox rabbi Henry Siegman, executive director of the Synagogue Council of America, who was not a Breira member but also publicly advocated a withdrawal by Israel to its pre-1967 boundaries, "with the exception of Jerusalem and minor border rectifications."[44] More sympathetic publicity of Breira followed. The following week, a *New York Times* editorial noted that Breira was "picking up wide support among influential Jewish intellectuals in its criticism of Gush Emunim, overcoming as well the misapprehension of many Jewish Americans that criticism of Israeli policies would be seen as a rejection of Israel."[45] However, and although Rabbi Alexander M. Schindler, chairman of the Presidents of Major American Jewish Organizations, said at the time that there was "a new openness to divergent viewpoints and I am determined to keep that openness alive," and Rabbi Siegman agreed that American Jews were currently experiencing "a new openness and willingness to criticize certain specific issues" within Israel, there were powerful indicators that this optimism would prove premature, and that a tightening of the reins on dissent was already underway.[46]

Several leading Jewish communal figures stepped forward to condemn the April 7 letter. These critics used diverse strategies to deflate Breira's impact. Rabbi Stanley Rabinowitz, president of the Rabbinical Assembly, said of Breira members, "It is arrogant of them to sit in their ivory towers and pass judgement, with nothing to lose by making the wrong choice." Rabbi Israel Klavan, executive vice president of the Rabbinical Council (Orthodox), stated: "What they are doing is weakening Israel's bargaining position." And (although in 1972 he had warned that "American Jewry will not become a 'colony' of Israel. We insist on the right to criticize Israel when criticism is needed, even if that criticism is likely to be exploited by Israel's enemies"), Rabbi Arthur Hertzberg now observed that public criticism of Israeli policy inadvertently fed into anti-Israeli propaganda, citing as an example how a critical statement he had once made about Israel had been manipulated by an Arab U.N. delegate.[47]

Almost all at once Breira experienced its first real hostile backlash. Within weeks, several more Jewish communal leaders now publicly excoriated Breira. Hyman Bookbinder, Washington representative of the American Jewish Committee, noted how there was "a shrillness, a self-righteousness, [and] a certitude" about the group that disturbed him. And Bookbinder harshly added, "I don't believe Israel needs to be lectured about morality."[48] A Hadassah newsletter slammed Breira members as "Cheerleaders for Defeatism," lumped Breira together with anti-Zionist groups, and warned that "every Hadassah member should be alerted to anticipate and reject the advances of these organizations with their dogmas that run counter to Israel security and Jewish survival."[49] Meanwhile, forty-seven rabbis published a signed statement that accused Breira of promoting a position "practically identical with the Arab point of view."[50] And also that May, Harold M. Jacobs, president of the Union of Orthodox Jewish Congregations of America, and Fred Ehrman, chairman of the UOJCA Israel Commission, issued a joint statement that demeaned Breira representatives Prinz and Brickner for their "diaspora mentalities" and for their "cheap shots at the Israeli government" that performed "a great disservice by highlighting to the American people the division that may exist within the Jewish community in regard to the administered territories." The UOJCA statement characterized Breira as "dangerous and divisive," charged that the group's public dissent was "undermining the morale of the American and Israeli Jewish communities," and recorded UOJCA's official support of Gush Emunim and the settlement movement.[51]

In June 1976, when more than one hundred representatives of the Conference of Presidents of Major American Jewish Organizations met in New York, "the debate over debate" dominated discussion, just as it also would that same month at annual meetings of the Synagogue Council of America and the American Zionist Federation. At the presidents' conference Eugene Borowitz spoke in favor of Breira, advocating an official policy endorsing the possibility of American Jewish dissent on Israeli policy, while Fabian Schonfeld defended Gush Emunim and challenged the right to dissent. By the end of the conference, Alexander Schindler sought middle ground when he suggested that criticism of Israel might be restricted to the Jewish press. However, this move at conciliation did little to reduce heightening animosity between supporters and critics of the right to American Jewish dissent on Israel.[52]

As controversy over its actions continued to heat up, Breira's newsletter *interChange* stayed on the offensive against its detractors. In May 1976 it had circulated a public letter, "The Time Has Come To Say NO to Gush Emunim," signed by over one hundred prominent Breira supporters. These supporters included Aviva Cantor, Phyllis Chesler, Leonard Fein, Betty Friedan, Vivian Gornick, Grace Paley, Muriel Rukeyser, Morris Schappes, Charles Silberman, Ted Solotaroff, I. F. Stone, and Alvin Toffler. The letter read in full:

> We American Jews who are ardent supporters of Israel's existence encourage all peace forces in Israel in their demonstration on the eighth of May against the proposed Jewish settlement in Kadum on the West Bank.
>
> Like our brothers and sisters in Israel, we feel that further Jewish settlement in the occupied territories is an obstacle to peace efforts.
>
> We will join with all people committed to a secure Israel in building a just and equitable peace.[53]

In the same issue, and reversing precisely the rhetoric of Breira's opponents, Balfour Brickner bluntly asserted: "It is neither distortion nor exaggeration to accuse the Gush Emunim and their supporters of undermining the security and threatening the survival of the State of Israel."[54] In June *interChange* opened with an Irving Howe essay entitled "For Free Discussion in the Jewish Community"; it also reprinted the *Post* article and the *New York Times* editorial and offered a concise summary of the anti-Breira UOJCA statement. In short, Breira appeared in little mood to be conciliatory toward its opponents.

In the later months of 1976, during a period that might have seemed like a lull, the storm over Breira was actually about to break. Right-wing American Jewish elements supportive of Gush Emunim and the settlement movement were moving ahead with an analysis that Breira provided aid and comfort to anti-Israeli forces and was thus not to be trusted. On this front the right-wing journal *American Zionist* took the lead, leveling accusations that—by going public with a private Jewish communal debate—it was Breira that directly threatened Israeli survival. Breira was an organization comprised not of doves, a first *American Zionist* essay sarcastically intoned, but really of pigeons, and it was well-known that flocks of pigeons "constitute a public health menace in many large cities, not to mention a public nuisance."[55] A second *American Zionist* article asserted: "American Jews are in accord that dissent is a vital democratic freedom. What troubles the Jewish community is not the right itself, but its abuse." And it was manifestly obvious to the *American Zionist* that Breira abused its right to free speech when it brought intra-Jewish disunity to the attention of the wider gentile world. "The Jews who cry 'Foul!' in public must realize the treacherous consequences of their efforts," the magazine concluded. "Ramifications are felt not by them, but by fellow Jews thousands of miles away."[56]

Such crass and seemingly over-the-top attempts to cast Breira's members as illegitimate—indeed, inauthentic, traitorous, and anti-Jewish—Jews did little to dampen the enthusiasm of the group, flush with what correctly must have seemed like the moment it stood on the threshold of both popular acceptance and widespread credibility. Yet the reversal of Breira's fortunes arrived swiftly. Few could have foreseen how close at hand the end turned out to be.

BREIRA MEANS SUICIDE

On November 1, 1976, in New York, and then again on November 15 in Washington, D.C., several American Jews met with Sabri Jiryis, an Arab Israeli author with close ties to the PLO, and Isam Sartawi, a leading Palestinian intellectual and (according to the State Department) a member of the Fatah Revolutionary Council. Among the Jews present at the meetings were Herman Edelsberg, recently retired director of the B'nai B'rth International Council, David Gorin, the newly appointed Washington area regional director of the American Jewish Congress, Olya Margolin, Washington representative of the National Council of Jewish Women, Rabbi Max Ticktin, assistant national director of the B'nai B'rth Hillel Foundations, and Arthur Waskow, resident fellow of the Institute for Policy Studies in Washington, D.C. Ticktin and Waskow were also members of Breira's executive committee, as well as members of Fabrangen. The meetings were arranged by the American Friends Service Committee, a Quaker organization. By mutual consent, the meetings were to be kept secret; additionally, the American Jews made it understood that they were present solely as private citizens, not as representatives of any agency or association.

On November 23 *Near East Report* editor Wolf Blitzer revealed in the *Jerusalem Post* that the meetings had taken place, and within days the meetings made headlines in the American Jewish press.[57] There followed a rapid flurry of condemnations. The Conference of Presidents of Major American Jewish

Organizations stated that it "vigorously opposes and deplores any meetings—official or unofficial—with the P.L.O." (Interestingly, borrowing and reconfiguring the language of Breira, its reasoning was that such contacts "could tend to undermine the peace process.")[58] B'nai B'rth, the American Jewish Congress, and the National Council of Jewish Women all issued policy statements that denounced the meetings; Gorin received a public reprimand from the AJCongress. Additionally, Stanley Rabinowitz charged that Breira now appeared to be "fronting for the PLO."[59] Unsurprisingly, the meetings were also seized upon by I. L. Kenen, Blitzer's colleague at *Near East Report*, who singled out Breira for censure, labeling it an American Jewish organization that "actually has undermined American support for Israel."[60]

At the same time, *Jewish Week* rethought any prior reluctance to rip into Breira; an editorial in January 1977 now queried in vitriolic near incoherence: "Why, of all the many millions of Arabs with whom one might seek dialogue, has the *Breira* inner dictatorship elected to approach the PLO? Is it not because these ideologists assume that peaceful and passive people are so unrepresentative of virtue as to be contemptible, while terrorists and murderers are so only because the holiness of their cause justifies and demands violence?"[61] Another editorial stated that "it is most obnoxious to find American Jews conferring with terrorist agents who state as their purpose the manipulation of American Jewish influence to shape Israel's policies."[62] And yet a third *Jewish Week* editorial upstaged the first two by adding a reference to Nazism into the equation: "There is no doubt that American Jews have 'the right' to question Israel's policies, but it is a certainty that they have a prior duty to unmask the brutal intransigence of Israel's Arab enemies, and to fight the appeasement mentality of a world that seems to have forgotten the massive price civilization paid for appeasement at Munich."[63]

Thus it was in this already overheated rhetorical tinderbox that the third and final phase of the Breira controversy was announced by a front-page headline in *Jewish Week* on January 27, 1977: "Scholar accuses Breira of pro-PLO 'obsession.' " The scholar in question was Rael Jean Isaac, described as "a scholar of Jewish affairs, whose earlier work was 'Israel Divided,' a study of the opposed forces in the Jewish state's political and social struggles."[64] The text in question was a thirty-page pamphlet, *Breira: Counsel for Judaism*, which argued that Breira had no authority to speak on behalf of the American Jewish community. The neutral characterization of its author served only to make her analysis of Breira appear that much more credible.

A closer look at Isaac's background, however, revealed a less than neutral observer. In her book, *Israel Divided: Ideological Politics in the Jewish State*

(1976), Isaac had detailed how the settlement movement in Israel drew upon what was "normative" in Jewish religious tradition. Acknowledging that it was "possible to view both the Land of Israel Movement and the peace movement as embodying deviant traditional perspectives within Zionism," Isaac's argument was that this was inaccurate. According to Isaac, "the chief strength of the Land of Israel Movement is that it represents in fact normative Zionism," while "the peace movement, on the other hand, derives from a deviant but traditional strain that saw the basic task of Zionism as reaching agreement with the Arabs." Isaac's thesis hinged on this distinction. It was to misread both Jewish history and religion, Isaac stated, if one failed to grasp that "while over a thousand years of Hebrew sovereignty in the Land of Israel boundaries expanded and contracted, the core area where Hebrew sovereignty was first asserted, maintained for the longest period, and reestablished after exile, was what is now Jerusalem and the Israeli-occupied West Bank." Moreover, one should not "look upon Zionism as yet another movement of national liberation—which can then be paralleled to the Arab nationalist movement which developed only slightly later," because such comparisons "ignore the foundation of modern Jewish nationalism in religious tradition."[65] Though Isaac sidestepped the successes the settlement movement had already made by 1976, and downplayed almost entirely the role of Gush Emunim, she nonetheless persuasively blurred the increasingly permeable boundaries between religion and politics—and between "normative Zionism" and authentic Judaism. Isaac's book offered scholarly legitimation to what was still a seldom discussed aspect of contemporary Jewish political life: the ascendance of a religious right both in Israel and the Diaspora. In retrospect, this would all fit neatly together with the news (belatedly disclosed) that Isaac belonged to Gush Emunim and served on its advisory board in the United States.[66]

At the time, however, the Isaac pamphlet carried no visible ideological baggage, and was interpreted rather as a balanced account of Breira and the key individuals who helped bring it into being. In a chatty and affable style, and with the stated goal of understanding better one "puzzling feature of Breira," namely the group's "overriding obsession . . . [that] the solution to the Arab-Israeli conflict is a PLO-dominated state on the West Bank and in Gaza," Isaac flashed back to the sixties:

> Breira is one of the many organizations which grew out of the social activist thrust in the United States that can be traced to the Civil Rights movement of the early 1960's. For some Jews the decisive experience was being pushed out of that movement. Jews were disproportionately prominent among whites

> within it, and when they found themselves accused by resentful blacks of usurping power in a movement that rightfully belonged to blacks, some of them began to reexamine and reassert the Jewish identity they had discarded in deference to universalist concerns for human justice and dignity. For others the decisive experience was not the civil rights movement but the anti-war movement and the student movement which it precipitated, and which led many to a whole new radical politics, that of the so-called New Left. In this political vision America, especially the government and the big corporations, became the fountainhead of all oppression, of her own people and of the third world with which those in these movements identified. And the task became creating a revolution that would transform Amerika, which the activists customarily spelled with a "k" to indicate its surrealistic evil character, into America. Racist, oppressive, corrupt, imperialist, capitalist Amerika, through the revolution, would be transformed into egalitarian, socialist, free America.

This paragraph represented "a detour," Isaac acknowledged, but it was "a detour that leads to the heart of our subject: we will be introducing leaders of Breira, their ideologies, and the methods by which they work to achieve their goals." Armed with a license to stray, Isaac then seized it—and launched ahead for twenty more pages to name-drop virtually every organization that Arthur Waskow had ever joined or been remotely affiliated with. What did the manifold left-liberal impulses of the sixties have to do with this one individual? According to Isaac, Waskow "was in fact an organizing genius for the whole network of associations whose personnel was eventually to become important in Breira."[67] These associations included Jews for Urban Justice, Fabrangen, the National Jewish Organizing Project, CONAME, MERIP, Clergy and Laity Concerned About Vietnam, and the Institute for Policy Studies. In every case Isaac pinpointed statements from individuals in each organization that voiced criticism of Zionism, criticism of Israeli government policy, or criticism of the United States government. Such statements were not difficult to locate; former *Guardian* journalist Barry Rubin proved himself especially quotable.[68]

But Isaac's real target was Waskow, because Waskow had made the mistake during the sixties of asserting radical New Left claims about Judaism itself. For instance, Isaac noted, "Waskow disrupted Yom Kippur services in 1969 at Washington's Tifereth Israel synagogue, calling for Jews to ask atonement for 'creating, owning and supporting a system of grocery stores that starve some children into apathy and death while our children get fat.'" Isaac observed that Waskow had written the Freedom Seder. And Waskow believed, as did all radical Jews (according to Isaac) that the state of Israel "far from advancing the distinctively Jewish mission, impeded it." Having arrived at this view, Isaac concluded that for the Jewish radical "the way was clear to supporting the political tastes of the far left for Arab over Israeli on Jewish religious grounds."[69] And it had been precisely such anti-Zionist sentiments among radical Jews that had led directly to a decision to establish Breira in the winter of 1973.

Isaac even connected the B'nai B'rth Hillel Foundations to this unholy Jewish anti-Israeli radical alliance because Max Ticktin belonged to Fabrangen and because Breira member Albert S. Axelrad, Hillel director at Brandeis, had also participated in the Jewish Campaign for the People's Peace Treaty. In other words, everyone was held accountable for everything they had ever said or done and for every statement or action taken by every radical group they had ever belonged to or been even tangentially affiliated with. For example, Waskow had never been part of MERIP, but somehow he was responsible for its misdeeds anyway because MERIP member Sharon Rose had been in JUJ with him. At times, it appeared as if merely being in the same room with someone who uttered something critical about Israel or Zionism was enough to win a permanent place in Isaac's anti-Zionist hall of shame. And this, of course, included just about every liberal or former radical Jew now associated with Breira.

Finally, Isaac dismissed in advance the countercharge that her opposition to Breira might be part of a "witchhunt" or due to "McCarthyism." As Isaac pithily noted, "The assumption in such a reaction is that there are no witches and the accusers are pursuing figments of their imagination." According to Isaac, however, Breira's record spoke for itself; what the group was actually accomplishing was a legitimization of American Jews' "growing sense of distance from Israel, the feeling in their bones that may never be allowed to consciousness that in the future Israel will be for them not a source of pride and a haven against possible storms but a burden, economically, politically, emotionally." If this was what Breira aimed to accomplish, Isaac concluded, then so be it. But members of such a group "should not be able to pass themselves off as 'prophetic' critics and dedicated guides" for Israeli policies: "If Jews want to organize on behalf of the Fatah, that is their privilege. But let them call it 'Jews for Fatah' and not 'Breira.'"[70]

Such rhetorical tactics resisted counterattack because everyone Isaac tarred with the brush of anti-Zionism *had* said what she said they said or been present at the meeting she said they attended. But there was little doubt as well that her guilt-by-association-with-Waskow strategy functioned above all as an attempt to destabilize the left-center, secular-religious, Zionist–non-Zionist coalition that Breira had sought to build. And the strategy worked.

Breira started to fall apart from within. Joachim Prinz and Jacob Neusner immediately made separate announcements that they had resigned from the group. Prinz had never agreed with the Breira position that Israel should return to pre-1967 borders, but shied away from direct criticism of the group; Neusner was more eager to publicize his current dislike for his former associates. At around the same time, Alan Mintz, a member of the Havurat Shalom in Somerville, Massachusetts, the first editor of *Response*, and the organizer of the Rutgers University's Hillel conference that had led to the founding of Breira, published a widely discussed critique of Breira. Most damaging may have been Mintz's charge that "Breira often seems simply out of touch with the emotional rhythms of the Jewish People." According to Mintz, Breira had become an organization insufficiently sensitized to "*ahavat yisrael*, unconditional love for the Jewish people."[71] Given the other difficulties experienced by Breira at that moment, such charges were even more wounding than they might have been otherwise.

Matters got worse still when the Jewish Community Council of Washington, D.C. passed a resolution stating that it "deplores Breira's methodology and platform" because its members "seek to divide and politicize American Jewish support of Israel."[72] However bitterly ironic such a resolution might have felt to die-hard Breiraniks (as they were sometimes called), the group was quickly losing its credibility as a voice of moderation within the Jewish community. Increasingly, and painfully, Breira was getting painted as a PLO front working for Israel's ultimate destruction.

On February 20, 1977, in Chevy Chase, Maryland, Breira convened its first national membership conference, attended by three hundred people. Outside the hall, Jewish Defense League members distributed the Isaac pamphlet, shouted slogans like "Hell no, we won't go from Hebron or Jericho," "There is no Palestine," and "We remember Munich," and waved placards that read, "Not One Inch of Retreat," "Death to Breira," "No Deals with Baby-Killers," "Breira is the Choice of Death," and "Breira Means Suicide" (figure 8.1). Inside the convention hall, however, there was little sign that Breira was prepared to back down. It reconfirmed its call for "the immediate cessation of Jewish settlement of the occupied territories" and proposed that "while Jerusalem will continue to serve as the capital of Israel, the Arab part of the city could become, after the establishment of peace, the capital of a Palestinian Arab state." It stated as well that it adopted these views because "we love Israel. We cherish the cultural treasures and the many moral examples it has given us. And we similarly affirm the richness of the Jewish experience in North America and are eager to explore and extend its possibilities." More-

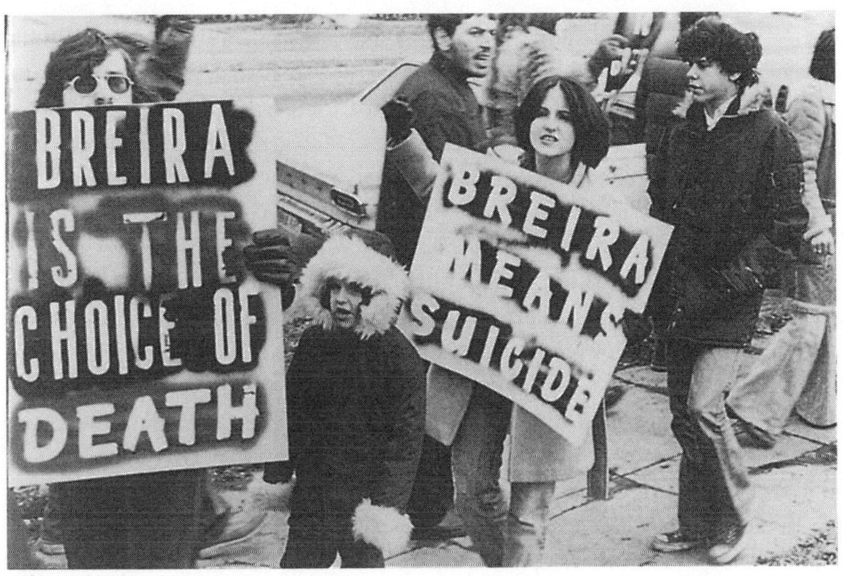

FIGURE 8.1 Jewish Defense League members protest outside the Breira national conference held in Chevy Chase, Maryland, in February 1977. Photograph by Bill Aron. Courtesy of Bill Aron.

over, and significantly, Breira declared its commitment to advancing domestic change. Its platform argued not only that "our Jewish prophetic values demand that we fight oppression and work to bring about economic and social justice in the American society in which we live." The platform also insisted that there was a need to eliminate "stereotyped sex roles in Jewish communal life" and support "non-sexist education; and the Jewish feminist movement." It contended as well that although "we endorse the forms of traditional Jewish family life . . . they are not the only legitimate social units for Jews in American society. We must pursue means of integrating Jews living in extended families, single people, and gays into the normative Jewish community."[73] However, the context for grasping the import of these policy statements was now being set not by Breira but rather by its ideological opponents. And in *that* context what Breira stood for was increasingly beginning to look more like unflattering caricature and less like real life.

For instance, *Reconstructionist* editor Ira Eisenstein, who made a point of noting that he'd quit Breira a year before, wrote in February 1977 that "there is a serious question whether safe and fairly prosperous American Jews, from their comfortable armchairs in the USA, have the moral right to urge policies upon Israelis which could well involve their very lives and the life of the State."[74] While defenders of Breira like historian Melvin I. Urofsky stated that the attacks on Breira were "creating a McCarthyite atmosphere" and serving only to "polarize the community between the young and the old, between liberals and conservatives," the innuendo that Breira represented an elite clique of radical chic intellectuals proved difficult to counter.[75] Here was an antileft technique as old as the cold war itself; as discussed in chapter 1, it had served successfully to mobilize popular class resentments against American leftists and their sympathizers already since the late 1940s. Those who denounced Breira therefore portrayed themselves also as crucially more in touch with an imagined Jewish public. Oftentimes their armchairs were just as comfortable as those of the Breira members they criticized. And yet it was the elitist image of Breira that stuck.

In short, Breira was losing the public relations battle over its own image. In April 1977 *Commentary* picked up the anti-Breira cause, citing at length what it characterized as "a well-documented pamphlet" and recycling once again (and repeatedly) the claim that Arthur Waskow was a PLO supporter. Author Joseph Shattan saw Breira's perspectives in the years since the Yom Kippur War as particularly unfortunate since during this period "the political fortunes of the state of Israel have reached perhaps an all-time low," adding that since 1973 "Israel has become increasingly isolated in the world as a whole, shunned even by many of its former friends and treated as a pariah by the community of nations." Hewing closely to the analysis served up by Rael Jean Isaac, Shattan delivered yet another installment in *Commentary*'s ongoing project of assessing Jewish left-liberalism in psychopathological terms, explaining how so many otherwise seemingly well-intentioned Jewish leaders could allow themselves to get lured into Breira in the first place:

> Liberal guilt, a desire to be on the side of "liberation" and "progress," a weariness at having to uphold Israel's cause when that cause has gone out of odor or has come to seem hopeless, even an unconscious and paradoxical wish to be, for once, on the side their government may be leaning toward. . . . [But] what strikes the observer above all in such mental maneuvers is the unspoken desire, born, perhaps, of the feeling that Israel has become an intolerable burden, to distance oneself as a Jew from Israel's fate. Because this desire cannot be confronted honestly, reality is denied or redefined, one's intentions become cloaked in the language of moral rectitude, and a conviction takes hold that the "solution" to Israel's dilemma is both simple and at hand.[76]

Despite continued and concerted efforts by the dwindling number of Breira members to counter these charges, largely by accusing their accusers of orchestrating a campaign to destroy them, these countercharges tended to get written off and proved largely ineffective. By late 1977 Breira was dead.[77]

ONE PEOPLE?

It would be hard not to conclude that the hawks had triumphed over the doves. Breira had been destroyed, and in subsequent years its collective memory would for the most part be lost. In retrospect, given that the 1970s were a decade marked primarily by widespread Jewish communal retreat from issues of social justice, the Breira controversy and its outcome might appear almost inevitable. Yet it is important also to recall that there emerged numerous American Jewish forums to replace Breira, notably the progressive broad-based coalition New Jewish Agenda (formed in 1980), *Tikkun* magazine (founded in 1986 as the liberal-left Jewish alternative to *Commentary*), as well as a variety of Jewish peace groups, like Americans for Peace Now, Jewish Peace Lobby, and Jewish Peace Network, established throughout the U.S. during the next quarter century.[78] At the same time, it is crucial to register the ongoing vitality of a right-leaning, religiously inflected American Zionism.[79]

Despite definite indications that renewed left-liberal activity within the American Jewish community followed the death of Breira, then, it would also be an error to underestimate how that death did represent "a watershed in contemporary American Jewish life," as Jacques Kornberg predicted in 1978. The shutting down of dissent around Breira so disturbed Irving Howe that it led him to remark: "Now I remember why I had nothing to do with the Jewish community all these years."[80] Although labeled a pro-PLO front, what Breira truly represented, according to Arnold Jacob Wolf speaking at the annual convention of the Rabbinical Assembly in May 1977, was a national Jewish group that had "recovered more young Jews, more 'New Left' Jews, more angry Jews, more intellectual Jews than any organization in the recent history of the United States."[81] And although several groups subsequently emerged to promote the causes of Breira, it is not at all certain they could really claim the same. Instead, American Jews turned primarily inward, not only away from social justice but also away from one another. This did not signal necessarily any loss in Jewish faith or Jewish conviction; on the contrary, the decades that ensued saw continued religious renewal within the community. But those decades also witnessed a profound splintering; this occurred to such an extent that the community—if it ever had been a community—could scarcely again even pretend to speak in one voice, believe in one faith, or act as one people. Thus, the 1970s may well have been the decade when American Jews moved subtly but conclusively from being One People (*K'lal Yisrael* in Hebrew) to becoming many peoples.

In *Number Our Days* (1978), her brilliant observer-participation study of elderly Jews living our their lives at the Aliyah Senior Citizen's Center in Venice, California, anthropologist Barbara Myerhoff described at length how much anger and negative emotion these old people expressed toward one another. Bitter quarrels and outright conflicts were a fact of life deeply lamented by these old people yet in which they nonetheless engaged with ritualized regularity. In her analysis of their angers Myerhoff also offered possible insight into the role infighting may have played in postwar conflicts over liberalism and antiliberalism in American Jewish life:

> Anger is a powerful indication of engagement between people, the very opposite of indifference. It may be regarded as the most dramatic proof of responsiveness and caring. . . . It is a basic form of remaining attached. And among people who are not inevitably bound together, anger may become a refutation of the possibility of separating. Anger is a form of social cohesion, and a strong and reliable one. To fight with each other, people must share norms, rules, vocabulary, and knowledge. Fighting is a partnership, requiring cooperation. A boundary-maintaining mechanism—for strangers cannot participate fully—it is also above all a profoundly sociable activity.[82]

By the end of the 1970s American Jews still fought, and continued to fight, with one another. And they would fight, and continue to fight, with one another into the twenty-first century and right up to the present day. But there appeared a noticeable change. The fighting remained fierce, but not quite so fierce as it had been in the past; across ideological divides, American Jews seemed just to have less to express to one another altogether. They simply shared less than they once did. Organizations and groups have proliferated, but they coexist more than conflict. The possible links between religious and political identifications are subject to far less debate than they once were. And with the loss of shared norms, the anger that had served—however paradoxically—as a distinctive and reliable form of social cohesion lessened as well, and that collectivity known as a Jewish people also came closer to an end.

Notes

"MAKING MY JEWISHNESS TOO VISIBLE": AN INTRODUCTION

1. Oestreicher quoted in Malka Zedek, "The Canning of Chaplain Goldman," *Jewish Liberation Journal* no. 2 (June 1969): 15; and the letter from the Rabbinical Alliance (signed by Rabbi David Weinberger) quoted in "Rabbis Ask Columbia to Repudiate Advice to Jewish Students," *Jewish Press*, April 19, 1968, p. 2. It should also be pointed out that Rev. William F. Starr was simultaneously dismissed from his chaplain's position at Columbia by the Ecumenical Foundation for Ministry to Higher Education in Metropolitan New York, but did not contest his dismissal. Rev. Starr summarized the reasons he was fired: "I was a co-belligerent with radical students on the campus, I was critical of the administration. I was arrested in the math building." Starr quoted in "Jewish and Protestant Chaplains Dismissed," *Jewish Currents* 23 (May 1969): 31.

2. The letter from the Rabbinical Alliance quoted in "Rabbis Ask Columbia," p. 2.

3. Sulzberger also reportedly intervened to prevent Goldman from getting a position at Wesleyan University. See "Sulzberger Accused by Fired Rabbi," *Jewish Week*, June 5, 1969, p. 1.

4. "Pickets Aid Goldman," *Jewish Post and Opinion*, May 30, 1969, p. 2.

5. Jewish Committee for Self-Determination broadside quoted in Jean Herschaft, "Confusing Case of Ousted Rabbi," *Jewish Post and Opinion*, May 2, 1969, p. 2.

6. Zedek, "The Canning of Chaplain Goldman," pp. 12, 20–21.

7. Quoted in "Sulzberger Accused by Fired Rabbi," p. 1.

8. Oestreicher quoted in Herschaft, "Confusing Case of Ousted Rabbi," p. 2, and Zedek, "The Canning of Chaplain Goldman," p. 20; and Goldman quoted in Zedek, "The Canning of Chaplain Goldman," pp. 13–14, 20.

9. Texts that offer significant interpretations of twentieth-century American Jewish history include Charles S. Liebman, *The Ambivalent American Jew: Politics, Religion, and Family in American Jewish Life* (Philadelphia: Jewish Publication Society of America, 1973); Irving Howe, *World of Our Fathers* (New York: Harcourt Brace Jovanovich, 1976); Chaim I. Waxman, *American Jews in Transition* (Philadelphia: Temple University Press, 1983); Charles E. Silberman, *A Certain People: American Jews and Their Lives Today* (New York: Summit, 1985); Arthur Hertzberg, *The Jews in America: Four Centuries of an Uneasy Encounter* (New York: Simon and Schuster, 1989); Edward S. Shapiro, *A Time for Healing: American Jewry Since World War II* (Baltimore: Johns Hopkins University Press, 1992); Benjamin Ginsberg, *The Fatal Embrace: Jews and the State* (Chicago: University of Chicago Press, 1993); Murray Friedman, *What Went Wrong? The Creation and Collapse of the Black-Jewish Alliance* (New York: Free, 1995); Gerald Sorin, *Tradition Transformed: The Jewish Experience in America* (Baltimore: Johns Hopkins University Press, 1997); Stuart Svonkin, *Jews Against Prejudice: American Jews and the Fight for Civil Liberties* (New York: Columbia University Press, 1997); Seth Forman, *Blacks in the Jewish Mind: A Crisis of Liberalism* (New York: New York University Press, 1998); Arthur A. Goren, *The Politics and Public Culture of American Jews* (Bloomington: Indiana University Press, 1999); and Marc Dollinger, *Quest for Inclusion: Jews and Liberalism in Modern America* (Princeton: Princeton University Press, 2000). An important analysis of the prewar decades is provided by Hasia R. Diner, *In the Almost Promised Land: American Jews and Blacks, 1915–1935* (Westport, Conn.: Greenwood, 1977). The two books that place intra-Jewish conflict at the center of their stories are Jack Wertheimer, *A People Divided: Judaism in Contemporary America* (New York: Basic, 1993); and Samuel G. Freedman, *Jew vs. Jew: The Struggle for the Soul of American Jewry* (New York: Simon and Schuster, 2000). Both books emphasize intra- and interdenominational conflicts from the 1960s to the 1990s.

10. Shapiro, *A Time for Healing*, p. 213.

11. Gabriel Schoenfeld, "Death Camps As Kitsch," *New York Times*, March 18, 1999, p. A25.

12. He goes on to say that, "from the 1970s on," the Holocaust became "ever more central in American public discourse—particularly, of course, among Jews,

but also in the culture at large. What accounts for this unusual chronology?" Peter Novick, *The Holocaust in American Life* (Boston: Houghton Mifflin, 1999), p. 1.

13. Howe, *World of Our Fathers*, p. 627.

14. Svonkin, *Jews Against Prejudice*, p. 17.

15. Jeffrey Shandler, *While America Watches: Televising the Holocaust* (New York: Oxford University Press, 1999), pp. 46–47.

16. Jonathan Sarna, "Introduction," in *The American Jewish Experience*, ed. Jonathan Sarna (New York: Holmes and Meier, 1986), p. xvi.

17. Silberman, *A Certain People*, pp. 22, 57.

18. Norman Podhoretz, *Making It* (New York: Random House, 1967), p. 50.

19. Riv-Ellen Prell, *Fighting to Become Americans: Jews, Gender, and the Anxiety of Assimilation* (Boston: Beacon, 1999), p. 5.

20. Abraham J. Heschel, "Central Problem of Our Time," *National Jewish Monthly* 75 (October 1960): 9.

21. Arthur Hertzberg, "The Present Casts a Dark Shadow," *Jewish Heritage* 6 (Winter 1963–64): 12–15.

22. Seymour Martin Lipset, "The Activists: A Profile," in *Confrontation: The Student Rebellion and the Universities*, ed. Daniel Bell and Irving Kristol (New York: Basic, 1969), p. 52.

23. Jonathan Braun, "Bagels and Lox Judaism: Neglecting the Jewish National Experience," *Flame* 3 (February 1970): 1, 7.

24. Yaakov Jacobs, "To Picket . . . Or to Pray?" *Jewish Observer* 5 (April 1968): 3.

25. Bernard Weinberger, "Orthodox Query Jews' Role in Rights Struggle," *Jewish Week*, October 17, 1968, p. 4.

26. Mordecai Gifter, "Why the Restlessness?" *Jewish Observer* 5 (March 1968): 11.

27. Jacobs, "To Picket . . . Or to Pray?" p. 6.

28. Michael Tabor, "The Jewish Youth Scene," *Jewish Currents* 24 (October 1970): 18.

29. "Jews for Urban Justice: Principles and Goals," *Jewish Currents* 22 (October 1968): 15.

30. See Bruno Bettelheim, *The Informed Heart: Autonomy in a Mass Age* (New York: Free, 1960); Hannah Arendt, *Eichmann in Jerusalem: A Report on the Banality of Evil* (New York: Viking, 1963). For early critiques, see especially Norman Podhoretz, "Hannah Arendt on Eichmann: A Study in the Perversity of Brilliance," *Commentary* 36 (September 1963): 201–8; and Alexander Donat, *Jewish Resistance* (New York: Warsaw Ghetto Resistance Organization, 1964).

31. Nat Hentoff, "Introduction," in *Black Anti-Semitism and Jewish Racism*, ed. Nat Hentoff (New York: Baron, 1969), p. xvii.

32. Bill Novak, "The Failure of Jewish Radicalism," in *Jewish Radicalism: A Selected Anthology*, ed. Jack Nusan Porter and Peter Dreier (New York: Grove, 1973), p. 309. Novak's article originally appeared in the April 8, 1971 issue of *Genesis 2*.

33. Rabbi Alvin S. Roth quoted in "Rabbi Recommends 4-Children Family," *Jewish Post and Opinion*, February 19, 1971, p. 3.

34. Quoted in "Radical Students Plan New Confrontation," *Jewish Post and Opinion*, May 22, 1970, p. 3.

35. Nathan Glazer, "Blacks, Jews and the Intellectuals," *Commentary* 47 (April 1969): 33–39.

36. Nathan Glazer, "Jewish Interests and the New Left," *Midstream* 17 (January 1971): 34.

37. Joel Walters, "Community Forum," *Cleveland Jewish News*, May 5, 1972, p. 20; and Edwin Jacobs, "Community Forum," *Cleveland Jewish News*, May 12, 1972, p. 14. Also see Mike Tabor, "Kent State Hillel Head's Letter Revealing," *Jewish Post and Opinion*, July 21, 1972, p. 7. For background on Hillel director Walters's New Left politics and his recommitment to Judaism in the context of a visit to Israel, see Jerry D. Barach, "One of 'New Breed' of Hillel Directors," *Cleveland Jewish News*, February 18, 1972, p. 11.

38. Yaakov Riz, "Breira Rabbis Should Be Asked to Resign or Be Thrown Out" (letter to the editor), *Jewish Post and Opinion*, December 20, 1974, p. 5.

39. Meir Kahane, "Small Voice," *Jewish Press*, October 11, 1968, p. 34.

1. "THE RACISTS OF AMERICA FLY BLINDLY AT BOTH OF US": ATROCITY ANALOGIES AND ANTICOMMUNISM

Epigraph from Marie Syrkin, "On Hebrewcide," Jewish Frontier *12 (July 1945): 10.*

1. In this discussion of the racial politics of Miami Jews, I owe much to Deborah Dash Moore, *To the Golden Cities: Pursuing the American Jewish Dream in Miami and L.A.* (Cambridge: Harvard University Press, 1994), especially pp. 169–87. However, Moore does not mention King's 1958 visit to Miami Beach.

2. Martin Luther King, "In Peace and in Dignity," *Congress Bi-Weekly* 35 (May 6, 1968): 16–17.

3. Stuart Svonkin, *Jews Against Prejudice: American Jews and the Fight for Civil Liberties* (New York: Columbia University Press, 1997), especially pp. 113–77.

4. See Lunabelle Wedlock, *The Reaction of Negro Publications and Organiza-*

tions to German Anti-Semitism (Washington, D.C.: Howard University Studies in the Social Sciences, 1942), pp. 91, 105. Wedlock is quoting from the *Afro-American* (October 14, 1933) and the *Washington Tribune* (June 23, 1933). Although it was scarcely her central intention to do so, Wedlock's study provides invaluable documentation of how routinely African American periodicals analogized German fascism and American racism in order morally to advance the cause of black civil rights. For numerous examples of the German fascism/American racism analogies, see especially pp. 90–115. For instance, this is from the *Amsterdam News* (February 11, 1939): "The only difference between the oppression of the unfortunate Jews in Naziland and the colored citizens here is that oppression in Germany is comparatively new, while the Negro has always been victimized in a thousand and one ways here." Quoted in Wedlock, *The Reaction of Negro Publications*, p. 114.

5. Kelly Miller, "Race Prejudice in Germany and America," *Opportunity* 14 (April 1936): 105. Or, as an *Opportunity* editorial from January 1939 put it: "The fascist governments of the world view American indignation over racial oppression with wonder and bewilderment. They can not understand why America should be so concerned with racial persecution in Europe and yet defend it with such vigor within its own borders." Quoted in Wedlock, *The Reaction of Negro Publications*, p. 103.

6. See "Negroes! Jews! Catholics!" *Crisis* 52 (August 1945): 217–19, 237–38. Also see Leonard Dinnerstein, *Antisemitism in America* (New York: Oxford University Press, 1994), pp. 135–36.

7. Quoted in Edward S. Shapiro, "Anti-Semitism Mississippi Style," in *Anti-Semitism in American History*, ed. David A. Gerber (Urbana: University of Illinois Press, 1986), p. 141.

8. "Race Hate First on Agenda of U.S. Congress," *Crisis* 52 (August 1945): 216.

9. "Terror in Tennessee," *Crisis* 53 (April 1946): 105. For a discussion of violent attacks in 1946 against African Americans (and the political response to them), see Donald R. McCoy and Richard T. Ruetten, *Quest and Response: Minority Rights and the Truman Administration* (Lawrence: University Press of Kansas, 1973), especially pp. 43–46.

10. "Massacre," *Crisis* 54 (August 1947): 233.

11. "Southern Schrecklichkeit," *Crisis* 53 (September 1946): 276.

12. "Editorial Roundup," *Crisis* 53 (October 1946): 291. See also, in the same issue, Harold Preece, "Klan 'Murder, Inc.,' in Dixie," pp. 299–301. For instance, Preece notes: "All, every one, of the official Nazi excuses for killing a prisoner are being invoked by the police murder ring to justify the slaughter of Negroes. When Gestapo captors wanted to get rid of a man whom they were transporting

to jail, they simply shot him down and wrote on the official records that he was 'killed while trying to escape.' " Ibid., p. 301.

13. "Lily-White Pepsodent," *Crisis* 53 (May 1946): 137.

14. See Hasia R. Diner, *In the Almost Promised Land: American Jews and Blacks, 1915–1935* (Westport, Conn.: Greenwood, 1977), especially pp. 118–42.

15. According to Murray Friedman, the NAACP had no black lawyers on its staff as late as 1933. Murray Friedman, *What Went Wrong? The Creation and Collapse of the Black-Jewish Alliance* (New York: Free, 1995), p. 106.

16. In addition to the discussions of Jews in the NAACP in Diner and Friedman, see Robert G. Weisbord and Arthur Stein, *Bittersweet Encounter: The Afro-American and the American Jew* (Westport, Conn.: Negro University Press, 1970), especially pp. 145–47.

17. Werner J. Cahnman, "Race Riots in the Schools," *Jewish Frontier* 12 (November 1945): 16, 18.

18. Leo Pfeffer, "Defenses Against Group Defamation," *Jewish Frontier* 13 (February 1946): 6.

19. Charles Abrams, "Homes for Aryans Only," *Commentary* 3 (May 1947): 421. Abrams would subsequently make an important contribution with his *Forbidden Neighbors: A Study of Prejudice in Housing* (New York: Harper, 1955).

20. Felix S. Cohen, "Alaska's Nuremberg Laws," *Commentary* 6 (August 1948): 136. As Cohen wrote: "What is done to Indians or Eskimos in Alaska today can be done to Negroes in the South tomorrow, and to Jews, Catholics, or descendants of non-Anglo-Saxon strains the day after tomorrow." Ibid., p. 137.

21. James A. and Nancy F. Wechsler, "The Road Ahead for Civil Rights," *Commentary* 6 (October 1948): 304.

22. Arthur M. Schlesinger Jr., *The Vital Center: The Politics of Freedom* (Boston: Houghton Mifflin, 1949).

23. "The NAACP and the Communists," *Crisis* 56 (March 1949): 72.

24. Quoted in Martin Bauml Duberman, *Paul Robeson* (New York: Knopf, 1988), p. 342. Actually, Duberman concludes that Robeson did *not* speak these words in his 1949 Paris speech—and so did not urge African Americans to avoid participation in a war against the Soviet Union. Ibid.

25. "Robeson Speaks for Robeson," *Crisis* 56 (May 1949): 137. The gratuitous slap at Paul Robeson Jr. is noteworthy in light of Paul Jr.'s marriage the following month to a Jewish woman, Marilyn Paula Greenberg, whom he had met while both were students at Cornell University. See Duberman, *Paul Robeson*, p. 355. Also see Tom Wolfe, "Radical Chic: That Party at Lenny's," *New York* (June 8, 1970), reprinted in Wolfe, *Radical Chic and Mau-Mauing the Flak Catchers* (New York: Farrar, Straus, and Giroux, 1970); and on the politics of radical chic,

see Michael E. Staub, "Black Panthers, New Journalism, and the Rewriting of the Sixties," *Representations* 57 (Winter 1997): 52–72.

26. As Michael Kazin points out, the VFW and the American Legion were at the forefront of the postwar anticommunist campaign. See Michael Kazin, *The Populist Persuasion: An American History* (New York: Basic 1995), pp. 178–83. By the early fifties, more than one hundred thousand American Legionnaires served as unpaid informants for the FBI. See Athan Theoharis, "The FBI and the American Legion Contact Program, 1940–1966," *Political Science Quarterly* 100 (Summer 1985): 271–86.

27. This discussion of the Peekskill riots is largely indebted to the account in Duberman, *Paul Robeson*, pp. 364–72. "God Bless Hitler . . . " is quoted from Howard Fast, *Peekskill: USA* (New York: Civil Rights Congress, 1951), p. 29.

28. Robeson and Dewey quoted in Duberman, *Paul Robeson*, p. 370.

29. Moses Miller, "Victory and Omen," *Jewish Life* 3 (October 1949): 3. Notably, Miller also condemned Jewish organizations like the American Jewish Committee and the Anti-Defamation League for their complete silence after the riots. Ibid., p. 4.

30. Howard Fast, "We Will Never Retreat," *Jewish Life* 4 (November 1949): 14.

31. Fast, *Peekskill: USA*, p. 40.

32. "Jewish Life," *Jewish Life* 1 (November 1946): 3.

33. Arthur D. Kahn, "The American SS," *Jewish Life* 1 (November 1946): 19.

34. "Dewey and Martin," *Jewish Life* 1 (December 1946): 22.

35. Mark Isaacson, "Numerus Clausus," *Jewish Life* 1 (February 1947): 18.

36. "Look Out America!" *Jewish Life* 1 (May 1947): 3–4.

37. "Anti-Communism, Anti-Semitism, and America," *Jewish Life* 1 (February 1947): 4.

38. Moise Katz, "A Warning Against Race Hatred," *Jewish Life* 1 (August 1947): 25.

39. L. Singer, "Jews of the USSR: Post-War Reconstruction," *Jewish Life* 3 (March 1949): 25.

40. For a brief and helpful summary of this history, see David A. Hacker, "*Jewish Life/Jewish Currents*," in *Encyclopedia of the American Left*, ed. Mari Jo Buhle, Paul Buhle, and Dan Georgakas (New York: Garland, 1990), pp. 390–91. Also see Vivian Gornick, *The Romance of American Communism* (New York: Basic, 1977).

41. "The Peekskill Riots," *Crisis* 56 (October 1949), p. 265.

42. Shlomo Grodzensky, "The Peekskill Affair," *Jewish Frontier* 16 (October 1949): 7.

43. Ibid., pp. 7–8.

44. Ibid., p. 8.

45. James Rorty and Winifred Raushenbush, "The Lessons of the Peekskill Riots," *Commentary* 10 (October 1950): 309, 314, 316–17, 321.

46. Ibid., pp. 319–21. Also see James Rorty and Moshe Decter, *McCarthy and the Communists* (Boston: Beacon, 1954).

47. Although *Commentary*'s editorial policy maintained independence from the American Jewish Committee, Stuart Svonkin argues that the Peekskill article "mirrored the views held by members of the committee staff." Svonkin notes: "The fact that the AJC prepared reprints of the Rorty-Rauschenbush article for mass distribution confirms that the authors' conclusions corresponded with the committee's official position on the riots." Svonkin, *Jews Against Prejudice*, p. 141.

48. Charles Abrams, "The Time Bomb that Exploded in Cicero," *Commentary* 12 (November 1951): 408. *Jewish Life* reported that the Cicero riots had prompted a Chicago Jewish newspaper, the *Sentinel*, to head a full-page editorial with "Prelude to Pogroms?" The *Sentinel* reminded Jewish readers that although "this time it was a Negro veteran seeking a place to live," "next time, it may well be a Jewish businessman opening a store in a non-Jewish neighborhood." See Carl Hirsch, "Terror in Cicero," *Jewish Life* 5 (September 1951): 12. However, the *Commentary* essay avoided the Nazism analogy. In another essay on Cicero, Hirsch argued that Americans are "not yet so far gone that they will accept genocide. They will not accept the mass murder of America's 15 million Negroes as so many Germans tolerated the killing of six million Jews." Carl Hirsch, "Cicero As Symptom," *Jewish Life* 6 (December 1951): 20.

49. James Rorty, "Desegregation Along the Mason-Dixon Line," *Commentary* 18 (December 1954): 503.

50. Elliot E. Cohen, "The Free American Citizen, 1952," *Commentary* 14 (September 1952): 221, 223.

51. Sidney Hook, "Why Democracy Is Better," *Commentary* 5 (March 1948): 203–4.

52. Sidney Hook, "The Fifth Amendment—a Moral Issue," *New York Times Magazine* (November 1, 1953); and Alan P. Westin, "Do Silent Witnesses Defend Civil Liberties?" *Commentary* 15 (June 1953): 537–46. Also see Ellen W. Schrecker, *No Ivory Tower: McCarthy and the Universities* (New York: Oxford University Press, 1986), pp. 191–92.

53. Notable examples include Melvin Lasky, "Why the Kremlin Extorts Confessions," *Commentary* 13 (January 1952): 1–6; Paul Kecskemeti, "How Totalitarians Gain Absolute Power," *Commentary* 14 (December 1952): 537–46; Peter Meyer, "Stalin Follows in Hitler's Footsteps," *Commentary* 15 (January 1953): 1–18; and Julius Margolin, "Do We Leave the Russian Jews to Their Fate?" *Commentary* 16 (October 1953): 321–27.

54. Robert Bendiner, "Civil Liberties and the Communists," *Commentary* 5 (May 1948): 430–31. For another version of this same argument, also see Robert Bendiner, "Has Anti-Communism Wrecked Our Liberties?" *Commentary* 12 (July 1951): 10–16.

55. Irving Kristol, " 'Civil Liberties,' 1952—A Study in Confusion," *Commentary* 13 (March 1952): 234–35. Kristol's reflections continued: "No doubt there are some present members of the Communist party who would, in a showdown, break free of the Idea and rally to the democratic cause. Unfortunately, we have no way of knowing who they are. No doubt there are some present members and fellow-travelers of the Communist party who would sooner or later get disillusioned with Communism if they were permitted to hold down their present job as teachers, civil service workers, etc., whereas they are likely to harden in the face of persecution. Unfortunately, it is quite as impossible to tell the citizens of Oshkosh, some of whom have suffered personal loss as a result of the war in Korea, that there is no harm in having their children taught the three R's by a Communist, as it would have been to persuade the citizens of Flatbush in 1939 that there was no cause for excitement in their children being taught by a Nazi." Ibid., pp. 235–36. This essay sparked tremendous (and overwhelmingly appreciative) response from readers. See the "Letters from Readers" (along with Kristol's rejoinder) in *Commentary* 13 (May 1952): 491–500. See also two efforts to challenge Kristol from within a liberal anticommunist perspective. Alan F. Westin, "Our Freedom—And the Rights of Communists," *Commentary* 14 (July 1952): 33–40; and Arthur Schlesinger Jr., "Liberty and the Liberal" (letter to the editor), *Commentary* 14 (July 1952): 83–84. Not long after this, Kristol moved to England to found the journal, *Encounter*. It was later disclosed that *Encounter* had received extensive funding from the Central Intelligence Agency. See Christopher Lasch, "The Cultural Cold War: A Short History of the Congress for Cultural Freedom," in *Towards a New Past: Dissenting Essays in American History*, ed. Barton J. Bernstein (New York: Pantheon, 1968), pp. 322–59; and Peter Steinfels, *The Neoconservatives* (New York: Simon and Schuster, 1979), pp. 83–90.

56. Joyce Antler, "A Bond of Sisterhood: Ethel Rosenberg, Molly Goldberg, and Radical Jewish Women of the 1950s," in *Secret Agents: The Rosenberg Case, McCarthyism, and Fifties America*, ed. Marjorie Garber and Rebecca L. Walkowitz (New York: Routledge, 1995), p. 208. As Antler also writes, "After the death penalties were handed down, Jewish organizations came out strongly in favor of the sentences." Ibid., 207–8. Also see Deborah Dash Moore's conclusion that the Rosenberg case "helped to make opposition to Communism a criterion of Jewish communal membership," even as it "hastened and legitimated the purge of the Jewish left from the organized Jewish community." Deborah

Dash Moore, "Reconsidering the Rosenbergs: Symbol and Substance in Second-Generation American Jewish Consciousness," *Journal of American Ethnic History* 8 (Fall 1988), p. 26. Note as well historian and rabbi Louis Ruchames's bittersweet description of Rabbi Abraham Cronbach as "a professor of Social Studies at the Hebrew Union College since 1922 who capped a lifetime of service to unpopular causes by championing the cause of Ethel and Julius Rosenberg and delivering the eulogy at their funeral." Louis Ruchames, "Jewish Radicalism in the United States," in *The Ghetto and Beyond: Essays on Jewish Life in America,* ed. Peter I. Rose (New York: Random House, 1969), p. 249.

57. Lucy S. Dawidowicz, " 'Anti-Semitism' and the Rosenberg Case," *Commentary* 14 (July 1952): 44.

58. Ibid., pp. 41–42.

59. Andrew Ross, *No Respect: Intellectuals and Popular Culture* (New York: Routledge, 1989), p. 19.

60. Dawidowicz, " 'Anti-Semitism' and the Rosenberg Case," pp. 41, 45. As the editorial remarks introducing Dawidowicz's essay made clear, *Commentary* felt that the convictions of the Rosenbergs were a good example of how American society "had dealt justly with a case of high treason." *Commentary* expressed incredulity at the way American communists "after a period of absolute silence, suddenly discovered that the trial was nothing less than a nefarious anti-Semitic plot by the American government!" And the magazine saw this as "one of the most brazen recent efforts of the Communist apparatus to exploit 'minority' fears and sympathies for its own purposes." Editorial introduction, ibid., p. 41. Also see Lucy S. Dawidowicz, "The Rosenberg Case: 'Hate-America' Weapon," *New Leader* 35 (December 22, 1952): 13.

61. Robert Warshow, "The 'Idealism' of Julius and Ethel Rosenberg," *Commentary* 16 (November 1953): 417. In particular, Warshow was responding to the publication of *Death House Letters of Ethel and Julius Rosenberg* (New York: Jero, 1953). The Rosenbergs' letters make frequent reference to their own Jewish heritage. Also see Leslie Fiedler's scathing assessment of the Rosenbergs in "A Postscript to the Rosenberg Case," *Encounter* 1 (October 1953): 12–21; as well as S. Andhil Fineberg, *The Rosenberg Case: Fact and Fiction* (New York: Oceana, 1953). A staff member of the American Jewish Committee, and a Reform rabbi, Fineberg denied that antisemitism played any role in the case against the Rosenbergs.

62. Sam Pevzner, "The Way of Brotherhood," *Jewish Fraternalist* 6 (January 1950): 2.

63. Louis Harap, "Lessons in Resistance: Is American Jewry Prepared?" *Jewish Life* 4 (January 1950): 15. For an earlier attack on *Commentary* in *Jewish Life*, also see Louis Harap, "X-Ray on *Commentary*," *Jewish Life* 1 (July 1947): 19–23.

64. As anticommunism intensified in the fifties, *Jewish Life* would accuse *Commentary* editor Elliot Cohen of "treachery" toward the American Jewish community. It explained, "He pooh-poohs the danger of McCarthyism. The effect of such playing down of the threat of fascism in our country is to facilitate its coming." See "Elliot Cohen and McCarthyism," *Jewish Life* 7 (November 1952): 5.

65. "Human Dignity Will Not Die!" *Jewish Life* 7 (July 1953): 3.

66. "Jewish Security and Negro Liberation," *Jewish Life* 6 (February 1952): 3.

67. Louis Harap, "Stalin and the Jewish People," *Jewish Life* 7 (April 1953): 4.

2. "LIBERAL JUDAISM IS A CONTRADICTION IN TERMS": ANTIRACIST ZIONISTS, PROPHETIC JEWS, AND THEIR CRITICS

Epigraph quoted in Melissa Fay Greene, The Temple Bombing *(Reading, Mass.: Addison-Wesley, 1996), p. 189.*

1. Max Nussbaum, "Dr. Prinz at 60," *Congress Weekly* 29 (June 25, 1962): 5–6.

2. Joachim Prinz, "America Must Not Remain Silent . . . ," *Congress Bi-Weekly* 30 (October 7, 1963): 3. Reprinted as "The Issue Is Silence," in *The Dynamics of Emancipation: The Jew in the Modern Age*, ed. Nahum N. Glatzer (Boston: Beacon, 1965), pp. 252–53.

3. Prinz, "America Must Not Remain Silent . . . ," p. 3.

4. See "The Embattled Minority," *Reconstructionist* 28 (June 2, 1962): 4.

5. Richard L. Rubenstein, "The Rabbis Visit Birmingham," *Reconstructionist* 29 (May 31, 1963): 5.

6. Rabbi Marc H. Tanenbaum quoted in Ruth Gruber Michaels, "March on Washington," *Hadassah Magazine* 44 (September 1963): 40.

7. For a classic and eloquent formulation of the post-sixties American Zionism that is most familiar to the contemporary reader, see Hillel Halkin, *Letters to an American Jewish Friend: A Zionist's Polemic* (Philadelphia: Jewish Publication Society of America, 1977).

8. Israel Goldstein, "Areas of Jewish Concern," *Congress Weekly* 23 (April 23, 1956): 3.

9. See *Against the Stream: Seven Decades of Hashomer Hatzair in North America*, ed. Ariel Hurwitz (Tel Aviv: Association of North American Shomrim, 1994).

10. Quoted in Albert Vorspan and Eugene J. Lipman, *Justice and Judaism: The Work of Social Action* (New York: Union of American Hebrew Congregations, 1956; 4th rev. ed., 1959), p. 21.

11. Rabbi Maurice N. Eisendrath, "Introduction," in Vorspan and Lipman, *Justice and Judaism*, pp. xi–xii.

12. Naomi W. Cohen, *Not Free to Desist: The American Jewish Committee, 1906–1966* (Philadelphia: Jewish Publication Society of America, 1972), p. 393.

13. For an excellent summary by a contemporary of southern Jews' hesitations about desegregation activism, see James A. Wax, "The Attitude of the Jews in the South Toward Integration," *CCAR Journal* 26 (June 1959): 14–20. Wax confirmed that "a large segment of the Jews in the South are segregationists." Ibid., p. 17. For a balanced and thoughtful discussion of southern Jews' ongoing resistance to antiracist activism in the early 1960s, see Debra L. Schultz, *Going South: Jewish Women in the Civil Rights Movement* (New York: New York University Press, 2001), especially pp. 91–100.

14. Cohen, *Not Free to Desist*, p. 393.

15. Quoted in "The Desegregation Problem," *American Judaism* 6 (Rosh Ha-Shono, 1956): 19.

16. Greene, *The Temple Bombing*, p. 5.

17. See Stuart Svonkin, *Jews Against Prejudice: American Jews and the Fight for Civil Liberties* (New York: Columbia University Press, 1997), p. 134; and Deborah Dash Moore, "Reconsidering the Rosenbergs: Symbol and Substance in Second Generation American Jewish Consciousness," *Journal of American Ethnic History* 8 (Fall 1988): 26.

18. Samuel Halperin, *The Political World of American Zionism* (Detroit: Wayne State University Press, 1961), p. 52. For a useful discussion of the American Jewish Committee's ambivalence toward Zionism (as well as its early opposition to independent Jewish statehood), see ibid., pp. 114–44.

19. Svonkin, *Jews Against Prejudice*, p. 23.

20. Max Lerner, "Role of the American Jew," *Congress Weekly* 17 (January 16, 1950): 7–10.

21. Ibid. Note also that by the time he died in 1992 Lerner had become a Reagan supporter. On the political evolution of Lerner (and much else besides), see Sanford Lakoff, *Max Lerner: Pilgrim in the Promised Land* (Chicago University of Chicago Press, 1998). Also see John Patrick Diggins, "The Possibilist," *New Republic*, November 16, 1998, pp. 42–45.

22. Vorspan and Lipman, *Justice and Judaism*, pp. 6, 24, 9–10, 107.

23. Quoted in Albert Vorspan, "Segregation and Social Justice," *American Judaism* 7 (January 1958): 11. Also see Ruth Silberstein, "A Southern Rabbi Takes a Stand," *Congress Weekly* 25 (January 20, 1958): 7.

24. Quoted in "The Crucial Test," *Congress Weekly* 25 (October 13, 1958): 3–4.

25. Charles Mantinband, "Integration and the Southern Jew," *Congress Weekly* 25 (June 16, 1958): 10.

26. Greene, *The Temple Bombing*, p. 178.

27. Nathan Glazer, *American Judaism* (Chicago: University of Chicago Press, 1957), pp. 134–36. See also the mixed review of Glazer's book by Conservative rabbi Robert Gordis, who argues "that the volume suffers from the fact that the author writes as an outsider"—"quite apart from the fact that Mr. Glazer is himself Jewish." Robert Gordis, "American Judaism in Tradition," *Congress Weekly* 24 (December 2, 1957): 8–10.

28. Seth Forman, *Blacks in the Jewish Mind: A Crisis of Liberalism* (New York: New York University Press, 1998), p. 46.

29. Quoted in Janice Rothschild Blumberg, *One Voice: Rabbi Jacob M. Rothschild and the Troubled South* (Macon: Mercer University Press, 1985), p. 68.

30. Quoted in Albert Vorspan, "A Visitor's Account," *Midstream* 2 (Autumn 1956): 47.

31. Harry L. Golden, "A Rabbi in Montgomery," *Congress Weekly* 24 (May 13, 1957): 8–9. Also see the letter from Irving London, former president of the Montgomery Congregation Agudath Israel. Addressing Golden, London wrote: "I am deeply upset over this distorted account of the dismissal here in Montgomery and I cannot help but feel that you have been victimized as an innocent bystander in an attempt to build up a rabbi who rode the coattails of a 'good cause' to cover up his own failings." Golden's sarcastic answer suggested that "if you do not believe I have given a true picture of the general attitude towards this problem prevailing now in the Jewish communities of the deep South, then perhaps I have been living on the planet Mars these last few years." See *Congress Weekly* 24 (June 17, 1957): 14.

32. Rabbi Abraham J. Heschel, "The Religious Basis of Equality of Opportunity—The Segregation of God," in *Race: Challenge to Religion*, ed. Mathew Ahmann (Chicago: Regnery, 1963), pp. 65, 69.

33. Quoted in Balfour Brickner, "Projects Under Synagogue Auspices," *Religious Education* 59 (January-February 1964), p. 77.

34. Ibid., pp. 76–77.

35. Louis Ruchames, "Parallels of Jewish and Negro History," *Negro History Bulletin* 19 (December 1955): 63.

36. "False Race Theories," *Congress Weekly* 23 (October 15, 1956): 3.

37. Cited in Forman, *Blacks in the Jewish Mind*, p. 42. Also see Arnold M. Rose, *The Negro's Morale: Group Identification and Protest* (Minneapolis: University of Minnesota Press, 1949), pp. 43–45.

38. Isaac Toubin, "A Message to Southern Jews: Recklessness or Responsibility?" *Congress Weekly* 25 (March 17, 1958): 5–6.

39. "Prinz Scores Hysteria Over Bombings," *Congress Record* 12 (November 24, 1958): 1.

40. See David Caplovitz and Candace Rogers, *Swastika 1960: The Epidemic of Anti-Semitic Vandalism in America* (New York: Anti-Defamation League of B'nai B'rith, 1961).

41. Tom Segev, *The Seventh Million: The Israelis and the Holocaust* (New York, Hill and Wang, 1993), pp. 327–28.

42. Milton Himmelfarb, "In the Community," *Commentary* 30 (August 1960): 160.

43. David Ben-Gurion, "The Personal Bond," *Jewish Frontier* 28 (February 1961): 8–9.

44. Joachim Prinz, "Beyond the Zionist Dream," *Congress Bi-Weekly* 28 (January 26, 1961): 5–7.

45. "B.G.'s War on Zionism," *Israel Horizons* 8 (April 1960): 3.

46. "Why Picket Woolworth?" *Jewish Frontier* 27 (April 1960): 3. Also see the critical letters in *Jewish Frontier* 27 (June 1960): 20–22. A second editorial repeated that "we questioned the expediency of picketing Northern stores which do not discriminate." It added rather testily: "The editorial stand of the *Jewish Frontier* on civil rights for Jews, Negroes or other groups requires no apologies." "Woolworth Again," *Jewish Frontier* 27 (June 1960): 3.

47. Shlomo Katz, "Notes in Midstream: Negroes and We," *Midstream* 6 (Spring 1960): 33.

48. Ted Dienstfrey, "A Conference on the Sit-ins," *Commentary* 29 (June 1960): 525.

49. Ruth R. Wisse, "The Maturing of *Commentary* and of the Jewish Intellectual," *Jewish Social Studies* 3 (Winter 1997): 34; and Forman, *Blacks in the Jewish Mind*, p. 115.

50. Lucy S. Dawidowicz, "Middle-Class Judaism: A Case Study," *Commentary* 29 (June 1960): 501–2.

51. Emil L. Fackenheim, "The Dilemma of Liberal Judaism," *Commentary* 30 (October 1960): 301.

52. Emil L. Fackenheim, "Apologia for a Confirmation Text," *Commentary* 31 (May 1961): 402, 404.

53. Theodore Solotaroff, "Harry Golden and the American Audience," *Commentary* 31 (January 1961): 12–13.

54. Milton Himmelfarb, "In the Community," *Commentary* 30 (August 1960): 158–59.

55. Norman Podhoretz, "The Issue: May 1960," *Commentary* 29 (May 1960): a.

56. Norman Podhoretz, "My Negro Problem—And Ours," *Commentary* 35 (February 1963): 98–101.

57. Ibid., pp. 98–101.

58.Daniel Rosenblatt, "The Demonology of the Superego," *Commentary* 29 (June 1960): 529.

59. See *Commentary* 35 (April 1963): 338–47; *Commentary* 35 (May 1963): 430–38; and *Commentary* 35 (June 1963): 525–30. For a representative letter of praise, see Gilbert A. Harrison, editor in chief of the *New Republic*, who wrote: "Norman Podhoretz's piece is a real landmark, and if I had a Pulitzer Prize to give, he'd have it." See "Letters from Readers," *Commentary* 35 (April 1963): 347.

60. Justine Wise Polier and Shad Polier, "Fear Turned to Hatred," *Congress Bi-Weekly* 30 (February 18, 1963): 5–6.

61. Ibid., pp. 6–7.

3. "ARTIFICIAL ALTRUISM SOWS ONLY SEEDS OF ERROR AND CHAOS": DESEGREGATION AND JEWISH SURVIVAL

Epigraph from Shlomo Katz, "Notes in Midstream," Midstream *8 (September 1962): 62.*

1. Manheim S. Shapiro, "Probing the Prejudices of American Jews: The Negro Revolution and Jews," *Jewish Digest* 10 (November 1964): 1–3.

2. Murray Friedman, "The White Liberal's Retreat," *Atlantic Monthly* 21 (January 1963): 44.

3. Albert Vorspan, "The Negro Victory and the Jewish Failure," *American Judaism* 13 (Fall 1963): 51, 54.

4. Fred Powledge, "Poll Shows Whites in City Resent Civil Rights Drive," *New York Times*, September 21, 1964, p. 26.

5. Richard C. Hertz, "Rising Tide of Negro-Jewish Tensions," *Ebony* 20 (December 1964): 118.

6. Rabbi Henry Cohen, "How Big Is the 'Jewish Backlash?' " *National Jewish Monthly* 79 (January 1965): 6.

7. A. James Rudin, "Thermostats or Thermometers? Does Judaism Reflect Change or the Status Quo?" *Jewish Digest* 11 (October 1965): 7.

8. Harry Tetelman, "Agrees with Criticism of Article" (letter to the editor), *National Jewish Monthly* 79 (May 1965): 6; and Sylvia Berlin, "Compares Negro Racists with the Nazis" (letter to the editor), *National Jewish Monthly* 79 (March 1965): 6. For Cohen's response, see Rabbi Henry Cohen, "Answers Critics of 'Backlash' " (letter to the editor), *National Jewish Monthly* 79 (May 1965): 6.

9. Robert Gordis, "Challenges That Face the Negro," *National Jewish Monthly* 79 (April 1965): 10, 38.

10. Richard G. Hirsch, "Judaism and the Political Process," *Dimensions in American Judaism* 3 (Fall 1968): 17.

11. Melvin M. Tumin, "Conservative Trends in American Jewish Life," *Judaism* 13 (Spring 1964): 136–39.
12. Ibid., pp. 138–40, 142.
13. "Conservative Trends in American Jewish Life: Discussion," *Judaism* 13 (Spring 1964): 149, 151, 147, 153.
14. Ibid., pp. 150–51.
15. Ibid., pp. 143–45.
16. Paul Lauter, "Reflections of a Jewish Activist," *Conservative Judaism* 19 (Summer 1965): 19.
17. Paul Cowan, *An Orphan in History: Retrieving a Jewish Legacy* (New York: William Morrow, 1996 [1982]), p. 6.
18. "Fourth Dialogue in Israel: The Challenge of Jewish Youth: Israel and America, 1965," *Congress Bi-Weekly* 32 (October 25, 1965): 19, 24.
19. Ibid., pp. 23–24, 13, 22.
20. Andre Ungar, "To Birmingham, and Back," *Conservative Judaism* 18 (Fall 1963): 1.
21. *Proceedings of the Rabbinical Assembly*, ed. Rabbi Jules Harlow (New York: Rabbinical Assembly, 1963), p. 243.
22. Ibid., p. 244.
23. Jack Bloom, "Journey to Understanding," *Conservative Judaism* 19 (Summer 1965): 11–12.
24. Ungar, "To Birmingham, and Back," p. 11. The *shtadlanim*, or "court Jews," traditionally functioned as intermediaries between the Jewish community and the European monarchs; they interceded on behalf of the community, but were also more privileged than that community.
25. Ungar, "To Birmingham, and Back," p. 17.
26. Richard L. Rubenstein, "The Rabbis Visit Birmingham," *Reconstructionist* 29 (May 31, 1963): 7. Also see Richard Rubenstein, "Why 19 Conservative Rabbis Went to Birmingham," *National Jewish Monthly* 77 (July-August 1963): 6–7.
27. Rubenstein, "The Rabbis Visit Birmingham," p. 9.
28. Ungar, "To Birmingham, and Back," p. 15.
29. Bloom, "Journey to Understanding," p. 16.
30. Ungar, "To Birmingham, and Back," p. 16.
31. Harold M. Schulweis, "Jewish Liberals, Alas!" *Jewish Spectator* 29 (February 1964): 9–10.
32. Ibid., p. 8–9.
33. Arthur Hertzberg, "America Is Galut," *Jewish Frontier* 31 (July 1964): 7–8.
34. Arnulf M. Pins, "Introduction: Changing Race Relations and Jewish Communal Service," *Journal of Jewish Communal Service* 41 (Summer 1965): 323.

35. Arthur Hertzberg, "Major Address: Changing Race Relations and Jewish Communal Service," *Journal of Jewish Communal Service* 41 (Summer 1965): 324–25.

6. Ibid., pp. 326–27.

37. Ibid., pp. 327–29.

38. Ibid., p. 331.

39. Ibid., pp. 329–30, 332–33.

40. For instance, see Glazer's contributions to "Liberalism and the Negro: A Round-Table Discussion," *Commentary* 37 (March 1964): 25–42.

41. Nathan Glazer, "Negroes and Jews: The New Challenge to Pluralism," *Commentary* 38 (December 1964): 30, 32.

42. Glazer, "Negroes and Jews," p. 34. In 1965, Glazer would query whether perhaps it was because blacks were "so unsuited for modern urban life, that we are confronted with enormous and new problems of assimilation?" Glazer, "Integration in the United States," *Jewish Frontier* 32 (April 1965): 8.

43. Nathan Glazer, "Effects of Emerging Urban-Suburban and Anti-Segregation Developments on Jewish Communal Service," *Journal of Jewish Communal Service* 41 (Fall 1964): 62–66. Glazer made his presentation to the Annual Meeting of the National Conference of Jewish Communal Service on June 3, 1964.

44. Albert D. Chernin, "Implications for Jewish Community Relations," *Journal of Jewish Communal Service* 41 (Summer 1965): 346–48.

45. Arnold Aronson, "Sectarianism in the American Society Today: Impact on Jewish Communal Service," *Journal of Jewish Communal Service* 42 (Winter 1965): 141, 150–51. Aronson presented this paper at the Annual Meeting of the National Conference of Jewish Communal Service on May 30, 1965.

46. See Albert Vorspan, "Ten Ways Out for Tired Liberals," *American Judaism* 14 (Fall 1964): 14–15, 57–58.

47. Albert Vorspan, "Negroes and Jews," *Journal of Jewish Communal Service* 42 (Spring 1966): 241–42. Vorspan presented his paper at the Annual Meeting of the National Conference of Jewish Communal Service on June 1, 1965.

48. Charles Miller, "The Impact of the Integration Struggle Upon Jewish Communal Service," *Journal of Jewish Communal Service* 41 (Fall 1964): 67, 74. Miller made his presentation to the Annual Meeting of the National Conference of Jewish Communal Service on June 2, 1964.

49. Morris Grumer, "Implications for Jewish Vocational Service," *Journal of Jewish Communal Service* 41 (Summer 1965): 334–5. Also see Morris Grumer, "Jewish Vocational Services in the American Jewish Community," *Journal of Jewish Communal Service* 40 (Winter 1963): 207–11.

50. Manheim S. Shapiro, "The Dilemmas of Jewish Agencies—Real and Un-

real," *Journal of Jewish Communal Service* 42 (Fall 1965): 18–9, 24. Shapiro made his presentation to the New York City Regional Meeting of the National Conference of Jewish Communal Service on March 30, 1965.

51. Ben Halpern, "Sectarianism and the Jewish Community," *Journal of Jewish Communal Service* 42 (Fall 1965): 9, 6, 13–14, 16. Halpern made his presentation to the Annual Meeting of the National Conference of Jewish Communal Service on May 29, 1965.

52. Eli Ginzberg, "The Agenda Reconsidered," *Journal of Jewish Communal Service* 42 (Spring 1966): 280–81. For several letters from communal service workers critical of Ginzberg's remarks, see Samuel Spiegler, "Fact and Opinion," *Journal of Jewish Communal Service* 43 (Fall 1966): 100–3. For the continuation of this debate, see Arnold Gurin, "Sectarianism: A Persistent Value Dilemma," *Journal of Jewish Communal Service* 43 (Fall 1966): 38–48; as well as Frank Fierman, "Discussion: The Impact on the Jewish Community of the Struggle for Equal Rights," *Journal of Jewish Communal Service* 43 (Fall 1966): 34–37.

53. Kurt Lang and Gladys Engel Lang, "Resistance to School Desegregation: A Case Study of Backlash Among Jews," *Sociological Inquiry* 35 (Winter 1965): 95–96. This essay is reprinted in *Problems and Prospects of the Negro Movement*, ed. Raymond J. Murphy and Howard Elinson (Belmont, Cal.: Wadsworth, 1966), pp. 145–66. The Langs had also previously presented a paper based on these findings at the Annual Meeting of the American Sociological Association in Montreal, September 1964.

54. Ibid., pp. 95–97.

55. Ibid., pp. 102, 106.

56. Ibid., pp. 100–1, 105, 103.

57. Myron M. Fenster, "The Princeton Plan Comes to Jackson Heights," *Midstream* 10 (March 1964): 77–78.

58. Ibid., p. 81.

59. Oscar Handlin, "Is Integration the Answer?" *Atlantic Monthly* 213 (March 1964): 52–53.

60. Abraham G. Duker, "On Negro-Jewish Relations—A Contribution to a Discussion," *Jewish Social Studies* 27 (January 1965): 20–29.

61. Marie Syrkin, "Can Minorities Oppose 'De Facto' Segregation?" *Jewish Frontier* 31 (September 1964): 6–9, 11–12.

62. Ibid., pp. 7, 9–10.

63. Ibid., pp. 10–11.

64. " 'De Facto' Segregation: A Discussion," *Jewish Frontier* 31 (November 1964): 7–9.

65. Ibid., pp. 9–10. On Rubenstein's subsequent disengagement from black civil

rights activism, see Richard L. Rubenstein, "Jews, Negroes, and the New Politics," *Reconstructionist* 33 (November 17, 1967): 7–16; and Michael E. Staub, " 'Negroes Are Not Jews': Race, Holocaust Consciousness, and the Rise of Jewish Neoconservatism," *Radical History Review* 75 (Fall 1999): 14–15.

66. " 'De Facto' Segregation: A Discussion," p. 5.

67. Ibid., pp. 6–7. There are some echoes between Bernstein's position and a prevalent view circulating in the early 1960s (and given impetus by the discussion surrounding Stanley M. Elkins's 1959 study, *Slavery*) that elaborated parallels between American blacks and Jewish concentration camp inmates. For one characteristic example, see Charles E. Silberman, "The Economics of the Negro Problem," in *The Negro Challenge to the Business Community*, ed. Eli Ginzberg (New York: McGraw-Hill, 1964), p. 18.

68. Milton Himmelfarb, "In the Community: How We Are," *Commentary* 39 (January 1965): 72–73.

69. Myron M. Fenster, "The Princeton Plan—One Year Later," *Midstream* 11 (June 1965): 68. For the larger context of the struggle against de facto segregation in New York City schools, see Charles Silberman, *Crisis in Black and White* (New York: Random House, 1964), pp. 285–307. Also see David Rogers, *110 Livingston Street* (New York: Vintage, 1969), especially pp. 75–78; and Steven Gregory, *Black Corona: Race and the Politics of Place in an Urban Community* (Princeton: Princeton University Press, 1998), especially pp. 78–82.

70. In 1964, after a morning spent interviewing several PAT members, journalist Harry Golden was finally moved to ask, "Are there any Gentile PAT's?" See Harry Golden in "Negro-Jewish Relations in America: A Symposium," *Midstream* 12 (December 1966): 41.

71. Fenster, "The Princeton Plan," p. 73.

4. "PROTECT AND KEEP": VIETNAM, ISRAEL, AND THE POLITICS OF THEOLOGY

Epigraph from Albert Vorspan, "Vietnam and the Jewish Conscience," American Judaism *15 (Passover 1966): 9.*

1. B. Z. Sobel and May L. Sobel, "Negroes and Jews: American Minority Groups in Conflict," *Judaism* 15 (Winter 1966): 16–17, 19.

2. Ibid., pp. 21–22.

3. Arthur Hertzberg, "The Changing American Rabbinate," *Midstream* 12 (January 1966): 22.

4. Ibid., pp. 23–25, 28.

5. Ibid., pp. 28–29. For a response to Hertzberg, see Myron M. Fenster, "Rabbi Hertzberg and the Rabbis," *Congress Bi-Weekly* 33 (February 21, 1966): 6–7.

6. Lucy S. Dawidowicz in "Negro-Jewish Relations in America: A Symposium," *Midstream* 12 (December 1966): 13–17.

7. Leslie A. Fiedler, ibid., pp. 23–25.

8. Ibid., pp. 27–28. These comments are perhaps particularly striking in light of the influential role Fiedler and especially his *Love and Death in the American Novel* (1960) have had on the evolving field of "whiteness" studies.

9. Avraham Schenker, "Dimensions of Jewish Existence," *Israel Horizons* 14 (March 1966): 7, 9–10, 12.

10. Arnold Jacob Wolf, "Vietnam," in *Unfinished Rabbi: Selected Writings of Arnold Jacob Wolf*, ed. Jonathan S. Wolf (Chicago: Dee, 1998), pp. 95–97.

11. Vorspan, "Vietnam and the Jewish Conscience," p. 9.

12. Quoted in Sam Pevzner, "Inside the Jewish Community," *Jewish Currents* 19 (December 1965): 28.

13. "Viet Nam and Peace: A Policy Statement Adopted by the Governing Council of the American Jewish Congress, January 30, 1966," *Congress Bi-Weekly* 33 (February 7, 1966): 3.

14. "Synagogue Council of America: Policy Statement on Vietnam," *Jewish Currents* 20 (March 1966): 4–6.

15. Balfour Brickner, "It Can't Be Left to 'Big Daddy,' " *Israel Horizons* 14 (March 1966): 5.

16. Quoted in "Religious Leaders on War and Peace," *Reconstructionist* 32 (March 18, 1966): 3–4.

17. Arthur J. Lelyveld, "Peace: Jewish Imperatives," *Congress Bi-Weekly* 33 (March 21, 1966): 8–10.

18. Vorspan, "Vietnam and the Jewish Conscience," pp. 9, 52.

19. Ellen Bernstein, letter to the editor, *American Judaism* 16 (Fall 1966): 4.

20. Trude Weiss-Rosmarin, "The Editor's Pages," *Jewish Spectator* 31 (January 1966): 3.

21. Michael Wyschogrod, "Peace: The Real Imperatives," *Congress Bi-Weekly* 33 (April 6, 1966): 8.

22. "No 'Jewish' Position on Vietnam," *Jewish Frontier* 33 (October 1966): 3.

23. Caliste J. Alster and Philip Milstein, letters to the editor, *American Judaism* 16 (Fall 1966): 4, 41.

24. "Peace: Jewish Dimensions," *Congress Bi-Weekly* 33 (March 7, 1966): 2. Also see "Religious Leaders on War and Peace."

25. "Jewish War Plea Vexes President," *New York Times*, September 11, 1966, p. 4.

26. For a summary of this controversy, see Phil Baum, "Johnson, Vietnam, and the Jews," *Congress Bi-Weekly* 33 (October 24, 1966): 7–9.

27. Rabbi Feuerstein quoted in Rabbi Arnold Pessin, "Rabbis As Political Activists: An Investigation," *Ideas* 1, nos. 3–4 (1969): 29.

28. Wyschogrod, "Peace: The Real Imperatives," p. 8. The full passage reads: "As Jews, we cannot be hawks. But neither can we be doves—we must be men." Ibid.

29. Michael Wyschogrod, "The Jewish Interest in Vietnam," *Tradition* 8 (Winter 1966): 5–7.

30. Ibid., p. 12.

31. Ibid., p. 13–16. Wyschogrod may also have been influenced by reports circulating at the time that the Palestine Liberation Organization was planning to send soldiers to fight alongside the North Vietnamese. See Michael Elkins, "Ahmed Shukeiry, Arab Dissension and the Viet Cong," *Midstream* 12 (October 1966): 14–22.

32. Wyschogrod, "The Jewish Interest in Vietnam," pp. 8–9.

33. Ibid., p. 17.

34. Charles S. Liebman, "Judaism and Vietnam: A Reply to Dr. Wyschogrod," *Tradition* 9 (Spring-Summer 1967): 159–61.

35. Michael Wyschogrod, "Communications," *Tradition* 9 (Fall 1967): 155–56.

36. Meir Kahane, "The Jewish Stake in Vietnam," *Jewish Press*, June 9, 1967, p. 38.

37. Walter Laqueur, "Russia Enters the Middle East," *Foreign Affairs* 47 (January 1969): 305.

38. Charles A. Weil, "Israel, Vietnam, and American Geostrategy," *Ideas* 2, no. 4 (1970): 18.

39. Quoted in Misha Louvish, "Israel," in *American Jewish Year Book 1968*, ed. Morris Fine and Milton Himmelfarb (New York: American Jewish Committee, 1968), p. 118.

40. I. F. Stone, "The Harder Battle and the Nobler Victory," *I. F. Stone's Weekly* 15 (June 12, 1967): 1–2. Stone's widely discussed *New York Review of Books* essay from later that summer opened with the provocative statement: "Stripped of propaganda and sentiment, the Palestine problem is, simply, the struggle of two different peoples for the same strip of land." I. F. Stone, "Holy War," *New York Review of Books* 9 (August 3, 1967): 6. For unsympathetic and dismissive reactions to Stone's post–Six-Day War arguments, see Robert Alter, "Israel and the Intellectuals," *Commentary* 44 (October 1967): especially 49–51; and Marie Syrkin, Joel Carmichael, and Lionel Abel, "I. F. Stone Reconsiders Israel," *Midstream* 13 (October 1967): 3–17. For instance, in her essay, Syrkin pithily observed: "Mr.

Stone finds nothing reprehensible in love of country if Arabs do the loving." Ibid., p. 8.

41. Lucy S. Dawidowicz, "American Public Opinion," *American Jewish Year Book 1968*, p. 205.

42. Quoted ibid., p. 211. Interestingly, portions of this same 1967 letter to the *Village Voice* also appear in Charles E. Silberman, *A Certain People: American Jews and Their Lives Today* (New York: Summit, 1985), p. 201; and in Jack Wertheimer, *A People Divided: Judaism in Contemporary America* (New York: Basic, 1993), p. 30.

43. Norman Podhoretz, "A Certain Anxiety," *Commentary* 52 (August 1971): 6.

44. Martin Peretz, "The American Left and Israel," *Commentary* 44 (November 1967): 27.

45. Balfour Brickner, "Vietnam and the Jewish Community," *Christian Century* 87 (April 29, 1970): 534.

46. Steven S. Schwarzschild, introduction to "Jewish Values in the Post-Holocaust Future: A Symposium," *Judaism* 16 (Summer 1967): 267–68.

47. Emil L. Fackenheim, contribution to "Jewish Values," pp. 272–73.

48. Schwarzschild and Fackenheim, discussion, ibid., pp. 287, 289–90.

49. Fackenheim, discussion, ibid., pp. 289–90.

50. Richard L. Rubenstein, "Imperatives of Survival: A Presentation," *Congress Bi-Weekly* 36 (February 24, 1969): 33–34, 37.

51. Ibid., pp. 35–37.

52. Steven S. Schwarzschild, "Discussion," *Congress Bi-Weekly* 36 (February 24, 1969): 40.

53. Ibid., p. 41.

54. Richard L. Rubenstein, "Discussion," *Congress Bi-Weekly* 36 (February 24, 1969): 42.

55. Emil L. Fackenheim, *God's Presence in History: Jewish Affirmations and Philosophical Reflections* (New York: Harper, 1970), pp. 70, 89, 79, 91. In the text the person Fackenheim imagined would be hesitant to shoot his gun is Amos Kenan, a left-wing secular Israeli writer, though it was clear that Fackenheim meant Kenan to stand in for progressive Jews in general.

56. For a compelling testimonial about his first experience in the southern civil rights movement, see Seymour Siegel, "Pilgrimage to Selma," *Congress Bi-Weekly* 32 (March 29, 1965): 5–6.

57. Seymour Siegel, "The Current Theological Situation," *Conservative Judaism* 23 (Summer 1969): 14–18. Also see Emil L. Fackenheim, "Jewish Faith and the Holocaust: A Fragment," *Commentary* 46 (August 1968): 30–36.

58. Emil L. Fackenheim, "On Jewish Radicals and Radical Jews," *Hadassah*

Magazine 50 (June 1969): 7, 32. For detailed articulation of Fackenheim's Zionism, see his *To Mend the World: Foundations of Post-Holocaust Jewish Thought* (New York: Schocken, 1982).

59. Michael Wyschogrod, "Faith and the Holocaust," *Judaism* 20 (Summer 1971): 288–89.

60. Michael Wyschogrod, "Some Theological Reflections on the Holocaust," *Response* 9 (Spring 1975): 67.

61. Wyschogrod, "Faith and the Holocaust," p. 288. Nor were Wyschogrod's conclusions solely a reaction against Fackenheim. See also his cautionary remarks soon after Israel's victory in the Six-Day War that "to make solid messianic claims and to tie the fate of Judaism to the fate of Israel, for whose preservation and prosperity we all fervently pray, is simply unauthorized and therefore irresponsible." Michael Wyschogrod, "The Religious Meaning of the Six Day War: A Symposium," *Tradition* 10 (Summer 1968): 10.

62. See Steven Schwarzschild, "Justice," in *Jewish Values*, ed. Geoffrey Wigoder (Jerusalem: Keter, 1974), pp. 194–98.

63. Quoted in James Finn, *Protest: Pacifism and Politics: Some Passionate Views on War and Nonviolence* (New York: Random House, 1967), p. 126. Also see Steven Schwarzschild, "Introduction," in *Roots of Jewish Nonviolence*, ed. Allan Solomonow (Nyack, N.Y.: Jewish Peace Fellowship, 1970), p. 4–5.

64. Steven Schwarzschild, "The Necessity of the Lone Man," *Fellowship* 31 (May 1965): 18.

65. Steven S. Schwarzschild, "The Religious Demand for Peace," *Judaism* 15 (Fall 1966): 412–13.

66. Menachem Kellner, "Introduction," *The Pursuit of the Ideal: Jewish Writings of Steven Schwarzschild*, ed. Menachem Kellner (Albany: State University of New York Press, 1990), p. 11.

67. Steven S. Schwarzschild, "On the Theology of Jewish Survival," in *The Pursuit of the Ideal*, pp. 90–96. Reprinted from *CCAR Journal* 63 (October 1968): 2–21.

68. Balfour Brickner, "My Zionist Dilemmas: Two Recent Cases," *Sh'ma* 1, no. 1 (November 9, 1970): 4–5.

69. Arnold Jacob Wolf, "Sandy Lee Scheuer, Zikhronah Livrakhah," *Sh'ma* trial no. 1 (May 22, 1970): 2–3.

70. Trude Weiss-Rosmarin, "Communications," *CCAR Journal* 65 (April 1969): 91.

71. Steven S. Schwarzschild, "The Radical Imperatives of Judaism," *Judaism* 21 (Winter 1972): 9, 11.

72. Richard L. Rubenstein, "The Politics of Powerlessness," *Reconstructionist* 34 (May 17, 1968): 14, 11, 8, 12, 15. For a response to Rubenstein's article that labels

its views "dangerous," see Inge Lederer Gibel, "The Possible Dream," *Reconstructionist* 34 (October 11, 1968): 16–23.

73. Judd L. Teller, "The Jewish Experience with Liberalism," *Judaism* 21 (Winter 1972): 44–48. Also see Jakob J. Petuchowski, "Left Turn! The Politics of American Reform Judaism," *Ideas* 2, no. 4 (1970): 47–54.

74. Richard G. Hirsch, "Toward a Theology for Social Action," *CCAR Journal* 60 (January 1968): 67–68, 74.

75. Richard G. Hirsch, "Social Values in Judaism and Their Realization in the Reform Movement," *CCAR Journal* 75 (October 1971): 41, 45.

76. Andre Ungar, "A Rabbi's Dilemma," *Jewish Spectator* 34 (April 1969): 10.

77. Avraham Schenker, "The New Left, Israel, and the Jewish People," *Diaspora and Unity* 9 (1969): 58.

78. Richard L. Rubenstein, "Liberalism and the Jewish Interests," *Judaism* 21 (Winter 1972): 16.

79. Jakob J. Petuchowski, "Prophetic Religion, Jewish Self-Interest and the American Scene," *Ideas* 4, no. 1 (1973): 33.

80. Jakob J. Petuchowski, "The Limits of Self-Sacrifice," in *Modern Jewish Ethics: Theory and Practice*, ed. Marvin Fox (Columbus: Ohio State University Press, 1975), p. 103.

81. Seymour Siegel, "What Direction for Jewish Social Ethics? A Case for Traditional Conservatism," *Conservative Judaism* 25 (Fall 1970): 65.

82. Seymour Siegel, "An Anatomy of Liberalism—A Conservative View," *Judaism* 21 (Winter 1972): 26, 30. Also see Seymour Siegel, "Danger on the Left, II," *Ideas* 2, nos. 2–3 (1970): 30–34.

5. "IF THERE WAS DIRTY LINEN, IT HAD TO BE WASHED": JEWS FOR URBAN JUSTICE AND RADICAL JUDAISM

Epigraph from "Jews for Urban Justice: Principles and Goals," Jewish Currents *22 (October 1968): 15.*

1. Judd L. Teller, *Strangers and Natives: The Evolution of the American Jew from 1921 to the Present* (New York: Delacorte, 1968), p. 226. Teller also observed: "The suburban Jew is different. God and faith are not part of his basic vocabulary; he gives them fleeting thought at best and may even be said to be unaligned in the eternal debate between believers and agnostic (there are no atheists in suburbia, or so it appears, because that would mean taking sides)." Ibid.

2. Edward S. Shapiro, *A Time for Healing: American Jewry Since World War II* (Baltimore: Johns Hopkins University Press, 1992), p. 150.

3. Quoted in Philip Slomovitz, "Is Youth Being Slighted?" *Detroit Jewish News*, October 16, 1970, p. 2.

4. The term *multi-particularist* appears in Arthur I. Waskow, *The Bush Is Burning! Radical Judaism Faces the Pharaohs of the Modern Superstate* (New York: Macmillan, 1971), p. 20.

5. Sharon Rose, "Anti-Racist Organizing in the Jewish Community: A Case Study," unpublished ms. (May 1970), p. 1. All unpublished papers cited in this chapter are from the private collection of Michael Tabor.

6. "An Open Letter to Members of the Washington Hebrew Congregation," September 24, 1966.

7. Quoted in Michael Tabor, "The Jewish Youth Scene," *Jewish Currents* 24 (October 1970): 13; and Rose, "Anti-Racist Organizing," p. 2.

8. Mike Tabor, "Jews for Urban Justice and Fabrangen: A Memoir," unpublished ms. (1972), p. 3. Also see Harold Goldberg, "A History of the Jews for Urban Justice, 1966–1969," unpublished ms. (1970), p. 3. At the time Goldberg was a graduate student in the Department of Near Eastern and Judaic Studies, Brandeis University. In 1970 Goldberg also contributed an occasional column on Jewish radical activism to the *Jewish Post and Opinion*. For example, see his "Jewish Ferment on Campus Defined," *Jewish Post and Opinion*, June 26, 1970, p. 2.

9. Rose, "Anti-Racist Organizing," p. 2.

10. "An Open Letter to Members of the Washington Hebrew Congregation," October 1967. The leaflet also contained this quotation: "Woe to him that gaineth evil gains for his house, that he may set his nest on high, that he may be delivered from the power of evil, thou hast devised shame to thy house, by cutting off many peoples, and has forfeited thy life. For the stone shall cry out of the wall, and the beam out of the timber shall answer it.—Habakkuk, the Prophet." Ibid.

11. Jason R. Silverman to Mike Tabor, letter, November 1, 1967. Also see Goldberg, "A History of the Jews for Urban Justice," p. 8.

12. Jews for Urban Justice to Jason Silverman, letter, November 15, 1967. Silverman wrote back that "not only do I think that you hurt your own cause—but more important, it is actually counter-productive of the goals we mutually seek to achieve." Jason R. Silverman to Michael Tabor, letter, November 20, 1967.

13. "Conclusions and Recommendations: JUJ Survey of the Jewish Community, May 1968," p. 1. Also see William R. MacKaye, "Plea for Social Action: Jewish Groups Called Unconcerned," *Washington Post*, May 23, 1968, p. B1; and "Young Adults Urge Action on Rights," *Jewish Week*, May 16, 1968, p. 1.

14. Quoted in " 'Urban Justice' Reactions Vary," *Jewish Week*, May 30, 1968, p. 3.

15. Quoted in MacKaye, "Plea for Social Action." Also see Milton Friedman, "Leaders Aghast at Activists," *Jewish Week*, May 30, 1968, p. 1.

16. Rabbi Bernard H. Mehlman, letter to the editor, *Jewish Week*, May 30, 1968, p. 4. An editorial that same day in *Jewish Week* also attempted to strike a more conciliatory tone. While on the one hand stating that the press conference to announce its survey had been "wrong," "a goof on the part of Jews for Urban Justice," and pointedly elaborating that "a goof is sometimes good for the soul, especially for a soul predisposed to self-righteousness, as activist souls so often are," *Jewish Week* also declared that "it is surely wholesome to have a Jewish organization devoting itself wholeheartedly in a specialized intensity to urban justice." See "Washing or Blackening the Linen?" *Jewish Week*, May 30, 1968, p. 4.

17. Tabor, "Jews for Urban Justice and Fabrangen," p. 11–12.

18. Quoted in Goldberg, "A History of the Jews for Urban Justice," p. 19. It was Arnold Sternberg who had come up with the idea for the *daven*-in. Sternberg was a Washington attorney and vice-chairman of the Urban Affairs committee of the Jewish Community Council. Ibid., p. 18–19.

19. Waskow, *The Bush Is Burning!*, p. 14.

20. "Jewish Groups Join Rally for Poor People," *Jewish Week*, June 27, 1968, p. 2. Although the American Jewish Congress sent two busloads of members to the march, and the American Jewish Committee and the Washington Board of Rabbis urged support, the Anti-Defamation League and B'nai B'rith did not endorse the march.

21. In the end the JCC building was sold to the group that would "do the greatest good for the largest portion of the community" (it became the Federal City College, the first four-year institution for higher education in the district), though the JCC never disclosed whether JUJ pressure contributed to this decision. See Goldberg, "A History of the Jews for Urban Justice," pp. 20–25. Also see "Center's Closing Is Proposed," *Jewish Week*, August 15, 1968, p. 1; Michael Tabor, "Discussing the Center," letter to the editor, *Jewish Week*, August 15, 1969, p. 4; and Michael Tabor, "Jews for Urban Justice," *Jewish Currents* 22 (October 1968): 16.

22. Within a short time, the discussion series became a major community event with talks by prominent speakers like performer Theodore Bikel, Jewish Community Council executive Isaac Franck, Harry Kaufman, president of the Orthodox Board of Rabbis, and the UAHC social activist Richard Hirsch. See "Urban Justice Group Details Latest Activities," *Jewish Week*, September 5, 1968, p. 5.

23. Tabor, "Jews for Urban Justice and Fabrangen," p. 15.
24. Ibid., p. 13.
25. "New Left Jews Split on Mideast," *Jewish Week*, January 30, 1969, p. 4.
26. Morris U. Schappes, "Around the World," *Jewish Currents* 22 (December 1968): 73.
27. The leaflet not only once again invoked the Holocaust but also elaborated parallels between Zionism and the grape workers' struggle:

> WHAT WILL *YOU* DO?
> What did the world do to prevent the holocaust? Nothing.
> Did the Allies bomb Nazi gas chambers in WWII? No.
> Who helped Israel in 1948? No one.
> Who helped Israel in 1967? No one.
> Who is helping the suffering grape workers?

See Jews for Urban Justice leaflet, 1969.
28. Morris U. Schappes, "Around the World," *Jewish Currents* 23 (March 1969): 46; and memorandum on the Giant position by Paul Scott Forbes, assistant to President Joseph Danzansky, quoted in Harold Goldberg, "A History of the Jews for Urban Justice," p. 32. Mike Tabor would later conclude in his memoir of Jews for Urban Justice that the local grape boycott campaign had been a failure. See Tabor, "Jews for Urban Justice and Fabrangen," p. 17.
29. Waskow, *The Bush Is Burning!* p. 18.
30. Rabbi Marc H. Tanenbaum, national director of the interreligious affairs department of the American Jewish Committee, quoted in "Tanenbaum Applauds California's Grape Strike Settlement," *Detroit Jewish News*, August 14, 1970, p. 31.
31. Waskow, *The Bush Is Burning!* p. 18.
32. "Draft: Criteria for Action by JUJ," 1969.
33. Invitation to the Freedom Seder, April 4, 1969.
34. Arthur Waskow, "A Radical Haggadah for Passover," *Ramparts* 7 (April 1969): 26.
35. Ibid., pp. 26, 28.
36. Ibid., pp. 19–20, 28–29.
37. Judith Coburn, "Passover in the Ghetto: This Year in Washington," *Village Voice*, April 10, 1969, p. 59.
38. David and Toby Brooks, letter to the editor, *Jewish Week*, April 24, 1969, p. 4.
39. Tabor, "Jews for Urban Justice and Fabrangen," p. 23. For Balfour Brickner's critically balanced but ultimately favorable reflections on his participation

in the Freedom Seder, see Balfour Brickner, "Notes on a Freedom Seder," *Reconstructionist* 35 (June 13, 1969): 15–19.

40. Waskow, "Radical Haggadah," pp. 30, 33, 26.

41. Quoted in "Negro Martyr Made Hero of New Haggadah," *Jewish Week*, March 20, 1969, p. 9.

42. Anita Miller and Fran Schreiberg, "Notes from Radnor," *Jews for Urban Justice Newsletter*, May 1969, p. 5.

43. See Goldberg's discussion of the Radnor Conference in "A History of the Jews for Urban Justice," pp. 39–40; and Miller and Schreiberg, "Notes from Radnor," pp. 5–6. Also see Robert Dudnick, "Jews Organize to Fight White Racism," *Guardian*, April 19, 1969, p. 15.

44. "Draft Statement for the Jewish Organizing Project," April 1969, p. 2.

45. "This Is the Bus to Auschwitz," leaflet/poem, June 1969. The poem is reprinted in Waskow, *The Bush Is Burning!* pp. 142–43.

46. Cited in Tabor, "Jews for Urban Justice and Fabrangen," p. 27.

47. Jews for Urban Justice statement quoted in "Tisha B'Av Service Held at Capitol," *Jewish Week*, July 31, 1969, p. 7.

48. Fran Schreiberg, "A Service to Commemorate the Fast of the 9th of Av," *Jewish Urban Guerrilla* 2 (September-October 1969). Two weeks later, on August 6, 1969, the anniversary of the Hiroshima atomic bomb, the Senate approved funding for the ABM system.

49. Fran Schreiberg, "Tisha B'Av: A News Story," *Jewish Urban Guerrilla* 2 (September-October 1969). Also see Arthur Waskow's comments quoted in "Urban Group Tactics Denounced by Rabbi," *Jewish Week*, August 7, 1969, p. 1.

50. Reprinted in Waskow, *The Bush Is Burning!* pp. 29–30.

51. Goldberg, "A History of the Jews for Urban Justice," pp. 50–51.

52. Ben J. Wattenberg quoted in Stephen D. Isaacs, *Jews and American Politics* (New York: Doubleday, 1974), p. 96. Wattenberg was a speech writer and influential Washington political analyst.

53. Report of the Special Committee on Kol Nidre Night quoted in Goldberg, "A History of the Jews for Urban Justice," p. 80.

54. Marilyn F. Pollin, Sidney Koretz, and Morris Goldman, letters to the editor, *Jewish Week*, April 3, 1969, p. 4. Also see the letter from Hyman J. Cohen, who writes "that I could not agree more with Morris Goldman" and that if "I knew his address, I would send him a note of thanks." Hyman J. Cohen, letter to the editor, *Jewish Week*, April 10, 1969, p. 4.

55. Haim Solomon, letter to the editor, *Jewish Week*, July 17, 1969, p. 4.

56. Harry Blum, letter to the editor, *Jewish Week*, October 23, 1969, p. 4; Ronald

S. Blum, letter to the editor, *Jewish Week*, October 2, 1969, p. 4; and David Ginsberg, letter to the editor, *Jewish Week*, October 16, 1969, p. 4.

57. Rabbi Kaufman had delivered a talk entitled "An Orthodox View of Social Justice" at the group's Monday evening discussion series on February 24, 1969. See the calendar in *Jews for Urban Justice Newsletter* (February 1969).

58. Kaufman statement quoted in "Urban Group Tactics Denounced by Rabbi," p. 1.

59. Emil L. Fackenheim, "On Jewish Radicals and Radical Jews," *Hadassah Magazine* 50 (June 1969): 7. For another critical (but also nonlocal) analysis of the Freedom Seder, see Itzhak Epstein, "This Year in Washington: The Waskow Haggadah and the 'Freedom Seder,'" *Jewish Liberation Journal* no. 2 (June 1969): 7–11. About the Freedom Seder, Epstein felt that "most of what was good in it was not new, and most of what was new in it was not very Jewish." Ibid., p. 8.

60. Fran Schreiberg, "Statement by Jews for Urban Justice," *Jewish Urban Guerrilla* 2 (September-October 1969).

61. Tabor, "Jews for Urban Justice and Fabrangen," p. 28. In June 1969 Mike Tabor also reflected in a short essay that unless American Jews grasped how "a radical ideology, a strong sense of social justice, disobedience to unjust laws and rules, and militant direct action are not inimical to Jewish tradition or law," the alternative would be the slow and painful death of Judaism "through a form of GENOCIDE much more effective than that ever dreamed of by all the 'anti-semites' in history." Mike Tabor, "The Final Solution," *International Jewish Conspiracy* 1 (June 1969): 2.

62. Monroe H. Friedman, letter to the editor, *Jewish Week*, October 9, 1969, p. 4.

63. See Mike Masch, "Anti-war Marchers Turn Out En Masse in Washington," *Jewish Exponent*, November 21, 1969. Masch's article was subsequently distributed as a leaflet for the National Jewish Organizing Project.

64. Tabor quoted in "'Massive Jewish Presence' Anticipated in Washington for Peace March: Prayers to Be Heard in Synagogues This Weekend," *Detroit Jewish News*, November 14, 1969, p. 33.

65. See "Activities Scheduled," *Jewish Week*, November 13, 1969, p. 1; Masch, "Anti-war Marchers"; and "National Fast for Jews Called by Jewish Radicals," *Jewish Post and Opinion*, November 28, 1969, p. 1.

66. See Tabor, "Jews for Urban Justice and Fabrangen," p. 35.

67. Albert Vorspan to Mike Tabor, letter, December 4, 1969.

68. For instance, thirty-three local rabbinic and community leaders had already endorsed the first moratorium, held in mid-October, as had the National Capi-

tal Chapter of the AJCongress. See "Moratorium Gains Community Support," *Jewish Week*, October 9, 1969, p. 1.

69. Seymour D. Wolf, letter to the editor, *Jewish Week*, November 27, 1969, p. 4. Before the moratorium/New Mobe weekend, Wolf had stressed that "Jewish students are coming here to express their feelings about war and peace as part of the American democratic tradition and Jewish tradition—in a peaceful, non-violent way. They are our sons and daughters, our nieces and nephews. We as a Jewish community must open the doors of our homes and of our institutions and welcome them, rather than have them roam the streets." In the protest's aftermath, however, Wolf was careful to correct "the impression that the Council had taken a position against President Nixon's policies concerning the war, and in support of the Moratorium. Such is not the case. The Council, after extensive discussion, did not arrive at any position on the war, and does not have a position at this time." A report in the *Jewish Post and Opinion* indicated that the D.C. Jewish Community Council's hesitation about taking a stand came in the wake of "hearing arguments that pressure on the U.S. to withdraw from Vietnam could also impel the government to reduce its armament assistance to Israel." See Wolf quoted in "Local Community Opens Doors to Incoming Student Participants," *Jewish Week*, November 13, 1969, p. 1; Wolf, letter to the editor, p. 4; and "Radical Jewish Coalition May Be Moratorium Product," *Jewish Post and Opinion*, November 14, 1969, p. 3.

70. See " 'Massive Jewish Presence,' " p. 33; and "Activities Scheduled," p. 1.

71. "Thousands Join Mass Anti-war Activities," *Jewish Week*, November 20, 1969, p. 1.

72. Judye Saypol and Groner quoted ibid.

73. Oscar Groner, "Not 'Jewish Radicals' but 'Radical Jews,' " *National Jewish Monthly* 85 (May 1971): 53.

74. "Mortgage Financing in the City and the Jewish Community: A Fact Sheet Prepared by Jews for Urban Justice," leaflet, November 1969, p. 2. See also Rose, "Anti-Racist Organizing," pp. 15–16; Goldberg, "A History of the Jews for Urban Justice," p. 33; Leonard Downie Jr., "Tiny Group Takes on Big S&L," *Washington Post*, January 22, 1970; and Harris Lyle, "Move for Inner City Effort Fails at Guardian Federal," *Washington Evening Star*, January 22, 1970.

75. See "Jewess on Vigil Hasn't Eaten for Days," *Jewish Post and Opinion*, February 20, 1970, p. 1; and "Jewish Girl in Vigil Ends 13-Day Fast," *Jewish Post and Opinion*, February 27, 1970, p. 1. When Rose ended her fast, Arthur Waskow took her place. See "Jewish Girl in Vigil Ends 13-Day Fast," p. 1. Other rabbis affiliated with CALCAV—which later changed its name simply to Clergy and Laity Concerned—included Roland B. Gittelsohn, Wolfe Kelman, and Arthur Lelyveld.

76. Lois D. Cohen, " 'Freedom Seder' a 7-Hour Happening with Many Doing Their Many 'Things,' " *Jewish Week*, April 30, 1970, p. 2. Also see "Freedom Seder Even Inspires One Male Nude," *Jewish Post and Opinion*, May 8, 1970, p. 2.

77. "Groups Plan March Against Amerikan and Soviet 'Pharaohs,' " JUJ press release, April 16, 1970. Also see "Soviet Jewry," *Voice of Micah* (December 1971): 3.

78. "For Peace and Justice in the Middle East" (JUJ statement), November 1970.

79. Tabor, "Jews for Urban Justice and Fabrangen," p. 34.

80. See "A Bund Haggadah" reprinted in David P. Shuldiner, *Of Moses and Marx: Folk Ideology and Folk History in the Jewish Labor Movement* (Westport, Conn.: Bergin and Garvey, 1999), p. 155–64.

81. Tabor, "Jews for Urban Justice and Fabrangen," p. 37. On JUJ's realization that Yiddish was also a language of political resistance, see Mike Tabor, "Young Jews Discover Their True Forebearers," *Jewish Post and Opinion*, June 18, 1971, p. 2. For summaries of the Bund that appeared on the movement's centennial, see Alisa Solomon, "Bund to the Future," *Village Voice*, October 7, 1997, p. 37–39, and Abraham Brumberg, "One Hundred Years of the Bund," *Dissent* 44 (Fall 1997): 105. Also see Karen Brodkin, *How Jews Became White Folks and What That Says About Race in America* (New Brunswick: Rutgers University Press, 1998), pp. 104–10.

82. "The Jewish Campaign for the People's Peace Treaty," reprinted in Waskow, *The Bush Is Burning!* pp. 117–19.

83. Arthur I. Waskow, "From Jewish Radical to Radical Jew," ibid., p. 28.

84. Ibid.

85. Paul Ruttkay and Robert Agus, "Proposal for *Fabrangen*," in *Contemporary Judaic Fellowship in Theory and Practice*, ed. Jacob Neusner (New York: Ktav, 1972), pp. 178, 180–81.

86. Chava Weissler, "The *Fabrangen* Experiment," *National Jewish Monthly* 86 (February 1972): 32.

87. Tabor, "Jews for Urban Justice and Fabrangen," p. 40.

88. George Johnson, "Proposal for a Summer Living-Working Experiment," *Jewish Urban Guerrilla* 3 (April 1971): 8.

89. Tabor, "Jews for Urban Justice and Fabrangen," p. 41.

90. Weissler, "The *Fabrangen* Experiment," p. 38.

91. Tabor, "Jews for Urban Justice and Fabrangen," pp. 42–43.

92. Weissler, "The *Fabrangen* Experiment," p. 38. Also see "Fabrangen: A Jewish Coming Together," *D. C. Gazette* 11 (June 21-July 4, 1971): 11; George E. Johnson, "*Fabrangen*: A Coming Together," in *Contemporary Judaic Fellowship in Theory and Practice*, pp. 185–88; and Arthur I. Waskow's account of his involvement with Fabrangen in *Godwrestling* (New York: Schocken, 1978).

93. Weissler, "The *Fabrangen* Experiment," p. 40.

94. Bertram Jonas, "When El Fatah Goes to Shul!" *Jewish Week*, September 2, 1971, p. 1.

95. See Carl Goldman, letter to the editor, *Jewish Week*, September 30, 1971, p. 5; and "The Editor's Chair," *Jewish Post and Opinion*, September 17, 1971, p. 6.

96. Quoted in "Lipman Wants Reversal of *Fabrangen* Decision," *Jewish Post and Opinion*, November 5, 1971, p. 3.

97. Mike Tabor, "Red-Baiting," *Jewish Post and Opinion*, October 1, 1971, p. 2. Also see Michael Tabor, "Distortion Charged," *Jewish Post and Opinion*, October 15, 1971, p. 2.

98. "Come On in, the Water's Fine," *National Review* 23 (March 9, 1971): 249.

99. Walter Laqueur, "Revolutionism and the Jews 1: New York and Jerusalem," *Commentary* 51 (February 1971): 42, 44–45.

100. Nathan Glazer, "Revolutionism and the Jews 3: The Role of the Intellectuals," *Commentary* 51 (February 1971): 57–58, 60–61.

101. Robert Alter, "Revolutionism and the Jews 2: Appropriating the Religious Tradition," *Commentary* 51 (February 1971): 48–51.

102. Norman Podhoretz, "The Tribe of the Wicked Son," *Commentary* 51 (February 1971): 10. Balfour Brickner was especially outraged at Podhoretz's charge that Jews like himself and Waskow were Jewish antisemites. Implicitly echoing the 1963 critique of Podhoretz written by Justine Wise Polier and Shad Polier, Brickner argued not only that Judaism did have "a particular social thrust" but also contended that the truly assimilationist and anti-Jewish Jews were those who

> betray an unutterable *chutzpah* in presuming to judge who among their fellow Jews is "kosher" and who is "*treif*"—who falls within the pale and who has strayed beyond the *Commentary* line—who should be tolerated and who should be wiped out. Editor Podhoretz has the litmus paper, and he gives out the new Jewish seal of Good Housebroken Approval. An intellectual, pseudo-Jewish McCarthyism, presided over by *Commentary*, is something new and ugly under the sun! That is what is anti-Jewish, masking in the guise of Jewish affirmation.

Brickner further suggested that "Love of Israel, commitment to the Zionist ideal, never did, and must not now, demand slavish silence, and one's credentials as a Jewish self-affirmer must not be held suspect because he is sometimes pained by what he sees and who, because of this pain, cries out within the bosom of the Jewish family. Candor is often more important than popularity." See Balfour Brickner, letter to the editor, *Commentary* 51 (June 1971): 8, 12. For the rebuttals by Robert Alter and Norman Podhoretz, see ibid., pp. 24, 26–28, 32–33.

103. Chava Alkon Katz, "Jewish Radical Zionists in the U.S.," *Encyclopaedia Judaica Year Book 1975/6* (Jerusalem: Keter, 1976), p. 127.

104. Stanley Rothman and S. Robert Lichter, *Roots of Radicalism: Jews, Christians, and the New Left* (New York: Oxford University Press, 1982), p. 137.

6. "WE ARE COMING HOME": NEW LEFT JEWS AND RADICAL ZIONISM

Epigraph from "We Are Coming Home," Brooklyn Bridge *1. no. 1 (February 1971): 1.*

1. David Weissman, "Radicals Invade Federation, Glue 200 Mezuzahs to Doors," *Jewish Post and Opinion*, November 14, 1969, p. 4.

2. Denise Baker, "Jewish Students List Demands," *Flame*, December 1969, pp. 1, 8. Also see Itzhak Epstein, "Demand Funds Act on Jewish Education," *Jewish Liberation Journal* no. 5 (November-December 1969): 1, 7. The full text of Levine's speech is reprinted as "To Share a Vision" in *Jewish Radicalism: A Selected Anthology*, ed. Jack Nusan Porter and Peter Dreier (New York: Grove, 1973), pp. 183–94.

3. Deborah Rosenthal, "The Jewish Youth Scene," *Jewish Currents* 24 (October 1970): 6. Julius Hoffman was a frequent target of radical Jewish mockery. For instance, in late 1969 the Jewish Liberation Project awarded Hoffman one of its prestigious Uncle Jake Awards, "presented to the Jew who has out-distanced all competitors in the imagination and creativity with which he has ass-licked the Establishment." The dedication continued, "Hoffman's claim to fame derives from his deft stage-managing of the conspiracy to deprive eight men of their constitutional rights under the First Amendment and to defame, bind and gag the anti-war movement." See "Uncle Jake Award," *Jewish Liberation Journal* no. 5 (November-December 1969): 2.

4. Bob Brown quoted in "Jewish Student Activists Speak Out," *Hadassah Magazine* 51 (June 1970): 9. Brown was active in the Jewish Student Union of Long Island University and coeditor of the student newspaper, the *Dawn*. Also see "Youth Occupy Federation," *Jewish Liberation Journal* no. 7 (April-May 1970): 1, 4.

5. "Students Stage Sit-In at NY Federation Charging 'Insensitivity'; 41 Arrested," *Detroit Jewish News*, April 17, 1970, p. 5. Also see "Forty-five Jewish Activists Arrested After Protest on Philanthropies," *New York Times*, April 9, 1970, p. 31;

and "Federation Is Target of Demands in New York," *Jewish Post and Opinion*, April 24, 1970, p. 12. For a radical Jewish analysis of the Jewish Federations, see Judah J. Shapiro, "The Philistine Philanthropists: The Power and Shame of Jewish Federations," *Jewish Liberation Journal* no. 4 (October 1969): 1, 4.

6. "'Emanuel' Leaves Reform Group in Protest Against Vietnam Stand," *Jewish Press*, May 12, 1967, pp. 1–2. In addition, the Radical Jewish Union distributed a "Jewish Manifesto," which, among other things, demanded that Temple Emanu-El "provide $1,000,000 in reparations to the National Jewish Liberation Movement so that we can begin to rebuild our lives in accordance with the real values of Judaism which have been denied us by those who purport to lead and represent us." Quoted in "Radical Students Plan New Confrontation," *Jewish Post and Opinion*, May 22, 1970, p. 3.

7. Morris U. Schappes, "Around the World," *Jewish Currents* 24 (July-August 1970): 46; and Rosen quoted in "Seminary Students for Peace to Lecture Against U.S. Policy in SE Asia," *Detroit Jewish News*, June 5, 1970, p. 14.

8. Quoted in Sharlene Kranz, "News from the International Jewish Conspiracy," *Jewish Urban Guerilla*, June 5, 1970, p. 8.

9. "Radical Jewish Union Reached Accord with Temple Emanu-El," *Detroit Jewish News*, June 19, 1970, p. 3; Morris U. Schappes, "Around the World," *Jewish Currents* 24 (July-August 1970): 46; and "Radical's Rabbi Raps Conviction of Girl on Temple's Complaint," *Detroit Jewish News*, June 18, 1971, p. 21.

10. *Havurot* were established all over the United States at the end of the 1960s and the early part of the 1970s. They varied tremendously from place to place, each expressing its own eclectic mixture of traditional and countercultural Jewish values. The *havurah* movement has received rich and extensive examination elsewhere. For a wonderful look at havurot compiled by individuals deeply involved in the movement, see *The First Jewish Catalog: A Do-It-Yourself Kit*, ed. Richard Siegel, Michael Strassfeld, and Sharon Strassfeld (Philadelphia: Jewish Publication Society of America, 1973); and numerous of the essays in *Contemporary Judaic Fellowship in Theory and in Practice*, ed. Jacob Neusner (New York: Ktav, 1972). The finest scholarship on the havurot is Riv-Ellen Prell, *Prayer and Community: The Havurah in American Judaism* (Detroit: Wayne State University Press, 1989).

11. "Federations Give Funds for Havurah," *Jewish Week*, June 18, 1970, p. 2.

12. Rafi Goldman, "Can Socialist-Zionists Live with the Jewish Establishment?" *Bagolah* 1, no. 1 (1970): 5.

13. Mike Masch, "Who Needs Jewish Liberation?" *Hayom* 2, no. 5 (February 23–March 9, 1972): 2.

14. "Radical Zionist Manifesto," *Genesis 2* 1 (April 1970): 8; and "Jewish Leftists

Form Anti-Establishment Body," *Jewish Post and Opinion*, February 27, 1970, p. 1. For a first-person response to the conference, see J. B., "A Search for Radical Zionism," *ACIID* 1, no. 3 (1970), p. 14.

15. Itzhak Epstein, "American Jewry: On the Barricades or on the Fence?" *Jewish Liberation Journal* no. 1 (May 1969): 6.

16. Quoted in "Hillel vs. the Elders," *Newsweek*, December 8, 1969, p. 118.

17. "Picket Marine Hq.," *Jewish Liberation Journal* no. 5 (November-December 1969): 8.

18. Joseph Kohane, "Jewish Activism," *Achdut* 1, no. 3 (March 1971), p. 6.

19. Jonathan Braun, "Bagels and Lox Judaism: Neglecting the Jewish National Experience," *Flame* 3 (February 1970): 1, 7. Also see Jonathan Braun, "The Student Revolt and the Jewish Student," *Midstream* 16 (March 1970): 41–44.

20. Amos Kenan, "New Left Go Home," *Jewish Liberation Journal* no. 2 (June 1969): 4.

21. Quoted in "Jewish Student Activists Speak Out," p. 26.

22. Al Taxim ben Moses, "Radical Activists Form New Independent Jewish Movement," *Ha-Orah* 2 (October 6, 1969): 6.

23. See Jack Nusan Porter and Peter Dreier, "Introduction: The Roots of Jewish Radicalism," in *Jewish Radicalism*, p. xxxi.

24. Aviva Cantor Zuckoff, "Oppression of Amerika's Jews," *Jewish Liberation Journal* no. 8 (November 1970): 1–2.

25. Ibid., p. 2.

26. It is worth pointing out that Zuckoff herself subsequently wrote a sharp critique of the passivity-under-Nazism thesis. See Aviva Cantor, "Blaming the Victim," *Jewish Women/Jewish Men: The Legacy of Patriarchy in Jewish Life* (San Francisco: Harper, 1995), pp. 391–94.

27. Zuckoff, "Oppression of Amerika's Jews," pp. 2–4. See also Itzhak Epstein and Aviva Zuckoff, "Jewish Liberation and the Fourth World," *Hayom* 1, no. 2 (May 1971): 3, 7.

28. Robert Alter, "Revolutionism and the Jews 2: Appropriating the Religious Tradition," *Commentary* 51 (February 1971): 53–54.

29. Jack Porter, "The New Left, the Blackman, and Israel in New View of Jewish Tom," *Ha-Orah* 1 (June 1969): 3–4. For a good example of a well-known Jewish New Leftist who severed his ties to the New Left in the wake of the New Politics convention, see the remarks of Martin Peretz quoted and discussed in Jonathan Kaufman, *Broken Alliance: The Turbulent Times Between Blacks and Jews in America* (New York: Scribner, 1988), pp. 207–12. Also see Arthur Liebman, *Jews and the Left* (New York: Wiley, 1979), pp. 568–71.

30. M. Jay Rosenberg, "To Uncle Tom and Other Such Jews," *Flame* 1 (March

26, 1969): 3. Rosenberg's essay originally appeared in the *Village Voice*, February 13, 1969.

31. Tsvi Bisk, "Uncle Jake, Come Home!" *Jewish Liberation Journal* no. 1 (May 1969): 7–14.

32. Ibid. Bisk was not only critical of New Left Jews but also of mainstream Jewish organizations: "Jewish institutional life is not characterized by a drive to be more Jewish, but rather by a drive to be more American. . . . Jewish institutions are in the forefront of the Jewish assimilative process." Ibid., p. 9.

33. The revised song read in part: "When Israel was in Soviet Union / Let my people go. / Oppressed so hard they could not stand / Let my people go. / Go down Moses, / Way down in Russia land. / Tell old Pharaoh / Let my people go." *Hayom* 1, no. 2 (May 1971): 5.

34. On the Jewish Student Press Service, see McCandlish Phillips, "Jewish Student Press Seeing Swift Growth," *New York Times*, March 13, 1971, pp. 31, 33.

35. Jerry Kirschen, "And Now . . . the Pig City Follies," *Hakahal* 1, no. 2 (March-April 1972): 7.

36. For an extended discussion of the "tough Jew" stereotype ascendant after 1967 but dating back also to the hugely successful novels of Leon Uris (*Exodus*, *Mila 18*), see especially Paul Breines's discussion of the "Rambowitz" genre in his *Tough Jews: Political Fantasies and the Moral Dilemma of American Jewry* (New York: Basic, 1990), pp. 171–230.

37. Yossi Klein, "Why I Sat In at Hadassah," *Achdut* 1, no. 4 (June 1971): 15. Klein returned to sit-in at Hadassah a second time in October 1971. For his account, see Yossi Klein, "Second Sit-in at Hadassah Ends Like the First One," *Jewish Post and Opinion*, October 22, 1971, p. 2. For an account of his long-standing (and largely ambivalent) connection to the JDL, see Yossi Klein Halevi, *Memoirs of a Jewish Extremist: An American Story* (Boston: Little, Brown, 1995).

38. Kahane's use of the expression "Nice Irvings" is cited in Klein Halevi, *Memoirs of a Jewish Extremist*, p. 79.

39. *The Jewish Defense League: Principles and Philosophies* (New York: Education Department of the Jewish Defense League, n.d.). This document appears to have been published around 1970. The same remarks appear in Meir Kahane, *Never Again! A Program for Survival* (Los Angeles: Nash, 1971), p. 275.

40. Meir Kahane, "Resistance for Jewish Honor," *Jewish Press*, March 1, 1968, p. 18.

41. Meir Kahane, "Our Treasures," *Jewish Press*, February 12, 1971, p. 9.

42. Meir Kahane, "A Small Voice," *Jewish Press*, July 26, 1968, p. 36.

43. "Fellow Jews! Stand Up and Fight Now!" *Jewish Press*, November 31, 1967, p. 10.

44. "Jewish Survival!" *Jewish Press*, July 5, 1968, p. 35.

45. For a typical headline ghostwritten by Kahane, see "N.Y. City Gives Funds to Racists: Anti-Semite Gets $200,000," *Jewish Press*, May 31, 1968, p. 1.

46. Meir Kahane, "Racist Leaflets in N.Y. Schools Warn White Teachers to Leave," *Jewish Press*, June 14, 1968, pp. 1–2. No one knew who had produced the antisemitic leaflets, which among other things accused Jewish teachers of being "The Middle East Murderers of Colored People," and of being "Responsible For The Serious Educational Retardation of Our Black Children." But it was the United Federation of Teachers that reprinted and distributed the leaflet by the hundreds of thousands (to "prove" the antisemitic nature of the community control movement). See Robert G. Weisbord and Arthur Stein, *Bittersweet Encounter: The Afro-American and the American Jew* (Westport, Conn.: Negro Universities Press, 1970), pp. 169–70; and Derek Edgell, *The Movement for Community Control of New York City's Schools, 1966–1970: Class Wars* (Lewiston, N.Y.: Mellen, 1998), pp. 303–6.

47. See Shlomo M. Russ, "The 'Zionist Hooligans': The Jewish Defense League" (Ph.D. diss., 1981, City University of New York), p. 68.

48. Murray Schneider quoted ibid., p. 70.

49. Russ, "The 'Zionist Hooligans,' " p. 40. As Russ recounts, Rackman later broke publicly with Kahane when the JDL began to advocate using more violent measures (like explosives) against Soviet groups and buildings in the United States. Ibid.

50. Clayborne Carson, *In Struggle: SNCC and the Black Awakening of the 1960s* (Cambridge: Harvard University Press, 1981), pp. 294–95. Carson notes that Forman's idea failed to attract widespread black support, citing how "SNCC itself refused to adopt it as a project." Ibid., p. 295.

51. A useful summary of the Forman incident appears in Sam Pevzner, "Inside the Jewish Community," *Jewish Currents* 23 (July-August 1969): 33–34.

52. "Is This Any Way for Nice Jewish Boys to Behave?" *New York Times*, June 24, 1969, p. 31. This ad went on to exclaim: "We Are Speaking of Jewish Survival! We Are Speaking of The American Dream!" Although in hindsight the men with their dark sunglasses and stern expressions may look rather more foolish than tough, at the time the photograph was certainly shocking to many.

53. Eisendrath and Kahane both quoted in Steven E. Frieder, "Intergroup Relations and Tensions in New York City," in *American Jewish Year Book 1970*, ed. Morris Fine and Milton Himmelfarb (New York: American Jewish Committee, 1970), p. 226. Also see Albert Vorspan, "Blacks and Jews," in Nat Hentoff, ed., *Black Anti-Semitism and Jewish Racism* (New York: Baron, 1969), p. 200.

54. Cited in "Activists' Calendar," *Jewish Press*, September 3, 1971, p. 11. The same calendar also announced for September 12, 1971: "JDL 'Jewish Is Beautiful'

Night at Manhattan Center at 5:00 P.M. A night of Jewish 'soul.' Special: Last speech of Rabbi Meir Kahane before his aliyah. Followed by a mass farewell to Rabbi Kahane at Kennedy Airport." Ibid.

55. Quoted in Janet L. Dolgin, *Jewish Identity and the JDL* (Princeton: Princeton University Press, 1977), p. 69.

56. JDL members quoted ibid., p. 160.

57. Quoted in Weisbord and Stein, *Bittersweet Encounter*, pp. 202–3.

58. Arnold Forster, general counsel of the Anti-Defamation League, quoted in Frieder, "Intergroup Relations and Tensions in New York City," p. 228.

59. Quoted in Zvi Lowenthal and Jonathan Braun, "Right On Judaism . . . JDL's Meir Kahane Speaks Out—An Interview," in Porter and Dreier, *Jewish Radicalism*, p. 280. This interview originally appeared in the *Flame* (Winter 1971).

60. Jonathan Goldin and Morris U. Schappes, "Dialogue with a Radical Jewish Student," *Jewish Currents* 24 (July–August 1970): 26–7. Goldin's letter is dated February 16, 1970.

61. Steven L. Gurner, "The Jewish Defense League: The Philosophy of the New Jews," *Kol Bo* 1 (February 16, 1971): 4. *Kol Bo* was published at Northwestern University in Evanston, Illinois.

62. Morris U. Schappes and Jack Nusan Porter, "That Jewish Defense League," *Jewish Currents* 25 (June 1971): 27–28. Only after *Jewish Currents* editor Morris U. Schappes had challenged him as to how "a Jewish radical [could] rush to the defense of Jewish reactionaries" did Porter acknowledge his error: "I sided with the JDL because of their activism—their ideology stinks and therefore I'm leaving it." Ibid. Meanwhile, even Yippie leader Abbie Hoffman was widely reported in the early 1970s as saying: "I approve of JDL's tactics but not of their goals." Cited in "Narishkeit (Strange but True)," *Achdut* 1, no. 3 (March 1971): 8.

63. Steve Cohen, "The JDL: Politics of Jewish Experience," *ACIID* 2, no. 4 (April 1971): 15.

64. Quoted in Dolgin, *Jewish Identity*, p. 115.

65. Debby Littman, "Jewish Militancy in Perspective," in Porter and Dreier, *Jewish Radicalism*, p. 295. Also see Stuart Starr, "A Critical Look at the Jewish Defense League," *Kol Bo* 1 (February 16, 1971): 4–5.

66. Quoted in Frieder, "Intergroup Relations and Tensions in New York City," p. 227.

67. "A Poll of Jewish Attitudes," *Newsweek*, March 1, 1971, 57.

68. Cited in Peter Novak, *The Holocaust in American Life* (Boston: Houghton Mifflin, 1999), p. 174.

69. Cantor, *Jewish Women/Jewish Men*, p. 364. Interestingly, Paul Breines's *Tough Jews* did not analyze the masculine styles of the Jewish Defense League.

70. On Doyle Dane Bernbach's advertising campaign for Volkswagen, see Thomas Frank, *The Conquest of Cool: Business Culture, Counterculture, and the Rise of Hip Consumerism* (Chicago: University of Chicago Press, 1997), especially pp. 67–68.

71. See Jerry Rubin, *We Are Everywhere* (New York: Harper and Row, 1971), pp. 72, 76.

72. Ed Richer, "No Jets for Israel," *Los Angeles Free Press*, June 19, 1970, p. 14.

73. "A Nice Jewish Girl," *Great Speckled Bird* 3, no. 40 (October 26, 1970): 14.

74. Ibid.

75. Ibid. This essay also appeared in a publication of the War Resisters League: Sharon Rose, "Zionism in the Mid-East," *Win* 6 (June 15, 1970): 8–9.

76. "Revolutionary Jewish Nationalism," *Brooklyn Bridge* 1, no. 4 (June 1972): 2.

77. "Our Brother's Keeper," *Brooklyn Bridge* 1, no. 3 (May 1971): 13.

78. "The Jewish Defense League," *Brooklyn Bridge* 1, no. 4 (June 1972): 3.

79. "We Are Coming Home," *Brooklyn Bridge* 1, no. 1 (February 1971): 2.

80. "Revolutionary Jewish Nationalism," *Brooklyn Bridge* 1, no. 4 (June 1972): 2. Members of the Brooklyn Bridge Collective seldom granted interviews to the mainstream Jewish press. A rare exception appears in Ray Kestenbaum, "Meet the Floating Commune!" *Jewish Week*, August 19, 1971, pp. 1, 5.

81. "Kaddish—for Our Sisters and Brothers Who Fought and Died in Warsaw and Attica," *Brooklyn Bridge* 1, no. 4 (June 1972): 28.

7. "ARE YOU AGAINST THE JEWISH FAMILY?" DEBATING THE SEXUAL REVOLUTION

Epigraph quoted in Gail Gianasi Natale, "Jews Must Have More Children," Cleveland Jewish News, *June 2, 1972, p. 6.*

1. Quoted in Vivian Witt, "Divinity, Sensuality, and Sexuality," *Cleveland Jewish News*, October 29, 1971, p. 18.

2. "Drugs and Family Problems Now Top Jewish Priorities," *Jewish Week*, August 12, 1971, p. 7.

3. Quoted in "Brides Rarely Virgins," *Jewish Post and Opinion*, February 19, 1971, p. 11.

4. Quoted in "Three Out of Four Coeds Have Had Sex Experience," *Jewish Post and Opinion*, October 6, 1972, p. 1. Also see Jack Segal, "Sex and the Jewish College Girl," *Jewish Digest* 18 (April 1973): 36–40. Conservative rabbi William Malev, also of Houston, thought Segal had not been condemnatory

enough in his attitude toward premarital activity and criticized what he saw as a new brashness and lack of shame among Jewish youth. Malev felt that the problem with Segal's premarital sex survey was that it failed to say "whether it (premarital sex) was right or wrong, proper, or improper. Nor was a word said about the Jewish tradition that sex must be sanctified by love, by commitment and by lifelong loyalty to the one whom we have chosen as our life partner." In his own sermon on the subject, Malev emphasized that one big difference between past and present attitudes toward premarital sex was that in the past it had "always been done surreptitiously and shamefacedly knowing that it was very wrong. Today, however, it is done openly and brazenly because, for the first time in the Judaeo-Christian tradition, it is being given sanction of religious authority by those who should know better." Quoted in "Pre-Marital Sex Survey of Jewish Coeds Wrong," *Jewish Post and Opinion*, November 24, 1972, p. 1.

5. "The Survey on Pre-Marital Sex," *Jewish Post and Opinion*, October 20, 1972, p. 6.

6. "Weaker Jewish Family Leads to Weaker Identity, Experts Say," *Cleveland Jewish News*, May 26, 1972, p. 23.

7. Emanuel Rackman, "The Jewish Father," *Jewish Week*, February 22–28, 1973, p. 10.

8. Quoted in "Rabbi Urges Conversion of JEWS to Judaism," *Jewish Week and American Examiner*, May 3–9, 1973, p. 8.

9. Rabbi Gilbert S. Rosenthal quoted in "Ailing Jewish Family Still Less Sick Than Most, Experts Agree," *Jewish Week and American Examiner*, November 2, 1974, p. 18.

10. Rabbi Simon Glustrom quoted in "Teenagers Told in Booklet How to Think Jewish," *Jewish Week and American Examiner*, August 9, 1975, p. 3.

11. Pinchas Stolper, *The Road to Responsible Jewish Adulthood: Jewish Insights Into Love, Sex, Dating and Marriage* (New York: Youth Division of the Union of Orthodox Jewish Congregations of America, 1967), p. 8.

12. This is evident not just in the book's self-presentation but also in its reception. For example, see the review pairing Mandel's text with those of such prominent rabbinical scholars on sex and marriage as Eugene Borowitz, David Feldman, Robert Gordis, and Norman Lamm. See "Scholarly Works Present Traditional Jewish Attitudes on Marriage, Divorce, Birth Control," *Detroit Jewish News*, April 10, 1970, p. 41.

13. Morris Mandel, *How to Be Married—and Happy* (New York: Jonathan David, 1968), pp. 56–57.

14. Ibid., pp. 57–59.

15. Ibid., pp. 74–75, 79, 91.
16. Morris Mandel, "Problems in Human Emotions," *Jewish Press*, August 23, 1968, p. 17.
17. Morris Mandel, "Problems in Human Emotions," *Jewish Press*, July 12, 1968, p. 20.
18. Morris Mandel, "Problems in Human Emotions," *Jewish Press*, August 20, 1971, p. 41.
19. Morris Mandel, "Problems in Human Emotions," *Jewish Press*, March 28, 1969, p. 15.
20. Morris Mandel, "Problems in Human Emotions," *Jewish Press*, December 17, 1971, p. 10.
21. Morris Mandel, "Problems in Human Emotions," *Jewish Press*, October 8, 1971, p. 8.
22. Morris Mandel, "Problems in Human Emotions," *Jewish Press*, July 30, 1971, p. 8.
23. Mandel, "Problems in Human Emotions," October 8, 1971, p. 8.
24. Mandel, "Problems in Human Emotions," August 23, 1968, p. 17.
25. Mandel, "Problems in Human Emotions," August 20, 1971, p. 41.
26. Mandel, "Problems in Human Emotions," July 12, 1968, p. 20.
27. Louis M. Epstein, *Sex Laws and Customs in Judaism* (New York, Ktav, 1967), pp. 144, 135–38.
28. Quoted in Jean R. Herschaft, "The Invisible Gay Rabbi: There Are Some," *Jewish Post and Opinion*, September 10, 1971, p. 4.
29. Quoted in David Rothenberg, "Conversations with a Closeted Gay Rabbi," *Gaysweek*, October 24, 1977, p. 14.
30. Norman Lamm, "A Rabbi Views Homosexuality: Fears Christian Lapse to Paganism," *Jewish Week*, February 22, 1968, p. 4. Also see "Tendency in Christianity to Approve Homosexuality Called Pagan," *Jewish Week*, February 1, 1968, p. 3.
31. Norman Lamm, "Judaism and the Modern Attitude to Homosexuality," *Encyclopaedia Judaica Year Book 1974* (Jerusalem: Keter, 1974), pp. 197, 203–5.
32. Quoted in Jean R. Herschaft, "Rabbis Give Their Views, But Disagree," *Jewish Post and Opinion*, September 24, 1971, p. 4.
33. Quoted in "Polygamy, Concubancy Are Not for Modern Jew," *Jewish Post and Opinion*, December 31, 1971, p. 3.
34. Robert Gordis, " 'Be Fruitful and Multiply'—Biography of a Mitzvah," *Midstream* 28 (August-September 1982): 25–26, 28.
35. Earl Raab, "Homosexuals and the Jews," *Jewish Digest* 18 (April 1973): 25–26. This essay originally appeared in the *San Francisco Jewish Bulletin*, May 26, 1972.

36. Will Herberg, "The Case for Heterosexuality: A Death-Defying Act," *National Review* 21 (October 7, 1969): 1007.

37. Quoted and discussed in Jack Wertheimer, *A People Divided: Judaism in Contemporary America* (New York: Basic, 1993), p. 106.

38. Chaim Dov Keller, "The Unbridgeable Gap: The Youth Culture vs. the Establishment," *Jewish Observer* 7 (May 1971): 10–13.

39. Emanuel Rackman, "Political Liberalism and Jewish Orthodoxy: Clashing Viewpoints Create Problems for Community," *Jewish Week and American Examiner*, September 28–October 4, 1975, p. 15.

40. For example, a 1970 survey made public by the American Jewish Committee found that almost 90 percent of Jewish college freshman favored legalized abortion. See Irving Spiegel, "Jewish Students Found Concerned," *New York Times*, December 4, 1970, p. 22. Also see Brant Coopersmith, " 'Elite' Jews Divide Sharply on Most Issues, But Agree Early Abortion Is a Right," *Jewish Week and American Examiner*, June 1, 1974, p. 10.

41. Quoted in "Orthodox Union Hits 'Indiscriminate' Abortions As Dangers to Morality," *Detroit Jewish News*, July 24, 1970, p. 17.

42. Quoted in Gunther Lawrence, "Abortions Cut Jewish Adoption Rate," *Cleveland Jewish News*, July 7, 1972, p. 18.

43. Quoted in Coopersmith, " 'Elite' Jews Divide Sharply on Most Issues," p. 10.

44. For example, see "Adoption Numbers Drop," *Detroit Jewish News*, November 27, 1970, p. 46.

45. See Lawrence, "Abortions Cut Jewish Adoption Rate," p. 18.

46. Walter S. Wurzburger, "Not Rated As 'Necessary Evil,' But 'Swinging Society' Is Out!" *Jewish Week and American Examiner*, June 7–13, 1973, p. 19.

47. Quoted in "Rabbi Denounces Jews Who Misstate Judaism's 'Abhorrence of Abortion,' " *Jewish Week*, January 29–February 4, 1976, p. 2.

48. David Kirshenbaum, *Mixed Marriage and the Jewish Future* (New York: Bloch, 1958), p. 10–12. While far from comprehensive, the following list offers a sampling of writings on this topic during the sixties: Charles E. Shulman, "Mixed Marriage, Conversion, and Reality," *CCAR Journal* 11 (January 1964): 27–32; Jacob Petuchowski, "Realism About Mixed Marriages," *CCAR Journal* 13 (October 1966): 35–38; Richard J. Israel, "A Note on Counseling Young People Contemplating Intermarriage," in *Campus 1966: Change and Challenge* (Washington, D.C.: B'nai B'rith Hillel Foundations, 1966), pp. 47–54; and Allen S. Maller, "Mixed or Mitzvah Marriages," *Jewish Spectator* 31 (March 1966): 8–9. A fine introductory survey of earlier literature on intermarriage is Ira Eisenstein, "Intermarriage," *Jewish Information* 7, no. 2 (1969): 49–59.

49. Mike Tabor, "Intermarriage Is a Lie," *Jewish Post and Opinion*, April 6, 1973,

p. 2. See also Mike Tabor, "Why All the Fuss About B.L.B.?" *Jewish Post and Opinion*, March 2, 1973, p. 6.

50. Quoted in "TV Mixed Marriage Just a Fantasy to Collegians," *Detroit Jewish News*, March 9, 1973, p. 33. This article went on to note that when several area college students were queried about the show none felt it posed a threat to the Jewish community or that it should be taken off the air.

51. "Latest News on Bridget," *Jewish Post and Opinion*, January 26, 1973, p. 1.

52. Betty Zoss, "Defending Freedom: Bridget Loves Bernie," *Sh'ma* 3 (March 30, 1973): 86.

53. "Bridget to Shift Emphasis," *Jewish Post and Opinion*, February 9, 1973, p. 3; and "Love of Bridget for Bernie to Die as CBS Axes Show," *Jewish Post and Opinion*, April 27, 1973, p. 2.

54. Quoted in "Network Says Bridget-Bernie Going off the Air, for Good!" *Jewish Week and American Examiner*, April 5–11, 1973, p. 1.

55. Tabor, "Intermarriage Is a Lie," p. 2.

56. Richard Yaffe, "Rabbis Alarmed by Soaring Rate of Mixed Marriages," *Jewish Week*, February 15–21, 1973, p. 1.

57. Quoted in "Rabbi Cohen Warns of Intermarriage Danger," *Cleveland Jewish News*, December 3, 1971, p. 19.

58. Quoted in "Who's Sleeping with Her Now?" *Jewish Post and Opinion*, August 17, 1973, p. 2.

59. "Judaic Studies: Another Look," *Jewish Observer* 8 (April 1972): 25.

60. Quoted in "Rabbi Cohen Warns of Intermarriage Danger," p. 19.

61. Rabbi Kalman Packouz, *How to Stop an Intermarriage: A Practical Guide for Parents* (New York: Feldheim, 1976; 2d rev. ed., 1984), p. 4.

62. "If You're Jewish Chances Are Your Grandchildren Won't Be," *Jewish Week*, September 18–24, 1975, p. 11.

63. Quoted in "Triennial '71,' " *National Jewish Monthly* 86 (November 1971): 16.

64. "After Intermarriage: 96% of Children Raised As Jewish," *Jewish Week*, September 27-October 3, 1973, p. 2. For a typical example of the earlier statistics, see "Rabbi Cohen Warns of Intermarriage Danger," p. 19.

65. For excellent examples of the ways intermarriage was seen above all as a crisis in parent-child relations, see the readers' letters on the subject excerpted in "We Are Many: Our Readers Speak on Intermarriage," *Moment* 2 (April 1977): 36–38.

66. Allen S. Maller, "Marriage: Mixed or Matched," *National Jewish Monthly* 86 (April 1972): 41.

67. Rabbi Herbert Baumgard quoted in "Rapid Rise of Jewish Divorces Alarms Rabbis," *Jewish Post and Opinion*, March 14, 1975, p. 1.

68. "Orthodox and Hassidim have 50% Divorce Rise; Parents Found at Fault," *Jewish Week and American Examiner*, June 28, 1975, p. 18.

69. Chaim I. Waxman, *America's Jews in Transition* (Philadelphia: Temple University Press, 1983), p. 164.

70. Marshall Sklare, "Intermarriage and Jewish Survival," *Commentary* 49 (March 1970): 53.

71. Brickner said, "You can't say that the world suffers from overpopulation and at the same time say Jews should ignore this. I don't want to put myself in the vulnerable position of saying it's good for Puerto Ricans and poor South Americans to cut back on their population and not the Jews. I've never thought for a moment that the way you insure Jewish viability is sheer weight of numbers." Quoted in Shirley Frank, "The Population Panic," *Lilith* 1, no. 4 (Fall/Winter 1977–78): 17.

72. Asher Bar-Zev, "ZPG and the Jewish Problem," *Conservative Judaism* 30 (Spring 1976): 76–77, 82, 78–79. For another reflection on proselytizing ("In this way, we would add to the Jewish population but not to the world's population"), see Jack D. Spiro, "'People Plague' and 'Birth Dearth,'" *Keeping Posted* 20 (April 1975): 20. For examples of others at this time who called for conversion and celebrated "Jews by Choice," see the discussion in Charles E. Silberman, *A Certain People: American Jews and Their Lives Today* (New York: Summit, 1985), pp. 274–324. Silberman himself was an enthusiastic endorser of the "Jews by choice" phenomenon.

73. Rabbi Baumgard quoted in "Sexual Revolution Seen 'Catastrophic' for U.S. Jews," *Jewish Week*, November 25–December 1, 1976, p. B10.

74. Rabbi David Wice quoted in Lawrence, "Abortions Cut Jewish Adoption Rate," p. 18.

75. Quoted in "Judaism Called Immunization Against Extremism of Lib," *Jewish Week and American Examiner*, October 25–31, 1973, p. 21.

76. Quoted in Irving Spiegel, "Rabbi Deplores Small Families," *New York Times*, January 24, 1974, p. 40. As Roth explained: "The Jewish population in the United States is the same now as it was 30 years ago. There should have been, if we had merely kept pace, 12 million Jews in America today, but there are only six million." Roth also asked: "Is it not obvious that in terms of Jewish survival, the European Holocaust [Nazi murders of Jews], of the war years and the Holocaust-size loss in America during the last three decades produced the same results?" Ibid.

77. H. J. Roberts, "Are the Jews Committing Jewish Genocide?" *Jewish Digest* 20 (March 1975): 37. Roberts made a direct connection between the low birth rate and feminism, noting critically that "many 'liberated' young Jewish wives no longer re-

gard the opportunities and responsibilities for rearing children, keeping a home, and engaging in constructive social or philanthropic work as sufficiently fulfilling." Observing that "procreation is the primary purpose of marriage," and that young Jews' disregard for this time-honored Jewish teaching resulted from "cultural illiteracy and the influences of various counter-cultures," Roberts concluded that "*parents, grandparents, concerned friends and confidants MUST impress upon gifted young couples the importance of bearing a reasonable number of children without undue procrastination.*" Ibid., pp. 39, 42. A longer version of Roberts's essay initially appeared as "Endogenous Jewish Genocide: The Impact of the ZPG-Nonparenthood Movement" in *Reconstructionist* 40 (November 1974): 8–17.

78. Quoted in "The Disappearing Jews," *Time*, July 14, 1975, p. 39.

79. Quoted in Frank, "The Population Panic," p. 13.

80. Milton Himmelfarb, "The Vanishing Jews," *Commentary* 36 (September 1963): 249.

81. Quoted in Natale, "Jews Must Have More Children," p. 6.

82. Milton Himmelfarb, *The Jews of Modernity* (New York: Basic, 1973), pp. 138–39. Also see the review of the book by William Novak, "The Achievement of Milton Himmelfarb," *Moment* 1 (July/August 1975): 69–72.

83. Quoted in "Dialogues," in *Zero Population Growth—For Whom? Differential Fertility and Minority Group Survival*, ed. Milton Himmelfarb and Victor Baras (Westport, Conn.: Greenwood, 1978), p. 169.

84. Quoted in " 'Contraceptive Virtuoso' Seen As Survival Threat," *Jewish Week*, February 20–26, 1975, p. 1.

85. Helen Cohen, "Court Ruling on Abortion," *Jewish Post and Opinion*, February 23, 1973, p. 10.

86. Quoted in "Low Jewish Birth Rate Seen As Family Suicide," *Jewish Week*, May 5–11, 1977, p. B2.

87. Quoted in "500 Women in Convention Demand Full Role in Jewish Resurgence," *Jewish Week and American Examiner*, February 26, 1973, p. 1.

88. Diane Levenberg, " 'Either I'm Neurotic or I Haven't Found the Right One Yet': Growing Up to Be Thirty, Single, Female and Jewish," *National Jewish Monthly* 93 (October 1978): 45, 48, 50–51.

89. Quoted in "Low Birth Rate Seen 'Demographic Disaster,' " *Jewish Week*, May 27–June 2, 1976, p. 9.

90. David M. Feldman, *Birth Control in Jewish Law: Marital Relations, Contraception, and Abortion As Set Forth in the Classic Texts of Jewish Law* (New York: New York University Press, 1968), p. 63.

91. Quoted in "Fun in the Bedroom Is the Jewish View," *Jewish Post and Opinion*, April 13, 1973, p. 3.

92. Quoted in "Breakdown of Morals Is Lambasted by Olan," *Jewish Post and Opinion*, August 13, 1971, p. 1.

93. Helen Cohen, "The Games Singles Play," *Jewish Post and Opinion*, August 24, 1973, p. 10. Also see Helen Cohen, "New Sex Hardly Utopia," *Jewish Post and Opinion*, February 9, 1973, p. 10.

94. Quoted in "Women's Sex Rights Held Traditional," *Jewish Week and American Examiner*, November 9, 1974, p. 23. For another Reform rabbi who effused that "one of the most progressive principles of Halakhah has been that women, as well as men, have sexual rights," see Eugene J. Lipman, "Women's Lib and Jewish Tradition," *Jewish Digest* 18 (October 1972): 67.

95. Robert Gordis, *Love and Sex: A Modern Jewish Perspective* (New York: Farrar, Straus Giroux, 1978), p. 101.

96. Wurzburger, "Not Rated As 'Necessary Evil,' " p. 19. Also see Walter S. Wurzburger, "What Jewish Values Tell Us About Sex," *Jewish Digest* 19 (March 1974): 27–30.

97. Norman Lamm, *A Hedge of Roses: Jewish Insights into Marriage and Married Life* (New York: Feldheim, 1966; 4th rev. ed., 1972), pp. 18, 21, 15, 25, 28.

98. Quoted in "Fun in the Bedroom Is the Jewish View," p. 3. Along similar lines, *Jewish Week* columnist Phineas Stone opined in 1973 that "Jewish tradition, which values sex as essential to human fulfillment, has not had any hangups about sex education. Physiological sex . . . is presented as a human need for women as well as men. It has been so taught through the ages, and Jewish tradition has rejected the notion that sex is always sinful except when required for procreation." Phineas Stone, "Sex Revolution May Be Another Fashion Sweep,"*Jewish Week and American Examiner*, April 5–11, 1973, p. 22.

99. Quoted in Julie Baumgold, "The Persistence of the Jewish American Princess," *New York*, March 22, 1971, p. 25.

100. Quoted in Susannah Heschel, "Introduction," in *On Being A Jewish Feminist: A Reader*, ed. Susannah Heschel (New York: Schocken, 1983), p. xix.

101. Rabbi Albert L. Lewis quoted in "Rabbi Bans Hot Pants, See-Through Blouses," *Jewish Post and Opinion*, July 30, 1971, p. 1.

102. Teryl Daskal, "Jewish American Princess," *Jewish Post and Opinion*, April 4, 1975, p. 2.

103. Neil Shister, "Sex: Professionals and Lay People," *Moment* 2 (December 1976): 21.

104. Susan Weidman Schneider, " 'In a Coma! I Thought She Was Jewish!' " *Lilith* 1, no. 3 (Spring/Summer 1977): 4–8. The title joke was this: "A prince enters a castle and finds a beautiful woman lying on a bed. He tiptoes into her room and ravishes her. As he leaves, he is approached by the lord of the castle. LORD

of CASTLE: 'Have you seen my poor daughter? She's been in a coma since her horse threw her last week.' PRINCE: 'In a *coma!* I thought she was *Jewish!*' " Ibid., p. 5.

105. Susan Weidman Schneider, *Jewish and Female: Choices and Changes in Our Lives Today* (New York: Simon and Schuster, 1984), pp. 217–19.

106. For example, see Bob Elias, "Fruma Buber—Girl Rabbi," *Davka* 1, no. 4 (Summer 1971): 12–14.

107. For example, see Daniel J. Elazar, "Women in American Jewish Life," *Congress Bi-Weekly* 40 (November 23, 1973): 10–11; and Lucy Dawidowicz's remarks quoted in Susannah Heschel, "Lucy Dawidowicz's Contempt for Her Own Sex," *Lilith* 1, no. 4 (Fall/Winter 1977–78): 44.

108. One classic expression of this view came from a male *Moment* reader who said that "if someone would teach Jewish girls how to use makeup and look attractive, teach them some manners, and how to be feminine instead of feminist, the intermarriage rate would plummet." See 'We Are Many: Our Readers Speak on Intermarriage," p. 37.

109. Quoted and discussed in Paula Hyman, "The Jewish Family: Looking for a Usable Past," in Heschel, *On Being a Jewish Feminist*, p. 20.

110. Judith Plaskow, "The Jewish Feminist: Conflict in Identities," in *The Jewish Woman: New Perspectives*, ed. Elizabeth Koltun (New York: Schocken, 1976), p. 4.

111. Rachel Adler, "The Jew Who Wasn't There: Halacha and the Jewish Woman," *Response* 18 (Summer 1973): 81.

112. Quoted in Anne Lapidus Lerner, " 'Who Hast Not Made Me a Man': The Movement for Equal Rights for Women in American Jewry," *American Jewish Year Book 1977*, ed. Morris Fine and Milton Himmelfarb (New York: American Jewish Committee, 1976), p. 35.

113. Heschel, "Introduction" to part 1, in Heschel, *On Being a Jewish Feminist*, p. 5.

114. Paula E. Hyman, "The Other Half: Women in the Jewish Tradition," *Conservative Judaism* 26 (Summer 1972): 14.

115. "Jewish Women: Life Force of a Culture?" *Brooklyn Bridge* 1, no. 1 (February 1971): 14.

116. Aviva Cantor Zuckoff, "The Oppression of the Jewish Woman," *Response* 18 (Summer 1973): 52–53.

117. Gloria Averbuch in "Ten Women Tell . . . the Ways We Are," *Lilith* 1, no. 2 (Winter 1976–77): 7.

118. Elenore Lester, "Women As Jews Demand More Progress," *Jewish Week and American Examiner*, May 3, 1975, p. 15.

119. Quoted in Aviva Cantor Zuckoff, "An Exclusive Interview with Dr. Phyllis Chesler," *Lilith* 1, no. 2 (Winter 1976–77): 26–27.
120. Susan Dworkin, "A Song for Women in Five Questions," *Moment* 1 (May/June 1975): 52–53.
121. Quoted in Frank, "The Population Panic," p. 14.
122. Ibid., pp. 15–6. The Himmelfarb quotation is from his "Population Fizzle," *Commentary* 32 (September 1961): 236.
123. Frank, "The Population Panic," pp. 14, 16–17.
124. Dworkin, "A Song for Women in Five Questions," p. 45.
125. Joyce Antler, *The Journey Home: Jewish Women and the American Century* (New York: Free, 1997), pp. 259–60.
126. For example, see the statements by Rachel Adler in "Ten Women Tell . . . ," pp. 4–5; the socialist Zionist feminist Sheryl Baron in her "National Liberation and the Jewish Woman," *Davka* 1, no. 4 (Summer 1971): 37–42; and Phyllis Chesler in "An Exclusive Interview with Dr. Phyllis Chesler," pp. 24–31.
127. Lev Raphael, "To Be a Jew," in *Wrestling with the Angel: Faith and Religion in the Lives of Gay Men*, ed. Brian Bouldrey (New York: Riverhead, 1995), p. 47. See also the related sentiments expressed by Batya Bauman in *Lilith*: "The Zionist movement, the women's movement and the gay liberation movement have been the most important factors in affirming myself and my identity as a Jew, as a woman and as a lesbian. Zionism brought me out as a Jew. The women's movement brought me out as a feminist. The gay liberation movement brought me out as a lesbian. All are self-affirming. All are life-affirming. All have made the difference between the denial of who I am and the affirmation of who I am." Bauman in "Ten Women Tell . . . ," p. 10.
128. Bauman in "Ten Women Tell . . . ," pp. 9–10.
129. Dworkin, "A Song for Women in Five Questions," p. 53.
130. Barry Alan Mehler, "Gay Jews," *Moment* 2 (February-March 1977): 23–24.
131. Bauman in "Ten Women Tell . . . ," p. 10.
132. Quoted in Tony Domenick, "Memorial to Holocaust Will 'Ignore' Gays," *Gay Community News* 5 (July 15, 1978): 1.
133. Quoted in Rothenberg, "Conversations with a Closeted Gay Rabbi," p. 15.
134. New Jewish Agenda, "Coming Out, Coming Home: Lesbian and Gay Jews and the Jewish Community" (New York: New Jewish Agenda, n.d.), pp. 3–6.
135. Edward S. Shapiro, *A Time for Healing: American Jewry Since World War II* (Baltimore: Johns Hopkins University Press, 1992), p. 249.
136. Silberman, *A Certain People*, p. 262.
137. Heschel, "Introduction," p. xxxiii.

8. "IF WE REALLY CARE ABOUT ISRAEL": BREIRA AND THE LIMITS OF DISSENT

Epigraph from Arnold Jacob Wolf, "American Jewry and Israel: The Need for Dissent," Conservative Judaism *31 (Winter 1977): 33.*

1. William Novak, "On Leaving the Havurah," *Response* 22 (Summer 1974): 107–15.

2. See *Unfinished Rabbi: Selected Writings of Arnold Jacob Wolf*, ed. Jonathan S. Wolf (Chicago: Dee, 1998), p. 245.

3. William Novak, "The Breira Story," *Genesis* 2, March 16, 1977, p. 6.

4. Quoted in Marla Brettschneider, *Cornerstones of Peace: Jewish Identity Politics and Democratic Theory* (New Brunswick, N.J.: Rutgers University Press, 1996), pp. 109–10.

5. Daniel J. Elazar, *Community and Polity: The Organizational Dynamics of American Jewry* (Philadelphia: Jewish Publication Society, 1995), p. 109.

6. Chaim I. Waxman, *America's Jews in Transition* (Philadelphia: Temple University Press, 1983), p. 223.

7. Brettschneider, *Cornerstones of Peace*, 41. Brettschneider builds on the analysis of Paul M. Foer. See his "The War Against Breira," *Jewish Spectator* 48 (Summer 1983): 18–23.

8. Jacques Kornberg, "Zionism and Ideology: The Breira Controversy," *Judaism* 27 (Winter 1978): 103.

9. Avi Shlaim, *The Iron Wall: Israel and the Arab World* (New York: Norton, 2000), p. 319.

10. Quoted ibid., p. 318.

11. Benny Morris, *Righteous Victims: A History of the Zionist-Arab Conflict, 1881–1999* (New York: Knopf, 1999), p. 404. Also see Seymour Hersh, *The Samson Option: Israel's Nuclear Arsenal and American Foreign Policy* (New York: Random House, 1991), pp. 225–40.

12. I. L. Kenen, "The Mood of Israel," *Near East Report* 17 (December 5, 1973): 193.

13. Morris, *Righteous Victims*, p. 437.

14. Ibid., p. 335. Also see Ian S. Lustick, *For the Land and the Lord: Jewish Fundamentalism in Israel* (New York: Council on Foreign Relations, 1988), and David Newman, ed., *The Impact of Gush Emunim: Politics and Settlement in the West Bank* (London: Croom Helm, 1985).

15. "Myths and Facts: 1970," *Near East Report* 14 (January 7, 1970): 3.

16. "Myths and Facts: 1974," *Near East Report* 18 (February 6, 1974): 36, 58, 60–61.

17. "Myths and Facts," *Near East Report* 11 (August 1967): B4, B13.

18. Don Peretz, "The Palestine Arabs: A National Entity," in *People and Politics in the Middle East*, ed. Michael Curtis (New Brunswick, N.J.: Transaction, 1971), pp. 69, 91.

19. Marie Syrkin, "Who Are the Palestinians?" in Curtis, *People and Politics in the Middle East*, p. 110. Also see Marie Syrkin, "The Claim of the Palestinian Arabs," *Midstream* 16 (January 1970): 3–14.

20. Balfour Brickner, "My Zionist Dilemmas: Two Recent Cases," *Sh'ma* 1 (November 9, 1970): 5.

21. Joachim Prinz, "An Agenda for the Jewish People," in *Proceedings of the Rabbinical Assembly*, ed. Jules Harlow (New York: Rabbinical Assembly, 1971), pp. 24, 21–22.

22. Michael P. Lerner, "Jewish New Leftism at Berkeley," *Judaism* 18 (Fall 1969): 477–78. While "the Jews have a right to an area in Palestine which can be their own, in which they are the majority, and can determine the nature of culture and style of political and social life," the statement from the Committee for a Progressive Middle East (Berkeley Chapter) also categorically declared: "Israel should give back the West Bank of Jordan, neutralize Gaza and the Golan Heights and perhaps Jerusalem—perhaps even shrink to a smaller size than the pre-1967 boundaries." "Statement on the Middle East," *Judaism* 18 (Fall 1969): 486.

23. Barry Rubin, contribution to "How American Radicals See the Resistance Dilemma," *Journal of Palestine Studies* 1, no. 4 (Summer 1972): 25–26.

24. Ben Halpern, "Israel and Palestine: The Political Use of Ethics," in Curtis, *People and Politics in the Middle East*, pp. 14–15.

25. Seymour Martin Lipset, " 'The Socialism of Fools': The Left, the Jews and Israel," *Encounter* 33 (December 1969): 32–33.

26. Sol Stern, "My Jewish Problem—and Ours: Israel, the Left, and the Jewish Establishment," *Ramparts* 10 (August 1971): 32.

27. M. Jay Rosenberg, "My Evolution As a Jew," *Midstream* 16 (August/September 1970): 53.

28. For instance, Americans for a Progressive Israel executive vice president David Tulin became Breira vice president, and Americans for a Progressive Israel national chairperson Inge Lederer Gibel was Breira treasurer. Rabbi Gerald Serotta, active in Americans for a Progressive Israel, also became a prominent member of Breira.

29. For a substantial list of rabbis who supported Breira, see "77 Rabbis on Breira Committee," *National Post and Opinion*, August 9, 1974, p. 1.

30. And here again there were strong ties between the Jewish Liberation Project and Americans for a Progressive Israel; the two would later merge.

31. See, for example, Arthur Waskow, "Draft of a Possible Position for Jewish Radicals in America, on 'The Diaspora, Zion, and Israel,' " *Response* 4 (Fall 1970): 72–75.

32. Kornberg, "Zionism and Ideology," p. 105.

33. Quoted in "How Breira's Director Sees It," *Village Voice*, March 7, 1977, p. 26. Loeb added: "We have people who consider themselves socialists, people who consider themselves the opposite. The issues that bring them together seem to cut across classic political lines." Ibid.

34. Novak, "The Breira Story," p. 6.

35. Quoted in Edward Tivnan, *The Lobby: Jewish Political Power and American Foreign Policy* (New York: Simon and Schuster, 1987), p. 91.

36. *Proceedings of Breira's First Annual Membership Conference: February 20–22, 1977* (New York: Breira, 1977), p. 4. Or as Robert Loeb, executive director of Breira, put it in testimony before the Near East Subcommittee of the U.S. Senate on July 23, 1975: "What must be understood, of course, is that in pursuit of reconciliation, Jews are not going to find Arab Zionists, nor are Arabs going to find Jewish Palestinian Nationalists, but what we may find are Israeli Jews and Palestinian Arabs who are willing to find practical ways to live together in peace for their mutual benefit. I believe it is the role of this committee, the Congress and the Administration to encourage such voices of moderation on all sides." Robert Loeb, "Beyond the Interim Agreement," *interChange* 1, no. 1 (September 1975): 8.

37. "Why We Fear Open Discussion," *Jewish Post and Opinion*, November 29, 1974, p. 6.

38. "Dissent and Enmity Not the Same," *Jewish Week*, September 2, 1971, p. 4.

39. "What Is the Breira Now?" *Jewish Week*, November 14–20, 1974, p. 12. Breira's public statement (dated November 4, 1974) on the reasons for its opposition to the "Rally Against Terror" appeared in *Jewish Post and Opinion*, November 15, 1974, p. 3.

40. See David Saperstein, "Jews Mustn't Let Themselves Be Blackmailed," *Jewish Week*, July 17–23, 1975, pp. 9, 11. Also see Herbert A. Fierst, "Our Military Strength: A New Jewish Concern," *Jewish Week*, June 26–July 2, 1975, p. 13.

41. Wolf I. Blitzer and David Saperstein, "Should U.S. Jews Urge Concessions? Pro and Con," *Jewish Week*, April 8–14, 1976, p. 18. Or as Saperstein also argued around this time: "We must make people understand that they can continue to be and will continue to be strong supporters of Israel even if they feel morally they must speak out for the national rights of the Palestinians." Quoted in "Breira Will Seek to Widen Publicity, Says Saperstein," *Jewish Week*, February 12–18, 1976, p. 2. Also see *Myths and Facts: A Concise Record of the Arab-Israeli*

Conflict, ed. Wolf I. Blitzer, (Washington, D.C.: Near East Research, 1976). Two "myths" in the Blitzer edition were "Israel has no right to hold on to the Golan Heights" and "Acquisition of territory by force is inadmissable." Thus, *Myths and Facts* (1976) left an impression that it tacitly endorsed Gush Emunim's goal to achieve annexation of the occupied territories. In an ambiguous turn of phrase, one reason *Myths and Facts* offered for retaining the Golan was that it represented "an area crucial for the safety of Israel's settlements." Ibid., p. 51.

42.See *interChange* 1, no. 5 (January 1976): 5. On the phenomenon of religious Zionism in the U.S., Israel Singer of the Judaic Studies Department at Brooklyn College wrote: "When one encounters the Gush Emunim here in the U.S., the modified feeling of admiration that one has for them in Israel dwindles. Only a sense of revulsion is left at the willingness of their counterparts in the U.S. to fight to the last Israeli." Israel Singer, "Moderation in Support of Redemption is No Vice," *interChange* 1, no. 6 (February 1976): 2.

43. See *interChange* 1, no. 8 (April 1976): 4.

44. Marjorie Hyer, "U.S. Jews Beginning to Go Public in Criticism of Israel," *Washington Post*, May 3, 1976, p. A2. Also see Henry Siegman, "For Zion's Sake: American Jews and Israeli Policy," *Moment* 1 (January 1976): 13–17.

45. "Israel's Dilemma," *New York Times*, May 11, 1976, p. 32.

46. Quoted in Hyer, "U.S. Jews Beginning to Go Public in Criticism of Israel," p. A2.

47. Rabinowitz and Klavan quoted ibid.; and Hertzberg quoted in Irving Spiegel, "American and Israeli Jews Reappraise Their Ties to the Left and Find They Are Now Tenuous," *New York Times*, August 8, 1972, p. 13.

48. Quoted in "Breira Is Self-Righteous, Bookbinder Says," *Jewish Week*, May 13–19, 1976, p. 7.

49. Quoted in "Controversy Over Breira," *New Outlook* 19 (July/August 1976): 6.

50. Quoted in "Protest Lashes Rabbi, Breira," *Jewish Post and Opinion*, June 18, 1976, p. 3. This protest occurred in the Los Angeles area and was directed principally against local Breira spokesperson Rabbi Leonard Beerman. Also see "Rabbis Come to Defense of Beerman and Breira," *Jewish Post and Opinion*, July 16, 1976, p. 3.

51. Quoted in *interChange* 1, no. 10 (June 1976): 7; and "Orthodox Groups Condemn Breira," *Jewish Week*, May 27–June 2, 1976, p. 14.

52. "No Agreement on Criticism," *Jewish Post and Opinion*, July 9, 1976, p. 1.

53. "The Time Has Come To Say NO To Gush Emunim," *interChange* 1, no. 9 (May 1976): 8.

54. Balfour Brickner, "Saying No to Gush Emunim," *interChange* 1, no. 9 (May 1976): 4.

55. Jacques Schwartz, "Why Our Doves Are Pigeons," *American Zionist* 67 (September 1976): 23.

56. Daniel Charles, " 'Breira': Alternative of Surrender," *American Zionist* 67 (November 1976): 17. Charles (a pseudonym) also said Gush Emunim represented "sincere if criticized militant Zionism," while Breira articulated a "nagging non-Zionism and pro-Palestinianism." Ibid., p. 16.

57. Wolf Blitzer, "Five Washington Jews Meet with PLO Representatives," *Jewish Week*, November 25–December 1, 1976, p. A1. A memorandum on the meetings had been prepared by Herman Edelsberg and delivered to the Israeli Embassy; the memo was then passed along to Blitzer. See David Szonyi, "What Happened When the P.L.O. Came to Town," *interChange* 2, no. 5 (January 1977): 5. For a first-hand account of the meetings, see Arthur I. Waskow, "Talking with the P.L.O.," *New York Times*, December 16, 1976, p. 47; and Arthur I. Waskow, "The Need to Talk with the PLO," *Nation*, February 12, 1977, pp. 178–80.

58. Quoted in Bernard Gwertzman, "American Jewish Leaders Are Split Over Issue of Meeting with P.L.O.," *New York Times*, December 30, 1976, p. 6.

59. Quoted in Marjorie Hyer, "Jews Ask Boycott of Meetings Here on Middle East," *Washington Post*, February 13, 1977, p. C8.

60. I. L. Kenen, "Monitor," *Jewish Week*, December 23–January 5, 1977, p. A8.

61. "Ain Breira in Breira," *Jewish Week*, January 13–19, 1977, p. A10.

62. "Damage Has Been Done," *Jewish Week*, December 9–15, 1976, p. A8.

63. "How Clever the Critics!" *Jewish Week*, January 20–26, 1977, p. A8.

64. "Scholar Accuses Breira of Pro-PLO 'Obsession,' " *Jewish Week*, January 27–February 2, 1977, p. A1.

65. Rael Jean Isaac, *Israel Divided: Ideological Politics in the Jewish State* (Baltimore: Johns Hopkins University Press, 1976), pp. 18, 25, 27. Nor did Isaac neglect (amidst her religious arguments) more conventional right-wing statements about Israeli security concerns: "Should Israel return to the old [pre-Six-Day War] borders she would greatly increase her vulnerability." Ibid., p. 159.

66. Isaac's affiliation with Gush Emunim is discussed in Leonard Fein, "The Assault on Breira," *Moment* 2 (May 1977): 49.

67. Rael Jean Isaac, *Breira: Counsel for Israel* (New York: Americans for a Safe Israel, 1977), pp. 2–4.

68. Singling out Barry Rubin for attack was misleading not least because Rubin had so persistently already since 1973 renounced his own former anti-Zionist perspectives. For Rubin's bitter response to "the spread of material aimed at ruining me," see his letter to the editor in *Commentary* 63 (June 1977): 4.

69. Isaac, *Breira: Counsel for Israel*, pp. 4, 6.

70. Ibid., pp. 26–28. For a recapitulation and elaboration of her argument, also

see Rael Jean Isaac and Erich Isaac, "The Rabbis of Breira," *Midstream* 23 (April 1977): 3–16.

71. Alan Mintz, "The People's Choice? A Demurral on Breira," *Response* 32 (Winter 1976–77): 8, 6. Also see the letters from William Novak, David M. Szonyi, and Jack Nusan Porter, as well as Mintz's reply to his critics in *Response* 34 (Fall 1977): 108–18.

72. Quoted in "Community Council Blasts Breira, Hits Contact with PLO," *Jewish Week*, February 3–9, 1977, p. 1.

73. *Proceedings of Breira's First Annual Membership*, pp. 15–16, 11, 9.

74. Ira Eisenstein, "The Breira Controversy," *Reconstructionist* 18 (February 1977): 4. For another contemporaneous critique, see Albert Vorspan, "Why I Have Not Joined Breira," *Reform Judaism* 5 (February 1977): 3. For a response to Vorspan, see Arnold Jacob Wolf, "Breira, Yes" (letter to the editor), *Reform Judaism* 5 (April 1977): 2.

75. Melvin I. Urofsky, "Breira Battle Turning Into a Witch-Hunt," *Jewish Observer and Middle East Review* 26 (March 31, 1977): 8, 18.

76. Joseph Shattan, "Why Breira?" *Commentary* 63 (April 1977): 60, 64–65.

77. As Brettschneider writes: "The attack on Breira was so intense and organized that many felt it had to have been orchestrated." Brettschneider, *Cornerstones of Peace*, p. 44.

78. On December 6, 2000, Jewish Peace Lobby circulated a statement signed by 101 rabbis, including quite a few former Breira members. The statement maintained that "the pursuit of both justice and lasting peace requires that, in some form, Jerusalem be shared with the Palestinian people." The statement focused attention on the sensitive issue of who would control a stone plateau in Jerusalem that is holy to both Muslims and Jews. Known as the Temple Mount to Jews, it is revered as the site of the First and Second Temples and the center of Jewish religious life. Known as Haram al Sharif to Muslims, it contains the sacred Al Aksa Mosque and the Dome of the Temple. The issue of sovereignty over the site had proven insurmountable during the exhaustive Israeli-Palestinian peace negotiations at Camp David in the summer of 2000. It was widely held that peace efforts had failed precisely because of the impasse created by the question of shared sovereignty over the sacred site. On September 28, 2000, right-wing Likud leader Ariel Sharon had visited the Temple Mount, an act interpreted by Palestinians as a blatant provocation. "It was no provocation whatsoever," Sharon averred. "A Jew in Israel has the right to visit the Temple Mount." Yet Sharon's visit sparked intense and immediate clashes between Palestinians and Israeli riot police. The violence quickly spread to East Jerusalem and to the West Bank town of Ramallah. Within days the Al Aksa intifada had broken out.

Sharon quoted in Joel Greenberg, "Sharon Touches a Nerve, and Jerusalem Explodes," *New York Times*, September 29, 2000, p. A10. Soon after the December 6 call for sharing the Temple Mount, Rabbi Avi Shafran of Agudath Israel of America described the rabbis who signed the Jewish Peace Lobby statement both of "hav[ing] done a disservice to the cause of Middle East peace" and of having "done a disservice to the cause of theological integrity." See Avi Shafran, letter to the editor, *New York Times*, December 11, 2000, p. A30.

79. For example, see the discussion in Jerold S. Auerbach, *Are We One? Jewish Identity in the United States and Israel* (New Brunswick: Rutgers University Press, 2001). In this context it is also not incidental to note that by 2001 the settlement movement numbered over two hundred thousand. See Anthony Lewis, "Is There an Answer?" *New York Times,* October 30, 2001, p. A25.

80. Quoted in Novak, "The Breira Story," p. 11.

81. Wolf, "American Jewry and Israel," p. 32.

82. Barbara Myerhoff, *Number Our Days* (New York: Simon and Schuster, 1978), p. 184.

Acknowledgments

IT IS A GREAT PLEASURE at long last to acknowledge the friends and colleagues who offered advice, support, and gracious assistance during the several years it took me to complete this work. At Bowling Green State University I am most grateful to Allan Emery, David Hampshire, Erin Labbie, Don McQuarie, Don Nieman, Kausalya Padmaraj, and Tom Wymer. The semester I was in residence at the Institute for the Study of Culture and Society proved especially valuable, and I owe a particular debt to its director, Vicki Patraka, for her generosity and encouragement. Researching and writing this book also put me into helpful conversation with numerous individuals both inside and outside a fluid field known as American Jewish studies. I benefited greatly from advice and criticisms from Rachel Adams, Adina Back, Hasia Diner, Leonard Dinnerstein, Carla Goldman, Susannah Heschel, Sydelle Kramer, Pam Nadell, and Gail Reimer. Sarah Barnard and Robin Judd assisted me with translations.

I am especially indebted to Joyce Antler, Paul Buhle, Marjorie Feld, Eric Goldstein, Deborah Dash Moore, Bill Novak, Riv-Ellen Prell, Jennifer Stollman, and Mike Tabor, each of whom offered invaluable critiques of all or some of the manuscript and whose collective commentary immensely improved the book. However, it is Michael Rogin who deserves special praise for his impeccable judgment and calm reassurance at critical junctions, and for believing I could and should do this work. At Columbia University Press I have been honored with an all-star cast of editors. Ann

Miller found me at a moment when I was not even looking. Without her tireless encouragement and precise guidance, I rather wonder whether this would have become a book at all. Helena Schwarz took a special interest in this work, which led to a number of wonderfully spirited exchanges and conversations. Wendy Lochner made incisive and thoughtful comments on the manuscript, and Susan Pensak, my ministering angel, offered lots of excellent suggestions and made everything better. Thanks to one and all.

Locating sources for this book represented an often difficult procedure, and I am grateful to the several libraries and archives that assisted me with my work. Staff at the Hebrew Union College Library, Cornell University's Olin Library, Judaica Division at Harvard University's Widener Library, the Bentley Historical Library at the University of Michigan, the Labadie Special Collections at the University of Michigan, and Bowling Green State University's Jerome Library were all extremely helpful. Bill Aron, Marion Bee, Renee Bomgardner, Heidi Coleman, Diana J. Davies, Yaakov Kirschen, and Paul Lauter all responded warmly to inquiries about locating or reprinting sources for this book. Bill Novak and Sharon Schumack assisted greatly with finding crucial sources on Breira. Most significantly, I owe a debt to Mike Tabor. The chapter on Jews for Urban Justice could never have been written if Mike had not opened his personal archives to me. It was a great gift, and I am immensely thankful.

Finally, I wish to acknowledge my family and our friends. First of all, to David Staub and Florence Staub I owe a tremendous debt for the countless conversations we had arguing the world while I was growing up in New York and on Long Island in the sixties and early seventies. I also wish to thank Kristin Herzog for her support through times both thick and thin. Jennifer Fleischner has been a trusted and valued friend throughout the years it took to complete this book. I thank her for her wise counsel and affection. Jim Henle has been a comrade so long it is hard to think when I did not know him. He has sustained me in my work and my life in ways that are almost impossible to put into words. I can only express sincerest gratitude. Arno Armgort, Amy MacKenzie, and Dianne Sadoff are good friends I hope to see more often now that this project is completed. Dora Gholson, Julie Seidel, and Sylvia Van Meerten provided remarkable assistance over three summers caring for the brave, exceptional, wonderful child to whom this book is lovingly dedicated. And to Dagmar Herzog there is nothing I can put into print that she does not already know so many times over—that this book would not exist without her and that it is hers as much as it is mine. I am thankful every day for her friendship, courage, and love.

Index